Growth of the AMERICAN REPUBLIC

SECOND EDITION

Fundamental Concepts in U.S. Government & Politics

Kendall Hunt
publishing company

E. Michael Young

To Erica and Micah

CONTENTS

Note to Readers   xiii

Note to Instructors   xv

UNIT ONE
Political Values and The Constitution   1

CHAPTER 1   What Is Government? 3

Preamble and the Purpose of Government 4
Aristotle 7
Types of Government 8
Final Thoughts 10

CHAPTER 2   What Are America's Original Political Values? 13

Roots of American Democracy 14
Social Contract Theory 18
Political Culture 20
The Declaration of Independence 20
American Creed 23
Final Thoughts 26

CHAPTER 3   What Happened at the Constitutional Convention? 29

The Articles of Confederation 30
The Constitutional Convention of 1787 31
Debates and Compromises at the Convention 33
Principles of the Constitution 37
A Brilliant Solution 38
Final Thoughts 40

CHAPTER 4 How Does the Constitution Change? 43

Ratification of the Constitution 44
Adding the Bill of Rights. 46
Amending the Constitution 48
Supreme Court Interpretations 49
Other Ways the National Government Has Changed beyond the Constitution . 52
Final Thoughts 55

CHAPTER 5 What Are America's Current Political Ideologies? 57

History of Liberalism in America 58
Contemporary Liberalism 61
History of Conservatism 63
Contemporary Conservatism 65
Other Ideologies 67
Final Thoughts 70

UNIT TWO
State and Individual Rights   73

CHAPTER 6 How Does Federalism Work?. 75

Definition of Federalism 76
Advantages of Federalism. 77
National Powers 78
State Powers 80
Shared Powers. 82
Summary of Federalism 83
Final Thoughts 83

CHAPTER 7 How Has the National Government Grown in Power over the States? 87

Two Metaphors of Federalism 88
Marshall Court 89
Era of Dual Federalism 91
Era of Cooperative Federalism. 93
New Federalism 96
Federalism Today 98
Final Thoughts. 100

CHAPTER 8 What Are My First Amendment Rights? 103

Freedom of Religion 105
The Supreme Court and the Establishment Clause 107
The Free Exercise Clause 109
Free Speech 111
Freedom of the Press 116
Right to Assemble and Petition 117
Final Thoughts 118

CHAPTER 9 How Does the Bill of Rights Protect Me? 121

The History of the Bill of Rights 122
Rights Imbedded in the Original Constitution 124
The Bill of Rights 127
1st Amendment 127
2nd Amendment 127
3rd Amendment 129
4th through 8th Amendments: Criminal Procedures 129
9th and 10th Amendments: Remaining Rights to People and the States . . . 132
Incorporation of the Bill of Rights 133
Right of Privacy? 134
Final Thoughts 136

CHAPTER 10 Have Americans Always Enjoyed Equal Rights? 139

Black Civil Rights from the Civil War to Jim Crow 141
The Civil Rights Movement 143
Discrimination and Classification 146
Affirmative Action 148
Women and Gay Rights 150
Final Thoughts 152

UNIT THREE
The Three Branches of Government   155

CHAPTER 11 What Are the President's Constitutional Powers? 157

Creating the Presidency 158
Three Major Powers of the Presidency 162
Other Presidential Powers 164

Impeachment and Succession 166
Presidential Issues and Controversies 167
Final Thoughts 169

CHAPTER 12   What Are the Keys to a Successful Presidency? 173
Presidential Leadership 174
The President and the Media 179
Presidential Party Politics 184
Final Thoughts 188

CHAPTER 13   What Are the Powers of Congress? 191
Congressional Constitutional Powers 192
Structure and Function of Congress 194
How the House of Representatives Works 196
How the Senate Works 197
Congressional Committees 199
Final Thought 202

CHAPTER 14   How Does a Bill Become a Law? 205
Running for Congress 206
Role of the Lawmaker 208
How a Bill Becomes a Law 209
What Influences a Lawmaker's Vote? 214
Problems and Suggested Reforms 216
Final Thought 217

CHAPTER 15   What Does the Supreme Court Do? 221
Constitutional Power of the Supreme Court 223
Structure of Federal Judiciary 225
The Political Ideology of the Supreme Court 226
Judicial Philosophy 228
The Politics of Appointing Judges 230
How the Supreme Court Works 233
Supreme Court Opinions 235
Final Thoughts 237

UNIT FOUR
Political Process   239

CHAPTER 16   Who Are the American People and What Are Their Political Opinions? . . . 241

Demographic Sketch of America. 242
US Public's Decline in Political Knowledge 243
Polling Public Opinion 245
Political Socialization 248
Red State versus Blue State America 249
Final Thoughts 253

CHAPTER 17   How Are American Elections Conducted? 257

Expansion of the Franchise. 258
Prominent Features of US Elections 260
Voter Turnout 262
The Electoral College 264
Final Thought 268

CHAPTER 18   How Do You Run for President? 271

Qualifications to Run for President 272
Managing a Presidential Campaign. 273
The Three Stages of Presidential Campaigns. 275
Voting Choice 285
Final Thoughts 287

CHAPTER 19   What Do Political Parties Do? 289

The Functions of Political Parties 290
The Two-Party System 292
What Role Do Third Parties Play? 295
Party Identification 297
Political Parties as Institutions. 299
Conventional and Unconventional Participation. 302
Final Thoughts 303

CHAPTER 20   What Is the Role of the News Media in Our Democracy?. 307

The Functions of a Free Press in a Democracy 308
History of News Media 310

Government Regulation of the Media 315
Where Do People Get Their News Today? 316
The Professional Press 317
News Bias 319
Final Thoughts 322

UNIT FIVE
Public Policy 325

CHAPTER 21 What Do Interest Groups Do? 327

Theories about Interest Groups 328
Interest Groups: the Good, the Bad, and the Billionaire 330
Types of Interest Groups 332
Campaign Finance Law 337
How Interest Groups Influence Public Policy 341
Final Thoughts 344

CHAPTER 22 How Is Public Policy Made and Implemented? 347

What Is Public Policy? 349
The Public Policy Process 349
Flaws in the Public Policy Process 351
How Does the Bureaucracy Make Law? 354
The Size of the Current Federal Bureaucracy 356
Problems with the Large Federal Bureaucracy 357
Reforming Bureaucracies 361
Final Thoughts 363

CHAPTER 23 What Is the US Economic Policy? 365

Economic Terms 365
Laissez-Faire versus a Controlled Economy 369
Monetary Policy 372
Supply-Side Economics 374
The Triumph of Keynesian Economics 376
Final Thoughts 378

CHAPTER 24 How Does the Government Make the Budget? 381

The Budget Process 382
Types of Taxes 384
Tax Issues 386
Government Spending 388
The Debt Problem 390
Final Thoughts 392

CHAPTER 25 What Is America's Foreign and Defense Policy? 395

Tools in Foreign Policy 396
The Constitution and Foreign Policy 400
Two Foreign Policy Approaches 403
Early American Foreign Policy 403
Modern US Foreign Policy 406
Final Thoughts 415

Appendix 419

A Controversial Social and Political Issues 419
B Landmark Supreme Court Cases 433
C Declaration of Independence (1776) 447
D The Constitution of the United States of America 451

Class Activities 467

Glossary 475

NOTE TO READERS

Even though this book is in textbook format, my hope is that the general reader who wants to learn about the fundamental concepts of US government will enjoy reading this book.

Judging from recent polls, it seems that today most Americans no longer know the ideas the American Republic is founded on or know how our system of limited government is designed to work. If American citizens lose this knowledge, the great American experiment will fail. This is why I consider this book to be so vitally important.

NOTE TO INSTRUCTORS

This textbook is conceived to be used differently than normal textbooks.

Each chapter is designated to be preparation reading for one lecture or one class period. It is recommended that you give the students a quiz on the chapter terms at the beginning of each class period.

Once the students know the fundamental concepts, you may focus your lecture on the things you consider most important and then devote the rest of the period to class activities and discussion. I consider the half-lecture/half-class activity format to be the most engaging for students.

Recommended Course Schedule

1. **US Govt Freshman College Course:** I recommend that instructors complete Units 1–4 for a semester course. Individual topics in Unit 5 may be used for student projects. Also, instructors may wish to alternate each semester to make things more interesting for them: Units 1–4 one semester, and Units 1, 2, 3, and 5 the next.

2. **US Govt College Course with State Government:** Some colleges combine federal and state government topics in one course. For example, US and Texas Constitutions and US and Texas Governments. For this format, I would teach Units 1 and 2 for constitution, and Units 3, 4, and 5 for government, leaving the rest of the course to state topics.

3. **High School and AP:** Instructors should cover Units 1–5 for the school year.

4. **Home School:** Parent/instructors should teach the entire book.

Note on Appendix: There are two very important chapters in the Appendix: "Controversial Social and Political Issues" and "Landmark Supreme Court Cases." Both can be used as reference resources, but I recommend that the instructor assign them for students to get started on term papers or class debates.

UNIT ONE

POLITICAL VALUES AND THE CONSTITUTION

CHAPTER 1

What Is Government?

TOPICS

- ▶ Preamble and the Purpose of Government
- ▶ Aristotle
- ▶ Types of Governments
- ▶ What Is Good Government?

LEARNING OBJECTIVES

When you finish reading this chapter, you will be able to:

1. Define government.
2. Cite the basic purposes of government.
3. List Aristotle's different types of governments.
4. Discuss Aristotle's ideas on direct democracy and good government.

WHAT IS GOVERNMENT?

Throughout world history there have been many different types of governments: tribal, theocratic, aristocratic, democratic, monarchical, totalitarian. Even the family might be described as a basic form of government. How can we define something so amorphous or changeable that it can take so many different forms? Later in this chapter we will describe Aristotle's six forms of government, but for now we will define **government** *as an entity that uses legitimate force to make policy, conducts affairs of the state, and enacts laws guiding its citizens.*

Government

an entity that uses legitimate force to make policy, conducts affairs of the state, and enacts laws guiding its citizens

PREAMBLE AND THE PURPOSE OF GOVERNMENT

Thomas Jefferson, in his first inaugural address, outlined what he thought was the proper purpose of Government. "A wise and frugal government," asserted Jefferson, "which shall restrain men from injuring one another, shall leave them otherwise free to regulate their own pursuit of industry and improvement, and shall not take from the mouth of labor the bread it has earned. This is the sum of good government."

Another American wrote a brief and poignant description of the purpose of government that has inspired America for centuries. At the Constitutional Convention of 1787, Gouverneur Morris was assigned to a committee to write a final, polished draft of the Constitution. Feeling the Constitution needed some sort of introduction, he wrote a preamble. The Preamble of the US Constitution not only succinctly lists the basic functions of any government, but it also gives us some indication of the nature of America's unique form of government.

The Preamble of the US Constitution: "We the People of the United States, in Order to form a more perfect Union, establish Justice, insure domestic Tranquility, provide for the common defense, promote the general Welfare, and secure the Blessings of Liberty for ourselves and Posterity, do ordain and establish this Constitution of the United States of America."

The Preamble of the Constitution.
©larry1235/Shutterstock.com

"We the People": The first three words of the US Constitution, "we the people," sent a shock wave across monarchical Europe when they were first read. The authority of the new American government rests not on one individual, as do monarchies, or on a privileged few, as do aristocracies, but instead on *the people*. This indicates that our government is democratic in nature; it is ruled by the people. These words also echo a sentiment expressed in the Declaration of Independence, written about a decade earlier: "Governments are instituted among Men, deriving their just powers from the *consent of the governed*." No government is legitimate unless it serves the people and is supported by the people.

"In Order to Form a More Perfect Union": The American people who first read this in 1787 would have understood it differently than we do today. The US Constitution was replacing America's first government, the Articles of Confederation. This implied that government under the Confederation was imperfect, that it was a failure. One of the main reasons that the Confederation failed was that the individual states had too much power and the central government was not strong enough to unite the country. At the time the Preamble was written, America was filled with strife and on the verge of fragmentation. This new Constitution promised to form a better government, one that provided unity, order, and stability. *Governments provide armies, laws, and police to protect people and property in order to establish* **order***. Order is the primary function and responsibility of government.* For if a government fails to maintain order, the country will no longer exist.

Order

the primary function and responsibility of government. Governments provide armies, laws, and police to protect people and property in order to establish *order*

Government needs to provide law and order.
©Jane Kelly/Shutterstock.com

"Establish Justice": Another key function of government is to establish and maintain a legal system. Governments make laws that guide the people and bind the whole country together. Law is a rational set of rules that everybody must follow. The legislature makes laws; the police enforce the laws; and judges interpret laws and punish wrongdoers. Our Constitution establishes the fundamental law and framework of our government. Without laws, there would be chaos. The Revolutionary Generation fought against the "arbitrary" rule of the British monarch and said there is no liberty without established, impartial law.

"Insure Domestic Tranquility": Local governments have police, states have the National Guard, and the Constitution gives the national government control over all state militias. So the government can always call up troops to quell threats and restore domestic order. Also, after the terrorist attacks of 9/11, the federal government created the Department of Homeland Security to fight against internal terrorist threats. Governments must have the power to quell internal insurrections, riots, and looting.

"Provide for the Common Defense": It is an essential duty of government to protect and defend the country. Traditionally, this has been considered the primary responsibility of the executive, be it a king or a president. Currently, America has five branches of the armed services (the Army, Navy, Air Force, Marines, and Coast Guard), and sixteen intelligence agencies, including the CIA. All countries must allocate some of their resources to defend the nation.

Promote the General Good

providing for the best long-term interest for the greatest number of people in the country

"Promote the General Welfare": Originally the concept was a limiting one—the national government will do what is best for the whole (general) country, not special geographical or financial interests. In recent times, however, this concept has expanded tremendously. "General Welfare" is now understood to mean that the government should spend money to provide services to **promote the general good:** *providing for the best long-term interest for the greatest number of people in the country.* Building schools, maintaining national parks, providing food stamps, inspecting meat, and erecting bridges are merely a few examples of the many services government provides for its citizens. The government uses its coercive power to raise money by taxing the citizens in various ways in order to finance these services. *Coerce* means that the government can force you to do something. If you do not pay your taxes, for example, you can be sent to prison.

"And Secure the Blessings of Liberty to Ourselves and Our Posterity": The Revolution was fought in the name of liberty, and one of the primary objectives of the Framers was to establish a government that protects individual freedom. This is another important function of government. Governments help teach or socialize new generations about certain values. The Founders believed it was essential to teach future generations to cherish liberty otherwise our republic would vanish. Noah Webster believed that through common schools we could teach Americans liberty and republicanism. Others believed that national documents, such as the Declaration of Independence, and national monuments, such as the Statue of Liberty, would also teach future generations to cherish liberty.

"Do Ordain and Establish this Constitution for the United States of America": This government is legitimate because it was established by "We the People" in democratically constituted ratifying conventions. Our country will be called "The United States of America." And our government is a federal system where the *states* share power with the federal government. It is interesting to note that in the early years of American history people often referred to the US in the plural, emphasizing the many states. For example, they would say "these United States of America are." Today we think of America as one entity and say "the United States of America is."

Five Basic Functions of Government: So, as we can see, the Preamble outlines five basic objectives of government. Governments must provide **order** by protecting life and property and setting up the rules by which the government will operate. Governments must **establish justice** by providing and maintaining a legal system. It must **defend** the country against external and internal threats. Governments must provide services to **promote the general good**. And governments engage in **socialization**: *they teach or socialize proceeding generations certain values that society holds dear.*

Preamble Today: Today, when modern liberals or conservatives cite the Preamble, they tend to emphasize different parts of it. Conservatives value order and liberty, so they like to focus on "insure domestic tranquility," "provide for the common defense," and "secure the blessings of liberty." Liberals, on the other hand, value social justice and equality, so they focus on "establish justice" and "promote the general welfare." The remarkable thing about our founding documents is that the ideas they express still inspire modern Americans all across the political spectrum.

ARISTOTLE

The American Founding Generation was highly influenced by their readings of ancient Greek and Roman writers. Perhaps the most influential ancient writer in Western Civilization was Aristotle.

Aristotle (384–322 BC) *was a Greek philosopher who taught in ancient Athens in the school he established, the Lyceum.* One of the greatest thinkers of all time, this polymath was authoritative in a wide variety of fields, including poetry, zoology, logic, metaphysics, ethics, music, physics, linguistics, and

Socialization

teaching or socializing proceeding generations certain values that society holds dear

Aristotle

a Greek philosopher who taught in ancient Athens in the school he established, the Lyceum

Aristotle (384–322 BC)
©MidoSemsem/
Shutterstock.com

biology. One of Aristotle's most famous works is the *Politics*. Although written a long time ago in a culture much different than ours, the *Politics* still has much to say about human nature and the difficulty of establishing good government. Aristotle said "man is a political animal," meaning people naturally function in social groups; therefore, it is important for us to understand the best way to order ourselves into political communities. This is what the study of government is all about.

TYPES OF GOVERNMENT

Six Types of Governments: Aristotle identifies six fundamental types of government: three good and three bad. Good governments, according to Aristotle, do three things: they follow the law, provide for the common good, and select the best people to public office. Good governments can be ruled by one (**Monarchy,** *power given to a hereditary king or queen*); the few (*Aristocracy,* power is given to the noble, educated class); or the many (*Polity,* a mixed democracy that served the public good). Bad governments serve only the selfish interests of the rulers. Bad governments can be ruled by one (**Tyranny,** *a selfish, autocratic ruler*); or by a few (**Oligarchy,** *rule by the few, usually the rich*); or by the many (**Democracy,** *rule by the people*).

Totalitarianism: In Aristotle's day, there were many governments ruled by tyrants in an autocratic fashion in which the leader has supreme power and ruled without regard to established laws or public opinion. We might also use the words such as dictator, strongman, or despot. In the modern world, with the advent of mass media, vast standing armies, and secret police, we have seen the rise of a new type of tyranny: **totalitarian government**—*a political system that has total authority over all aspects of society, including the economy, the military, the press, education, the arts, and the legal system.* Governments like the Nazis under Adolph Hitler or the Soviet Union under Joseph Stalin were totalitarian. Through a single political party, Hitler and Stalin controlled all aspects of life. This made political opposition nearly impossible.

Direct Democracy: Aristotle made many interesting comments about democracies, but before we discuss these we should understand what a democracy was in his time. Aristotle lived in ancient Athens, the world's first democracy. Athens was what we call today a **direct democracy**: *the people made the laws and determined policy by immediate majority vote, sometimes without regard to established law.* The Athenian citizens met in the assembly and made law by majority vote. The citizens also served on juries and in other government bodies. To be a full citizen, however, one had to be an adult male who had completed his military training and whose parents were both born in Athens, which actually excluded a majority of the Athenian residents

Monarchy

power given to a hereditary king or queen

Tyranny

government by a selfish, autocratic ruler

Oligarchy

rule by the few, usually the rich

Democracy

rule by the people

Totalitarian Government

a political system that has total authority over all aspects of society, including the economy, the military, the press, education, the arts, and the legal system

Direct Democracy

the people made the laws and determined policy by immediate majority vote, sometimes without regard to established law (including women and slaves). For its time, however, Athens was a brave democratic experiment in an era when most countries were ruled by kings.

Why Aristotle Thought Direct Democracy Was Bad: Many students are puzzled when they learn that Aristotle considered democracy to be a bad form of government, but he was referring to *direct democracy*. Aristotle believed that to run a government an individual needs specialized skills and knowledge. Even a shoemaker needs specialized skills and training for his job, and running a government is far more complex. Aristotle simply thought that the people were not knowledgeable and virtuous enough to make these difficult decisions required when running a government. In his life, Aristotle witnessed direct democracies devolve into mob rule, where the majority did whatever they wanted regardless of the laws. They even killed the great philosopher Socrates.

Aristotle essentially believed that only educated people with property should rule. But remember, he lived in a time before public education. In the ancient world, only people with property had the time and wealth to educate their children. Aristotle felt that property ownership was an essential prerequisite to full citizenship because land owners were experienced in managing an estate and taking responsibility. Landowners also had a "stake in the country," meaning they were more connected to the nation than a transient worker. This idea of a property qualification for full citizenship would still hold sway in the early years of the American Republic.

In ancient Athens, the people had the power to make their own laws.
©Dimitrios/Shutterstock.com

What Aristotle Liked about Democracy: In the *Politics*, however, Aristotle made many comments that revealed that he thought democracies had several virtues and that perhaps one day it could be made to work. He said that democratic governments produce the most freedom and prosperity. This prosperity leads to a large middle class of farmers, artisans, and professionals. This is important. Good government, declared Aristotle, should be supported by the large middle, not merely the rich or the poor. He also said it was good that democracies promote equality. Moreover, although Aristotle doubted that the common man had the knowledge and skill to run government, he did believe in the "wisdom of the majority," that the people could elect good public officials. Therefore, Aristotle hinted that he believed a "polity," some sort of mixed democracy that represented the people but placed the aristocrats in important positions, might work if it followed the law and provided for the common good.

Preserving Democracies: In Book Six of the *Politics*, Aristotle outlined several things that Democracies must do to avoid destruction. First, democratic governments must educate the people to lead virtuous lives, respect justice, and learn democratic values. Second, he warned, "watch out to ensure there are no transgressions of the laws, and above all be on guard against small ones." Aristotle knew that once government officials got accustomed to bending the law, it could lead to the unraveling of constitutional government. Third, don't allow popular leaders to confiscate property in an effort to gain favor with the poor. Aristotle called this a "punctured jar," the more public assistance you give the poor the more they will want. And fourth, the best way to keep a democracy healthy is to promote general prosperity in order to bring the poor into the middle class.

FINAL THOUGHTS

Aristotle made another interesting declaration about good governments—that they lead to greater happiness. Aristotle believed that the proper goal in life is individual happiness; and, therefore, the proper goal for the government is to promote the happiness of its citizens. Aristotle did not mean a sort of superficial happiness of fun and amusement as we might use the term today. He meant the deep well-being a person experiences when he or she leads a virtuous life well lived. If a government is properly organized, provides good moral and educational institutions, fosters the arts and sciences, and promotes the prosperity needed for each individual to find a rewarding occupation that contributes something positive to society, then government can foster the happiness of the people. The American Founders also believed good government will lead to the happiness of the people.

NOTES

Aristotle. *The Politics*. Translated by Carnes Lord. Chicago: University of Chicago Press, 1984.

ESSAY QUESTIONS

1. What are the five functions of government outlined in the Preamble of the US Constitution? And which one do you think is most important?
2. What is considered the primary function of government, and why?
3. What were Aristotle's criticisms of Direct Democracies?
4. List Aristotle's criteria for good government regardless of the type.
5. What did Aristotle think was the ultimate goal of good government?

TERMS

Aristotle: _____

Democracy: _____

Direct Democracy: _____

Government: _____

Monarchy: _____

Oligarchy: _____

Order: _____

Promote the General Good: _____

Socialization: _____

Totalitarian: _____

Tyranny:_____

CHAPTER 2

What Are America's Original Political Values?

TOPICS

► Roots of American Democracy
► Social Contract Theory
► Political Culture
► The Declaration of Independence
► American Creed

LEARNING OBJECTIVES

When you finish reading this chapter, you will be able to:

1. Differentiate between a direct democracy and a republic.
2. List some of the major historical influences on the Founders.
3. Compare the Social Contract Theory of Hobbes and Locke.
4. Recognize the political values of the American Creed.

WHAT ARE AMERICA'S ORIGINAL POLITICAL VALUES?

Before one studies the laws of a country, one should first understand that country's culture. The people of Italy, Japan, and Libya, for example, have very different cultures, and, not surprisingly, their laws and constitutions are also very different. This is why we will study America's political culture before we study the US Constitution. Once we understand the history of America's political culture and ideas, then we will better understand our governmental institutions.

This chapter consists of three sections. First we will discuss the historical influences on the people who helped form the American government, whom will be referred in this textbook as "the Revolutionary Generation," "the Framers," or "the Founders." Then we will discuss Social Contract Theory, which also had a profound influence on the Founders. Lastly, we will study the core traditional American political values, sometimes referred to as the American Creed.

ROOTS OF AMERICAN DEMOCRACY

The US Constitution did not spring fully formed from the minds of the Framers during the Federal Convention of 1787, as the adult Athena was said to have sprung from the head of the Greek god Zeus. Early US history textbooks often depicted the framing of the Constitution as a divinely inspired flash of creativity. The fact is that centuries of history went into the crafting of the Constitution. Through their education and reading, the Founders were influenced by many ideas about government from the ancient world to contemporary Great Britain.

Judeo-Christian Belief: Many fundamental concepts about government and social justice come from the Old and New Testaments that were very familiar to the Revolutionary Generation. In Luke 20:25, Jesus says "render therefore unto Caesar the things which be Caesar's, and unto God the things which be God's," establishing the idea of the separation of church and state. Judeo-Christian doctrine holds that all people are equal in the eyes of God. The Bible, especially the Torah and the Minor Prophets, assert that humans have God-given rights and that all people—rich and poor, free and slave— must be treated fairly, establishing the idea of equality under the law. The Bible also teaches that good governments have the consent of the governed and that the sanctity of contracts should not be violated. Taken together, the political concepts described in the Bible established for the Revolutionary Generation the concept of fundamental law, a core set of laws set up by God that form the basis of human law and individual rights. This concept was referred to in the Declaration of Independence as the "laws of nature."

Ancient Athens: As we learned in Chapter 1, ancient Athens practiced *direct democracy*. Democracy literally means "rule by the people." All Athenian citizens had the right to attend the assembly and laws were made by majority vote. The Founders liked many aspects of democracy, but from their reading of the Greek historians they perceived much danger in direct democracy. During stressful times, direct democracies could quickly transform into mob rule. The rights of the minority or individuals were unprotected in this system. Often the majority could be swayed by a **demagogue**: *politicians with*

Demagogue

politicians with great rhetorical skills that appealed to the public's baser emotions of greed and fear *great rhetorical skills that appealed to the public's baser emotions of greed and fear.* So the Founders sought to avoid the pitfalls of direct democracy.

Ancient Rome: While the American Founders distrusted direct democracy as practiced in Athens, they greatly admired the Roman Republic. The Romans understood the word republic to mean government that had no king, that follows the rule of law, and that provided the people with the ultimate control over the government. Their constitution consisted of a very complex system of democratic assemblies, the aristocratic Senate, and magistrates (administrators). Polybius, in his influential book, *Histories*, said that the Roman constitution was a mixed government consisting in "the Senate proposing, the people resolving, and the magistrates executing the law." The Framers borrowed many aspects of the Roman republican system: separation of powers with checks and balances, limited government, the rule of law, consent of the people, and the executive and Senate in control of foreign affairs.

An indication of how much the Revolutionary Generation was inspired by Roman history was the fact that they often used pseudonyms of legendary republican figures in their writings, such as Brutus, Publius, and Cincinnatus. The Founders were especially influenced by the idea of *Republican virtue*: the courage, duty, simplicity of manners, self-sacrifice, dignity, and civic virtue of a man who would energetically serve the Roman Republic. For example, George Washington was often called the "American Cincinnatus," referring to

Roman Forum: The American Founders greatly admired the Roman Republic.
©Cris Foto/Shutterstock.com

the Roman leader who protected the nation from invasion and then returned to his farm to lead a simple life. It must be remembered that the Framers never referred to the government they created as a "democracy," but always as a **Republic,** *a representative form of government in which elected officials make laws on behalf of the people.*

Martin Luther and the Protestant Reformation: In 1517, Martin Luther, a German Catholic monk and professor, nailed his *95 Thesis* on the door of the Wittenberg Church. This led to a series of actions resulting in the formation of several Protestant denominations in northern Europe, which split from the Roman Catholic Church. Protestant comes from the words "to protest." Luther influenced people to protest against the Catholic Church and to protest against the kings that support the Church. In doing this, Luther also encouraged people to take control of their own lives, to think about individual rights, and to change society if it did not properly follow the teachings of the Bible. This led to the idea that people can govern themselves. The Puritans came to America to forge a society based on their interpretation of Protestantism. The Revolutionary Generation highly identified with the Protestant movement in England.

English Common Law: The Founders were highly versed in English constitutional history. A 1334 version of the Magna Carta (originally published in 1215) stated: "No freeman shall be captured or imprisoned...except by the lawful judgment of his peers...nor without the due process of the law." This establishes the English constitutional tradition of limited government and individual rights. Other rights included in the Magna Carta were that churches shall be independent, equal justice under the law, government must compensate an individual for confiscated property, the right to a writ of habeas corpus, a prohibition against excessive fines, and the guarantee that taxes could not be levied without the consent of the people through their representatives. England has no written constitution. If enough people follow a law, it becomes "common law" on the basis of precedent. Much of our legal system is based on English Common Law.

Colonial America: North America was colonized by England in the seventeenth century. The Thirteen Colonies developed their own government with many democratic elements. In 1619, Virginia established the House of Burgesses, the first representative assembly in North America. In 1641, the Massachusetts Bay Colony promulgated its own legal code, the Body of Liberties. In New England, the people gathered together to discuss important issues and decide policy based on majority rule in *Town Hall Meetings.* Pennsylvania, with its frame of government written by William Penn, was known for its religious tolerance. Anxious to make their rights as Englishmen clear, all the

Republic

a representative form of government in which elected officials make laws on behalf of the people

**People in New England would gather in town halls
to debate the issues facing the community.**
©holbox/Shutterstock.com

colonies established governments with *written* constitutions, often including a bill of rights. So, by the time of the Revolution, the colonies had a long-established tradition of self-elected assemblies that made local law and oversaw civil and criminal courts. The American Revolution was conservative in that the colonists fought to retain their original freedoms.

The English Constitution: By the 1700s, Englishmen in the mother country and in the American colonies had come to accept and admire the idea of the "British Constitution." Although unwritten, the British government was based on certain accepted principles and traditions. Exemplifying the *balanced constitution*, the British government was based on the idea that the "three estates" or social classes would be reflected in government: the king represents the royal family, the House of Lords represents the aristocracy, and the House of Commons represents the common people. In this mixed system, the virtues of the three forms of government are balanced: monarchy (power), aristocracy (wisdom), and democracy (liberty). Further, the British Bill of Rights limited the monarchy and protected individual rights. And Parliament, as representative of the people, is sovereign. By the time of the Revolution, most Americans had come to believe a corrupt circle of royal advisors had defiled this fundamentally good system.

SOCIAL CONTRACT THEORY

Another major influence on the Founders was the intellectual history of Social Contract Theory. First expressed by Aristotle and later expanded on by Thomas Hobbes and John Locke, **Social Contract Theory** *states that people must give up certain liberties when they enter into society, but the resulting order and safety is worth the loss of freedom.* Not necessarily to be taken literally, Social Contract Theory was a way for these writers to express the theoretical origin of government.

Thomas Hobbes published the *Leviathan* in 1651 in order to defend the divine right of the British monarchy. In this highly influential book, Hobbes emphasized the primary importance of order in society. He said that when man lives in nature, outside of government, he lives as in a state of war and life is "solitary, poor, nasty, brutish, and short." He believed it is necessary to give a single ruler absolute power to protect the citizens and maintain order. In essence, Hobbes asserted that people make a sort of bargain or contract: that to have the privilege of living in a civil society of order and safety, they pay the price of submitting to a government of strict law. But the price was steep. In Hobbes' *Leviathan* a citizen must give up his personal freedom, control of his possessions, free speech, free trade, and the legal right to defend himself. The Founders rejected Hobbes idea of the divine right of kings and the need for absolute government control.

John Locke, living a generation after Hobbes, published *Two Treatises on Government* in 1690. In this book he rejected the concept of the divine right of kings and instead supported a powerful legislature (the lawmaking branch), as long as it received the consent of the people and followed established law. Locke also rejected Hobbes's overly pessimistic view of human nature. As demonstrated by the American Indian, people in nature mostly get along with each other. True, humans can be selfish and brutal, but they can also use their foresight, charity, and goodwill to make a just society.

No other writer had more influence on the Revolutionary Generation than Locke, who was frequently quoted or alluded to in pamphlets and in the Declaration of Independence. Locke's most influential idea was that man is born with certain divine rights, including "life, liberty, health, limb, and goods of another (property)." All humans are naturally free, equal, and sovereign over their own bodies, thus they do not have the power to forfeit their lives and freedom to government. This is the basis of the concept of limited government. Government is instituted to protect man's God-given rights, provide for the safety and happiness of the people, and rule by impartial laws crafted by a legislature supported by the consent of the governed; and, if governments fail to do these things, then the people have the right to rebel.

Social Contract Theory states that people must give up certain liberties when they enter into society, but the resulting order and safety is worth the loss of freedom

Central to Locke's political philosophy was the concept of private property and that a person must be free to enjoy the fruits of one's labor. "The labor of his body and the works of his hand," said Locke, "we may say, are properly his." And no other person can lay claim to it. Locke asserted that if government could arbitrarily take away a person's property, or unfairly tax him, he has no real freedom and is little more than a slave. In other words, there is no political freedom without economic freedom. Further, private property fosters the virtues of industriousness and rationality. And the hard work and enterprise resulting from property rights will improve the whole society. The writings of Locke, along with other eighteenth-century thinkers, such as Adam Smith, Jean-Baptiste Say, and David Ricardo, form the foundation of **Classical Liberalism**, *which holds that limited government should leave citizens free to further their individual pursuits, which will enhance the public good in the aggregate.*

John Locke was the thinker that had the most influence of the Founders.
©Everett Historical/Shutterstock.com

Charles de Montesquieu, a Frenchman, wrote the *Spirit of the Laws* in 1749. Like Locke, Montesquieu rejected Hobbes's overly pessimistic view of human nature. He remarked that if humans were so horrible, why do people flock together and form cities? He also agreed with Locke that economic freedom improves the character of the individual and benefits society. "The spirit of commerce," said Montesquieu, "brings with it a spirit of frugality, economy, moderation, work, wisdom, tranquility, order, and rule." He went on to say that "in a nation that is in servitude, one works more to preserve than to acquire; in a free nation, one works more to acquire than preserve." In the *Spirit of the Laws,* Montesquieu emphasized the importance of culture on law and government. A republic could only work in a nation whose culture reflected democratic virtues. He also said that the government should always make reforms through moderation, gently persuading the people that new laws are needed.

Montesquieu was the most quoted author by the delegates at the Constitutional Convention. The delegates shared Montesquieu's concern about thwarting despotic government and protecting individual liberty, and so they adopted his concept of separating the branches of government. "When the legislative power is united with executive power in a single person or in a simple body of magistry, there is no liberty, because one can fear that the same monarch or Senate that makes tyrannical laws will execute them tyrannically." And the Framers adopted many other principles of Montesquieu's, including

Classical Liberalism

holds that limited government should leave citizens free to further their individual pursuits, which will enhance the public good in the aggregate divided government, checks and balances, decentralization, an independent judiciary that interprets not makes law, and the importance of impartial laws. But the Framers ended up rejecting Montesquieu's idea that republics can only work in small geographical areas—an idea Madison refutes in *The Federalist #10* (which will be discussed in Chapter 4 and Chapter 21).

POLITICAL CULTURE

Political culture *refers to the widely shared beliefs, values, and norms concerning the relationship of citizens to their government and to one another.* In these next sections we will discuss America's unique political values, often referred to as the American Creed. Alexis de Tocqueville, a French aristocrat who toured America in the early 1830s, believed that political culture was the primary engine of good government. In *Democracy in America,* he said, "I am convinced that the luckiest of geographic circumstances and the best of laws cannot maintain a constitution in despite of mores (culture), whereas the latter can turn even the most unfavorable circumstances and the worst laws to advantage." What he meant was that the political culture of a country constantly guides the creation and adherence to the law, and that a country with a flawed political culture will quickly dismantle good law. So, political culture is the foundation of a country's laws and government.

Political Culture

refers to the widely shared beliefs, values, and norms concerning the relationship of citizens to their government and to one another

THE DECLARATION OF INDEPENDENCE

The first place to look for some idea of America's original political culture is in its founding document, the Declaration of Independence. Chiefly written by the young Thomas Jefferson in 1776, it declared to the world that America is now a free and independent nation and no longer a British colony. But it also expresses the political values of the newly formed nation.

Declaration of Independence: **"We hold these truths to be self-evident, that all men are created equal, that they are endowed by their Creator with certain unalienable Rights, that among these are Life, Liberty and the pursuit of Happiness.—That to secure these rights, Governments are instituted among Men, deriving their just powers from the consent of the governed,—That whenever any Form of Government becomes destructive of these ends, it is the Right of the People to alter or to abolish it, and to institute new Government, laying its foundation on such principles and organizing its powers in such form, as to them shall seem most likely to effect their Safety and Happiness . . ."**

Thomas Jefferson was the primary author of the Declaration of Independence.
©vkilikov/Shutterstock.com

Liberty is the primary American political value. Liberty was the rallying cry of the American Revolution. Patrick Henry said, "Give me liberty or give me death." Besides the flag, the Statue of Liberty is the most recognizable symbol of America. The inscription on the Liberty Bell reads: "Proclaim LIBERTY throughout the land unto all the inhabitants thereof, Lev 25.10." Jefferson wrote in the Declaration that all people "are endowed by their Creator with certain inalienable rights that among these are life, *liberty*, and the pursuit of happiness." **Liberty** *is individual freedom from undo government interference and the freedom to pursue happiness.* The Framer's main fear was that an overweening government would restrain individual freedom.

Equality: Jefferson said, "We hold these truths to be self evident, that all men are created *equal*." In 1776, all Americans would have understood that this reflected the Judeo-Christian tradition which held that all humans have equal value in the eyes of God. And this idea had social implications as well. Americans have always believed in social equality and rejected the concept of an aristocratic class of privilege. European aristocrats traveling through America were often taken aback by the assertiveness of all Americans to be treated equally, regardless of income or social rank. Jefferson said, it is a "palpable truth, that the mass of mankind has not been born with saddles on their backs, nor a favored few booted and spurred." The American government was based on the idea that the wealthy and privileged should not hold a political monopoly.

Liberty

is individual freedom from undo government interference and the freedom to pursue happiness

The Founders understood "equality" in two senses. **Political equality**: *all Americans should enjoy equal protection under the law, equal voting rights, and equal access to office.* And they believe in **equal opportunity**: *Regardless of wealth or background, all people should have an equal chance in life.* America is the land of opportunity and no matter where you start out in life, through hard work and talent, one can become anything he or she desires. The president born in a log cabin became a great symbol of American opportunity. Abraham Lincoln said, "when one starts poor, as most do in the race of life, free society is such that he knows he can better his condition; he knows that there is no fixed condition of labor for his whole life." The concept of equal opportunity is coupled with the idea of liberty, that each individual has the ability to take advantage of life's opportunities.

Natural Rights: The Declaration asserts that the "Creator" has granted certain rights and liberties to all people and that they are "unalienable," meaning they cannot be taken away. This is an important political concept. If governments grant your rights and freedoms, then they can take them away. But if they are granted by God, then your rights and freedoms are prior to and separate from government and government cannot take them away. This concept forms the foundation of limited government: that there are certain things that the government cannot do.

Democracy: The Declaration of Independence states that the only legitimate governments are those that receive the "consent of the governed." Americans believe in everybody having a say and in majority rule. If the majority of Americans think a certain way about something, we feel the politicians should listen. Bills become law through the democratic process in Congress. We elected officials through the democratic method in free elections. We hate any system where the minority of elites have all the power. America has a representative form of government, but *ultimate power resides in the people. This is known as* **popular sovereignty**. As Lincoln said, ours is a "government of the people, by the people, [and] for the people."

Pursuit of happiness: Notice that Jefferson did not write that there is a right to happiness, but instead wrote that we have the right to <u>pursue</u> happiness. Pursue is an active verb, meaning to engage in, to hunt, and to work at. Only some sort of utopian government would promise the right to happiness. Instead, the Founders created a

Political Equality

all Americans should enjoy equal protection under the law, equal voting rights, and equal access to office

Equal Opportunity

regardless of wealth or background, all people should have an equal chance in life

Popular Sovereignty

ultimate power resides in the people

The Statue of Liberty is a symbol of American liberty and its openness to immigrants.
©Luciano Mortula/Shutterstock.com

totally different kind of government, one based on liberty. People will have the liberty to pursue their own happiness, to make their own life, to discover their talents, to earn their success, and to figure out how they can contribute to society. This is the deep, Aristotelian sense of happiness as described in Chapter 1; what psychologists call today "self-actualization," discovering your potential. But being allowed to pursue your own happiness also implies that there will be trials and errors. A free society must allow people to fail and learn from their mistakes.

AMERICAN CREED

Besides the ideas expressed in the Declaration of Independence (liberty, equality, natural rights, democracy, and the opportunity to pursue happiness), there were other aspects of America's original political values, often called "the American Creed." European travelers, such as the oft quoted Alexis de Tocqueville, noted how different America's political culture was from Europe's. The American Creed is also referred to as "American Exceptionalism," meaning that these are the cultural aspects, good and bad, that made America different, unique, or exceptional.

Protestant Ethic: Historians call the unique form of culture that dominated colonial America and the early years of the Republic as the **Protestant Ethic**: *A set of virtues especially strong in Puritan America that valued hard work, self-reliance, thrift, honesty, religiosity, and moderation.* The America Founders strongly believed that limited government was contingent upon America's unique culture. Patrick Henry said, "No free government, or the blessing of liberty, can be preserved to any people but by a firm adherence to justice, moderation, temperance, frugality, and virtue." Besides limited government, these cultural values helped foster free market capitalism. Max Weber, in his seminal work, *The Protestant Ethic and the Spirit of Capitalism (1905)*, said that modern capitalism developed in America due to the Protestant Ethic.

Individualism: In America we celebrate the individual. In other parts of the world, people feel a strong identity or attachment to their clan, class, sect, village, region, or ancestry. In China, for example, people use their family name first, reflecting the primacy of family in the Chinese culture. Americans believe in the individual and self-determination: a person's success in life depends on their efforts, talents, and luck. The "self-made man" is an American hero. People come to America from all over the world to start a new life and forge a new identity.

Today, however, there is a tendency to look at people not as free individuals but as members of their race, class, and gender. Modern Progressives talk of equality as equality of conditions or *equal outcome*: the attempt to achieve

Protestant Ethic

a set of virtues especially strong in Puritan America that valued hard work, self-reliance, thrift, honesty, religiosity, and moderation equal economic conditions. In order to achieve material equality, governments should initiate some sort of redistribution of wealth through a progressive tax and a generous welfare state. The American Founders were opposed to this type of egalitarianism. As Jefferson said, "to take from one, because it is thought that his own industry and that of his father's has acquired too much, in order to spare to others, who, or whose fathers, have not exercised equal industry and skill, is to violate arbitrarily the first principle of association, the guarantee to everyone the free exercise of his industry and the fruits acquired by it."

A Nation of Immigrants: Unlike any other country, the United States of America is a nation of immigrants. People come from all over the world to pursue their own happiness and seek economic opportunity. It takes great courage to break free from one's own country and start a new life in a foreign land. The Immigrant experience has also contributed to the American culture of rugged individualism. By coming to America, immigrants helped break down the frontier, struggled to build a farm or start a business, and scratched out a life for themselves that was better than the one they would have had had they stayed in the land of their birth. America has benefited from people of independent spirit and initiative that came to America.

E Pluribus Unum

Latin for "from the many one." The American motto that represents the idea that individuals with a diversity of backgrounds come together to form one nation

One of the mottos of America is "**E Pluribus Unum**," *which is Latin for "from the many one."* It is printed on every US coin. The concept of one America, made up of people from all walks of life, is the social glue that holds us together. Foreign travelers are often astounded by how quickly newcomers are accepted as fully American by the American people. In contrast, if somebody from Africa moved to Japan, for example, they might never be accepted as "Japanese." But in America we quickly accept people who want to become American as Americans. E Pluribus Unum means that each individual is unique but that we can all come together as Americans.

Respect for the Common Man: Americans trust the common sense, decency, and wisdom of the common people. In contrast, we often feel distrustful of the intellectual or social elite. Our government, based on open elections and majority rule, is founded on the concept that we can trust the wisdom of the masses. The Jeffersonian Republicans trusted the yeoman farmer. The Jacksonian Democrats trusted the "common man." The Populists trusted the small famer and laborer against the financial elites. Today nobody can successfully win the presidency if they fail to connect with the average person. This is why candidates are often depicted going to county fairs, flipping pancakes, or

"From the many one": Americans come from many different backgrounds but together they form one America.
©rorem/Shutterstock.com

going to ball games. In America, being accused of being a snob or an elitist is political death. This accounts for one reason Donald Trump won the presidential election: he ran a populist campaign that appealed to the "forgotten man."

Capitalism: Adam Smith's *Wealth of Nations* was published in 1776, the same year as the Declaration of Independence. The founding generation believed in private property and that private institutions should be run to generate profits. They fought the Revolution against Great Britain, in part, to protest the English system of mercantilism: an economic system based on government control and privilege. The Founders strongly believed that there is no political freedom without economic freedom. In the **capitalistic system**, *free enterprise sets prices, allocates natural resources, establishes wages, distributes goods and services, and regulates production, while providing the individual with the incentive to succeed.*

Millions of immigrants come to this country in pursuit of the "American Dream," which is open to all who work hard, take initiative, and who play by the rules. America is the land of opportunity where anyone can own a house, start a business, and earn a good living. Free enterprise capitalism, based on the freedom of the individual to innovate and take risk, has lifted the most people out of poverty than any other system in world history.

Pluralism: One of the key aspects of American society that surprised Tocqueville the most was the ability of the American people to form groups to achieve different goals. He said Americans exhibit a "can do spirit" by spontaneously forming groups to, for example, distribute free Bibles, gain the vote for women, provide for orphans, beautify the parks, or represent textile manufacturers. What Tocqueville described became known as a *pluralistic democracy:* a democracy which allows the free association of groups to pursue various social, economic, and political goals. Instead of relying on a centralized government to do things, Americans formed groups or used local government to solve problems. In our federal system, these groups serve an important function as an intermediary between the national government, the states, and the individual. Americans have always had a great knack for forming groups and taking care of their own problems.

In God We Trust: This is one of the mottos of the United States. "In God We Trust" is printed on all US currency and is inscribed above the rostrum in the US Congress. The President ends each important address with "God bless America." Every presidential inaugural address since 1789 has included the word God. These references to God

> **Capitalistic System**
>
> free enterprise sets prices, allocates natural resources, establishes wages, distributes goods and services, and regulates production, while providing the individual with the incentive to succeed

"In God We Trust" is engraved on all US coins.
©Steve Allen/Shutterstock.com

make western Europeans uncomfortable, but it has been a core principle in America's culture and history. Many of the colonial settlers, such as the Puritans, Quakers, and Methodists, came to America seeking religious freedom. And today a higher percentage of Americans believe in God and regularly attend church than in any other industrialized nation.

Although some of the American Founders held unorthodox Christian views, especially Thomas Jefferson and Benjamin Franklin, they all shared a core set of religious beliefs that helped shape their understanding of the proper role of government. The Founders believed our rights are granted by God and that each life is equally precious; that there is no objective good and evil without God; and that God judges people and nations. And consistent with Judeo-Christian belief, the Founders believed that human nature is morally flawed. This understanding had two important consequences. The Founders believed that government must be checked and limited to guard against abusive government officials. And the people, especially a people granted so much freedom, must be morally instructed by religion. But they firmly believed that religion must be a free choice and not dictated by the state.

The Rule of Law: Order has historically had a negative connotation in America. It summons images of intrusive government. Except in times of war or crisis, few American politicians call for a need for order. Yet, Americans have always possessed a profound trust in law and order. Tocqueville said, "sooner or later all American political controversies are settled in the courts, which the people abide by." Of the three branches of government, recent polls show that Americans trust the judicial branch the most. This is because they understand the role of the Supreme Court as the maintainer of the rule of law. We might not always agree with the Court's ruling, but we understand that one institution must have the final say to maintain order.

FINAL THOUGHTS

The premise of the chapter is that culture dictates what type of government a society will establish. America's unique form of culture made America's government based on individual freedom possible. But the Founders were a bit worried about their experiment in liberty. If people are going to be granted so much freedom, including economic, political, and social freedom, then this should be counter-balanced by some institutions that instill restraint, moderation, and charity. This is why the Founders emphasized the importance of law and religion in society. The law restrains people and teaches them right conduct. And religion teaches people humility and goodwill. John Adams said:

"we have no government armed with power capable of contending with human passions unbridled by morality and religion. Avarice, ambition, revenge, or gallantry would break the strongest cords of our Constitution as a whale goes through a net. Our Constitution was made only for a moral and religious people. It is wholly inadequate to the government of any other."

The title of this textbook is *Growth of the American Republic*. We will see that as American culture has changed over time, and that the American government has adopted to these changes. The Framers were correct, the constitutional Republic they created was based on a culture that valued individual freedom and limited government. Today, in our post-industrial society, we have a different political culture and a different view of the proper role of government. Yet, through all these changes, we still have retained many of the elements of the Founder's original vision.

NOTES

Arthur Brooks, *The Road to Freedom*. New York: Basic Books, 2012.

Hobbes, *The Leviathan*. London: Penguin Classics, 1982.

Locke, *Second Treatise on Civil Government*. New York: Prometheus Books, 1986.

Charles de Montesquieu. *Spirit of the Laws*. Translated by Thomas Nugent. New York: Cosimo Classics, 2011.

Polibius, *Histories*. Translated by Robin Waterfield. Oxford, Oxford University Press, 2010.

Dennis Prager, *Still the Best Hope*. New York: Harper Collins, 2012.

Alexis de Tocqueville, *Democracy in America*. Translated by George Lawrence. New York: Harper Collins, 1969.

Steven Waldman. *Founding Faith*. New York: Random House, 2009.

Jordon Wood, *The Idea of America: Reflections on the Birth of the United States*. London: Penguin Books, 2012.

ESSAY QUESTIONS

1. Cite some of the important historical roots of American Democracy.
2. Describe Social Contract Theory and explain how Hobbes and Locke differ.
3. Define the core values of the American Creed: liberty, equality, individualism, Democracy, Capitalism, "In God We Trust," and E Pluribus Unum.
4. What type of equality did the Founders believe in?

TERMS

Capitalistic System: _____

Classical Liberalism: _____

Demagogue: _____

Equal Opportunity: _____

E Pluribus Unum: _____

Liberty: _____

Political Culture: _____

Political Equality: _____

Popular Sovereignty: _____

Protestant Ethic: _____

Republic: _____

Social Contract Theory: _____

CHAPTER 3

What Happened at the Constitutional Convention?

TOPICS

▶ The Articles of Confederation
▶ The Constitutional Convention of 1787
▶ Debates and Compromises at the Convention
▶ Principles of the Constitution
▶ A Brilliant Solution

LEARNING OBJECTIVES

When you finish reading this chapter, you will be able to:

1. Discuss the flaws of the Articles of Confederation.
2. Describe the three major compromises made at the Constitutional Convention.
3. Outline the major principles of the Constitution.
4. Explain some of the fears the Framers expressed about the Constitution.
5. Demonstrate how the Constitution guides the democratic process.

WHAT HAPPENED AT THE CONSTITUTIONAL CONVENTION?

The summer of 1787 is a defining moment in American history. Delegates representing the newly formed states convened to write a constitution and establish a new government. But these delegates were well prepared. Over the last several years, a period called the "era of constitutionalism," Americans framed several constitutions. The former English colonies, now American states, each wrote a constitution. And the national government wrote a constitution, called the Articles of Confederation. This presented a wonderful time of trial and error in which the Founding Generation learned what worked and what did not work. Equipped with this valuable experience and the knowledge gained from their extensive readings of history, the fifty-five delegates arrived in Philadelphia in May of 1787 to craft a new form of government. But it was not without much debate, frustration, and compromise.

THE ARTICLES OF CONFEDERATION

Most people do not know that the US Constitution is actually America's second attempt at forming a government. The first attempt, the Articles of Confederation, failed. The Confederation was America's functioning constitution from 1777 to 1788. Historically, a *confederation* is a league of smaller states that form an alliance, especially for defensive purposes. The Articles of Confederation declared that the thirteen states are entering into a "league of friendship . . . for their common defense . . . and their mutual and general welfare." Leaving most of the powers in the hands of the states, this league of friendship created a weak central government that did not maintain order or fulfill most of the other traditional objectives of government.

Unicameral

a legislative branch with only one chamber

State Constitutions: As America declared independence from Great Britain and prepared for war, each state drafted its own constitution. In January 1776, even before the Declaration of Independence was written, New Hampshire became the first state to adopt a constitution. South Carolina quickly followed, and in June of that year Virginia and New Jersey approved their constitutions. The state constitutions shared several similarities: a weak governor, a strong legislative branch, one-year terms of office, a republican form of government, and written constitutions (unlike Britain's). Penned by George Mason, Virginia was the first state to adopt a bill of rights, called the Virginia Declaration of Rights. Soon nearly all the states approved a bill of rights, usually placed at the beginning of their constitutions.

How the Confederation Worked: With each state retaining most of its sovereignty, government under the Articles of Confederation was highly decentralized. The Confederation Congress was **unicameral**, *meaning the legislative branch had only one chamber*. The delegates representing one of the thirteen states sat at a table together, sharing one vote. If nine of the thirteen states voted for a proposal, it became law. There were no separate executive or judicial branches: these duties were conducted by legislative committees. For example, Robert Morris headed a committee on finance which administered most of the government's financial duties. And in order to add an amendment

The Articles of Confederation was our constitution during the Revolutionary War.
©Victorian Traditions/Shutterstock.com

to the Articles, all thirteen states had to unanimously agree, something the highly independent states were never able to do.

Weaknesses of the Articles: Probably the greatest flaw of the Articles was its weak tax authority. As citizens, we do not like to pay taxes. But as we learned in Chapter 1, governments must supply armies and provide many other services for its citizens. Governments need a steady source of revenue to do these things. Under the Articles of Confederation, states were requested to pay taxes to the national government, yet many states ignored these requests. As a result, America could not pay its debts, which were extensive due to the Revolutionary War. Further, the Articles contained many other weaknesses: each state printed its own money, no national judiciary existed to resolve mounting interstate disputes, different states made their own trade agreements with foreign countries, and because we had no president, no national leader guided the country. In summary, the government failed to provide order, causing some to fear that the thirteen states might break up.

THE CONSTITUTIONAL CONVENTION OF 1787

After several years under the Articles, more and more people understood the fundamental flaws of a confederate form of government. Men like George Washington, Alexander Hamilton, and James Madison started discussing ways to strengthen the national government. After only five states showed up at a conference in Annapolis, Maryland, to discuss interstate commerce,

The Framers met in Independence Hall in 1787.
©f11photo/Shutterstock.com

Madison called for another convention "to take into consideration the situation of the United States, to devise such further provisions as shall appear to them necessary to render the constitution of the Federal Government adequate to the exigencies of the Union . . . and to correct such defects as may be discovered to exist." Most understood this to mean they were to *revise* the Articles of Confederation. Subsequently, Congress authorized a convention to meet in Philadelphia in May 1787.

Who attended the Constitutional Convention? Within days, the men that met in Philadelphia decided that a whole new constitution needed to be written. A total of fifty-five delegates from twelve states (Rhode Island refused to send delegates) attended the convention, but a core of about thirty completed most of the work. They were young, the average age was forty-three, and highly educated, most went to college, which was unusual at that time. But their key characteristic was that they were highly experienced. All the delegates had experience writing a constitution (either for their state or the Confederation), serving in the state or national legislature, or serving in the military during the Revolution. About a third of the delegates were lawyers, a third were merchants (businessmen), and a third were farmers (most of whom owned slaves). All of them were wealthy, accomplished men.

A few prominent revolutionaries did not attend the Convention. Samuel Adams and John Hancock stayed in Massachusetts. Thomas Jefferson and John Adams, who dearly wanted to participate in crafting a new government, were serving as ambassadors in Europe. Patrick Henry, a supporter of the Confederation and state's rights, refused to attend, stating that he "smelt a rat." But many of the important leaders of the Revolution did attend, such as James Madison, Alexander Hamilton, George Mason, James Wilson, and Robert Morris. Most significantly, the two most famous Americans, George Washington and Ben Franklin, attended the Convention. This was important. The presence and eventual approval of the Constitution by those two eminent men gave the American people confidence that the Constitutional Convention was necessary and legitimate.

The Beliefs of the Delegates: The delegates argued heatedly over many issues, but there were topics that they did not debate because they were in agreement. The delegates agreed that they had to restore order to America by giving more power to the central government and taking power away from the states. They agreed that they wanted a republican form of government, not a direct democracy. Due in large part to their reading of Montesquieu's *Spirit of the Laws* and John Adam's *Thoughts on Government*, they agreed that they wanted a federal government with three branches and *a legislature with two chambers*, **bicameral.** And significantly, they seemed to share a cautious understanding of human nature. They knew that if you give one person or a group of people power they will eventually abuse that power or want more power. This realistic view of human nature posed a real problem: how were they going to create a stronger government when they didn't trust people with governmental power?

Bicameral

a legislature with two chambers

The Great Dilemma: After the Convention, James Madison described the historic conundrum the delegates faced. In *Federalist #45* he said: "but what is government itself but the greatest of all reflections on human nature? If men were angels, no government would be necessary. If angels were to govern, neither external nor internal controls on government would be necessary. In framing a government which is to be administered by men over men, the great difficulty lies in this: you must first enable the government to control the governed; and in the next place obligated to control itself."

So the great challenge for the delegates arriving in Philadelphia that fateful summer was how were they going to create a stronger central government when they did not trust government officials with power? And how were they going to create a democratic form of government when they did not always trust the opinion of the majority? These were the great problems they faced, problems nations had been struggling with for centuries.

DEBATES AND COMPROMISES AT THE CONVENTION

The Federal Convention convened at the Pennsylvania State House, today called Independence Hall, on May 25. For the next four months the delegates argued over many topics. Confined in one large room during the notoriously hot and humid summer months of Philadelphia, tempers flared, accusations were hurled, and many delegates threatened to dissolve the United States. But because their collective desire to build a stronger union outweighed their many individual differences, they were able to produce a document by making important compromises on three difficult issues: state representation, slavery, and the presidency.

Virginia's Big State Plan: James Madison, a scholarly, soft-spoken man and son of a wealthy Virginian tobacco planter, arrived early to the convention and drafted a plan of government. Afraid few would listen to him due to his diminished statue and young age (he was 5 feet 4 inches and 36 years old), he asked the commanding governor of Virginia, Edmund Randolph, to present his plan to the Convention.

Madison's plan called for a federal system, dividing power between the states and the national government. It had three separate branches: a legislative, executive, and judicial. It derived its ultimate authority from the people, but in a very indirect way. Only members of the lower house of the legislature would be chosen by the people. In turn, the members of the upper house would be selected by the members of the lower house. And together, the legislature would select the president and national judges. In a remarkable support of a powerful national government, Congress would have the right to veto state laws. The fifteen articles of the Virginia Plan became the working blueprint from which the delegates framed the Constitution, but ultimately they changed many of its features. The aspect of the **Virginia Plan** that initially provoked the most discussion was the proposal that *representation in Congress should be based on the population of the states, thus giving large states more power*.

The New Jersey Small State Plan: Because each state had a unique colonial history, the people felt a much stronger personal attachment to their state than we do today. When the Virginian delegation presented its plan of government in which the large states would have more representatives in Congress, the smaller states were fearful that they would be stripped of their current power. In response to the Virginia Plan, William Patterson of New Jersey presented the **New Jersey Plan**, *which would retain equal state representation in the legislature just as they did under the Articles of Confederation*. Patterson confessed that the Articles were flawed, so to make up for its weaknesses he proposed giving the national government more power over taxes, commerce, and foreign affairs. But

Virginia Plan

a plan written by James Madison and presented at the Constitutional Convention that specified that representation in Congress should be based on the population of the states

New Jersey Plan

which would retain equal state representation in the legislature just as they did under the Articles of Confederation

James Madison crafted the Virginia Plan.
©Dawn Hudson/Shutterstock.com

when the New Jersey Plan came up for a vote, it was soundly defeated. The delegates may have had doubts about the Virginia Plan, but they knew that they did not want to go back to a confederate form of government.

1) The Compromise between the Big and Small States: The debate between the big and small states went on for several frustrating weeks. Finally, it was proposed that a committee composed of one delegate from each state chaired by Ben Franklin should meet in private to resolve this issue. Here Roger Sherman of Connecticut proposed the compromise that would eventually be accepted by the Convention. The **Great Compromise** *stated that each state will have an equal vote in the Senate* (as the New Jersey Plan proposed) *and representation in the House will be based on population* (as the Virginia Plan proposed). Members of the Senate will serve a six-year term; members of the House will serve a two-year term. And in order to know how many people live in each state, a census will take place every ten years to count the population. Originally, each member of the House of Representatives represented 30,000 people.

Debate between the Free and Slave States: After the Revolution, the northern states started the process of freeing their slaves. The northern states never had large slave populations, and they were moving toward a diverse manufacturing and commercial economy based on free labor. The South, on the other hand, remained an agricultural economy based on slave labor. The nation was deeply split between these two economic systems. At the Convention, the debate on slavery was closely linked to the debate on representation in Congress. Whenever it was proposed that representation in Congress should be based on the population of the state, it presented the problem of whether the state's slave population should be counted in the census.

Great Compromise

stated that each state will have an equal vote in the Senate and representation in the House will be based on population

The debate on slavery became so heated that at several points it threatened to terminate the Convention. Gouverneur Morris said slavery was immoral and slaves should not be counted in the census, after all slaves were treated as property not citizens. George Mason said slavery will "bring the Judgment of Heaven on a country . . . [for its] national sins." Other delegates defended slavery and argued that slaves should be counted in the census. Charles Pinckney of South Carolina said slaves produced the wealth and power of the southern states, and a state's power should be reflected in Congress. If slavery is not protected in the Constitution, Pinckney warned, the southern delegates will leave the convention and go home. It would simply be impossible to get the southern states to ratify a constitution that did not protect their economic interests.

2) Compromise between the Free and Slave States: In his notes of the convention speeches, Madison wrote on June 30 that "the great division of interests in the United States . . . did not lie between large and small states; it lay between the northern and southern [states]." So although the differences between the free and slave states ran deeper than the differences between the large and small states, the delegates finally hammered out three major compromises over slavery. (1) **The Three-Fifths Compromise** *stated that for purposes of representation five slaves will be counted as three citizens*; (2) The international slave trade will end in twenty years, in 1808; and (3) The Fugitive Slave Clause stated that if a slave escaped from a Southern state, Northern states were obligated to return the runaway slave.

The Three-Fifths Compromise is often mischaracterized as something that increased the power of the slave states. This is not true. At the Constitutional Convention, the slave states wanted 100% of the slaves to be counted for representation in Congress, but the northern states rejected this. The Three-Fifths Clause REDUCED the power of the slave states by reducing the number of representatives they would have had in Congress and the Electoral College.

The Three-Fifths Compromise

a phrase in the original Constitution that stated that for purposes of representation in Congress five slaves will be counted as three citizens in the census

Unlike the Great Compromise, this compromise had only a short-term success. Many delegates understood that the compromise on slavery violated America's founding principles of liberty and equality as expressed in the Declaration of Independence. But these delegates came to Philadelphia to strengthen the Union, not dissolve it. If the Southern delegation were allowed to depart, it would mean the end of the Union. The delegates who were opposed to slavery simply hoped that within a generation or two the institution of slavery would die on its own, as it appeared to be doing in the North. But by imbedding this compromise with slavery in the text of the Constitution, they made a legal solution impossible. Eventually these three provisions will be removed from the Constitution but only after the Civil War, the bloodiest conflict in American history which cost over 620,000 lives.

3) Compromise on the Presidency: America had just won a rebellion against a tyrannical monarch, the King of Great Britain. This experience gave them great trepidation in creating a strong executive branch. Indeed, most of the state constitutions had created a very weak executive, and the Articles had no executive branch at all. But after ten years without strong national leadership, most delegates realized a strong executive was needed. Afraid to give one man too much power, Ben Franklin proposed creating a council of several executives. Alexander Hamilton, on the other hand, recommended a single, powerful president elected for life. Surprisingly, Hamilton got much of what he wanted.

Alexander Hamilton wanted a strong presidency.
©Everett Historical/Shutterstock.com

The Constitution created a strong, unitary president, but with appropriate limits. A president could serve for life as Hamilton wanted, as long as he was reelected every four years. The president would be the commander in chief of the military, but only Congress could declare war. The president would take the lead in foreign affairs, but the Senate would approve his appointments and treaties. And the president was given a qualified veto, which Congress could override it with a two-thirds vote. So, considering the fear the Framers had of a strong executive, they created a surprisingly capable president, but much of the powers of the office would not become apparent until many years later.

PRINCIPLES OF THE CONSTITUTION

Assigned to the Committee of Style, Gouverneur Morris wrote one of the final drafts of the Constitution, polishing the language and organizing it logically into seven articles. The first three articles correspond to the three branches of government: Article I describes the legislative powers, Article II describes the executive powers, and Article III describes the judicial powers. Other articles deal with various issues. How the states are to relate to each other is contained in Article IV. The procedure to add amendments is included in Article V. And how the Constitution is to be ratified is explained in Article VII. The supremacy clause, stating that "This Constitution . . . shall be the supreme Law of the Land," is found in Article VI.

Constitutional Principles: The Constitution is based on several basic principles. The Framers created a *Republican* form of government, in which the people are the ultimate sovereigns. Representatives serve the people and are held accountable by free elections. *National and states governments share power in this* **federal system**. Unlike the Articles of Confederation, the new government is controlled by a powerful central government, while allowing limited state authority. But in order to limit the power of the national government, the Framers created a system of **separation of powers** *with three branches of government: executive, legislative, and judicial.*

The Constitution gives each branch the ability to protect itself from the other two branches. This is called **checks and balances**: *each branch of government has some power over the other branches.* In *Federalist #51*, Madison said, "The great security against a gradual concentration of the several powers in the same department consists in giving to those who administer each department the necessary constitutional means and

Federal System

national and state governments share power

Separation of Powers

with three branches of government: executive, legislative, and judicial

Checks and Balances

each branch of government has some power over the other branches

LEGISLATIVE

EXECUTIVE

JUDICIAL

The three branches of government have the power to check each other.
©JPL Designs/Shutterstock.com

personal motives to resist encroachments of the other . . . Ambition must be made to counter ambition." Madison said that mere words on a constitution, what he called "parchment barriers," would never last long. Eventually one branch of government would ignore or misinterpret those words. Instead, we must equip each branch with actual power to defend itself from the encroachment of another branch.

A BRILLIANT SOLUTION

As delegates were leaving the Philadelphia State House after signing the Constitution, a lady came up to Benjamin Franklin and asked, "Well Doctor, what have we got—a Republic or a Monarchy?" "A Republic," responded Franklin, "if you can keep it." Franklin's reply exemplifies a common belief held by the Framers. From their reading of the history, they thought that the reason Republics failed, particularly the Roman Republic, was that the people and their leaders lost the virtues necessary to maintain self-government: patriotism, self-reliance, austerity, courage, self-sacrifice, and industry. Many of the Founders believed that the American Republic would be short-lived because eventually the prosperity and abundance that America offered would result in luxury, self-centeredness, and complacency. John Adams echoed Franklin's sentiment when he said, "Democracy never lasts long . . . there was never a democracy yet that did not commit suicide."

Ben Franklin wondered how long the American Republic would last.
©Eduard Moldoveanu/Shutterstock.com

Madison's Fears: James Madison may have been slightly more optimistic than Adams, but on June 26 during the Constitutional Convention he made an ominous speech. Madison said that in "all civilizations . . . there are debtors and creditors . . . rich and poor." The poor will always be more numerous than the rich. In a republic, the majority rules; and one day, Madison warned, the people might be motivated by a "leveling spirit" and vote for an "equal distributions of [the country's] blessings." Decades later, Alexis de Tocqueville expressed this fear in more direct language when he said, "The American Republic will endure until the day Congress discovers that it can bribe the public with the public's money." So how would the Constitution prevent the *people* from making what Madison called "temporary errors"?

The Brilliant Solution: The Framers solved two problems that had stumped political thinkers for centuries:

First, how do you create a government powerful enough to accomplish the necessary goals and responsibilities of government without giving government officials unlimited power? In other words, how do you guard the guardians? And the second problem they solved was how do you create a democratic form of government which will prevent the majority from trampling on individual and minority rights? That is, how do you prevent mob rule?

The Framers put in place several mechanisms to prevent government officials from abusing and expanding their powers. The central government will be divided into three branches, and each will be given the ability to check the other's power. Second, the legislative branch will further be divided into two branches to provide more deliberation. Third, they created two levels of government: one national government and several state governments. And the states will retain their powers except for the ones explicitly granted to the national government. To make this clear, the powers of the national government will be specifically listed or enumerated. This way the people will know exactly what the national government is permitted and forbidden from doing. And lastly, they added a Bill of Rights to further limit the national government and proscribe its powers, for example Congress cannot limit freedom of the press.

And the Framers erected a system to thwart mob rule. The people will vote, but representatives will make the laws. Ideally, these representatives will be persons of intelligence, experience, and virtue that will do what is right even if against popular opinion. This will be especially true of the Senators whose six-year terms give them time to think about the long-term interest of the nation. Further, the immediate passions of the people will be thwarted by staggered elections by different constituent groups. Representatives are elected every two years by the voters of their congressional district. Senators are selected every six years by the legislators of their state (and only one-third of the Senate is up for election at any one time). And the president is elected every four years by the Electoral College. Finally, judges are selected for life, giving them the ability to properly interpret the Constitution and the Bill of Rights, which protects the rights of individuals and minorities against the will of the majority.

A Democratic Process: Certainly, the Constitution the Framers built sounds like a complicated machine with many moving parts and internal friction. But this machine is the vehicle by which the nation can solve its problems in a democratic manner. The Framers knew that the best solution to a difficult issue is seldom the result of initial impulse. We have all had the experience of being confronted by something new and allowing our knee-jerk reaction to lead us into making a bad decision. The Framers created a structure by which the nation will deliberate and debate issues in enough time to arrive at the proper solution or perhaps the least worse solution. Through free speech and elections, political contests and factional conflict, the country will grapple its way to the right solutions. Often the political process looks messy and inefficient, but that is the way the Framers wanted it.

FINAL THOUGHTS

If you ask the average person on the street what kind of government the Framers created, they will likely say that we are a democracy. Although true, this is not the most accurate way of describing our system of government. Our government has three aspects. We are a *republic*: the people vote for representatives that make the law and set the policies on behalf of the people. We are a *democracy*: The people are the ultimate sovereigns and we vote by majority rule. And we are a *constitutional* government: Congressmen, the President, and judges must all abide by the limits of the Constitution. We are a country of laws. Therefore, the best way to describe our government is to call it a **Constitutional Democratic Republic.**

NOTES

Alexander Hamilton, John Jay, and James Madison. *The Federalists.* Indianapolis: Liberty Fund, 2001.
James Madison. *Notes of Debates in the Federal Convention of 1787.* New York: Norton & Company, 1966.

ESSAY QUESTIONS

1. What were the weaknesses of the Articles of Confederation?
2. Describe how the Great Compromise worked.
3. List the three major compromises on slavery.
4. Describe the major principles of the constitution: checks and balances, three branches, and federalism.
5. What were the two historic problems the Framers sought to solve?
6. Why is "Constitutional Democratic Republic" the best way to describe the US government?

TERMS

Bicameral: _____

Checks and Balances: _____

Constitutional Democratic Republic: _____

Federal System: _____

Great Compromise: _____

New Jersey Plan: _____

Separations of Powers: _____

Three-fifths Compromise: _____

Unicameral: _____

Virginia Plan: _____

CHAPTER 4

How Does the Constitution Change?

TOPICS

- ► Ratification of the Constitution
- ► Adding the Bill of Rights
- ► Amending the Constitution
- ► Supreme Court Interpretations
- ► Other Ways the National Government Has Changed beyond the Constitution

LEARNING OBJECTIVES

When you finish reading this chapter, you will be able to:

1. Describe the conflict between the Federalists and Anti-Federalists.
2. Explain how amendments are added to the Constitution.
3. Define judicial review.
4. Outline some of the ways the government has changed since the founding.

HOW DOES THE CONSTITUTION CHANGE?

Aware that they may have made mistakes and that society is constantly evolving, the Framers set up an amendment process in order to change the Constitution. Indeed, as part of a political compromise during the ratification debates, many Framers agreed to add amendments to the Constitution in order to win support for the new government. Since the time the Constitution was ratified in 1788, twenty-seven amendments have been added to it. And beyond the amendment process, our government has changed over the last two centuries in ways the Framers could never have imagined. This chapter will outline how the Constitution was ratified, how amendments are added to the Constitution, and how our government has evolved since the original Constitution.

RATIFICATION OF THE CONSTITUTION

From the moment the Constitution was made public, people wanted to change it. After nearly four months of wrangling and arguing at the Constitutional Convention, during which several delegates went home in frustration, the remaining thirty-nine delegates signed the Constitution on September 17, 1787. The Constitution was then sent back to the Confederation Congress, and consequently they transmitted it to the thirteen states for ratification. The Framers decided that the new Constitution would be adopted if nine states, in popularly elected ratification conventions, approved it. This method would insure that the new government would obtain the "consent of the governed," and thus receive the legitimacy of popular sovereignty.

But even before the state ratification conventions formed, many people, such as Richard Henry Lee, Patrick Henry, and George Mason, called for accepting the Constitution only with recommended amendments. Soon two broad camps developed across the nation. The **Anti-Federalists** *were either outright opposed to the Constitution or would approve it only with certain amendments.* And the **Federalists** *approved of the Constitution as it stood.* Yet, many of the Federalists agreed to eventually add amendments as part of a compromise to attract supporters.

The Federalists were people who favored the Constitution. It was a stroke of promotional genius to adopt this name, which emphasized the concept of state confederation. They included members of the Convention such as George Washington, James Madison, and Alexander Hamilton, and other men of high reputation. Federalists tended to be wealthy, landed, creditors, urban, and professional men who desperately wanted a restoration of order. Better organized, they dominated most state ratifying conventions. The Federalists sometimes conceded that the new Constitution was not perfect, but they insisted that continuing with the Articles of Confederation would certainly be disastrous. Individual liberty, they argued, could only be preserved in an environment of order and stability.

The Federalist Papers *are the most famous Federalist essays written in support of the new Constitution.* Under the pseudonym "Publius," James Madison, Alexander Hamilton, and John Jay composed eighty-five political essays published in four New York newspapers in late 1787 and early 1788. Most of the essays were written by Hamilton and Madison. Ironically, the project was

Anti-Federalists

during the debate to ratify the Constitution, they were either outright opposed to the Constitution or would approve it only with certain amendments

Federalists

during the debate to ratify the Constitution, they approved of the Constitution as it stood

The Federalist Papers

are the most famous Federalist essays written in support of the new Constitution proposed by Hamilton even though the Constitution differed greatly from his own political views—he admired the English system. Yet he was certain that the Articles of Confederation, if allowed to continue, would soon lead to chaos and ruin, so he put his considerable intellectual powers behind the effort for ratification of the new government.

James Madison helped write the Constitution, the Federalist Papers, and the Bill of Rights!
©Everett Historical/Shutterstock.com

The *Federalist Papers* were organized into several themes: a general discussion of government, the defects of the Articles of Confederation, and then discourses on different aspects of the Constitution. Many historians and judges consider it the most authoritative writing on the theory of American government. Along with Madison's *Notes of the Debates at the Federal Convention*, it provides the best source for an understanding of the Framer's rationale for creating the structure of the Constitution, such as separation of powers, checks and balances, and limited government. As you have already seen, the *Federalist Papers* are often quoted in this book.

Anti-Federalists were the people who opposed the new constitution. In general, they tended to be small farmers, debtors, rural folk, poorer, and less educated people. Many prominent figures, however, filled the ranks of Anti-Federalists, such as Patrick Henry, Richard Henry Lee, George Mason, John Hancock, and Sam Adams. Their positions ranged from outright rejection of the Constitution to adding amendments before ratification. The Anti-Federalists believed in a weaker central government and stronger state sovereignty in order to preserve individual liberty. They warned that the president will eventually become monarchical, the Senate aristocratic, and the Supreme Court too powerful. They believed a republic can only work in a small country where local interests were represented in the assembly.

Brutus: Thousands of pamphlets were published during the national debate on whether to adopt or reject the new Constitution. Today, the *Federalist Papers* are the most famous pro-Constitution writings, but at the time of the debate Anti-Federalist pamphlets like the *Cato letters* and *Federal Farmer* were better known to the public. Perhaps the most influential Anti-Federalist essays were *Brutus*. Many historians believe *Brutus* was written by Robert Yates. A New York delegate to the Constitution Convention, he left Philadelphia because he thought the Convention was going beyond its mandate to merely "revise" the Articles. The sixteen essays of *Brutus* were published in the New York papers at the same time as the *Federalist Papers*.

Brutus made several compelling arguments for why the proposed Constitution was flawed. He argued that the federal government would eventually gain too much power, destroying state sovereignty. He predicted that Congress's unlimited power to "borrow money on the credit of the United States" and to collect tax revenue would eventually be abused. (We now have a national debt of over $20 trillion.) And in *Essay 11*, Yates wrote: "in their decisions, [the Supreme Court] will not confine themselves to any fixed or established rules, but will determine, according to what appears to them, the reason and spirit of the Constitution. The opinions of the Supreme Court…will have the force of law; because there is no power provided in the Constitution that can correct their errors." Today, many libertarians and conservatives believe his predictions came true as they watch activist judges broadly interpret the "Living Constitution."

Ratification: The first state to ratify the new government was Delaware, on December 7, 1787. Soon after, four more states ratified, but the contest intensified after this. Virginia and New York had very heated debates and ratification was achieved only by slim margins. One argument the Anti-Federalists made that carried a lot of weight was that the Constitution did not have a Bill of Rights. In *Federalist #84*, Hamilton argued that the Constitution contained an internal Bill of Rights. Its protection against Habeas Corpus, its explicitly written limits, its federal system, and its checks and balances, he contended, would amply protect individual rights. Many states, however, would not accept Hamilton's arguments and demanded a Bill of Rights. So, leading Federalists promised to add one in the first session of Congress. With the promise of a Bill of Rights, New Hampshire (the ninth state), ratified the Constitution on June 21, 1788. Later, the rest of the states ratified.

ADDING THE BILL OF RIGHTS

Madison was originally in agreement with Hamilton in his opposition to a Bill of Rights. In *Federalist #48*, Madison argues that no "parchment barriers" (rules written on paper) could ever protect the people against tyrannical government. "It will not be denied," wrote Madison, "that power is of an encroaching nature." That is, powerful governmental institutions tend to grow in power. Madison then gave several examples of when state governments, with the backing of the majority of the people, disregarded their written bill of rights and broke the law. The only solution, Madison argued, is to divide government so that if one branch tries to transcend its constitutional limits, the other branches will fight back.

History shows that Madison was at least partly correct. Throughout US history, when one branch overstepped its constitutional limits, the other branch tried to check it. But there are many examples of times when *all three* branches of the US government violated the rights of individuals or minority groups without regard to the Bill of Rights. The most obvious examples would include the establishment of Jim Crow laws, the passage of the sedition acts of 1799 and 1918, and the internment of Japanese Americans during World War II. However, without a Bill of Rights, there may have been many more violations of civil rights and civil liberties, and the Bill of Rights certainly helped create a roadmap for the country to rectify those wrongs and return to a nation of just laws.

Madison Crafts the Bill of Rights: As one of the leaders of the Federalists, in order to achieve ratification, Madison eventually agreed to support the adoption of a Bill of Rights. Madison was elected to the House of Representatives of the First Congress in 1789. As a congressman, Madison collected over a hundred proposals for amendments to be included in a bill of rights. He crafted nineteen amendments and submitted them to the House, twelve of which (with some rewriting) eventually passed both chambers. Of these original twelve, the states ratified ten. These ten amendments became part of the Constitution in 1791, collectively known as the Bill of Rights.

The Bill of Rights, *in general, protects the individual against the encroachment of the federal government.* These rights were understood by the Framers to be natural, inherent, or God-given rights, or, as the Declaration of Independence states, the "unalienable rights" possessed by each human being. These rights are not granted by government but exist prior to or separate from government; therefore, governments cannot rescind these rights.

The Bill of Rights

consisting of the first ten amendments to the Constitution, it protects the individual against the encroachment of the federal government

The Bill of Rights were ratified in 1791.
©Cheryl Casey/Shutterstock.com

The US Bill of Rights includes freedom of speech, freedom to assemble, freedom to protest, freedom of religion, and the right to bear arms. The government must respect an individual's privacy: it can't quarter troops, search one's property without a warrant, or force somebody to testify against himself. The government must follow certain legal procedures: jury trial, grand juries, no excess bail, and no unusual punishment. Fearful that future generations might construe the Bill of Rights as a complete list of individual rights, the 9th Amendment states that all rights not listed in the Constitution are "retained by the people." Likewise, the 10th Amendment states that all rights not prohibited by the states, nor exclusively delegated to the federal government, are "reserved to the states."

AMENDING THE CONSTITUTION

The Framers knew that they may have made some mistakes when they prepared the Constitution. And they understood that future generations would want to make changes to the government as society developed new issues and problems. By allowing amendments to the Constitution, the government would be flexible enough to adopt to change. "Amendments will therefore be necessary," said George Mason at the Constitutional Convention, "and it will be better to provide for them in an easy, regular and Constitutional way than to trust to chance and violence."

One of the major flaws of the Articles of Confederation was that it made it too difficult to add amendments by requiring the unanimity of all the states. The Framers sought to hit the right balance. If it is too hard to add amendments, the Constitution will eventually be discarded because it will fail to address new problems. On the other hand, if it is too easy, soon the original Constitution will be buried under a pile of amendments and lose its meaning and integrity. Most constitutional scholars believe the Framers successfully established the right method: not too easy and not too hard. The fact that the US Constitution is the longest surviving written Constitution in the world seems to support this contention.

How to Add Amendments: Article V of the Constitution sets up a two-step process for adding amendments: proposal and ratification. There are two methods of proposal. *Method One Proposal:* The first way, and the only way it has been done so far, is for a member of Congress to submit a proposed amendment to Congress and for it to be approved by two-thirds of each chamber. This has been done thirty-three times. *Method Two Proposal:* The second method is for Congress to call a convention by the request of two-thirds of the state legislatures. This has never been done. People have been afraid that this would open up the whole Constitution to radical changes.

And there are two methods of ratification. ***Method One Ratification*****:** If three-fourths of the state legislatures ratify a proposal, it becomes an amendment. This has been done twenty-six times. ***Method Two Ratification***: Three-fourths of the states hold conventions. This has only been done once, for the 21st Amendment. This might sound a bit confusing, so for the purposes of the test just remember this **formula for adding amendments**: *A proposal must pass two-thirds of both chambers of Congress, and it must be ratified by three-fourths of the state legislatures.*

Formula for Adding Amendments

a proposal must pass two-thirds of both chambers of Congress, and it must be ratified by three-fourths of the state legislatures

Constitutional Amendments: One way to think about the process of amending the Constitution is that it requires two supermajorities from a wide number of bodies (the House, the Senate, and state legislatures). Interestingly, the president plays no part in the process. Throughout our history, Congress has proposed thirty-one amendments, and twenty-seven have been ratified. But Congress has considered over 11,000 proposals. The Supreme Court has said that ratification must be completed in a reasonable period of time. Usually Congress gives the states seven years. Since the ratification of the first ten amendments (the Bill of Rights), there have been only seventeen additional amendments added to the Constitution.

What Have the New Amendments Accomplished?
The seventeen amendments added since the Bill of Rights can be placed into three broad categories. Some amendments make public policy: The 16th created an income tax, the 18th prohibited alcohol, and the 21st repealed prohibition. Some amendments clarified or improved provisions in the original Constitution: the 12th requires electors to vote separately for president and vice president, the 17th allowed the people of a state to vote for senators, the 22nd limits the president to two terms, and the 25th established a procedure for presidential succession. And the remaining amendments protect civil liberties and civil rights: the 13th prohibited slavery, the 14th established that all people must be treated equally under the law, the 15th states that the right to vote cannot be denied on the basis of race, the 19th gave women the right to vote, and the 26th lowered the voting age to eighteen.

In 1920, the 19th Amendment gave women the right to vote.
©catwalker/Shutterstock.com

SUPREME COURT INTERPRETATIONS

The Framers established the amendment process in order to make changes to the Constitution. But since 1788 there has been another way the Constitution has changed: by judicial interpretation. Judges have changed the meaning of the words in the Constitution in order to allow for new policies. This is something the Framers did not fully anticipate. Progressive Justice Charles Evan Hughes (in office 1862–1948) famously said, "The Constitution is what the judges say it is." Liberal Justice Thurgood Marshall (in office 1967–1991) said, "You do what you think is right and let the law catch up." So, does this mean the Supreme Court can do whatever it wants to do by interpreting the document as they deem fit? In Chapter 15 (How Does the Supreme Court Work?) we will discuss the different approaches to constitutional interpretation. For now, we will merely explain how the Court established for itself the power to interpret the Constitution.

Origins of Judicial Review: *The power of the Supreme Court to declare a congressional act null and void if it is found to be unconstitutional is called* **Judicial Review.** It is clear from the Constitution that the Framers intended the Supreme Court to have the power to declare state laws unconstitutional, but less clear if they intended the Supreme Court to have this authority over Congressional law. In America, both colonial and state courts had exercised the power of judicial review. And in debates at the Constitutional Convention, several delegates argued that the Supreme Court ought to have this power. But fearful of the implications of judicial power, in a vote on August 15 the delegates rejected a motion to provide the federal judiciary with the power to review all congressional bills before it becomes law. Instead they decided that it will be the president's responsibility to veto any unconstitutional laws Congress may pass.

So, by the end of the constitutional convention, many delegates thought it was the responsibility of the President to protect the integrity of the Constitution. This especially made sense since the president was required to takes an oath to uphold the Constitution. Yet, in 1799 this concept proved to be weak. Congress passed and President John Adams signed the Alien and Sedition Act which clearly violated the First Amendment's free speech clause by making it a crime to criticize the government. In response to this, James Madison and Thomas Jefferson, in the Virginia and Kentucky Resolutions, hinted that the states should have the power to nullify unconstitutional Congressional laws. But most people felt that if the states had nullification power it would lead to chaos and eventually disunion as each state picked which national laws they would follow or ignore.

Judicial Review: Others had always believed that by implication the structure and language of the Constitution grants the Supreme Court the power of judicial review. Alexander Hamilton argued that America's system of government makes judicial review by the Supreme Court absolutely necessary. In Britain, whatever law the Parliament passes is by definition constitutional: this is the essence of *parliamentary supremacy*. In America, however, we have

Judicial Review

the power of the Supreme Court to declare a congressional act null and void if it is found to be unconstitutional a "limited constitution," which means that Congress does not have the power to do whatever it wants. For example, Congress cannot unilaterally make a treaty with a foreign nation because this is explicitly a power of the president.

In *Federalist #78*, Hamilton asserts that the whole concept of a limited constitution hinges on the role of the Supreme Court to interpret the Constitution and to nullify breaches by Congress, the president, or by the states. The proper role of the judiciary, explains Hamilton, is to interpret the law. And Article VI states that the "Constitution is the supreme Law of the Land." Therefore, it is the job of the Supreme Court to interpret the Constitution. This means that a judge must compare a congressional act to the Constitution and if they are in conflict, the act must be declared null and void. Hamilton concluded that "No legislative act contrary to the constitution can be valid" or soon the Constitution would become a dead letter.

The Supreme Court established the power of judicial review for itself in the landmark case **Marbury v. Madison (1803).** In this case Chief Justice John Marshall quoted Hamilton extensively and made a strong case for why the Supreme Court must have the power to declare congressional acts unconstitutional in order to preserve our structure of limited government. This is one of the most important Supreme Court cases in history and you can read a full description of this case and other important cases in the Appendix, "Landmark Supreme Court Cases."

Marbury v. Madison

in this landmark case, the Supreme Court established the power of judicial review

The Supreme Court has the power to nullify unconstitutional laws.
©fstockfoto/Shutterstock.com

The Court's Power of Interpretation: By claiming and winning the power of judicial review, it eventually became routine for the Supreme Court to nullify congressional law based on its interpretation of the Constitution. It is difficult to overestimate this power. One example will demonstrate the far-reaching power of the Supreme Court as a result of judicial review. In *Dred Scott v. Sanford (1857),* the Supreme Court sparked a firestorm of protest by the way it interpreted the Constitution. Chief Justice Roger Taney ruled that Congress could not prohibit slavery in the territories and that blacks, as a permanent slave class, could never be US citizens. Taney arrived at this conclusion by making up words that were not in the text of the Constitution and by misrepresenting history. This ruling was so controversial that it helped spark the Civil War. So the power of judicial review has become another source of political conflict as different groups debate the correct interpretation of the Constitution.

Trend of Judicial Power: Although few cases are as infamous as *Dred Scott,* it is clear that judicial review has indeed given the Supreme Court tremendous power. Over the last two centuries, there have been several trends that characterize the way the Court exercises this power. First, the Court is normally averse to going strongly against public opinion and social norms. In 1896 (*Plessey v. Ferguson*), racism was strong in America and most people supported segregation, so the Court did not rule against it. But by 1854 (*Brown v. the Board of Education*), public opinion was becoming more tolerant of blacks, so the Court declared segregation unconstitutional.

Furthermore, the Supreme Court has tended to support federal power over state's rights. Since the 1930s, the Court has justified almost all expansion of federal power to regulate business with a broad interpretation of the commerce clause. Also the Supreme Court usually supports decisions by the president, especially related to national security. And lastly, in the modern era, the Court has also supported more individual rights and has mandated that the federal Bill of Rights also applies to state governments. So, today most people see the Supreme Court as the protector of the individual rights—something the Framers had not comprehended.

OTHER WAYS THE NATIONAL GOVERNMENT HAS CHANGED BEYOND THE CONSTITUTION

Why has the Constitution survived for more than two centuries? Part of the reason that the Constitution is still strong is that all segments of society—liberal and conservative, progressive and traditional, secular and religious, immigrant and native born—still revere it for its original design and principles: limited government, checks and balances, protection of individual liberty, rule of law, and equality under the law. The Constitution established the skeletal framework, but still allows society to evolve. This is the overarching theme of this book: How has our government changed since its establishment in 1789? We will describe new developments in America's government in more detail in later chapters, but for now we will focus on six major ways our government has changed since the founding:

The Rise of National Political Parties: There is nothing in the US Constitution that relates to political parties, but today government is dominated by partisan party politics. Beyond campaigns and the election process, today political parties play a central role in how the national government operates: the president appoints executive department officials based on party affiliation, federal judges are appointed based on unspoken assumptions about their political ideology, and congressional leadership and committee membership is based on what party dominates either chamber. For better or worse, today when people think of government they most likely think of Republicans versus Democrats.

17th Amendment

gave the people of the state the power to vote for their two US Senators, not the state legislatures

More Direct Democracy: The Framers were afraid of direct democracy, in fact "democracy" was something of a bad word for them; they preferred to use "republic." But since 1789 our system of government has allowed for more democracy. Originally the Electoral College was to be a temporary body of wise men to choose the president, but very quickly it changed to a system in which *the people* elected their president. The passage of the **17th Amendment** *gave the people of the state the power to vote for their two US Senators, not the state legislatures.* About a third of the states have the initiative and

Today party conflict dominates government.
©Lightspring/Shutterstock.com

referendum, essentially allowing the people to craft their own laws. For example, in 2012 the people of Colorado voted for the initiative to legalize recreational marijuana. So, today our government is more democratic than the original Constitution allowed for.

Growth of the Bureaucratic State: As society and the economy modernized and became more complex, Congress created independent government agencies to oversee corporations. Now regulatory agencies oversee almost all aspects of life, including businesses, education, transportation, communications, labor, healthcare, public safety, and the environment. This started when Congress created the Interstate Commerce Commission (ICC) in in 1887 to regulate the railroads. Now these agencies have tremendous power as they set up the rules and regulations that affect every citizen. Currently, there are about fifty major federal regulatory agencies and they enforce over 150,000 pages of rules.

Changes in Media: Today the media plays a much more important role in our government than the Framers ever could have imagined. The modern press considers its role so important that they often refer to themselves as the "fourth branch of government." The news media indeed plays a central role in our government by giving the people the information necessary to make informed votes, serving as a watchdog on government officials and programs, and providing the environment in which the candidates spar with each other. Now the media is a constant and ever pervasive presence in modern life as newspapers, internet news sites, social media, talk radio, and cable news shows fill our consciousness on an almost hourly basis.

Growth of the Welfare State: In the years of the Early Republic, it was assumed that responsibility for the poor and disabled fell on state and local governments and private charity. Local governments often supported orphanages and homes for elderly widows with taxpayer money. And thousands of associations and charitable organizations took care of the poor and needy. But now the national government assumes this responsibility. One explanation for why government took over this role is that the economy has changed. When America was primarily an agricultural economy, during economic recessions poor families could at least feed themselves by growing food and raising livestock. After the industrial revolution, when a factory worker lost his job he had no way to support his family. During the Great Depression, a majority of Americans realized the need for things like unemployment insurance, old age pensions, and aid to poor families.

Growth of Presidential Power: The Framers designed the executive branch to be the second branch of government. Congress had the power to make laws, and the president would merely execute or administer those laws. But over the years, the president has become the most powerful person in Washington, DC. The president now established the national agenda and forces Congress to pass his proposals. And instead of waiting for Congress to declare war, in recent decades the president goes to war without an official congressional declaration.

Related to the growth of the power of the president, is the growth of other aspects of the executive branch. Currently, the president heads the fifteen branches of the executive branch with several million civilian and military personnel. The president issues **executive orders,** *executive branch directives that have the force of law,* which can have a major impact on American society. And in recent years, presidents have appointed "**czars,**" *executive department officials appointed by the president with ad hoc responsibilities, such as "drug czar" or "environmental czar."* These are examples of the president taking over powers that were originally designated only to Congress: the power to make law and the power to create government departments.

Theodore Roosevelt helped create a more powerful Presidency.
©catwalker/Shutterstock.com

Executive Orders

executive branch directives that have the force of law

Czars

executive department officials appointed by the president with ad hoc responsibilities, such as "drug czar" or "environmental czar"

FINAL THOUGHTS

The Framers thought that future generations should have the power to alter the Constitution, and so they created the amendment process. Since 1791, twenty-seven amendments have been added to the Constitution, most importantly the Bill of Rights. But most changes have occurred extra-constitutionally—outside the Constitution. Political parties and the press dominate the political process. The Supreme Court has discovered new rights in the Constitution that the Founders would never have imagined. And the Presidency and the bureaucratic state seem to be growing and growing. Today, much of the political debate centers on people's attitudes regarding these changes. Liberals tend to be more optimistic and view these changes as good. Conservatives, on the other hand, tend to fear these changes and advocate a return to limited government.

NOTES

Code of Federal Regulations, found at the US Government Publishing Office (www.gpo.gov).

Alexander Hamilton, John Jay, and James Madison. *The Federalists*. Indianapolis: Liberty Fund, 2001.

History of constitutional and amendments, found at www.constitutionfacts.com.

Richard Labunski. *James Madison and the Struggle for the Bill of Rights*. Oxford: Oxford University Press, 2006.

James Madison. *Notes of Debates in the Federal Convention of 1787*. New York: Norton & Company, 1966.

ESSAY QUESTIONS

1. Describe the difference between the Federalists and Anti-Federalists.
2. How was the Constitution ratified?
3. What, in general, does the Bill of Rights do?
4. Describe the main way amendments have been added to the Constitution.
5. How does judicial review give the Supreme Court power over Congress?
6. Of the three branches, which branch has grown the most since the writing of the Constitution?

TERMS

Anti-Federalist: _____

Bill of Rights:: _____

Czars: _____

Executive Orders: _____

Federalists: _____

Federalist Papers: _____

Formula for Adding Amendments: _____

Judicial Review: _____

Marbury v. Madison: _____

17th Amendment: _____

CHAPTER 5

What Are America's Current Political Ideologies?

TOPICS

- ► History of Liberalism
- ► Contemporary Liberalism
- ► History of Conservatism
- ► Contemporary Conservatism
- ► Other Ideologies

LEARNING OBJECTIVES

When you finish reading this chapter, you will be able to:

1. Define political ideology.
2. Describe the core tenants of modern American liberalism.
3. Describe the core tenants of modern American conservatism.
4. Compare the ideas of other political ideologies, such as libertarianism and socialism.
5. Cite recent polls on American's views on government.

WHAT ARE AMERICA'S CURRENT POLITICAL IDEOLOGIES?

Political ideology *is a consistent set of values and beliefs about the proper purpose and scope of government.* Today, America is dominated by two political ideologies: liberalism and conservatism. In 2016, a Gallup poll that tracks American's political ideology reveals that 37% identify as conservative, 35% as moderate, and 24% as liberal. So, the vast majority of Americans are conservative to moderate. And many people hold a variety of liberal and

Political Ideology

is a consistent set of values and beliefs about the proper purpose and scope of government conservative views. But in this chapter we will describe pure liberalism or Leftism and pure conservatism so that the student can clearly understand the distinction. But there are also smaller groups of people that believe in other ideologies, such as communism, socialism, environmentalism, libertarianism, and anarchism.

HISTORY OF LIBERALISM IN AMERICA

Liberals *believe in the positive use of government to promote economic and social equality.* This ideology was a departure from the political ideology of the Founders, which was based on individual liberty and limited government. In the decades after the Civil War, some Americans advocated for a larger role for the government to solve various social and economic issues. Many of these proto liberals were influenced by new European thinkers. One European that had particular influence was Otto Von Bismarck. The Chancellor of Germany from 1871 to 1890, Bismarck established the world's first welfare state, which included an old age pension and public health insurance. Another influence was the socialist movement in Europe that was inspired by the writings of Karl Marx (1818–1883). Although few Americans supported Marx's call for the abolition of private property, many early Leftists were attracted to Marx's goal of achieving material equality and protecting the labor class, and they also shared his hostility to big business and capitalism.

Liberals

believe in the positive use of government to promote economic and social equality

Populism: American liberalism has its roots in the Populist Movement of the late 1880s and early 1890s. Due to advancements in agricultural technology and transportation, large farms were producing a surplus of food, resulting in the lowering of food prices (deflation). Small farmers couldn't compete and were struggling to keep their land. They organized themselves into groups such as the Grange and the Farmers' Alliance to figure out ways to help each other economically and to seek political advocacy. In common cause against big business and industrialization, soon these farmer's groups united with organized labor to form the People's Party or the Populist Party.

One of the most influential Populist's was Ignatius Donnelly. He helped organize the Minnesota Farmers' Alliance and in 1892 he wrote the preamble of the Populist Party's Omaha Platform. In the platform, Donnelly wrote that "the fruits of the toil of millions are boldly stolen to build up colossal fortunes for the few," and as a result America is quickly becoming a country of "two great classes—tramps and millionaires." This expresses an

In 1896, Williams Jennings Bryan brought the populist movement into the Democratic Party.
©Everett Historical/Shutterstock.com

aspect of early liberalism called **populism**: *a political approach that appeals to the concerns and prejudices of the ordinary people against the financial or cultural elites*. The Omaha Platform proposed several initiatives designed to help the poor farmer and laborer: a progressive income tax, the legal recognition of labor unions, a paper currency based on silver to spur inflation (which they thought would help indebted farmers), and the government takeover of the banks, railroads, and telegraph companies.

Donnelly was also the author of one of the most successful books in the 1890s, *Caesar's Column*, which sold over 250,000 copies. It was a science fiction novel about a workers' revolt against a global oligarchic government. Donnelly was influenced by another blockbuster publishing success with populist themes, *Looking Backward* by Edward Bellamy. Set in the year 2000, this book described a future without private property where all people were provided with free transportation and housing and everybody received the same income. And because there was material equality, there was no cause for jealousy and all people lived in peace and harmony. This book is an example of Leftist Utopian literature. *Utopia* is an ideal government system that creates a perfect social world. There is a utopian strain in liberalism that hopes to use government to perfect the world and eradicate all social, political, and economic problems.

Progressivism: During the 1896 election, the Democratic Party "fused" with the Populist Party when it nominated William Jennings Byron for president. Byron lost the election, but populist ideas lived on in the Progressive Era (1900 to 1921). The **progressives** *believed good laws and institutions could eradicate corrupt business and government and aid the enlightened progress of mankind*. The Republican president Theodore Roosevelt and the Democratic president Woodrow Wilson implemented many progressive laws: The Pure Food and Drug Act, which regulated the pharmaceutical industry; the Meat Inspection Act, which regulated the meat industry; and the Hepburn Act, which regulated the railroads. They created the Federal Trade Commission to oversee business, instituted the Federal Reserve to set monetary policy, and implemented the progressive income tax, taxing the wealthy to supply revenue for government programs.

And in order to eradicate corruption in government, they introduced more direct democracy into America's political system. They passed the 17th Amendment, allowing the citizens of each state to vote for their senators instead of the state legislators; they created the initiative and referendum, giving the people the power to make their own laws; and

Populism

a political approach that appeals to the concerns and prejudices of the ordinary people against the financial or cultural elites

Progressives

believed good laws and institutions could eradicate corrupt business and government and aid the enlightened progress of mankind

A progressive, Woodrow Wilson won the presidency in 1912.
©Olga Popova/Shutterstock.com

they established the direct primary, giving the people the power to nominate the party candidates and thus taking power away from party leaders. Like the populists, the progressives disagreed with the premise of classical liberalism. Instead of fearing a powerful central government, the progressives sought to give government more power in order to protect and aid the individual.

Today liberals often call themselves progressives, but they might be surprised by the religious fervor of the original progressives. Theodore Roosevelt campaigned for president on the "Ten Commandments and the Golden Rule." The musical theme of the 1912 Progressive National Convention was "Onward Christian Soldier." Woodrow Wilson told a YMCA groups that "the mighty task before us . . . is to make the United States a mighty Christian Nation, and to Christianize the world." Historians now recognize that the Progressive Movement grew out of the Third Great Awakening, a period of renewed religious activity. This helps explain their passionate mission to eradicate evil from society.

Safety Net

a set of government programs designed to catch Americans if they fall on hard times and to provide basic support for the poor

New Deal: Liberalisms moved into the mainstream during the New Deal Era in the 1930s. In response to the Great Depression, Franklin D. Roosevelt advanced populist and progressive ideas by providing aid to the poor, the elderly, the unemployed, the small farmer, and the laborer. The New Deal established the minimum wage, recognized labor unions, guaranteed farm prices, and created federal jobs for the unemployed. Roosevelt's greatest success was Society Security, which provided a pension for the elderly, implemented unemployment insurance, and created welfare (Aid to Families with Dependent Children).

Social Security and other New Deal programs were a radical departure from the Founder's ideal of government. The American Republic was established on the idea of limited government, individualism, and personal responsibility. It was the duty of the family, charities, and local government to help the poor and elderly. And in the land of opportunity, with its abundance of cheap land, poverty was considered to be a result of poor character, such as laziness or drunkenness. But the Great Depression changed that perception. Suddenly millions of able men were unemployed through no fault of their own. Now it was the responsibility of the federal government to provide for the unemployed, poor, handicapped, and elderly. This support is often referred to as the **safety net**: *a set of government programs designed to catch Americans if they fall on hard times and to provide basic support for the poor.*

Lyndon Johnson created the Great Society to fight poverty in America.
©catwalker/Shutterstock.com

The Great Society: These liberal programs were expanded during Lyndon Johnson's administration (1963–1968) with the Great Society. Launching a "war on poverty," Johnson pushed through Congress dozens of laws expanding welfare by creating food stamps, offering school lunches, providing public housing, increasing pensions for government workers, and supplying day care for low-income families. The Great Society expanded health care benefits for the poor with Medicaid, and it expanded health care benefits for the elderly with Medicare. The Great Society marked the development in America of the modern **welfare state**: *a government that uses the progressive income tax to distribute wealth and provide cradle to grave service to its citizens* by providing food, day care, education, health care, transportation, housing, job training, pensions, and other services to its citizens.

The Johnson administration also oversaw the desegregation of the South by passing the Civil Rights Act of 1964, making racial discrimination a federal crime. And Johnson pushed the Voting Rights of 1965 through Congress, making voting discrimination a federal crime. Up to this time, most black Americans voted for the Republicans, the party of Abraham Lincoln. Then starting in the 1960s, over 90 percent of blacks voted for the Democratic Party. And by the end of the 1960s, the Democratic Party became more liberal as it appealed to ethnic minorities, the youth, recent immigrants, feminists, religious minorities, gays and lesbians, labor unions, and government workers. *Political activity that appeals to a citizen's identity as a member of an ethnic or social group and its perceived mistreatment is known as* **identity politics**.

Welfare State

a government that uses the progressive income tax to distribute wealth and provide cradle to grave service to its citizens

Identity Politics

political activity that appeals to a citizen's identity as a member of an ethnic or social group and its perceived mistreatment

CONTEMPORARY LIBERALISM

We will look at modern liberalism in three areas: political, social, and economic ideology.

Liberal Political Ideology: The Left wishes to use government as a tool to transform society and promote greater social and economic equality. Like the social democracies of Western Europe, the American Left wishes to implement cradle-to-grave government programs that insure greater economic security and comfort, such as child care, school lunches, free education, government-run health care, generous worker's benefits, public transportation, affordable housing, and old age pensions. In order to implement these programs, the central government needs to be large and powerful. But the one area where liberals cut the federal government is in the military. Since the Vietnam War, liberals have become more pacifistic. It is a liberal slogan that "war never solves anything." So liberals seek to solve international conflicts through global organizations such as the United Nations. Liberals also tend to be uncomfortable with displays of patriotism and nationalism.

Liberalism and Society: American Leftists often call themselves "progressives," meaning they advocate societal change and progress. Liberals tend to be suspicious of traditions and established institutions, claiming that they are used by powerful elements in society to retain privilege and control. The Left supports a secular society and often protests religious symbols in the public sphere. Liberals highly value tolerance, compassion, and feelings. They support multi-culturalism and highlight the importance of ethnic, social, and gender identity. Liberals support feminism and the right to have an abortion. Because the Left believes that society and genetics plays a prominent role in a person's behavior, they do not give an individual as much credit for his or her success or failure. In like manner, liberals are more lenient toward criminals and oppose the death penalty. The left advocates strict gun control. Since the Left believes in social progress, they often accuse conservatives of being intolerant, sexist, xenophobic, homophobic, Islamophobic, racist, bigoted, small-minded, anti-science, and anti-intellectual.

Equal Outcome

the attempt to achieve equal economic conditions

Liberalism and Economics: While still supporting private property rights, liberals advocate increasing regulations on business and the economy. To achieve a more egalitarian society, they advocate a progressive tax in which the rich pay higher rates to fund the welfare state. Liberals are more likely to believe poverty is a result of social wrongs, not individual choices and character. Liberals are suspicious of the profit motive and feel animus toward corporations. They see pure capitalism as defective. Since the New Deal, liberals have supported more central government planning of the economy and Keynesian economics (see Chapter 23). One reason liberals do not like pure capitalism is that it creates winners and losers, which is contrary to its central value of equality. Liberals tend to want to protect the environment with industrial regulation and the reduction of fossil fuels. They are more likely to believe in man-made global warming.

Liberalism and the American Creed: While conservatives still hold to the American Creed as described in Chapter 2, liberals reject or have reinterpreted America's original political values. Instead of economic and personal liberty, liberals support social liberty (gay marriage, radical ideologies, alternative lifestyles, legalization of drugs). Instead of equal opportunity and equality under the law, they believe in **equal outcome**: *the attempt to achieve equal economic conditions*. Instead of individualism, they emphasize the importance of

Liberals value equality and diversity.
©stournsaeh/Shutterstock.com

social groups. Instead of E. Pluribus Unum, liberals value a heightened ethnic and cultural identity. Instead of "In God we Trust," liberals favor a secular society. Instead of free market capitalism, liberals support a more regulated economy with high taxes. And while conservatives talk of "restoring America," liberals talk of "fundamentally changing America."

HISTORY OF CONSERVATISM

Definition of a Conservative: A **conservative** *believes in limited government, traditional values, and personal responsibility and liberty, especially economic liberty.*

Classical liberalism: The political ideology founded by the eighteenth-century English thinkers John Locke and Adam Smith who advocated *that limited government should leave citizens free to further their individual pursuits, which will enhance the public good in the aggregate is called* **Classical Liberalism**. John Locke rejected the notion of the divine rights of kings. He believed government is limited and cannot infringe on the God-given rights of life, liberty, and the protection of property. Locke believed there is no political freedom without economic freedom. Adam Smith believed in free market capitalism within the context of limited government that did not grant privilege. He believed that government should protect the nation and set up fair and sound laws, but beyond that they should leave the individual free to innovate and compete. By allowing the individual the freedom to enjoy the fruits of his hard work and creativity, the whole society will progress technologically and develop a higher standard of living for all.

Industrial Conservatism: Before the Industrial Revolution in America, the ideas of Classical Liberalism were nearly universally accepted in the United States. But during the Gilded Age (about 1870 to 1900), the rise of big business caused populists and progressives to question the premises of our founding ideas. William Graham Sumner, author of *The Forgotten Man* and *What Social Classes Owe Each Other*, and the industrialist Andrew Carnegie, author of *Triumphant Democracy*, sought to defend these traditional ideas in the context of the Industrial Age. They rejected European socialists and American Progressives who argued for a redistribution of wealth. Instead, they argued for the maintenance of the status quo and **laissez-faire economics**: *The idea that government should not interfere with the economy.*

Conservative

believes in limited government, traditional values, and personal responsibility and liberty, especially economic liberty

Classical Liberalism

limited government should leave citizens free to further their individual pursuits, which will enhance the public good in the aggregate

Laissez-faire Economics

the idea that government should not interfere with the economy

Andrew Carnegie was a great advocate for the virtues of American capitalism.
©Everett Historical/Shutterstock.com

Sumner and Carnegie argued that if you take away the profit motive it would destroy the astonishing economic engine that is reducing poverty and creating so much technological progress in America, making it the richest country in the world. And they contended that government aid to the needy would undermine America's traditional Protestant Ethic of hard work, thrift, temperance, and self-reliance. These values were also celebrated by the popular juvenile fiction writer of the era, Horatio Alger. Through such books as *Ragged Dick* and *Luke Larkin's Luck*, Alger instructed boys that the best way to get out of poverty was to work hard, stay out of trouble, and make your own luck. In other words, virtue and self-improvement was the key to success. Progressives, however, dismissed Alger as promoting the "myth of success."

Opponents of the New Deal and the Great Society: Conservatism remained the favored ideology of white Protestants, the middle and upper classes, and many business leaders, but the average voters began to accept more progressive ideas after the turn of the century. In the 1920s, conservatives enjoyed their last heyday with the Calvin Coolidge administration, which reduced the national debt, cut government spending, and slashed taxes. But that period was short-lived. In the 1930s, Franklin Roosevelt built the modern Democratic Party by gaining the loyalty of several groups that were attracted to the liberal promise of government, known as the New Deal Coalition (the poor, labor unions, ethnic minorities, immigrants, small farmers, urban dwellers, and government workers). In the 1960s a small resurgence of conservatism was led by people like Senator Barry Goldwater and writer William F. Buckley Jr., the founder of *National Review* magazine. They criticized large government and the Great Society for its incompetence and corruption, and blamed the welfare state for destroying the American family and eroding public morals.

Frederick Hayek: Perhaps the one writer that revived conservatism after it became moribund during the 1930s and World War II was Frederick Hayek with the publication of *The Road to Serfdom* in 1944. Written as an attack on socialistic planned economies, Hayek argued that not only is socialism less economically efficient than democratic capitalistic systems, it is also morally inferior because it necessarily denies human freedom. In a centrally planned economy, Hayek argued, the individual loses his liberty and becomes a piece in the planner's scheme. But Hayek was not for laissez-fair. He believed the government must maintain the rule of law, create a safety net, and establish the market rules that enable fair competition. But individualism and competition must be at the heart of the system because it is the source of innovation and progress. Hayek's conservative model allows greater human dignity because the individual is given the "opportunity peacefully and in freedom to build up his own little world."

The Conservative Resurgence: Conservatism was the minority ideology from the 1930s through the 1970s; then in the 1980s, with the election of Ronald Reagan, conservatism enjoyed a major political comeback. This was remarkable considering that much of the press and popular culture advocated liberal ideas. In his presidential campaign, Reagan preached the ideas of classical liberalism by saying, "the government that governs least governs best." Known for his humor, he also said, "The most terrifying words in the English language are: I'm from the government and I'm here to help." This quip was an attack on a core liberal assumption: that government officials are competent and effective. But by 1980, many had seen that large government could also be wasteful, incompetent, and could enact laws with terrible unintended consequences. For example, conservatives said welfare destroyed the inner-city family and Medicaid increased health costs. And by 1980, people saw that Social Security, Medicare, Medicaid, and welfare accounted for more than 50 percent of the federal budget, growing an enormous national debt.

CONTEMPORARY CONSERVATISM

The Three Legs of Modern Conservatism: Reagan possessed enormous political skills that have become more apparent since he left office. No conservative since has been able to garner as much success as him due to the inherent tensions within the conservative movement. Today political scientists often talk of the "three legs of the stool of conservatism": traditional conservatives, social conservatives, and libertarian conservatives. Reagan, with his ability to articulate the weakness of liberalism and communism, his sense of humor, and his instinct to avoid certain issues, was the last politician to successfully attract all three types of conservatives. Although they share a common belief in limited government, individual responsibility, and economic freedom, each type of conservative emphasizes different values, sometimes in direct contradiction to one another.

Traditional Conservatives like George H. W. Bush, Reagan's vice president and the forty-first President of the United States, believed in cutting government waste, but opposed dismantling the New Deal safety net. Traditional conservatives believe in private property rights, free trade, less regulation, a balanced budget, and law and order. They instinctively believed in traditional Protestant values, but are uncomfortable with evangelical Christians and are sometimes neutral on abortion. Believing that the primary responsibility of the federal government is to protect the nation, they support a strong defense and an interventionist foreign policy to assert American interests and values overseas. Opposed to marijuana and

Ronald Reagan was able to get the support of all three types of conservatives.
©Olga Popova/Shutterstock.com

other recreational drugs, Bush 41 launched a "war on drugs" by appointing a Drug Czar. To combat poverty, Bush advocated economic growth and private charity, which he called "a thousand points of light." Traditional conservatives are sometimes called "country club Republicans" or "establishment Republicans."

Social Conservatives like George W. Bush, the forty-third President of the United States, identify strongly with their religion. As Christians, they believe in the sanctity of all human life and therefore oppose abortion and euthanasia. They often talk in terms of "good" and "evil," which makes the Left uncomfortable. To protect children, they favor restrictions on pornography and drugs. They are more comfortable with religious expressions in the public sphere and support religious schools and church-based interest groups. Afraid that gay marriage would undermine the family unit, they reserve the term "marriage" to unions of one man and one woman. Social conservatives became a potent political force after the Supreme Court case *Roe v. Wade* (1973), which made it illegal for states to ban abortions. In 2012, 78 percent of voters who self-identified as born-again Christians voted for the Republican presidential candidate.

Ayn Rand defended libertarianism and free market capitalism in such novels as *Fountainhead* and *Atlas Shrugged*.
©catwalker/Shutterstock.com

Libertarian Conservatives adhere most closely with the Classical Liberalism. They focus on drastically shrinking the federal government in order to maximize individual liberty and responsibility. As strict constructionists, they believe in faithfully adhering to the Constitution. They believe in free market capitalism and very small taxes to fund the few valid responsibilities of the federal government, like national defense. But unlike traditional conservatives, they oppose an interventionist foreign policy, believing the military should only be used to defend the country. On social issues, they tend to be neutral on abortion, gay marriage, and recreational drug use, saying the individual is free to pursue their own happiness as long as they take responsibility. In 2012, Ron Paul ran for the Republican presidential nomination as a libertarian conservative. He angered many traditional conservatives for attacking America's eagerness to engage in foreign wars and for its strict drug laws.

Summary of Conservatism: Conservatives want to "conserve" or keep traditions, seeing wisdom and value in traditional institutions like marriage and the church. Believing state and local governments are better suited to serve the needs of the people, conservatives want a less powerful central government. They believe free market capitalism is the best path to prosperity because it provides incentives to hard work and to innovate. Conservatives believe overbearing government bureaucracies and regulations stifle freedom, innovation, and economic growth.

Conservatives believe the welfare state has changed human behavior by destroying self-reliance and encouraging a sense of entitlement. They also blame the liberal welfare state for running up a massive national debt. Conservatives feel that the church, as the only institution dedicated to teaching morality, is an irreplaceable institution in society. And they are more comfortable with religion in public spaces. Conservatives think that government laws and policies should be colorblind and college admission, for example, should be based on merit alone. Conservatives believe in law and order, strictly following the Constitution, harsher criminal penalties, the death penalty, and gun rights. Conservatives believe a strong defense ensures peace.

OTHER IDEOLOGIES

Although most Americans identify as liberals or conservatives, some believe in other ideologies. Today most liberals vote for Democrats and most conservatives vote for Republicans, but in every election there are several other parties on the ballot. This section will describe some of the other political ideologies in America today. These ideologies can be placed on a political spectrum of those advocating the largest role for government up to those advocating the smallest role for government. This spectrum would be arranged in this order: communism → socialism → environmentalism → American liberalism → American conservatism → libertarianism → anarchism.

The Linear Political Spectrum

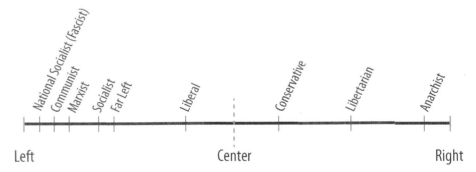

Communism: This ideology advocated the largest role for government. Modern communism was inspired by the writings of Karl Marx. Marx wrote that the only way to achieve real equality is to abolish private property. **Communism** *is a political system in which the central government owns the means of production (factories and farms) and uses a central government to allocate resources and manage the economy.* Marx wrote that the communist state is a result of a class conflict in which the working class rise up and overcome the property-owning class. Religion is usually banned because it offers another ideology and authority in contrast to the government, which is run by a single political party, the Communist Party. Free speech is banned so that the government can indoctrinate the people to reject bourgeois (capitalistic) beliefs. Today in America, only 2,000 people are registered members of the Communist Party USA (CPUSA).

Marxism had a tremendous influence around the globe in the twentieth century. The idea of material equality and anti-capitalism was very attractive to many intellectuals and common people around the world. But the moral record for communism is a poor one. Historians estimate the communist governments were responsible for the deaths of over 100 million people: the Soviet Union, 20 million; China, 65 million; Vietnam, 1 million; North Korea, 2 million; Eastern Europe, 1 million; Latin America and Cuba, 150,000; Africa, 1.7 million; and Afghanistan, 1.5 million.

Communism

is a political system in which the central government owns the means of production (factories and farms) and uses a central government to allocate resources and manage the economy

Stalin was the leader of the Soviet Union, the communist government of Russia.
©Alexey Borodin/Shutterstock.com

Bernie Sanders is the most successful socialist running for president since Eugene Debbs in 1912.
©Crush Rush/Shutterstock.com

Socialism: This ideology advocates a very large government, but smaller than communism. Wishing to achieve greater equality, **socialism** *asserts that strong central government authority is needed to regulate private property, to nationalize industry, and to distribute the wealth in order to achieve equality.* Socialist governments implement very high taxation and offer a wide variety of cradle to grave benefits, including generous pensions, government health care, schooling allowances, and mandatory extensive vacations. The economy is centrally planned and many important industries are owned by the government, but unlike communism private property still exists. Many European countries function on this model. Few Americans vote as Socialists in recent decades; however, in 2016 Bernard Sanders, the only Socialist member of the US Senate, ran for president as a Democrat.

Environmentalism: As a political movement, **environmentalists** *support a liberal agenda with the primary focus on protecting the environment* by highly regulating industry, reducing the use of fossil fuels, eradicating pollution and harmful pesticides, and educating the public on recycling and sustainability. The platform of the Green Party of the United States says they support "grassroots democracy, social justice, equal opportunity, ecology, non-violence, feminism, and diversity." In 2012, the Green Party candidate Jill Stein won nearly 470,000 votes.

American Liberalism: Advocates large, centralized government but would keep capitalism, although highly regulated.

Socialism

asserts that strong central government authority is needed to regulate private property, to nationalize industry, and to distribute the wealth in order to achieve equality

Environmentalists

support a liberal agenda with the primary focus on protecting the environment

American Conservatism: Advocates smaller government, lower taxes, a strong defense, and more free enterprise, but would not dismantle the safety net.

Libertarianism supports very limited government. It most closely follows the Classical Liberalism of Adam Smith and John Locke. **Libertarians** *believe that the federal government should be limited to the most essential functions in order to protect individual liberty.* They believe in free markets and free trade. Libertarians cherish liberty as the most important political value. Recognizing that individual freedom entails individual responsibility, libertarians would legalize drugs and tend to avoid social issues. They would end almost all welfare state programs and abolish the income tax. In foreign policy, they are isolationists. Libertarians would make major cuts in the defense budget, end the CIA, dismantle the IRS, end public education, and pull the US out of the United Nations. In 2012, the Libertarian Party candidate Gary Johnson won over 1,257,000 votes.

Anarchism: Technically, **anarchists** *oppose government in any form.* Government, they argue, is inherently oppressive and thus should be eliminated. State authority or any type of hierarchical organization is harmful to human relations. In practice, they tend to oppose capitalism, industrialization, and modernism. Anarchists protest against multinational corporations, sometimes in violent ways.

Libertarians

believe that the federal government should be limited to the most essential functions in order to protect individual liberty

Anarchists

oppose government in any form

FINAL THOUGHTS

When Donald Trump won the presidential election in 2016, it surprised so many political pundits because nobody was sure what groups would come out and vote for him. Trump ran on an agenda of enforcing immigration laws and building a wall on the Mexican border, stimulating the economy through tax cuts and deregulation, ending unfavorable trade deals that undermined American manufacturing, building a strong defense while avoiding unnecessary wars, restoring law and order, especially in the inner cities, and rebuilding the nation's infrastructure. Pundits called Trump a "populist nationalist." He was a populist because he appealed to blue collar voters who had lost their

Trump chose Mike Pence, a social conservative, as his running mate. This helps explain why Trump won so many votes from Christian conservatives.
©Evan El-Amin/Shutterstock.com

jobs in the rust belt, and because Trump would rail against the media elites and corrupt Washington politicians. And he was a nationalist because he talked about "Making America Great Again," his campaign slogan.

Although this sounds like a conservative platform, as a life-long Democrat with a personality that seemed more suited for reality-television than politics, Trump did not fit into any of the three types of conservatives. Traditional conservatives felt uncomfortable with his politically incorrect speech and lack of knowledge in many policy areas. Indeed, Trump seemed to spend as much time attacking establishment Republicans than Hillary Clinton. And libertarian conservatives were afraid that he talked too much of expanding executive powers and not enough time talking about reducing the deficit. Surprisingly, social conservatives were Trump's strongest supporters, even though Trump never attended church on a regular basis. And liberals liked Trump's plan to rebuild the infrastructure. In the end, according to exit polls Trump won 81% of the conservative vote, 41% of moderates, and 10% of liberals.

NOTES

On statistics that communism has killed 100 million people see Stephane Courtois et al. *The Black Book of Communism*. Cambridge, MA: Harvard University Press, 1999.

ESSAY QUESTIONS

1. Define a liberal's beliefs.
2. Define a conservative's beliefs.
3. What are the "three legs" of American conservatism?
4. Compare communism with socialism.
5. Compare libertarianism with anarchism.

TERMS

Anarchism: _____

Classical Liberalism: _____

Communism: _____

Conservatives: _____

Environmentalism: _____

Identity Politics: _____

Laissez-faire Economics:: _____

Libertarianism: _____

Liberals: _____

Political Ideology: _____

Populism: _____

Progressives: _____

Safety Net: _____

Socialism: _____

Welfare State: _____

UNIT TWO

STATE AND INDIVIDUAL RIGHTS

CHAPTER 6

How Does Federalism Work?

TOPICS

- ► Definition of Federalism
- ► Advantages of Federalism
- ► National Powers
- ► State Powers
- ► Shared Powers
- ► Summary of Federalism

LEARNING OBJECTIVES

When you finish reading this chapter, you will be able to:

1. Define federalism.
2. Explain the significance of implied powers and the supremacy clause.
3. List the benefits of federalism.
4. Delineate the powers granted to the national and state government by the Constitution.
5. Delineate the powers denied the national and state government.

HOW DOES FEDERALISM WORK?

American democracy started at the local and state levels before it developed nationally. The colonies created their own democratic institutions centuries before the United States declared independence in 1776. After independence, each state wrote its own constitution. America's first national constitution, the Articles of Confederation, came last and maintained the sovereignty established by the states. It soon became apparent, however, that this confederation of autonomous states couldn't keep the country united. With the nation on the verge of economic and political chaos, tilting toward fragmentation, fifty-five delegates met in Philadelphia in the summer of 1787 to frame a new government. One of their primary tasks was to find the right balance between national and state power. The result was the federal system, the subject of this chapter.

DEFINITION OF FEDERALISM

In order to achieve more order, the Framers of the Constitution took some power away from the states and gave it to the national government. But to maintain a degree of local rule, they allowed the states to retain many functions and responsibilities. This is known as a **Federal System** of government: *a division of power between regional (state) governments and a central (national) government*. America was actually the first country to adopt a federal system. Most countries, such as Great Britain, France, and China, have a **Unitary System**: *one central government has the ultimate authority and control to run all regions of the country*. Of the 193 governments in the world, only 25 have federal systems, including Canada, Australia, Mexico, and Russia.

Federal System

a division of power between regional (state) governments and a central (national) government

Unitary System

one central government has the ultimate authority and control to run all regions of the country

Number of Governments in Federal System

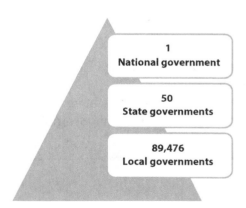

1
National government

50
State governments

89,476
Local governments

Governments using the federal system are inherently more complex. The national government has ultimate authority in some areas, the states in other areas, and in several areas they share power. This complexity has led to many disputes between the states and the federal government, which the Supreme Court has often had to resolve. And throughout US history, the Court's interpretation of federalism has changed. Today, many contentious political and social controversies involve different understandings of federalism. For example, are abortion laws a state responsibility or a national one? How about gun laws, prostitution, alcohol, marijuana, or gay marriage? As you read this chapter, think about these issues and how they fit into the federal system.

ADVANTAGES OF FEDERALISM

The Framers never considered completely abolishing state governments because they saw many advantages to maintaining state power under the umbrella authority of the national government. Perhaps the primary advantage in their minds was to check the power of the central government. For the public at the time of ratification, state sovereignty was associated strongly with individual liberty. This notion was so popular that supporters of the Constitution wisely adopted the name "Federalist," implying strong state sovereignty. But besides protecting individual liberty, the Framers saw several other advantages of federalism.

It is a check on Tyranny: The Framers believed that federalism would help prevent tyranny. The Framers always favored a diffusion of power. Just as the principle of checks and balances has been applied to the three branches of government, federalism was another way to prevent a concentration of power that could eventually be abused. Unless the states agree, it makes it harder for the national government to enact a policy. And the federal system even implies that the states' militias could fight a tyrannical president if he took over the US military.

Federalism Allows Unity without Uniformity: The central government in Washington, DC, can focus on the big national issues, and the states can deal with lesser issues, like education, maintaining roads, and issuing marriage licenses. Texas, for example, might have very different gun laws than New York, but this doesn't have to draw in the rest of the country. The national politicians can agree on big issues and not fight over every local issue.

Federalism Encourages Experimentation: James Madison famously said federalism creates "laboratories of democracy." Each state can experiment by trying new policies and seeing how they work. Georgia was the first state to give 18-year-olds the right to vote. Massachusetts passed mandatory health care insurance. Colorado legalized recreational marijuana. The federal system gives other states and the federal government the opportunity to watch these experiments and see if they work before they adopt them.

Federalism Allows Different Regions to Make Their Own Laws: Local government allows citizens with knowledge of their own local culture, history, and circumstances to craft laws that make sense for that community. Different regions of the country have different political cultures. Laws that make sense in San Francisco might not make sense in Atlanta. Laws are not always "one size fits all."

Federalism Is Quicker and More Efficient: Imagine if you saw a pothole in front of your house but you had to wait for a bureaucracy in Washington to fill it. It would take forever. Things get done a lot faster if local people can fix their own problems. Big businesses have also learned this truth. Corporations like McDonalds or GM have long learned that if you give local managers and workers the power to fix problems and make suggestions, the whole corporation becomes more efficient and innovative. This is also true for governments. Massive central bureaucracies are less efficient than smaller, local organizations.

Federalism Promotes Democracy: And lastly, federalism benefits citizens by making them feel empowered and responsible for their own communities. If an individual became conditioned to think the national government is responsible for everything, then he or she would become complacent. Alexis de Tocqueville, who came from France (a unitary government), thought that the great virtue of federalism is that it taught Americans practical democracy. "Local freedom," explained Tocqueville, "leads a great number of citizens to value the affections of their neighbors and forces them to help one another." He believed that local government encourages people to run their own affairs, solve their own problems, and look after their neighbor.

In 2012, the people of Colorado legalized marijuana.
©ducu59us/Shutterstock.com

NATIONAL POWERS

In the federal system, some powers are allocated to the national government, some are allocated to the state governments, and others are shared by both. These are called "concurrent powers." In America, each citizen can actually be taxed by five different governments: federal, state, county, city, and the school district. Taxation is an example of concurrent or shared powers—unfortunately, many governments have the shared power to tax you! In this section we will outline the national powers, and in the next sections we will summarize state and concurrent powers.

Expressed National Powers: We can divide the powers the Constitution grants the national government into three categories, the most clear-cut being the expressed powers. *The Constitution explicitly enumerates or lists the exact powers of the national government*, these are called the **expressed powers.** Many of these are stated in Article I, Section 8, which include the power to coin money, to declare war, to regulate interstate state and foreign commerce, to maintain a military, to make foreign treaties, to make post offices, and to tax and borrow.

Expressed Powers

the Constitution explicitly enumerates or lists the exact powers of the national government

The national government conducts foreign affairs, not states. Here is President Trump talking with the president of France, Emmanuel Macron.
©Frederic Legrand – COMEO/Shutterstock.com

Implied National Powers: The Constitution also grants the national government certain **implied powers**, *powers not enumerated in the text of the Constitution but implied as a means of carrying out the expressed powers*. The constitutional basis of implied powers is the **necessary and proper clause** *found in the last sentence of Article I, Section 8. It states that the national government possesses the power "to make all laws which shall be necessary and proper for carrying into Execution the foregoing powers, and all other Powers vested by this Constitution."* For example, Article 1, Section 8 states that the national government has the power to collect taxes, coin money, and regulate interstate commerce. This implies that the national government has the power to create a national bank in order to carry out those explicit powers. So Congress had the authority to establish the Federal Reserve in 1913, even though the power to make a national bank is not listed in the Constitution.

Inherent National Powers: And the Supreme Court has also recognized that the Constitution grants the national government certain **inherent powers**: *powers not expressed or implied in the text of the Constitution, but inherent in the function and responsibility of the office*. This is especially the case with the executive branch and its inherent powers to defend the nation. Traditionally, the primary responsibility of the executive office, be it a king or a president, is to protect the country, otherwise the nation may no longer exist. Recognizing this historical fact, the Supreme Court has granted presidents certain leeway in defending the country, even if it may temporarily

Implied Powers

as articulated in the necessary and proper clause, these are powers not enumerated in the text of the Constitution but implied as a means of carrying out the expressed powers

Necessary and Proper Clause

found in the last sentence of Article I, Section 8. It states that the national government possesses the power "to make all laws which shall be necessary and proper for carrying into Execution the foregoing powers, and all other Powers vested by this Constitution"

Inherent Powers

powers not expressed or implied in the text of the Constitution, but inherent in the function and responsibility of the office bend the Constitution. Obviously, this concept is controversial, and if abused, dangerous. For example, after the terrorist attack on 9-11, the Supreme Court upheld parts of Patriot Act, which expanded federal power to fight terrorism.

Supreme Law of the Land: Another important part of the Constitution that strengthens federal power over the states is the supremacy clause. Article VI contains the **Supremacy Clause**, *which states that "This Constitution and the laws of the United States. . . . shall be the supreme laws of the land."* In areas of vital national powers, when state law conflicts with national law, national law is supreme.

STATE POWERS

Much of the state's role in the federal structure is implied in the original Constitution. The Framers thought it would be too difficult to actually enumerate the numerous state powers, so they left it implied. The Framers thought it would be understood that the states retained a large degree of sovereignty when they joined the Union. The task at hand at the Constitutional Convention was to carve out the primary powers of the central government, but they thought it was clear that the states remained sovereign in all areas not relinquished to the central government.

Supremacy Clause

states that "This Constitution and the laws of the United States. . .shall be the supreme laws of the land."

Powers Denied to the National Government: The US Constitution does not merely grant the national government supreme power; it limits national power as well. The Constitution says that Congress cannot favor one state over another state, nor can it tax imports. The national government cannot grant titles of nobility or accept gifts and money from foreign countries. The national government cannot pass a bill of attainder (punishing an individual or group without a trial), make ex post factor laws (make something illegal retroactively), or deny a writ of habeas corpus (hold somebody in jail without telling them what they were arrested for). And then with the addition of the Bill of Rights, more explicit limits on national power were added, which we will discuss in Chapters 8, 9 and 10.

Powers Granted to the States: Although the bulk of state powers are not enumerated, the Constitution does list a few specific powers reserved to the state. The states can set the time and manner of elections, select electors, choose senators, and ratify constitutional amendments. Although the state powers for the most part are not listed, traditionally the law has recognized state supremacy in several areas. The traditional areas of state authority include local law enforcement, public safety, education, family law, property law, occupational regulations, commerce within the state, and road and land use. The primary state powers are often referred to as "police powers."

Local governments, like City Hall, are usually responsible for things like road maintenance, law enforcement, and providing clean water and garbage service.
©Vadik Swenson/Shutterstock.com

Originating from the ancient Greek word *polis*, or city-state, **police powers** *are the traditional state powers related to the health and safety of its citizens.*

Powers Denied to the States: Considering the fact that excessive state powers represented one of the chief flaws of the Confederation, it is not surprising that the Framers explicitly listed powers denied to the states. In Article I, Section 10, the states are prohibited from making treatise with foreign governments, authorizing pirates, coining money, taxing imports and exports, taxing foreign ships, keeping troops (except state militia), and engaging in war (unless attacked and an immediate response is necessary). States must also form a "republican form of government."

Tenth Amendment: One of the primary fears of the Anti-Federalists during the ratification debates was that eventually the national government would dominate the states and strip them of their rights. The 10th Amendment was included in the Bill of Rights to make what was implied in the original Constitution crystal clear. The **10th Amendment** states that *"the powers not delegated to the United States by the Constitution, nor prohibited to the states, are reserved to the states respectively, or to the people."* By joining the Union the states did not forfeit all of their rights. The 10th Amendment makes it clear that the national government and the state governments have equal autonomy in their respective spheres.

Police Powers

are the traditional state powers related to the health and safety of its citizens

10th Amendment

states that "the powers not delegated to the United States by the Constitution, nor prohibited to the states, are reserved to the states respectively, or to the people"

Senators Represent Their State: Lastly, the Framers gave the states another tool to protect themselves against the encroachment of the national government. The original Constitution stipulated that senators shall be selected by the state legislatures. The idea was that senators would be ambassadors of the states they represented, and they would vote against any congressional bills contrary to the interest of the states. This role of the Senate, however, was stripped away with the passage of the 17th Amendment in 1913. Now senators are popularly elected.

SHARED POWERS

Besides the powers of the national government and the powers of the state government, the Constitution recognizes a third category in the federal system: shared powers. These are the powers that the states share with other states and that states share with the national government.

Interstate Relations: A few clauses in the Constitution deal with how the states must relate with each other. *The Full Faith and Credit Clause* (Article IV, Section 1) requires state courts to enforce the civil judgments of the courts of the other states and accept their public records and acts as valid. It does not require one state to enforce the criminal laws or legislation or administrative acts of another state. The *Interstate Privileges and Immunities Clause* (Article IV, Section 2) says states must extend to citizens of other states the privileges and immunities granted to their own citizens, including the protection of the laws, the right to engage in peaceful demonstrations, access to courts, and freedom from discretionary taxes.

Federalism

NATIONAL POWERS	SHARED POWERS	STATE POWERS
► Declare war	► Maintain law and order	► Establish and maintain schools
► Maintain armed forces	► Levy taxes	► Establish local governments
► Regulate interstate and foreign trade	► Borrow money	► Regulate business within the state
► Admit new states	► Charter banks	► Make marriage laws
► Establish post offices	► Establish courts	► Provide for public safety
► Set standard weights and measures	► Provide for public welfare	► Assume other powers not delegated to the national government of prohibited to the states
► Coin money		
► Establish foreign policy		
► Make all laws necessary and proper for carrying out delegated powers		

Concurrent Powers: Lastly, *as long as there is no conflict, powers not exclusively given to the national government may be exercised concurrently by the states are known as* **concurrent powers.** As stated above, citizens can be taxed by five governments. This demonstrates that the power to levy a tax is a concurrent power shared by national, state, and local government. The Supreme Court has ruled that a state may tax the same item the federal government taxes, as long as it does not pose an "undue burden" or threaten to undermine the federal tax. Other concurrent powers include borrowing money, setting up courts, making laws, charting banks and corporations, and spending money on the general welfare—inherent powers of all governments.

SUMMARY OF FEDERALISM

In *Federalist #45*, James Madison summed up the federal system with these words: "The powers delegated by the proposed Constitution to the federal government are few and defined. Those which are to remain in the state governments are numerous and indefinite. The former will be exercised principally on external objects, as war, peace, negotiations, and foreign commerce; with which last the power of taxation will, for the most part, be connected. The powers reserved to the several states will extend to all the objects which, in the ordinary course of affairs, concern the lives, liberties, and properties of the people, and the internal order, improvement, and prosperity of the state."

Concurrent Powers

as long as there is no conflict, powers not exclusively given to the national government may be exercised concurrently by the states

We can clarify Madison's summary by making six points: (1) The Constitution lists the express powers of the national government, but it also possesses certain implied and inherent powers. (2) Within the scope of its vital functions, the national government is supreme. (3) State governments retain the powers not exclusive to the national government, except those prohibited to the states by the Constitution. Traditionally, the states have primary authority in education and "police powers" of public health and safety. (4) Some powers are expressly denied to both the national and state governments by the Constitution and the Bill of Rights. (5) The states recognize each other's laws and try to work together. (6) And, some powers are concurrently shared by the national and state governments.

FINAL THOUGHTS

The above summary of the federal system may seem clear enough, but it should be understood that there is plenty of room for interpretation. Many of the most heated political debates in American history have resulted from different interpretations of what powers the Constitution grants the states and national government. The greatest conflict over federalism was the Civil War.

The Confederate States thought slavery was a states' rights issue dealing with labor laws and property, and the North thought slavery was a human rights issue, protecting each person's right to life, liberty, and the pursuit of happiness. This tragic conflict over federalism cost hundreds of thousands of lives.

Although not nearly to the extent of the Civil War, today we are still fighting over issues related to federalism. For example, should each state be allowed to make it own abortion laws? After all, abortion falls under the traditional scope of "police powers," concerning public health and safety. Others argue that the right to have an abortion is a right protected by the Bill of Rights, which applies to all US citizens. What about gay marriage? Marriage and family law has always been under the purview of the states. Or do all citizens have an equal right to marry whoever they wish? How about the legalization of marijuana? Are federal marijuana laws supreme over state drug laws, or should the people of each state decide whether they want to criminalize recreational marijuana? Questions like these go to the heart of the complexity of the federal system and insure that there will always be some tension between the state and the national governments.

NOTES

Alexander Hamilton, John Jay, and James Madison. *The Federalists*. Indianapolis: Liberty Fund, 2001.
Alexis de Tocqueville, *Democracy in America*. Translated by George Lawrence. New York: Harper Collins, 1969.
Of 193 nations, 25 have a federal system. See the World Factbook (www.cia.gov).

ESSAY QUESTIONS

1. What did the Framers think were the advantages of federalism?
2. Explain the significance of the Supremacy Clause and 10th Amendment.
3. Describe the traditional "police powers" of the states, and list the powers the Constitution denies the states (Art 1, sect 10).

TERMS

Concurrent Powers: _____

Expressed Powers: _____

Federal System: _____

Implied Powers: _____

Inherent Powers: _____

Necessary and Proper Clause: _____

Police Powers: _____

Supremacy Clause: _____

10th Amendment: _____

Unitary System: _____

CHAPTER 7

How Has the National Government Grown in Power over the States?

TOPICS

- ▶ Two Metaphors of Federalism
- ▶ Marshall Court
- ▶ Era of Dual Federalism
- ▶ Era of Cooperative Federalism
- ▶ New Federalism
- ▶ Federalism Today

LEARNING OBJECTIVES

When you finish reading this chapter, you will be able to:

1. Compare Dual Federalism with Cooperative Federalism.
2. Explain the significance of *McCulloch v. Maryland* and *Gibbon v. Ogden*.
3. Describe how the New Deal led to a greater role for the federal government.
4. Discuss how conservatives in the 1980s and 1990s tried to restore some state power.

GROWTH OF THE NATIONAL GOVERNMENT

At the Constitutional Convention of 1787, the Framers invented the concept of federalism by carefully balancing the powers of the national government and the state governments. The national government was to have supreme power in its vital areas of responsibility, such as in foreign affairs, national defense, and in regulating commerce between the states and with foreign countries.

And the state governments were allowed to keep their sovereignty with local matters, especially with education, health and public safety, roads, public morals and criminal law. But as the country modernized and the problems facing the nation became more complex, the national government's powers and responsibilities expanded as those of the state governments diminished. This chapter will outline the history of the expansion of national power.

TWO METAPHORS OF FEDERALISM

Over the years, constitutional scholars have developed two metaphors to describe federalism. These models serve as a tool to help people visualize federalism and understand how it has evolved in American history.

The Layer Cake Metaphor: This was the old model of federalism that prevailed from 1789 to 1932. Like a layer cake, this metaphor depicts the American system with two separate and independent layers of government, with the national government on top and the state governments below. Also known as **dual federalism,** *the national government operates only within its limited enumerated powers while the states retain their sovereign powers, and the two layers of government have separate functions and responsibilities.* For example, the national government conducts foreign affairs, and the state governments run the local schools. Designed to protect state's rights, this model implies a basic level of tension between the state governments and the national government.

Dual Federalism

the national government operates only within its limited enumerated powers while the states retain their sovereign powers, and the two layers of government have separate functions and responsibilities

American Federalism
Marble Cake or Layer Cake?

Marble Cake Federalism is based on concept of cooperative federalism.

ffolas/Shutterstock.com

Layer Cake Federalism is based on the concept of dual federalism.

Paul Tessier/Shutterstock.com

The Marble Cake Metaphor: This new model developed during the New Deal and expanded through the 1960s and 1970s. Like a marble cake, the responsibilities and functions of the national and state governments swirl together. Also known as **cooperative federalism**, *the national government and the state governments cooperate and work together to serve the public.* For example, the states may run the public schools, but the national government provides some funding and sets education standards. This model provides for a greater role for the national government to operate within state boundaries.

Cooperative Federalism

the national government and the state governments cooperate and work together to serve the public

MARSHALL COURT

So the question is: how did America change from a layer cake to a marble cake? Much of this growth has been due to Supreme Court interpretations of the Constitution. In general, in disputes between the national government and the states, the Supreme Court has supported the federal government. Although much of this expansion started in the 1930s, the Marshall Court established the intellectual foundation of Cooperative Federalism in the beginning of the nineteenth century.

John Marshall

serving as Chief Justice from 1801 to 1835, John Marshall was the most influential jurist in Supreme Court history

Marshall Court: *Serving as Chief Justice from 1801 to 1835,* **John Marshall** *was the most influential jurist in Supreme Court history.* No other Chief Justice has done more to augment the power and prestige of the Supreme Court. Like Alexander Hamilton, Marshall was a Federalist that supported a stronger national government, as opposed to his distant cousin, Thomas Jefferson, who was a Republican that supported greater state's rights. Through several landmark Supreme Court decisions, Marshall interpreted the Constitution in a way that had long-term consequences for federalism, tilting the scales of power in the direction of greater national power. He did this by broadly interpreting the necessary and proper clause, the supremacy clause, and the commerce clause.

McCulloch v. Maryland

in this case, the Marshall Court established the constitutional approach to federalism that would guide the national government for centuries by upholding the establishment of a national bank

McCulloch v. Maryland **(1819):** *In this landmark Supreme Court case, Marshall established the constitutional approach to federalism that would guide the national government for centuries.* ***McCulloch v. Maryland*** involved the Bank of the United States (BUS). America's first central bank was established in 1791 by an act of Congress, which at the time was controlled by the Federalist Party. Republican politicians in Maryland opposed the BUS and passed a law levying a $15,000 annual tax on all banks not incorporated in Maryland. They argued that the Constitution does not explicitly grant Congress the power to create banks and therefore the BUS is invalid.

John Marshall was the most influential Chief Justice in history.
©Everett Historical/Shutterstock.com

John Marshall, writing a unanimous decision, sided with Congress by using the *necessary and proper clause* (implied powers) and the *supremacy clause* (national supremacy) cited in Chapter 6. Marshall said that the implied powers clause must be interpreted by the means-ends test. If the national government ends are one or more of the expressed powers in the text of the Constitution, then the means are valid. In this case, creating a national bank is the proper means for carrying out the expressed powers of Congress to collect taxes, to borrow money, and to coin money; thus, it is constitutional. Marshall also said that "the power to tax can be used as a power to destroy" and the state of Maryland cannot destroy a congressional law. As the supremacy clause asserts, when in conflict national law is supreme over state law.

Gibbons v. Ogden (1824): In this case, *Marshall established for the national government far-reaching powers to regulate business and the economy under the commerce clause.* The state of New York granted Robert Fulton and his franchisees a charter with the exclusive rights to run all ferries operating on waters within the state. Under this charter, Aaron Ogden, one of Fulton's franchisees, ran a lucrative ferry rout from a city in New York to a city in New Jersey. One day Thomas Gibbons showed up and started running his ferry on the exact same route. As a result, Ogden sued Gibbons. But Gibbons possessed something very important—a federal coastal license granted by the US Congress.

Chief Justice Marshall decided the case in favor of Gibbons. He based his ruling on a broad interpretation of the **commerce clause,** which in Article I, Section 8 states that *Congress shall have the power to "regulate commerce . . . among the several states."* He said that Gibbons' federal coastal license superseded Ogden's New York state monopoly because the national government has sole authority in regulating interstate commerce. In the most forceful language possible, Marshall asserted the national government possesses nearly unlimited power to regulate commerce between two or more states. The power of Congress to regulate commerce "is complete in itself" asserted Marshall, and "may be exercised to its utmost." But within a state, Marshall explained, commerce "carried on between man and man in a state, or between different parts of the same state, and which does not extend to or affect other states," then the national government has no power.

On the surface, Marshall's opinion seemed to clearly define the limits of national power as extending only to commerce *between* two or more states. But his language opened the door for future courts to allow the federal government to regulate commerce inside a state. He did this in two ways. First, he broadly defined the word "commerce." At that time, commerce usually meant "trade," but Marshall defined it as all economic "intercourse." This expansive term can be interpreted to include almost any type of commercial behavior. Second, Marshall said the national government could regulate commerce that

Gibbons v. Ogden

Marshall established for the national government far-reaching powers to regulate business and the economy under the commerce claus

Commerce Clause

Congress shall have the power to "regulate commerce . . . among the several states" could "affect other states." So even if it this economic intercourse took place within a state, if it *affected* another state, then the federal government could regulate it. Eventually, Congress will use Marshall's broad interpretation of the commerce clause to regulate nearly all economic activity in a state.

ERA OF DUAL FEDERALISM

Although the Marshall Court established the constitutional foundation for the expansion of the national government and Cooperative Federalism, during the 1800s the federal government was small and Dual Federalism was the model accepted by most politicians and judges. Advocates of Dual Federalism believed it was the best system to protect individual liberty and state's rights. But in several important cases, the Supreme Court misinterpreted the Constitution, undermining the credibility of Dual Federalism.

Pre-Civil War Era: In 1835, Roger Taney succeeded John Marshall as Chief Justice. He was appointed by Andrew Jackson and served into the early years of the Civil War. The Taney Court forged the concept of Dual Federalism, in which both the states and the federal government had equal powers, and the federal government should not exceed its constitutional limits. Senator John C. Calhoun of South Carolina, in an effort to support slavery, used this concept to buttress the *nullification doctrine*: if Congress passes an unconstitutional law, the states could nullify the act. In essence, the debate on slavery was a debate on federalism. Some in the North wanted the national government to ban slavery because it violated basic individual rights, but Southern apologists for slavery argued that the states had the right to manage their own local laws and labor system.

Dred Scott v Sanford

the Supreme Court declared a congressional act unconstitutional—the Missouri Compromise, which prohibited slavery in the Northern territories

Dred Scott: In an attempt to resolve the issue of slavery in the territories, Roger Taney exercised judicial review for only the second time in the Court's history. In ***Dred Scott v Sanford*** (1857), *the Supreme Court declared a congressional act unconstitutional—the Missouri Compromise, which prohibited slavery in the Northern territories.* This case involved a slave, Dred Scott, who had resided with his master for several years in the free territory of Wisconsin and the free state of Illinois before returning home to the slave state of Missouri. After his master died, Scott sued for his freedom on the grounds that he had lived outside of a slave state for many years.

This is considered one of the worst decisions in the history of the Supreme Court. In *Dred Scott v. Sanford*, Taney not only denied Scott his freedom, but ruled that no black man could set foot in a federal court because they were a perpetual slave race that could never retain US citizenship. Taney cited the Fifth Amendment, which prohibits the federal government from depriving people of their "life, liberty, or property, without due process." And since slaves are private property, argued Taney, any congressional act that prohibited slavery in the territories was unconstitutional.

Taney's ruling was filled with all sorts of factual errors and logical inconsistencies. He said blacks could never be citizens because at the time of the framing of the Constitution, no blacks were citizens. This is not true. By 1787, five of the thirteen states had either freed their slaves or started the process of gradual emancipation. And he ignores the clear meaning of Article IV, vesting Congress with the power to "make all needful rules and regulations" respecting the territories. Roger Taney's activist opinion, which radically misinterpreted the text of the Constitution in order to further his own political agenda, caused a firestorm of protest. In his attempt to maintain Dual Federalism and state's rights, he went too far and denied the national government a power enumerated in the Constitution (that it could regulate the territories) and implied that any state that prohibited slavery violated the Constitution.

In *Dred Scott v. Sanford* the Supreme Court ruled that Congress cannot prohibit slavery in the territories.
©Everett Historical/Shutterstock.com

The Civil War and Reconstruction: Instead of resolving the slave issue, *Dred Scott* actually helped precipitate the Civil War. During the conflict, President Abraham Lincoln and the national government exercised its tremendous war powers. Before the end of the war, the 13th Amendment was ratified, prohibiting slavery in America. And after the war, in a period known as Reconstruction, the former Confederate States in the South refused to protect the civil rights of the freed slaves. As a result, the North passed two more amendments that were *directed at the states*. The 14th Amendment said that all people born in America were citizens and that the states must treat all citizens equally under the law. And the 15th Amendment required that the states could not deny somebody the right to vote based on their color or ethnicity. These amendments were a blow to Dual Federalism. It was understood that a strong national government was needed to protect African-American civil rights.

The Gilded Age: But during the Gilded Age (1877–1900), the concept of Dual Federalism returned to preeminence, especially with regard to private property and economic matters. In 1892, the government sued E. C. Knight Company for violating the Sherman Anti-Trust Act, which outlawed monopolies on the grounds that it restricted trade between the states. At this time, E. C. Knight controlled about 90 percent of the sugar refineries in America. But in *United States v. E. C. Knight* (1895), the Supreme Court ruled on the side of the sugar company by strictly interpreting the commerce clause.

The Court ruled that E. C. Knight was a sugar *manufacturing* company, not a commercial or trade company. Under the Dual Federalism model, the Court ruled, the national government has the power to regulate trade between the states, but only the state governments have the power to regulate manufacturers as part of their traditional police powers.

Also during the Gilded Age, the Supreme Court refused to accept the original meaning of the 14th Amendment, which sought to protect the rights of the freed slaves. Instead, they interpreted it as a way to protect property rights. In cases such as the *Slaughter House Cases* (1873) and *Lochner v. New York* (1905), the Supreme Court established the doctrine of *substantive due process*: The Court read the due process clause of the 14th Amendment, which says that no state shall "deprive any person of life, liberty, or property, without the due process of the law," as containing fundamental individual rights, in this case of the protection of private property and contracts. This was a departure from the traditional understanding of due process as granting only procedural rights: the government had to follow certain procedures when arresting or fining a person. So, during the Gilded Age the 14th Amendment was actually used by the Court not to protect black civil rights as it was intended, but instead to protect corporations from federal regulations!

This refusal to recognize the clear meaning and intent of the 14th Amendment continued with *Plessy v. Ferguson* (1896). By this time, the Southern states implemented segregation, forcing the separation of blacks from the white population. When travelling, for example, blacks had to ride on the black designated ("colored") train car. And black children had to go to the black only public schools. In *Plessy*, the Court refused to rule that segregation violated the equal protection clause of the 14th Amendment. This ruling allowed the states to continue *Jim Crow laws* that isolated the black population and intimidated them from political participation.

ERA OF COOPERATIVE FEDERALISM

By the end of the 1800s, Dual Federalism was under attack. To many it seemed to be an intellectual tool used by conservative judges to protect corporations from regulation and to allow Southern states to continue to deny Black Americans their rights. During the Progressive Era (1900–1921), the federal government concentrated its powers in many important ways, but the powers of the federal government still fit into the model of Dual Federalism. But starting in the New Deal (1932–1941), and running through the Great Society (1964–1968) and into the 1970s, the nation switched to Cooperative Federalism. Broadly speaking, a majority of the American people came to believe that if left alone that state governments were incapable of addressing four areas of concern: regulating business, providing welfare to the poor and elderly, defending civil rights, and protecting the environment.

Regulating Business: Franklin D. Roosevelt was elected president in 1932. He pushed through Congress many reforms designed to fight the Great Depression, but the Supreme Court declared some of them unconstitutional. But by 1937, after FDR threatened to increase the number of justices sitting on the Supreme Court (in the "Court Packing Scheme"), and after he was able to make some of his own appointments, the Court started to uphold the New Deal laws. The Court accepted these new laws by broadening their interpretation of the commerce clause.

One of FDR's landmark New Deal reforms was the Wagner Act of 1935, which, among other things, mandated that if a majority of workers voted to unionize, the company must oblige. It also created National Labor Relations Board (NLRB), a federal government agency to enforce the many labor laws included in the Wagner Act. In *NLRB v. Jones and Laughlin Steel Corporation* (1937), the Supreme Court ruled that it was wrong for the steel company to fire ten workers who were trying to unionize and that the federal government could regulate internal labor practices of a corporation. By establishing a new interpretation of the commerce clause, the Court reversed itself in *E. C. Knight*. The national government, the Court declared, can now regulate corporations within a state whether they participate in *trade* or *manufacturing*. From this point on, the Court never ruled that administrative agencies that regulated private business or the economy had too much power.

Another landmark New Deal law was the Agricultural Adjustment Act of 1938 (AAA). Its purpose was to reduce crop and livestock production so that there would be less food sold on the market, thus increasing the price and providing farmers with more profits. The law was controversial because as millions of people were on the brink of starvation during the Great Depression, the government was killing livestock and plowing crops under the ground. In *Wickard v. Filburn* (1942), the Supreme Court ruled on the constitutionality of the AAA. This case concerned a small dairy farmer in Ohio, Roccoe Filburn, who was fined under the AAA for growing wheat on his own land to feed his family and livestock. The Court ruled that even though the farmer did not sell the wheat, by growing his own wheat he did not have to buy wheat on the open market, and this *indirectly* affected interstate commerce.

Conservatives were shocked that the Supreme Court ruled that under the commerce clause the national government can fine a person for growing crops for his own use. But these two cases mark a turning point in the nation's understanding of the proper role of the federal government. During the Great Depression, a majority of the people came to believe that the US needed a national policy to combat a national crisis. If each state could regulate private business, as they did under the Dual Federalism model, the nation would be thwarted in addressing problems that affected the whole country. Cooperative Federalism seemed to be a better model to deal with national economic issues.

Providing Welfare to the Poor and Elderly: Perhaps the most important New Deal law was the Social Security Act of 1935. Social Security provided an old age pension, unemployment insurance, and welfare for poor families and the disabled. Previously, the Supreme Court had declared other New Deal programs unconstitutional, and so many liberals were nervous about whether the Court would strike down the Social Security Act too. If the Court would uphold Social Security, they wondered, on what constitutional grounds would they do it? Nothing in the Constitution expresses or even implies that the national government must provide things like old age pensions or unemployment insurance. In *Helvering v. Davis* (1937), the Supreme Court used the *General Welfare Clause* to uphold the Social Security Act. The general welfare clause, in Article 1, Section 8, states that Congress shall have the power to tax in order to pay national debts and "provide for the . . . general welfare of the United States."

Originally the general welfare clause was understood to mean that the government must pay for the expressed items listed in Article 1, Section 8, but the new broad interpretation of the general welfare clause provided the foundation for the expansion of the modern welfare state in America. As part of a "war on poverty," these welfare programs substantially increased during the Great Society of the late 1960s. Spearheaded by Lyndon Johnson, the Great Society instituted dozens of programs designed to help the poor: food stamps, school lunches, public housing, job training, day care, welfare, Medicare (medical benefits for the elderly), and Medicaid (medical benefits for low income families). Traditionally, state and local governments, with the help of private charity and churches, were responsible for the poor. But by the 1960s, a majority of the population accepted the idea that only the federal government could properly provide for the general welfare of the country.

An important tool of the Great Society's war on poverty was federal grants to poor states. Since the adoption of the **16th Amendment** (*which created the income tax*), the national government has had much more money than the states, which often seek this money to supplement their budgets. Grants are designed to distribute wealth from high-income states to low-income states in order to help people living in poor regions of the country. Increasingly these grants came with more and more federal regulations. In other words, if the states accepted this money, then they had to accept numerous federal regulations. **Categorical grants** *are federal monetary grants to the states for specific purposes, which comes with federal rules and regulations.* For example, if states

16th Amendment

created the income tax

Categorical Grants

are federal monetary grants to the states for specific purposes, which comes with federal rules and regulations accept federal money for road construction, they must set the alcohol drinking age at 21. This is why all fifty states have the same drinking age, when in the past each state set its own drinking age.

Civil Rights: The third problem that Dual Federalism failed to solve was civil rights. After the Civil War, the 14th Amendment (promising equality under the law) and the 15th Amendment (promising equal access to the voting booth) were ratified, but the Southern states ignored these by passing Jim Crow laws. Nearly a hundred years after the Civil War, African-Americans still had not been granted political equality. Finally, in 1954 the Supreme Court reversed itself and declared in *Brown v. the Board of Education* that segregation did indeed violate the equal protection clause. Ten years later, Congress passed the *Civil Rights Act of 1964*, making it a federal crime to discriminate. And the following year Congress passed the *Voting Rights Act of 1965*, making it a federal crime to prevent somebody from voting. So, once again it took a national policy to address an issue (civil rights) that the states were unwilling to address.

Environmental Laws: The fourth area that Dual Federalism seemed incapable of addressing was protecting the environment. By the early 1970s, cities across America were choked by smog and many lakes and rivers were polluted. Richard Nixon created the Environmental Protection Agency (EPA) by executive order, which was later established by Congress in 1971. This federal agency was charged with protecting human health and the environment. The EPA was also given the task of implementing and enforcing the Clean Air Act of 1970 and the Clean Water Act of 1972. Together, these environmental laws and agencies reflect the belief of the public that the US needed a national environmental policy because state laws and regulations were not doing the job. Since the 1970s, pollution has been greatly reduced.

The EPA enforces the Clean Water Act of 1972.
©Perry Correll/Shutterstock.com

NEW FEDERALISM

Instinctively, many conservatives opposed this expansion of federal powers. Eventually, however, mainstream conservatives accepted a role of the national government to provide an economic "safety net," enforce civil rights, regulate the economy, and protect the environment. But by the 1980s, a large proportion of the public began to see problems with the immense federal bureaucracy. Conservatives like Ronald Reagan argued that an overweening federal government had many unintended consequences. The massive welfare state threatened to erode personal responsibility. Excessive government regulations, punitive environmental laws, and high taxes hampered economic growth. Categorical grants forced the states to deal with national goals, not local problems. And because the federal government promised to take on so many problems, the national debt skyrocketed. The conservative attempt to push back on the continued growth of the national government was called the **new federalism**: *a conservative effort to restore some power and responsibility to the states.*

Rehnquist Court: From the New Deal through the 1980s, the Supreme Court consistently supported congressional expansion of power by broadly interpreting the commerce clause. But by the 1990s, Republican presidents were able to select enough conservative justices on the Supreme Court to establish a majority block. And the Court was led by the first conservative Chief Justice in over a half-century, William Rehnquist. First appointed to the Supreme Court by Nixon in 1972, Rehnquist was made chief justice by Reagan in 1986.

In *United States v. Lopez* (1995), for the first time since the 1930s, the Supreme Court struck down a congressional act on the grounds that it violated the limits of the commerce clause. After a rash of school shootings, Congress passed the Gun Free Zone Law, making it a federal crime to carry a firearm within 1,000 feet of a public school. Most states had already created gun free zones, but Congress wanted to pass a federal statute. In the majority opinion, Rehnquist said that this was a state responsibility, falling squarely under local police powers, and he declared the law unconstitutional because Congress failed to demonstrate any "substantial effect on commerce." This, however, was merely a temporary victory for state's rights advocates. Congress passed a new Gun Free Zone Law, this time stating that it applies to "firearms in… interstate commerce." This new law has not been overturned.

The Rehnquist Court tried to establish the New Federalism in other decisions as well. The Court overturned the *Brady Bill*, a congressional law requiring local law enforcement officials to conduct background checks on people purchasing guns. The Supreme Court ruled that Congress cannot "commandeer" or force local administrators to carry out federal law. Also, the Rehnquist Court overturned the Violence Against Woman Act of 1994. In a 5 to 4 decision, the Court ruled that Congress once again exceeded its power under the commerce clause. By no stretch of the imagination does sexual assault constitute economic activity. Punishing rape, they argued, is a responsibility of local law enforcement. So, in these cases the Rehnquist Court recognized that these laws may have good intentions, but it is up to the states to enact and enforce these types of laws.

New Federalism

a conservative effort to restore some power and responsibility to the states

Block Grants: Another strategy of New Federalism was to reduce categorical grants. Starting in the 1970s with Richard Nixon, and expanded by Reagan in the 1980s, conservative presidents substituted more block grants for categorical grants. **Block grants** *are federal monetary transfers to states with no strings attached to be used for general purposes.* While still providing income distribution from the wealthy states to the poorer states, block grants afford the states with the freedom to run their local affairs more efficiently.

Prohibiting Unfunded Mandates: States love *block grants* because they can spend the money how they wish with no strings attached. States like *categorical grants* less because they have to comply with federal regulations. But states absolutely hate **unfunded mandates**: *laws passed by Congress requiring the states to do something without providing the funds to do it.* As part of Newt Gingrich's *Contract with America*, Congress passed a law in 1995 making unfunded mandates illegal. In part, this law was in response to the Americans with Disabilities Act (ADA), which was signed into law by George H. W. Bush in 1990. Part of the law required local and state governments to provide proper accommodations to make sidewalks and public and private facilities accessible to the disabled. This law cost local and state government billions of dollars. Now when Congress passes a law forcing the states to do something, they must also provide the funds.

FEDERALISM TODAY

Today, federalism is a fundamental part of the political debate between liberals and conservatives. Since the 1930s, liberals have advocated more centralization (a stronger national government) and conservatives have advocated more decentralization (stronger states governments). Liberals support a strong central government because they want to use government to promote greater social justice and equality. Conservatives support enough centralization to provide the national government with the ability to defend the country, provide law and order, and guide economic growth, but not so much power that it strips away individual and state freedoms. Conservatives feel that because humans are flawed, human institutions will also be flawed. They say it is wiser to distribute power to local entities, rather than one centralized bureaucracy.

The above represent the ideology and political rhetoric of liberals, who tend to be Democrats, and conservatives, who tend to be Republicans. In reality, however, both parties in recent decades have supported greater centralization. Whether a Democrat or Republic controls the White House, the federal government has steadily grown in power over the states.

Block Grants

are federal monetary transfers to states with no strings attached to be used for general purposes

Unfunded Mandates

laws passed by Congress requiring the states to do something without providing the funds to do it

The Bush Era: George W. Bush, a Republican serving as president from 2000–2008, halted if not killed the New Federalism movement. Bush sponsored three laws that augmented the scope of the national government. First, in response to the terrorist attacks of September 11, 2001, Bush implemented the *Homeland Security Act.* In conjunction with the Patriot Act, this law dramatically increased the size and scope of the federal domestic police agencies, a domain previously controlled by the states. Second, *No Child Left Behind* was a federal program that placed strict national standards on all public schools. Previously, education was considered a state responsibility. And lastly, in 2003 Bush pushed through Congress the *Medicare Modernization Act*, which provided federal assistance for the elderly to buy prescription drugs. So, in three areas where the states had traditionally exercised primary responsibility—police, education, and public health—George Bush had expanded federal authority.

The Roberts Court: John Roberts, selected by Bush, became Chief Justice in 2005. Known for having a conservative judicial philosophy, when Roberts replaced William Rehnquist, constitutional scholars wondered if he would continue to advance Rehnquist's New Federalism. One of Robert's first major cases, *Rapanos v. United States* (2005), centered on questions related to federalism. In 1994 John Rapanos was arrested for moving some dirt on his own land without the proper government permits. Rapanos discovered that he violated the Clean Water Act, enforced by the EPA, because he moved a "pollutant," which can include sand, into a ditch, which was considered "navigable water," even though his property was twenty miles from the nearest river. The Supreme Court, in a show of support for state's rights, sided with Rapanos and rejected the broad definition of "navigable water" because it would give the federal government too much control over private land within a state.

Barack Obama was elected president in 2008. Obama implemented the Patient Protection and Affordable Care Act (ACA), which mandates that all US citizens buy health insurance. To date, this represents the last major expansion of federal power. In *National Federation of Independent Business v. Sebelius* (2012), Florida and twenty-five other states brought action against the ACA, in particular the mandate to buy insurance. In this case Chief Justice Roberts used all his intellectual ability to preserve aspects of the New Federalism without overturning an act passed by Congress. Roberts ruled that the national government does not have the power to make people buy insurance under the *commerce clause* or the *necessary and proper clause*, but it does under the *taxing power*. So, he supported a key objective of New Federalism by limiting the scope of the commerce clause, but he ended up giving the national government the power to regulate the massive health care industry.

Sanctuary Cities: In 2017, Donald Trump's justice department threatened to withhold federal funds to sanctuary cities: cities that refuse to turn over illegal immigrant criminals to ICE (Immigration Customs Enforcement) for possible deportation. This is another example of a contention federalism issue. Many cities and the state of California have sued the justice department for this action.

If this case goes to the Supreme Court, the justices would likely look first at Article 1, Section 8, which reads: "Congress shall have the power…to establish a uniform Rule of Naturalization." The Constitution gives the national government the exclusive power to determine immigration law, which makes sense otherwise if each of the 50 states set their own immigration policy, there would be chaos. The states in support of sanctuary cities, however, have one possible constitutional argument in their defense. In recent years the Supreme Court has established the anti-commandeering doctrine, which holds that the national government cannot force local police to enforce federal laws. But this doctrine hasn't been clearly articulated and everyday local and state police cooperate with federal law enforcement. So, like many political issues in America, we will have to wait and see how the Supreme Court rules.

FINAL THOUGHTS

Today Cooperative Federalism reigns supreme as Dual Federalism languishes in a grave. Simply put, a large majority of Americans expect the federal government to solve the problems facing the country. Evidence of this is provided by the typical presidential or congressional campaign wherein the candidate promises to solve every problem without regard of whether it is considered a local or state issue, such as crime, public roads, or education. Today it is hard to imagine any area of life that the federal government does not regulate. If you look around your classroom, there are probably hundreds of federal regulations related to everything you can see: the paint on the walls, the material in the carpet, the electricity going into the lights bulbs, the type of light bulbs, everything.

Another way to view how dramatically the US has shifted from Dual Federalism to Cooperative Federalism is to look at federal spending and regulations. In 1930, the federal government spent 3.4 percent of GDP, and in 2010 the government spent 24 percent of GDP. As a result of the increased spending of the federal government, and its expanding role to finance more and more programs, in 2016 the national debt reached nearly $19 trillion, over 100 percent of GDP. And federal regulations have increased just as dramatically as spending. In 2010, for example, the national government enacted 3,573 new regulations that the American people and businesses must follow.

All federal regulations are reported in the *Federal Register*, which today has over 81,000 pages.

In summary, the liberals were right that when left alone, the states failed to solve many important problems. And today the conservatives are right that the central government is trying to do too much, and as a result the national debt is skyrocketing and the economy is burdened by excessive regulations. The Framers established the federal system to provide limits on centralized power. Now that the nation has discarded Dual Federalism and adopted Cooperative Federalism, we are struggling to find the proper limits of federal power.

NOTES

To find the full text of Supreme Court opinions: Findlaw.com: US Supreme Court Opinions.

For stats on growth of Federal government: Arthur Brooks, *The Road to Freedom*. New York: Basic Books, 2012.

Adam Freedman. *The Naked Constitution*: *What the Founders Said and Why it Still Matters*. New York: Broadside Books, 2012, p. 52.

Alfred H. Kelly et al. *The American Constitution: Its Origins and Developments*. Vol I & II. New York: Norton & Co., 1991.

Michael Les Benedict. The *Blessings of Liberty: A Concise History of the Supreme Court*. Boston: Wadsworth, 2006.

The Heritage Guide to the Constitution: Washington, DC: The Heritage Foundation, 2005.

William M. Wiecek. *Liberty under Law: The Supreme Court in American Life*. Baltimore: Johns Hopkins University Press, 1988.

ESSAY QUESTIONS

1. Explain the difference between dual federalism (layer cake) and cooperative federalism (marble cake).
2. Describe the significance of *McCulloch v. Maryland* and *Gibbons v. Odgen*.
3. List four societal problems that the states could not deal with and so the federal government had to step in.
4. Define a categorical grant, block grant, and unfunded mandate.
5. Define New Federalism and cite at least one Supreme Court case in which the Court tried to achieve the goals of the New Federalism.
6. Explain the advantages and disadvantages of greater government centralization.

TERMS

Block Grant: _____

Categorical Grant: _____

Commerce Clause: _____

Cooperative Federalism: _____

Dred Scott v. Sanford: _____

Dual Federalism: _____

Gibbons v. Ogden: _____

John Marshall: _____

McCulloch v. Maryland: _____

New Federalism: _____

16th Amendment: _____

Unfunded Mandates: _____

CHAPTER 8

What Are My First Amendment Rights?

TOPICS

- ► Freedom of Religion
- ► The Supreme Court and the Establishment Clause
- ► The Free Exercise Clause
- ► Free Speech
- ► Freedom of the Press
- ► Right to Assemble and Petition

LEARNING OBJECTIVES

When you finish reading this chapter, you will be able to:

1. Discuss the Framers' original ideas about freedom of religion.
2. Compare the establishment clause and the free exercise clause.
3. List how government can limit free speech.
4. Describe the importance of free speech and a free press in a democracy.
5. Explain significance of the right to assemble and petition the government.

WHAT ARE MY FIRST AMENDMENT RIGHTS?

Perhaps before we ask *what are my first amendment rights?*, we should ask *what are rights*? This is a difficult philosophical question. Today we hear people bandy this word around freely: "I have a right to marry who ever I want," "It is my right to have purple hair," "All children have the right to be happy." The concept of rights is often used to assert one's freedom to do whatever they want, but it also has a deeper political meaning. For this course, we will discuss political rights and their relationship to government. **Rights** *are the legal freedoms or entitlements that structure the form of government and the content of the laws.*

Rights Granted by Government: Another fundamental question is whether rights are granted by governments or by God. Some argue that rights are merely the liberties and civil protections granted to the people by the government. And as society has evolved over the centuries, people have struggled and fought for a more enlightened government that recognizes more human rights. Thus, rights are merely a legal arrangement and the rules by which the government must abide by. For example, governments have agreed that citizens have a right to a jury trial, the right of a free speech, and the right to an education.

Rights Granted by God: The Founders would have disagreed with the notion that rights are granted by government, otherwise they would not have been able to justify the rebellion against Great Britain. In the Declaration of Independence, Thomas Jefferson wrote, "We hold these truths to be self evident; that all men are created equal, that they are endowed by their Creator with certain unalienable rights, that among these are Life, Liberty, and the pursuit of Happiness." Jefferson went on to say that "whenever any Form of Government becomes destructive to these ends, it is the right of the people to alter or abolish it." In other words, if all rights are derived by government, then they have the right to do whatever they please, such as executing all political opponents. But if rights are granted by God, then they become an objective reality and a valid check on tyrannical government.

The First Amendment: Now that we have thought a little about the nature of rights, let's look at the specific rights enumerated in the 1st Amendment. As part of the Bill of Rights, the 1st Amendment was ratified by the states and added to the Constitution in 1791, during the First Congress. Although his words were altered by various congressional committees, James Madison was the primary author of the 1st Amendment, which reads as follows: **"Congress shall make no law respecting the establishment of religion, or prohibiting the free exercise thereof; or abridging the freedom of speech, or of the press, or the rights of the people peaceably to assemble, and to petition the government for a redress of grievance."**

The 1st Amendment actually contains six distinct ideas, coupled into three categories. Freedom of religion: Congress shall not establish a religion nor prohibit people from freely practicing their religion. Freedom of speech: Congress shall not abridge the freedom of speech of the people or of the press. And Freedom to Politically Organize: Congress shall not abridge the right of the people to form groups to protest or lobby the government. These six rights represent the core functions needed in a free democracy. No government can

Rights

The legal freedom or entitlements that structure the form of government and the content of the laws.

call itself democratic if the people are not free in their thoughts, religion, and speech. No government can call itself democratic if people cannot form groups to initiate political reform. These rights are so important that they are clustered into the very first section of the Bill of Rights.

FREEDOM OF RELIGION

The Framers were aware that religious freedom played an important role in colonial history. Many members of religious groups—such as the Puritans, Quakers, Baptists, Methodists, Catholics, Jews, and Mennonites—came to America to escape religious persecution. Religious liberty, they believed, should be protected. They also believed that the national government should be neutral toward religion and not promote one official state church. These two concepts are imbedded in the Constitution in the *establishment clause* and the *free exercise clause*.

The Establishment Clause: The **establishment clause** *of the 1st Amendment states that "Congress shall make no law respecting the establishment of religion."* The Framers were reacting to the English system wherein the King of England, as the leader of the Anglican Church (also called the Church of England) was the official head of the government AND of the church. All citizens were required to attend the Anglican Church, and all public officials were required to take an oath to the Church of England. Moreover, taxpayer's money supported the church and paid for the minister's salaries. Besides

Establishment Clause

of the 1st Amendment states that "Congress shall make no law respecting the establishment of religion"

Can a city government put up Christmas decorations or does this establish the Christian religion?
©Kenneth Sponsler/Shutterstock.com

prohibiting the national government from establishing an official national church, the Framers held two other ideas related to the establishment clause: they considered it a state's rights provision, and they thought it still allowed government to promote religion in a general way.

The Framers understood the establishment clause as an important element of the federal system. The original point of the establishment clause was to protect state government from religious interference by the national government. Supreme Court Justice Joseph Story, in his *Commentaries on the Constitution* (1833), wrote that in order to avoid the dangers of religious persecution and religious rivalry, the "whole power over the subject of religion is left exclusively to the states." Evidence that the establishment clause was understood to be only a limit on the national government is the fact that half a dozen states, including Massachusetts, had an established church for many decades after the ratification of the 1st Amendment. Story also wrote that the government has "a duty of supporting religion," but if it supports one religion over all others, it will create more "indignation" toward religion.

Madison expressed this same idea in *Federalist #51* when he wrote that the best way to protect "religious rights" is to promote a "multiplicity of sects." Religious freedom will keep religion strong by allowing churches to change and divide as they try to serve the needs of the people. So the Framers did not understand the establishment clause as a prohibition on the government to promote religion in society. It was only a prohibition against raising one official church over all others. The First Congress, which drafted the 1st Amendment, engaged in several efforts to promote religion. They authorized President Washington to establish the first Thanksgiving Day, in which the nation thanked God for all its blessings. They paid for a Senate and House chaplain. And they reauthorized the Northwest Ordinance, which ordered territorial government to teach "religion [and] morality" because they are "necessary to good government and the happiness of mankind."

Strict Separation of Church and State

this view states that the government should do nothing to aid any religious activity and that government and public spaces ought to be secular

Two Interpretations of the Establishment Clause

Today, establishment clause activists and jurists fall into two opposing camps, although there are plenty of people in the middle.

1. **Strict Separation of Church and State:** *This view states that the government should do nothing to aid any religious activity and that government and public spaces ought to be secular.* Advocates of this position argue that the traditional interpretation of the establishment clause was fine when America was a Christian nation, but today it should be interpreted in such a way as to fit into our modern, multicultural society, which includes many non-religious people.

They often cite Jefferson's letter to the Danbury Baptist Church, in which Jefferson wrote that the 1st Amendment "formed a separation of church and state." Over the last few decades, separation of church and state interest groups have sought to secularize the public sphere by supporting such things as a ban on all religion symbols in public, revoking tax breaks for churches, taking God out of the Pledge of Allegiance, and deleting "In God We Trust" from the currency.

2. **Accommodationism:** *This view of the establishment clause allows government to aid any or all religious groups as long as it does not favor one church over another or establish an official religion.* While secular liberals tend to hold the separation of church and state position, religious conservatives tend to support accommodationism. This view is more in line with the original understanding of the establishment clause held by the Framers. Advocates of this view maintain that government should promote religion, in a general way, because it is one of the few institutions that fosters morality and public virtue, which is a legitimate objective of government. They support, for example, tax breaks for churches, generic prayer at school functions, and allowing school vouchers to be used at parochial schools.

THE SUPREME COURT AND THE ESTABLISHMENT CLAUSE

For the last half century, the Supreme Court has struggled to formulate a coherent establishment clause doctrine. This is due to the fact that several justices have held separation of church and state views, such as Ruth Baber Ginsberg and Beyer. And several justices have held accommodationist views, such as Clarence Thomas and Antonin Scalia. And a few justices have wavered in-between the two camps, such as Sandra Day O'Conner and Anthony Kennedy. As you will see, Supreme Court opinions have flip-flopped back and forth over religious issues as moderate jurists swing back and forth between the two camps.

***Everson v. Board of Education of Ewing Township* (1947):** In *Everson*, the Court rejected the traditional interpretation of the establishment clause that had been accepted for over 150 years. Arch Everson sued his town for providing school buses for all the school-age children, including the ones going to the local Catholic school. He claimed this violated his first amendment rights. In the majority opinion, Hugo Black, referring to Jefferson's letter to the Danbury Baptist Church, said the "First Amendment created a wall between church and state. The wall must be high and impregnable." Black went on to say that "no tax in any amount, large or small, can be levied to support any

Accommodationism

this view of the establishment clause allows government to aid any or all religious groups as long as it does not favor one church over another or establish an official religion religious activity or institutions" and state governments must be *neutral* in its relations between groups of believers and non-believers. The logic of the opinion seemed to be heading toward striking down the town's transportation policy, then suddenly at the end of the opinion Black ruled against Everson.

Although *Everson* seemed to be a victory for those who supported the traditional interpretation of the establishment clause, the *neutrality doctrine* established in *Everson* would be used in future cases to drive religion out of the public schools. In **Engel v. Vital (1962):** *The Supreme Court ended prayer in all US public schools.* In *Wallace v. Jaffe* (1985), the Court ruled that an Alabama law that permitted one minute for prayer or meditation was unconstitutional. In *Lee v. Weisman* (1992), the Court banned clergy-led prayers at graduation ceremonies. And in *Sante Fe ISD v. Doe* (2000), the Supreme Court banned student-led prayers at high school football games. In *Weisman*, Justice Kennedy wrote that a public prayer would make non-believers feel "coerced," thus establishing the "coercion test." So, within 200 years the establishment clause went from prohibiting the federal government from establishing a national church, to protecting the feelings of non-believers at high school ceremonies.

Should "under God," be taken out of the Pledge of Allegiance?
©tobkatrina/Shutterstock.com

Lemon v. Kurtzman (1971): Aware that the Supreme Court had failed to develop a consistent doctrine with regard to the establishment clause, in *Lemon v. Kurtzman the Court tried to formulate clear establishment clause guidelines for legislatures to follow, called the "Lemon Test."* In the majority opinion, the Court struck down a state law that used revenue from a cigarette tax to pay for parochial school teacher's salaries and textbooks. The Court then listed three guidelines for Congress and state legislatures: (1) all laws must be secular in purpose, (2) they must neither advance nor inhibit religion, and (3) they must avoid "excessive government entanglement with religion." Laws that incidentally aid religious institutions are permitted, but all laws should be secular in nature. At the time, the ruling seemed clear enough, but the Lemon Test proved to be harder to apply in practice.

Engel v. Vital

the Supreme Court ended prayer in all US public schools

Lemon v. Kurtzman

the Court tried to formulate clear establishment clause guidelines for legislatures to follow, called the "Lemon Test"

Inconsistent Rulings: With regard to religious symbols in public, the Supreme Court has issued a series of inconsistent rulings. In 1984, the Supreme Court ruled that a nativity scene sponsored by a city in Rhode Island was unconstitutional. In the majority opinion, Sandra Day O'Conner wrote that this "endorsement" by the government "sends a message to a non-adherent that they are outsiders." In *Court in McCreary County v. ACLU of Kentucky* (2005), in a 5-4 decision, the Court ruled that a privately donated picture of the Ten Commandments, as part of a 300-picture display outlining the history of law, was unconstitutional. Yet, in another 2005 case, they permitted a monument of the Ten Commandments to be displayed next to the Texas Capitol building. (Incidentally, the Supreme Court building has the Ten Commandments displayed in its pediment and on its door.) And in 2010, in another 5-4 decision, the Court ruled that it was okay to erect a high cross in memory of World War I veterans in a state park. So again, the Court has failed to establish a consistent doctrine.

THE FREE EXERCISE CLAUSE

The Supreme Court, however, has formulated a more consistent doctrine in free exercise clause cases. The **free exercise clause** *states that "Congress shall make no law . . . prohibiting the free exercise thereof (of religion)."* This establishes the fundamental right for an individual to hold or practice any religious belief she or he wishes. The establishment clause cases described above usually involve religion and public institutions, such as public schools and courthouses. Free exercise cases often pertain to religious acts by members of a minority religion that conflicts with mainstream social customs.

Although both clauses are designed to protect religious freedom, there is some tension between the establishment clause and the free exercise clause. The establishment clause bans the government from helping religious institutions, and the free exercise clause bans government from enacting laws prohibiting the free exercise of religion by individuals. If a government bans some religious activity, is it interfering with the free exercise of some individuals? For example, if a public college provides funds to run all the school newspapers, should public funds also go to support a Christian school paper? In *Rosenberger v. University of Virginia* (1995), the Court said yes: the college must also provide funds to the Christian students otherwise their right to free exercise will be infringed.

Free Exercise Test: Starting in the 1960s, the Supreme Court demanded *strict scrutiny* of free exercise cases. Because religious liberty is a fundamental individual right, the Court uses the highest level of scrutiny when examining laws that may infringe on a person's right to freely worship. The strict scrutiny test has two components: First, the government must demonstrate a compelling interest to justify actions that might infringe on somebody's religious activities. And second, the government must prove that there was no less burdensome way to achieve that end.

Jehovah's Witnesses Cases: From the 1930s to the 1950s, there were over forty cases dealing with the Jehovah's Witnesses. One issue involved communities that passed laws designed to limit the activities of Jehovah's Witnesses,

Free Exercise Clause

states that "Congress shall make no law. . .prohibiting the free exercise thereof (of religion)" such as posting signs prohibiting door-to-door solicitation. In *Lovell v. City of Griffin* (1938), the Court said it was unconstitutional for a community to require Jehovah Witnesses to obtain a permit in order to distribute religious pamphlets.

Sherbert v. Verner **(1963):** This is another landmark case in which the Supreme Court protected the religious practices of members of a minority religion. Adell Sherbert worked for a company that switched from a five-day to a six-day work week, but because she was a member of the Seventh-day Adventist Church that holds its Sabbath on Saturdays, she refused to work and was fired. When a South Carolina employment commission denied her unemployment benefits, she sued. The Supreme Court overruled the state commission's order. Justice William Brennan, who wrote the majority opinion, said that a claimant must show that the government violated her free exercise rights by proving that the action infringed upon is a "sincerely held belief" and that government action places a substantial burden on an individual to act on that belief. Since holding a Saturday Sabbath was central to her church's doctrine, the government action did infringe on Sherbert's religious liberty.

Church of Lukumi Babalu Aye v. City of Hialeah **(1993):** This case involved members of the Santeria religion. Practiced in the Caribbean and South America, this religion descends from African traditions and used animal sacrifice in many of its ceremonies. Soon after they learned that a Santeria church was planning on relocating to its town, the city council of Hialeah, Florida, passed an ordinance forbidding the "unnecessary" killing of "an animal in a public or private ritual or ceremony not for the primary purpose of food consumption." The Supreme Court struck down this ordinance and ruled that the members of the Santeria religion should be free to conduct rituals in accordance to their religious practices.

In *Employment Division v. Smith* **(1990):** We will conclude our discussion of the free exercise clause with the unusual case of *Smith v. Employment Division*. Alfred Smith failed a drug test and was fired from his job as a counselor in a private drug rehabilitation clinic. Smith, however, was a member of the Native American Church that uses peyote as part of the religious ceremonies. When the state of Oregon denied his unemployment benefits, Smith sued. Normally, the conservative block of the Supreme Court is eager to protect religious activities, but in this case they ruled against Smith. Justice Scalia wrote that the state has a compelling interest to enforce state drug laws, which apply equally to everybody.

Many members of Congress felt that the conservative justice's antipathy to drugs prejudiced them from protecting the religious freedom of Native

Americans. Democrats and Republicans in both chambers of Congress passed the *Religious Freedom Restoration Act of 1993* (RFRA), which was signed by President Bill Clinton. The act tried to restore the compelling interest standard: explicitly saying that no local, state, or national government can limit a person's free exercise of religion unless government can demonstrate a compelling interest and it must do so in the least restrictive way. The Supreme Court, however, did not seem to like Congress telling them how they ought to decide cases. In *City of Boerne v. Flores* (1997), a case involving a Catholic priest in Texas who tried to expand his church in violation of city codes, the Supreme Court ruled that the RFRA was unconstitutional!

FREE SPEECH

After the two religious clauses, the 1st Amendment protects free speech: "Congress shall make no law . . . abridging the freedom of speech." This is a fundamental democratic right. In a true democracy, citizens must have the ability to speak freely, to criticize the government, and to openly campaign for changes in government policy.

Drawing the Line of Free Speech: Most Americans are for unrestricted free speech. If you ask somebody on the street to name a right contained in the Constitution, they will most likely say "freedom of speech." Yet there are many specific examples of when people think speech should be silenced. Should racist or violent speech be restricted? What about sexist speech at the workplace? Should websites showing how to make a bomb be outlawed?

Bad Tendency Test

permits restriction of freedom of speech by government if it is believed that speech has a sole tendency to incite illegal activity or bad morals

Recently, there has been a lot of debate on college campuses concerning free speech. On the nightly news this author recently saw a student from a prestigious university say that she supports "free speech," but not "hate speech." But who defines hate speech? Some people would say that those who advocate traditional marriage, enforcing immigration laws, and questioning climate speech are hate mongers. Others would say these are mainstream or traditional views. Actually, this debate on free speech represents a conflict between freedom of the individual and order of the society. In the past, the Supreme Court focused more on maintaining social order, but in recent decades the Court has protected individual free speech regardless of whether it disrupts society or not.

The Bad Tendency Test: For much of US history, the courts held a very narrow interpretation of free speech. Judges used to limit speech using the **bad tendency test**, *which permits restriction of freedom of speech by government if it is believed that speech has a sole tendency to incite illegal activity or bad morals.* This test comes from English common law that established that the government could reasonably ban speech which has a corrupting effect on society. In early American history, this was used to ban sexually suggestive literature. In *Abrams v. United States* (1919), the Court used the bad tendency test to uphold the conviction of a Russian immigrant who published and distributed leaflets calling for a general strike and otherwise advocated revolution, anarchism, and socialism.

The Clear and Present Danger Test: During World War I, the Supreme Court abandoned the bad tendency test for a new test that only recognized more tangible dangers. In **Schenck v. United States (1919),** *the Supreme Court established the clear and present danger doctrine to limit dangerous speech.* Charles Schenck, a leader in the Socialist Party, was arrested for distributing pamphlets to men waiting in a draft line. This violated the Espionage Act, a law forbidding activities that supported the enemy or interfered with military recruitment. Justice Oliver Wendell Holmes wrote the majority opinion, which upheld the Espionage Act. Holmes concluded that stopping the distribution of anti-war leaflets was constitutional because the government has the responsibility to stop speech if it logically can lead to harm—stopping the draft might weaken the war effort and place the country in *clear and present danger.*

Imminent Lawless Action Test (or Incitement Test): By the end of the 1960s, as the fear of a communist take-over subsided and anti-Vietnam War demonstrations became common, the Court allowed greater freedom of speech. In **Brandenburg v. Ohio** (1969), *the Supreme Court more narrowly interpreted the clear and present danger test to only include speech that can*

Schenck v. United States

the Supreme Court established the clear and present danger doctrine to limit dangerous speech

Brandenburg v. Ohio

the Supreme Court more narrowly interpreted the clear and present danger test to only include speech that can reasonably lead to imminent lawless actions

1st Amendment protects anti-war protests.
©Sage Ross/Shutterstock.com

reasonably lead to imminent lawless actions. In this case, the Court overruled the arrest of a Klan leader who said racist and anti-Semitic comments on TV while holding a gun. Ohio officials arrested him for posing a probable harm. But now the Court narrowed the clear and present danger test. Speech, the Court ruled, must present a high likelihood of imminent disorder or lawlessness in order to be censored. In other words, the speech must logically lead to placing somebody in imminent danger, like yelling "fire" in a crowded movie theater. Generalized, racist speech does not meet this test.

Symbolic Speech: The Court has also recognized that there is such thing as non-verbal and non-written speech. Protests such as flag-burning or wearing arm-bands are forms of free speech that is protected by the Constitution. In *Tinker v. Des Moines* (1969), the Court overturned the arrest of students wearing black arm-bands in protest of the Vietnam War. In *Texas v. Johnson* (1989), a man was arrested for burning a flag at the Republican National Convention. The Court overturned the man's conviction citing that flag-burning was symbolic speech. In reaction to this, Congress passed the Flag Protection Act making it a crime to burn the flag. But in *US v. Eichman* (1990) the Court, in a 5-4 decision, ruled that the act passed by Congress was unconstitutional.

Five Categories of Non-Protected Speech: The trend since the 1960s has been for the Supreme Court to expand freedom of speech. Today the Court broadly interprets the right of free speech as a vital function of our democracy that should very rarely be restricted. However, there are five categories in which courts have ruled that speech can be restricted by the government: (1) libel and slander, (2) obscenity and pornography, (3) fighting words, (4) commercials, and (5) politically incorrect speech.

> Libel
>
> is false *written* statements about others that harm their reputations

1. **Libel and Slander:** Libel *is false <u>written</u> statements about others that harm their reputations.* Slander is false *verbal* statements about others that harm their reputation. In America, if a person tries to sue somebody for libel they must prove there was malicious intent—know the accusations were false and recklessly publish them anyway. Truth is an absolute defense against libel, no matter how embarrassing or harmful the true statements are. It is much more difficult for public people or public officials to sue for libel. In *New York Times v. Sullivan* (1964), the Court said the newspapers cannot be sued unless it can be proven they had an actual malice or a knowing disregard for the truth. In *Hustler Magazine v. Jerry Falwell (1988)*, the Court said it is okay for the press to print malicious cartoons of public personalities, like the minister Jerry Falwell.

2. **Obscenity and Pornography:** When one considers nude paintings or romantic literature, it is hard to know where to draw the

line between pornography and art. What is obscene? Justice Potter Stewart famously answered, "I know it when I see it." In *Miller v. California* (1973), the Supreme Court defined obscenity as any work which (1) The average person using contemporary community standards finds that the work taken as a whole appeals to a prurient interest—that is, tends to excite unwholesome sexual desire. (2) The work describes or depicts, in a patently offensive style, a form of sexual conduct specifically prohibited by an anti-obscenity law. And, (3) The work, taken as a whole, lacks serious literary, artistic, political, or scientific value. Yet, even with this multi-part test, the Supreme Court has still found it difficult to know where to draw the line between free expression and obscenity.

In general, the Supreme Court has ruled that obscene or pornographic material can be censored, especially in public places and in order to restrict access to people under the age of 18. Cities may regulate porn theaters and strip clubs and ban obscene billboards. TV and radio stations are allowed to ban certain words and behavior. People under 18 cannot buy porn. And child pornography is banned. In recent years, however, the courts have allowed more public obscenity. In 2011, a federal appeals court overturned a $550,000 fine against CBS by the Federal Communications Commission (FCC) for failing to censor the exposure of Janet Jackson's breast during the Super Bowl halftime show. The court ruled that FCC rules regarding "fleeting material" were not clearly established. And in *Ashcroft v. Free Speech Coalition* (2002), the Supreme Court overturned a law that prohibited computer generated or virtual child pornography.

3. **Fighting Words:** The Supreme Court has ruled that fighting words (speech that inflicts injury or results in public disorder) can be banned. In *Chaplinsky v. New Hampshire* (1942), the Court concluded that fighting words which may instigate injury, anger, alarm, and resentment were not protected by the 1st Amendment. Walter Chaplinsky was arrested after making inflammatory comments to public officials. The Court upheld his arrest because certain words including "lewd and obscene, profane, libelous, and insulting or fighting words, by their very utterance inflict injury." These words in no way advance the democratic goals of free speech. In *Virginia v. Black* (2003), the Court ruled that cross burning by the KKK is not protected speech because the victim of the act can reasonably expect danger and harm.

4. **Commercial Speech:** Advertised statements that describe a product for sale can be restricted in order to protect public safety. States

may punish false or misleading advertising claims. Television, radio, or print ads must be true and backed up by scientific research. Because they pose a public harm, tobacco and hard liquor ads are often banned or restricted. But in recent years the Court has allowed less restricted speech for corporations and businesses. In *44 Liquormart v. Rhode Island* (1996), the Court struck down a law which forbids the advertising of the price of alcoholic drinks. In *Citizens United v. Federal Elections Commission* (2010), the Supreme Court ruled that corporate spending is protected under the First Amendment and therefore they can run political ads. (*Citizens United* will be discussed in more detail in Chapter 21, which discusses interest groups.)

5. **Politically Correct Speech:** Lastly, politically incorrect speech is often restricted in the workplace and college campus. Many public colleges have **speech codes:** *college policies that ban speech that may disparage somebody's race, ethnicity, gender, sexual orientation, or disability; or any speech that might be intimidating or offensive.* One example of an overbearing speech code is the University of Connecticut's ban on any speech that might undermine the "self-esteem" of another student. Also, many colleges have designated "free speech zones," small marked-off areas in which students are allowed to speak on political topics. Although the Supreme Court has not ruled on college speech codes or zones, many students have won lawsuits

Speech Codes

college policies that ban speech that may disparage somebody's race, ethnicity, gender, sexual orientation, or disability; or any speech that might be intimidating or offensive

Should colleges ban speech that makes students uncomfortable?
©a katz/Shutterstock.com

against colleges for violating their 1st Amendment rights. In 2014, a student won a $50,000 settlement against Modesto Junior College because he was stopped by the campus police for passing out copies of the Constitution outside of the tiny free speech zone.

The national government has also sanctioned censorship of other forms of politically incorrect speech. The federal Equal Employment Opportunity Commission (EEOC) has issued warnings to government employees that off-colored or sexual jokes in the workplace can constitute sexual harassment. As stated above, the Supreme Court prohibits students or clergy from saying prayers in public. And in a series of cases, including *Hill v. Colorado* (2000), the Court upheld state laws that created a no-speech zone around abortion clinics. Anti-abortion advocates were banned from speaking, holding signs, or protesting against abortion unless they were a certain distance from abortion clinics or people walking into the clinics. Then in 2014, the Supreme Court, in an unanimous opinion, reversed its previous rulings banning pro-life speech in buffer zones. In *McCullen v. Coakley*, Justice Scalia said in a concurring opinion, "Protecting people from speech they do not want to hear is not a function that the First Amendment allows."

FREEDOM OF THE PRESS

The 1st Amendment also states that "Congress shall make no law . . . abridging the freedom . . . of the press." A free press is essential to a functioning democracy. The people must have access to true and accurate information in order to cast an informed vote. Government actions and policies need to be examined. Public officials need the real facts in order to properly run the government. And the people need to be exposed to competing ideas and beliefs. This is known as the "market place of ideas." It is healthy for a society to conduct a public debate about issues affecting the country, including scientific

Without a free press, democracy won't work.
©Tupungato/Shutterstock.com

and culture ideas. Recognizing these democratic functions, the Supreme Court has consistently protected the freedom of the press. In Chapter 20 on the media, we explore freedom of the press in more detail but here we will make a few major points.

Prior Restraint: Because a free press is so important to the democratic process, the Supreme Court almost never allows the government to engage in *prior restraint*, preventing something to be published before it goes to print. In *Near v. Minnesota* (1931), the Court overruled Minnesota's decision to close down the *Saturday Press* for anti-Semitic stories. In 1971, the principle of prior restraint was reaffirmed in the controversial *New York Times Co. v. US*, commonly known as the "Pentagon Papers Case." Daniel Ellsberg, a government official, illegally photocopied top secret defense department documents about the Vietnam War and provided them to *The New York Times*, which published them over the objections of the Nixon administration. In a concurring opinion, Hugo Black wrote, "only a free and unrestrained press can effectively expose deception in the government." Newspapers, however, can be sued for libelous content *after* publication.

Does the Press Have the Right to Withhold Information? If a journalist is subpoenaed, can she withhold information from a grand jury or at a trial? Journalists argue that communications between a journalist and a source, such as a whistleblower who reveals government wrongdoing, should be confidential so that future sources will feel free to provide information. Courts have recognized other privileged communications, such as between a doctor and a patient, or a priest and a parishioner. But the Supreme Court has refused to recognize this journalistic right. This places journalists in a tough bind: do they reveal their source or go to jail? Journalist Judy Miller, in the Libby Stewart Case, refused to tell the special prosecutor that Stewart was her source and she went to jail. In recent years, however, many states have passed "press shield laws" protecting journalists.

RIGHT TO ASSEMBLE AND PETITION

The last two sections of the 1st Amendment state: "Congress shall make no law . . . abridging . . . the right of the people peaceably to assemble, and to petition the government for a redress of grievance." The right to petition the king goes back to the Magna Carta. In 1774, the First Continental Congress declared that the colonies "have a right peaceably to assemble, consider of their grievances, and petition the king." Up to the time of the Civil War, the US Congress took its duty to review petitions seriously and established committees to respond to each one. This commitment, however, was ignored in the 1830s when abolitionists sent Congress tens of thousands of petitions condemning slavery, and Congress refused to send them to committee.

In modern times, the Supreme Court usually treats democratic protest as freedom of speech and therefore there are few cases that deal explicitly with the right to assemble and petition. In *De Jonge v. State of Oregon* (1937), the Court recognized that "the right to peaceably assemble is a right cognate to those of free speech and free press and is equally fundamental." In other cases, the Supreme Court has ruled that it is permissible for cities to regulate the time, place, and manner of protests. So, as long as groups get the proper permit, they can conduct public protests even if it offends some groups. In *National Socialist Party v. Skokie* (1977), the Court ruled that the 1st Amendment allows the KKK to march through a Jewish neighborhood. And in *Boy Scouts of America v. Dale* (2000), the Supreme Court ruled that the freedom of association protects the Boy Scout's policy of excluding gay Scoutmasters. (Recently, the Boy Scouts have said they are reviewing this policy.)

FINAL THOUGHTS

It is interesting to note how interpretations of the 1st Amendment have dramatically changed over the history of the United States. In 1789, the First Congress, which drafted the 1st Amendment, passed a resolution allowing the President of the United States to proclaim a day of Thanksgiving in which the nation will "acknowledge the providence of Almighty God [and] obey His will." Yet by 2000, the Supreme Court banned students from leading a prayer at a high school football game. In the nineteenth century, courts routinely allowed censorship of material that undermined public moral. But by 2000, the Supreme Court ruled that the 1st Amendment protects virtual child pornography. During World War I, the Supreme Court prohibited people from protesting the war, and by the 1970s it allowed newspapers to print top secret military documents.

These rulings reflect how American society has changed in 225 years. One consistent theme in the history of the Supreme Court is that the Court seldom tries to move too far out in front of public opinion or too far behind it. Conservative jurists want the Court to remain true to the original constitutional principles established by the Framers. And liberals want the Court to change as society changes. In this regard, the First Amendment demonstrates that the Supreme Court has been a liberal institution that changes with society. The Court has consistently believed that in order for it to maintain its credibility it must remain within the mainstream of popular opinion.

NOTES

Erwin Chemerinsky. *Constitutional Law: Principles and Policies*. 3rd Edition. New York: Aspen Publishers, 2006.

Adam Freedman. *The Naked Constitution: What the Founders Said and Why it Still Matters*. New York: Broadside Books, 2012.

Alexander Hamilton, John Jay, and James Madison. *The Federalists*. Indianapolis: Liberty Fund, 2001.

Alfred H. Kelly et al. *The American Constitution: Its Origins and Developments*. Vol I & II. New York: Norton & co., 1991.

Michael Les Benedict. The *Blessings of Liberty: A Concise History of the Supreme Court*. Boston: Wadsworth, 2006.

Joseph Story, *Commentaries on the Constitution* (1833).

The Heritage Guide to the Constitution: Washington, DC: The Heritage Foundation, 2005.

ESSAY QUESTIONS

1. Cite and explain the six parts of the First Amendment.
2. Compare "Complete Separation of Church and State" and "Accommodationism."
3. Compare the free speech standards: Clear and Present Danger versus Imminent Lawless Action.
4. What five types of speech have the courts limited? Explain.
5. Define prior restraint and explain why the Supreme Court has refused to allow it.

TERMS

Accommodationism: _____

Bad Tendency Test: _____

Brandenburg v. Ohio: _____

Engel v. Vital: _____

Establishment Clause: _____

Free Exercise Clause: _____

Lemon v. Kurtzman: _____

Libel: _____

Rights: _____

Schenck v. United States: _____

Speech Codes: _____

Strict Separation of Church and State: _____

CHAPTER 9

How Does the Bill of Rights Protect Me?

TOPICS

- ► The History of the Bill of Rights
- ► Rights Imbedded in the Original Constitution
- ► The Bill of Rights
- ► 2nd Amendment
- ► 3rd Amendment
- ► 4th through 8th Amendments: Criminal Procedures
- ► 9th and 10th Amendments: Remaining Rights to People and the States
- ► Incorporation of the Bill of Rights
- ► Right of Privacy?

LEARNING OBJECTIVES

When you finish reading this chapter, you will be able to:

1. Explain the basic history of the Bill of Rights.
2. List the rights imbedded in the original Constitution.
3. Cite recent 2nd Amendment rulings.
4. Explain the significance of the Miranda Warnings.
5. Demonstrate constitutional foundation for the right to privacy.
6. Compare negative and positive rights.

HOW DOES THE BILL OF RIGHTS PROTECT ME?

The roots of the Bill of Rights go far back in English history, starting with the Magna Carta and continuing through the English Civil War and the Glorious Revolution of 1688. The basic idea of a bill of rights is that it protects the citizen against the government. It does this in two ways: It lists the procedures the government must take when arresting somebody or taking their property; for example, the police must get a warrant before they search your house. And the Bill of Rights establishes individual liberties that cannot be violated by the government, such as freedom of speech or freedom of religion.

THE HISTORY OF THE BILL OF RIGHTS

The bill of rights developed in English history as a struggle to define the powers of the king. In 1215, King John signed the Magna Carta with the local barons to establish the limits on monarchical power. The Magna Carta secured several rights that became the foundation of the bill of rights: punishment should properly fit the crime, a Sheriff cannot take property from a man without his consent (no taxation without representation), the right to a local trial, freedom from arbitrary imprisonment or trial, an accuser must produce a credible witness, a man cannot be punished or banned unless by a judgment of a lawful court of a jury of his peers, and the right to a speedy trial. As time went on, local judges made rulings based on legal concepts contained within the Magna Carta. These judicial precedents developed into a legal system known as *English common law*.

King John signed the Magna Carta in 1215.
©Everett Historical/Shutterstock.com

Eventually, all Englishmen came to believe that certain rights were a birth-right of English citizenship. The bill of rights tradition developed further during the English Civil War (1642–1651). The war started when the king refused to sign a petition granting all Englishmen certain rights, such as that no freeman could lose his life, liberty, or property without the due process of the law. The conflict ended with the execution of the king. After a period of time when Britain had no king, a new monarchy was established but again the crown refused to accept limits. This led to the Glorious Revolution of 1688, the result of which was that the new monarch had to sign the British Bill of Rights of 1689, established forever in England a constitutional monarchy in which the Parliament was supreme, the king had to operate under certain limits, and the citizens possess recognized rights.

American Revolution: To a large degree, the American Revolution was fought over the English bill of rights. The American revolutionaries were well versed in English constitutional history and asserted that the basic principles of a bill of rights must also apply to the English citizens living in the thirteen colonies, something the British government was unwilling to do. In hundreds of revolutionary pamphlets and "resolves," the colonies developed the idea that there is a natural or fundamental law that government couldn't violate. These writings, for example, often expressed the idea that the government must allow the accused to be tried by a jury of one's peers or that local representatives must approve taxes. The most eloquent and influential of the revolutionary writings that asserted the existence of natural rights was the Declaration of Independence, which pronounced that all men are "endowed by their Creator with certain unalienable Rights, among these are Life, Liberty, and the pursuit of Happiness."

George Mason: Often called the "father of the Bill of Rights," George Mason was the first American to write a comprehensive American bill of rights. Although he never practiced law, Mason was educated to be a lawyer and his studies focused heavily on English constitutional history. When the United States declared independence, each state, now that it was no longer a colony, had to prepare a state constitution. Virginia completed the Virginia Declaration of Rights and the Virginian Constitution in June of 1776. Mason was the primary author of both documents.

In the Virginia Declaration of Rights, Mason asserted that certain fundamental rights form the foundation of government. These include: (1) "All men are by nature equally free . . . and have certain inherent rights . . . , namely, the enjoyment of life and liberty, with the means of acquitting and possessing property." (2) All people have the right to "suffrage and cannot be taxed . . . without their own consent." (3) In all criminal cases, people have the right to confront their accuser, to have a speedy jury trial, and to not be compelled to give evidence against one's self. (4) Excessive bail and fines ought not be imposed, nor cruel and unusual punishment inflicted. (5) "Freedom of the press is one of the great bulwarks of liberty." (6) A well-regulated militia is the proper and safe defense of a free state. And, (7) "All men are equally entitled to the free exercise of religion." From this list, it is easy to see Mason's influence on the US Bill of Rights.

RIGHTS IMBEDDED IN THE ORIGINAL CONSTITUTION

George Mason was also one of the most influential delegates at the Constitutional Convention. When the delegates finally completed the task of producing the Constitution, Mason told them that he "wished that the plan be prefaced with a Bill of Right." Seeing a lack of enthusiasm, he said that by referring to the bill of rights in the various state constitutions, a national Bill of Rights could be produced "in a few hours." But the delegates

George Mason is often called the "Father of the Bill of Rights."
©Everett Historical/Shutterstock.com

demurred. After four long months of debate and conflict, they were too exhausted to start a new task as important as a Bill of Rights. Later, Alexander Hamilton would argue that the Constitution did not need a Bill of Rights because its very structure limited the national government. He also argued that the Constitution already contained many of the elements associated with the English bill of rights. This is true. The original Constitution contained the following rights:

Habeas Corpus: Article I, Section 9 of the Constitution states that "The Privilege of the Writ of Habeas Corpus shall not be suspended, unless when in Cases of Rebellion or Invasion the Public Safety may require it." The writ of habeas corpus is a great and ancient milestone of English common law originating in the Magna Carta. Literally meaning "you shall have the body," *the writ of **habeas corpus** means an official holding a person as prisoner must demonstrate the legal basis for continuing to hold that person.* In other words, officials cannot throw somebody in prison indefinitely and not tell him why he is being arrested or deny him a trial in a reasonable period of time.

habeas corpus

an official holding a person as prisoner must demonstrate the legal basis for continuing to hold that person

After the Revolution, several state constitutions included the right of habeas corpus in their bill of rights as a check against abusive government, and thus there was general agreement among the delegates to the Constitutional Convention that it should be included in the US Constitution. During the Civil War, Abraham Lincoln suspended the writ and held rebel prisoners without trial. Lincoln's executive action was criticized because the writ of habeas corpus is part of Article I, dealing with Congress, not Article II, describing the powers of the president. Later Congress did authorize it. During the War on Terror after 9/11, there was a debate about whether enemy combatants held in detention camps in Guantanamo Bay ought to be granted habeas corpus rights. In *Boumediene v. Bush* (2008), in a 5-4 decision, the Supreme Court ruled that habeas corpus is such a fundamental right that it cannot be denied even to suspected terrorists.

Bills of Attainder: The Constitution prohibits both Congress and state legislatures from inflicting punishment or fines on individuals or groups without a trial. In English common law, bills of attainder were used by Parliament to issue death warrants to enemies of the Crown. In America, however, **bills of attainder** have been interpreted more broadly to include any *punishment by a legislative body on an individual, including the confiscation of property*. It is a basic concept of the three branches of government that only the courts can punish a US citizen.

Ex Post Facto Law: The Constitution prohibits Congress and state legislatures from passing **ex post facto laws** *that retroactively punished an act that was legal at the time it was committed*. Ex post facto laws, meaning "after the fact," violates one of the most fundamental tenants of law: governments must propagate or make known all laws to the public so that an individual has a reasonable ability to know if he or she is breaking the law. In *Federalist #78*, Hamilton said, "the subjecting of men to punishment for things which, when they were done, were breaches of no law" is included among "the most formidable acts of tyranny."

Protection against the Impairment of Contracts: Article 1, Section 10 states that "No state shall . . . pass any . . . Law impairing the Obligation of Contracts." In general, this provision protects ordinary contracts between private persons and between corporations but also state charters. The Framers meant this clause to serve as a prohibition of the states to forgive debts. For most of American history, the Supreme Court has interpreted this clause to grant protection of private property. In *Federalist #44*, James Madison wrote that "Bills of attainder, ex post facto laws, and laws impairing the obligation of contracts, are contrary to the first principles of the social compact, and to every principle of sound legislation."

Trial by Jury: The Framers strongly believed that the right to a trial by a jury of one's peers was essential to a democratic form of government. Article III, Section 2 states: "The trial of all Crimes, except in Cases of Impeachment, shall be by jury; and such Trial shall be held in the state where the said Crimes shall have been committed." The jury is another fundamental right that goes back to the Magna Carta. And it held special importance in colonial history.

Bills of Attainder

punishment by a legislative body on an individual, including the confiscation of property

ex post facto Laws

retroactively punished an act that was legal at the time it was committed

Americans have the right of a jury trial.
©bikeriderlondon/Shutterstock.com

In the very first colonial settlement, as expressed in the Charter of the Virginia Company of 1606, the right to a jury was guaranteed. In the years leading to the Revolution, local juries served as democratic checks on unjust imperial laws. So, all the Founders, including Federalists and Anti-Federalists, thought that it was essential that the Constitution included the right to a local jury of one's peers.

No Religious Test for Holding Office: In Article VI, Clause 3, the Constitution states that "no religious Test shall ever be required as a Qualification to any Office or public Trust under the United States." This is one of the few references to religion in the original Constitution before amendments were added. The Framers sought to keep high office open to talented people of all sects, including those who were less religious. This provision also contrasted America with Britain's requirement that all public officials be pious members of the Anglican Church. In the early years of the Republic, however, the states did not think this prohibition applied to them. All the states had a religious test that required that only Christians could hold office.

Republican Form of Government: Lastly, the Constitution proscribes that the federal and state governments must protect individual liberty by maintaining a republican form of government. Article IV, Section 4, states that "The United States shall guarantee to every State in this Union a Republican Form of Government." In *Federalist #39*, James Madison wrote that a republic "was a government which derives all its power directly or indirectly from the great body of the people." This concept is bolstered by the Constitution's prohibition that "no title of Nobility" shall be granted by the federal or states governments. Inherent in these concepts is the idea of equality. The government will not create an aristocratic class, but instead all Americans will be equal in a republican form of government.

THE BILL OF RIGHTS

In America, the Bill of Rights refers to the first ten amendments to the Constitution. The general purpose of the US Bill of Rights was to protect the individual against government abuse. Primarily drafted by James Madison, they were proposed by the First Congress in 1789 and ratified by the states in 1791. The Bill of Rights does three things: (1) it guarantees a number of individual freedoms, (2) it requires the government to follow certain "due process" procedures when accusing a person of a crime, and (3) it reserves other rights and powers to the states and the people. The following sections will describe each of the first ten amendments.

1ST AMENDMENT

Chapter 8 was devoted to the 1st Amendment.

2ND AMENDMENT

The 2nd Amendment states: "A well regulated militia, being necessary for the security of a free state, the right of the people to keep and bear arms shall not be infringed." By the time the 2nd Amendment was adopted in 1791, the right to keep arms had been well established. The British Bill of Rights of 1689 said that Protestant subjects have the right to bear "arms for their defense." William Blackstone, in his famous *Commentaries on Laws of England* (1765), wrote that "the right of having arms for self defense" serves as a bulwark to protect "the three principle absolute rights (personal security, personal liberty, private property)." And several state constitutions included the right to bear arms in their constitutions. For example, the Vermont bill of rights of 1777 said that "The people have a right to bear arms for the defense of themselves and the state."

US vs. Miller (1939): Considering what a hot topic gun control is today, it is surprising that the Supreme Court has only addressed the 2nd Amendment a few times. In *Miller*, the Supreme Court heard a case related to the arrest of some mobsters for transporting sawed-off shotguns across state lines in violation of the National Firearms Act of 1934. By the time of the trial, Jack Miller had been killed and the defense never submitted a brief or sent a lawyer to argue their case. The Court, nevertheless, ruled that it was permissible for the national government to limit such guns because this weapon is not part of "ordinary military equipment" nor is it used for "the common defense." The Court took a collective interpretation of the 2nd Amendment and declared that the right to bear arms was only in the context of serving in a militia.

***District of Columbia vs. Heller* (2008):** In the 1970s, there was a spike in urban violence and many city governments passed strict gun control laws. In 1975, Washington, DC, banned private ownership of handguns except for on-duty law enforcement officers, and required all rifles and shotguns to be unloaded or bound by a trigger lock. Under the law, Dick Heller, a special police officer for the District of Columbia, was allowed to carry a handgun into federal buildings, but he could not bear arms to defend his own home, which was in a bad neighborhood.

McDonald v. Chicago

in this case, the Supreme Court upheld the right to keep and bear arms as an individual right applicable to the states

In *Heller*, the Supreme Court ruled for the first time that the right to bear arms was an individual right unconnected with service in a militia and that firearms can be used for traditionally lawful purposes, such as to defend one's home. In this case, there were forty-seven amicus briefs, revealing the intense national interest in the issue. Justice Scalia, who wrote the 5-4 opinion, declared that the DC law violated the 2nd Amendment and was thus voided. Scalia said the operative part of the sentence of the amendment is "the right of the people to keep and bear arms shall not be infringed," and the part of the sentence describing militia is merely a preface. When "the people" is used in the Constitution, Scalia said, it denotes individual citizens and individual rights. But Scalia also remarked that the government can set some reasonable regulations and limits on the types of guns people can own and where they can carry them.

McDonald v. Chicago* (2010):** The *Heller* case only referred to the nation's capital, the District of Columbia, and so gun rights advocated were anxious that the same opinion would also relate to state governments. In 2010, they got their wish. In ***McDonald v. Chicago*, with the justices again aligned 5-4, the Supreme Court upheld the right to keep and bear arms as an individual right applicable to the states.* This ruling overturned a 1972 Chicago ordinance that banned the registration of all handguns within the city.

The 2nd Amendments guarantees the right to keep and bear arms.
©patrimonio designs ltd/Shutterstock.com

Ironically, it is still difficult to buy a handgun in Chicago. After McDonald, the city council changed the law and permitted the registration of handguns after the applicant completed a one-hour course at a firing range. The only problem is that Chicago has not granted a license for anybody to operate a firing range in Chicago! In addition to firearms training, a person can only get a gun permit in Chicago after a criminal background check and the acquisition of a firearms owner's identification card, which requires further criminal and mental illness background checks. And all this requires several fees. This illustrated the point that even after the ruling in *Heller* and *McDonald* many cities across America have maintained strict gun control laws.

3RD AMENDMENT

The 3rd Amendment states: "No Soldier shall, in time of peace be quartered in any house, without consent of the Owner, nor in time of war, but in a manner prescribed by law." The inclusion of this amendment to the Bill of Rights received little debate during the ratification because resentments were still warm over the British practice of quartering troops in private homes as a punishment for the Boston Tea Party. The 3rd Amendment clearly states two prohibitions: the nonconsensual quartering of troops in private homes during peace and the unlawful quartering of troops during war. It also implies the sanctity of a person's private residence from government intrusion.

4TH THROUGH 8TH AMENDMENTS: CRIMINAL PROCEDURES

The 4th through 8th Amendments deal with how the government must operate in criminal and civil proceedings. They establish the **due process** rules that the government must abide by: *the procedures that governments must follow to protect individual rights and provide equal justice.* Again, the concept of due process goes back to the Magna Carta. It prohibited the king from acting arbitrarily when arresting people and proscribed that he must act according to the "law of the land." By the time of the writing of the Constitution, the concept of "the law of the land" was encapsulated by the legal term "due process." The 5th Amendment states: "No person shall be . . . deprived of life, liberty, or property, without the due process of the law."

Summary of the 4th–8th Amendments: The 4th through 8th Amendments list the due process procedures the government must follow when arresting a person or taking away their property. The 4th Amendment protects people from unwarranted search and seizures of their "person, houses, papers, and effects." The 5th Amendment provides the right of grand juries, double jeopardy (a person cannot be tried for the same crime more than once), imminent domain, and prohibits self-incrimination. The 6th Amendment outlines the rights of the accused in criminal proceedings, including the right to confront a witness and the right to a lawyer. The 7th Amendment guarantees the right to a jury trial in civil trials (the original Constitution already guaranteed this

Due Process

the procedures that governments must follow to protect individual rights and provide equal justice right in criminal trials). And the 8th Amendment protects against excessive fines, bail, and cruel punishment.

***Miranda v. Arizona* (1966):** In 1963, Ernesto Miranda confessed to kidnapping and raping an 18-year-old mentally handicapped girl. Later, he sued the police because they held him for a few hours and compelled him to write and sign a confession without telling him he could ask for a lawyer. The Supreme Court ruled in Miranda's favor. In **Miranda** the Court stated that *police must inform any person held in custody of their constitutional rights:* The *Miranda Warning* says: (1) You have the right to remain silent, (2) anything you say can be used against you, (3) you have a right to a lawyer, and (4) if you cannot afford a lawyer, one will be provided without charge. Miranda was very controversial at the time, but now people recognize that this merely informs individuals of their rights and protects them against overzealous interrogations.

Miranda Warning

police must inform any person held in custody of their constitutional rights

Exclusionary rule: In *Wolf v. Colorado* (1949), the Court said evidence obtained from following illegal search and seizures cannot be used in a trial. They ruled that this violates the defendant's 4th Amendment right against unwarranted search and seizure. In courts all across the country, it is very common for judges to throw out evidence that the judge thinks was collected without a proper warrant. This law occasionally sparks outrage when an obviously guilty criminal, even murderers, are let free. But most people agree that if the police did not have to follow strict rules, it would place all of us in danger of corrupt or overzealous law enforcement agents.

Police must inform a person taken into custody of their constitutional rights.
©Fisun Ivan/Shutterstock.com

Good Faith Clause: In *United States v. Leon* (1984), the Supreme Court slightly qualified the exclusionary rule. The Court ruled that if a judge issues a warrant for the police to search a specific area, and the police happen to come across illegal possessions in another area, and they were acting in good faith, then a judge could use this evidence in court. But it is up to the judge to use her discretion in the matter. In *Leon*, the Court said that if a judge follows the exclusionary rule too strictly, you punish society, not bad police. Because judges interpret this ruling differently, prosecutors tend to shop for judges that broadly follow the good faith clause, and defense attorneys try to find judges that closely adhere to the exclusionary rule.

Other Search and Seizure Issues: Because the police make thousands of arrests a day, the searches and seizures clause is the most litigatious part of the Bill of Rights. Over the years, the courts have established some basic rules regarding when police can search suspects: (1) Police must have probable cause to seek a warrant. (2) Illegal property can be seized without a warrant if it is in "plain view," and property can be searched if the individual gives verbal permission. (3) If a police officer has a reasonable suspicion of criminal activity, she can briefly stop and investigate a suspect. And (4), to deal with general, hidden criminal conditions, the police can conduct random searches, such as in a DUI checkpoint.

Recent Court cases have tried to clarify some areas related to searches and seizures in the modern world. For example, can police search your car? In *Arizona v. Grant* (2009), the Supreme Court reformulated the rules of warrantless searches of autos. In the course of a valid traffic stop, if the police come upon facts supporting reasonable suspicion of criminal or dangerous circumstances, then they can search a car in order to prevent evidence from being destroyed and to protect the safety of the officer. What about cell phones? In *Riley v. California* (2014), the Supreme Court ruled that the police need a warrant to search a cell phone because today this is where people store personal "papers and effects," as cited in the 4th Amendment.

Government Surveillance: As part of the war on terrorism, the supercomputers of the National Security Agency (NSA) scan certain digital communications, such as e-mails and cell phone calls, in order to discover terrorist activity. If these scans come across known phone numbers used by terrorists or if the computers come across certain words, such as "make a bomb" or "Al-Qaeda," it will set off red flags. Then a NSA agent must take the evidence to the **United States Foreign Intelligence Surveillance Court (FISA Court)**: *a special federal court established to grant surveillance warrants on suspected foreign intelligence agents or terrorists.* Once the FISA court grants the warrant, then the NSA (or other agency, such as the FBI or CIA) can conduct closer surveillance of the suspect. In recent years, some have accused the

United States Foreign Intelligence Surveillance Court (FISA Court)

a special federal court established to grant surveillance warrants on suspected foreign intelligence agents or terrorists

Supreme Court has ruled that cities can use eminent domain to eliminate blighted areas.
©jorisvo/Shutterstock.com

government of eavesdropping on American citizens in violation of the 4th Amendment.

Eminent Domain will be the final topic of this section. The 5th Amendment states: "Nor shall private property be taken for public use, without just compensation." **Eminent domain** *is the power of the government to take private property for public use as long as the government pays a fair market price.* Traditionally, this has been used by the government for public purposes, such as to build roads, construct dams, and erect public schools. Imminent domain suddenly became a controversial issue with the Supreme Court's ruling in *Kelo v. City of New London* (2005). The Court upheld the decision by a city council to authorize the taking of private property so that a contractor could build an office park, which they argued would enhance the "economic development" of the whole city. Previously, the Court had also ruled that towns can use eminent domain to eliminate "blighted areas." In response to *Kelo*, states like Texas passed a constitutional amendment banning the taking of property for "economic development."

Eminent Domain

is the power of the government to take private property for public use as long as the government pays a fair market price

9TH AND 10TH AMENDMENTS: REMAINING RIGHTS TO PEOPLE AND THE STATES

The Framers wrote the US Constitution and the Bill of Rights in order to restrain the federal government. They added the 9th and 10th amendments to make it clear that rights and powers not included in the Constitution are retained by the states and the people.

9th Amendment: "The *enumeration* in the Constitution, of certain rights, shall not be construed to deny or disparage others retained by the people." The Framers added this amendment so that future generations might not interpret all the rights explicitly listed in the Bill of Rights as representing the full and complete list of rights granted to the people. In other words, just because a right is not listed in the Bill of Rights, it does not mean that it doesn't exist.

10th Amendment: "The powers not delegated to the United States by the Constitution, nor prohibited by it to the States, are reserved to the States respectively, or to the people." With this amendment, the Framers sought to further protect the states against encroachment by the national government. The national government must operate by its expressed and implied powers, but the states retain all the traditional powers of local government.

INCORPORATION OF THE BILL OF RIGHTS

The purpose of the Bill of Rights was to place limits on the national government in order to protect individual rights. The whole focus of the Framers was on the national government. But every US citizen lives in a state. So the question eventually arose, does the Bill of Rights apply to the state and local governments as well? In the early years of American history, judges would have said no. But over the last hundred years, the Supreme Court has ruled that individual rights listed in the Bill of Rights do apply to the state governments as well as the national government. This is known as *incorporation*.

Selective Incorporation

the Supreme Court, on a case-by-case basis, has applied the Bill of Rights through the due process clause of the 14th Amendment to apply to the states

14th Amendment Applies Rights to the States: The 14th Amendment was passed in 1868 in order to protect the rights of the freed slaves. It stated that "No State shall make or enforce any law which abridges the privileges and immunities of citizens of the United States; nor shall any State deprive anyone of life, liberty or property, without due process of the law; nor deny any person within its jurisdiction the equal protection of the law." This broad prohibition that the states cannot violate a person's civil liberties and civil rights broadened the scope of the Constitution. But for many decades after the ratification of the 14th Amendment, federal judges did not change their view that the Bill of Rights only applied to the national government.

Selective Incorporation: Over the years, *the Supreme Court, on a case-by-case basis, has applied the Bill of Rights through the due process clause of the 14th Amendment to apply to the states*. For the most part, the Supreme Court started doing this after the 1920s. Here are a few examples: In 1925, the Supreme Court incorporated freedom of speech against the states (*Gitlow v. New York*). In 1931, freedom of the press was incorporated (*Near v.*

Minnesota). In 1940, the free exercise of religion was incorporated (*Cantwell v. Connecticut*). In 1967, the right to a speedy trial was incorporated (*Klopfer v. North Carolina*). The last right incorporated to the states was the right to bear arms (*McDonald v. Chicago*). As of today, nearly all the rights enumerated in the US Constitution have been incorporated and apply to state and local governments.

Increased Power of Supreme Court: Second only to the acceptance of judicial review, incorporation has augmented the power of the Supreme Court. Before incorporation, the role of the Supreme Court was largely to proscribe the limits of federal power. Since incorporation, the role of the Supreme Court has grown to include protecting the personal rights of every citizen. For many decades, Supreme Court justices resisted taking on this greater role. Today, people expect the Court to protect individual rights.

RIGHT OF PRIVACY?

Traditionally, the due process rights of the 5th and 14th amendments referred to procedures the government must follow, such as to grant a grand jury or to offer a speedy trial. But after the Civil War, the Supreme Court recognized certain *substantive due process rights*: fundamental individual rights contained in the due process clause. Conservative justices in the Gilded Age recognized the substantive due process right of private property, which they ruled the states cannot violate. Since the 1960s, liberal justices have recognized a new substantive due process right: the right to privacy, which the states also cannot violate.

In *Griswald v. Connecticut* (1965), the Court for the first time established the right to privacy. This case concerned a Connecticut law prohibiting the sale and distribution of birth control devices. The law also prohibited contraceptive counseling. Estelle Griswald, director of Planned Parenthood, was arrested for violating this law. Justice William O. Douglas, a FDR appointee, wrote the majority opinion. He famously said that "specific guarantees in the Bill of Rights have penumbras, formed by emanations from those guarantees that give them life and substance." This ruling sent hundreds of journalists to their dictionaries. A penumbra refers to the partial light seen around an eclipsed moon. Emanation is something emitted or radiating out from a source.

In common language, Douglas wrote that certain rights contained in the Bill of Rights, taken together, create a "zone of privacy." These include the 1st Amendment's rights of free speech, thought, and association; the 3rd Amendment's prohibition of quartering soldiers in a private house; the 4th Amendment's prohibition against unreasonable searches and seizures; the 5th Amendment's prohibition against self-incrimination; and the 9th

Since *Roe v. Wade* in 1973, the abortion debate continues.
©a katz/Shutterstock.com

Amendment, which places all un-enumerated rights with the people. The establishment of a right of privacy in *Griswald* would have far-reaching consequences in later cases.

Roe v. Wade **(1973)** *extended the concept of privacy to include the right to have an abortion.* The case dealt with a Texas law outlawing abortion. Roe (a pseudonym to protect the identity of Norma L. McCorvey) sued Dallas District Attorney Henry Wade because Texas law prevented her from having an abortion. The state argued that the life of the fetus is protected under the 5th Amendment: "no person shall be . . . deprived of life . . . without due process." In the Supreme Court's ruling, written by the newly appointed justice Henry Blackman, the Court addresses two constitutional rights: the fetus's right to life and the mother's right to privacy. Blackman ruled that in the first two trimesters, states cannot restrict abortion because it violates the mother's right to privacy. But in the third trimester, when the fetus could live outside of the woman's body, the fetus's right to life becomes substantial and states can restrict abortion.

Roe v. Wade

extended the concept of privacy to include the right to have an abortion.

Roe created a backlash toward the judiciary as many people thought the Court usurped the democratic process and violated the principle of federalism, which allows states to make laws dealing with public health and safety. By the early 1970s, as a result of a lively public debate on abortion, many state legislatures were passing liberal abortion laws. Still, most states still had anti-abortion laws on the books. Certain special interest groups, especially women's groups, began to use the courts to change their laws. And, as a result of *Roe*, the Supreme Court prohibited all the states from restricting abortions in the first two trimesters. Opponents of *Roe* said that it was undemocratic for five men in robes to stop the democratic process and make a ruling applying to all states, especially on such flimsy constitutional grounds as a "right to privacy."

***Planned Parenthood v. Casey* (1992):** Anger at *Roe* helped fuel support for the conservative movement that elected Ronald Reagan and George H. W. Bush. Conservatives argued that judges should strictly interpret the law, not make law based on broad interpretations of the Constitution. By 1992, when the Supreme Court heard another abortion case, *Planned Parenthood v. Casey*, many predicted that the new majority of conservative justices that were appointed by Republican presidents would overturn *Roe*. Instead, in a 5-4 ruling, the Court upheld *Roe*. The majority opinion was written by Sandra Day O'Conner, a Reagan appointee. She said that if *Roe* were overturned, and each state could make its own abortion laws, then it would place too much of a burden on a woman living in an anti-abortion state to travel to another state to get an abortion. Moreover, *Roe* had been the law of the land for so long that it would be too disruptive to society to change it.

FINAL THOUGHTS

Constitutional scholars often talk about two types of rights found in the bill of rights of countries around the world: negative and positive rights. The US Bill of Rights is mostly **negative rights**: *these are proscriptions that limit the government in order to protect individual rights.* These are rights that make no demands on the government to do something. The 1st Amendment, for example, says that the "the Government shall make no law abridging the freedom of speech or the press." The government does not have to provide anything, such as access to free radio broadcast or free Internet. The 1st Amendment simple limits the government from interfering with people's right of free speech. On the other hand, a **positive right** *is when the government must provide something to the people, as part of their human rights, such as education, medical support, housing, or welfare.*

This understanding of rights reveals another fundamental difference between conservatives and liberals. Conservatives, who are primarily concerned about limiting the power of the government in order to protect individual liberty, believe in negative rights. Liberals, who are primarily concerned with the expansion of government power to achieve greater social justice and equality, believe in positive rights. In 2012, Justice Ruther Baber Ginsburg, when asked if she thought new democracies like Egypt should use the US Constitution as a

Negative Rights

these are proscriptions that limit the government in order to protect individual rights

Positive Right

is when the government must provide something to the people, as part of their human rights, such as education, medical support, housing, or welfare model, said: "I would not look to the US Constitution if I were drafting a constitution in the year 2012. I might look at the Constitution of South Africa." As a liberal, Ginsburg admires the South African Constitution because it contains many positive rights, such as the right to housing, health care, food, social welfare, and the right to participate in the cultural life of one's choice.

The last time a president tried to transform the Bill of Rights by adding positive rights was Franklin Roosevelt. In FDR's 1944 State of the Union Address, he proposed a "*Second Bill of Rights*," which included the right to "a useful and remunerative job," "adequate food and clothing," "a decent home," "medical care," "a good education," and the "right to adequate protection from economic fears of old age, sickness, accident, and unemployment." Congress ignored this, but liberals have long praised FDR's attempt to expand the role of the national government to include providing each person with economic security. Conservatives scoffed at this attempt to expand government power, saying that it is impossible for government to provide all these things for each person. Only individuals, they argue, could properly look after themselves and the needs of their families.

NOTES

Erwin Chemerinsky. *The Case Against the Supreme Court.* New York: Penguin Books, 2014.

Adam Freedman. *The Naked Constitution: What the Founders Said and Why it Still Matters.* New York: Broadside Books, 2012.

Alexander Hamilton, John Jay, and James Madison. *The Federalists.* Indianapolis: Liberty Fund, 2001.

Alfred H. Kelly et al. *The American Constitution: Its Origins and Developments.* Vol I & II. New York: Norton & Co., 1991.

Michael Les Benedict. The *Blessings of Liberty: A Concise History of the Supreme Court.* Boston: Wadsworth, 2006.

The Heritage Guide to the Constitution: Washington, DC: The Heritage Foundation, 2005.

ESSAY QUESTIONS

1. List and explain the rights in the original Constitution.
2. Explain the significance of *McDonald v. Chicago.*
3. Cite Miranda Warning and explain what it does.
4. How are the Bill of Rights transferred to the states?
5. Discuss the origin of the concept of a right of privacy in *Griswold v. Connecticut.*
6. Compare negative and positive rights.

TERMS

Bills of Attainder: _____

Due Process: _____

Ex post facto laws: _____

FISA Court: _____

Habeas Corpus: _____

Imminent Domain: _____

McDonald v. Chicago (2010): _____

Miranda Warning: _____

Negative Rights: _____

Positive Rights: _____

Roe v. Wade (1973): _____

Selective Incorporation: _____

CHAPTER 10

Have Americans Always Enjoyed Equal Rights?

TOPICS

- ▶ Black Civil Rights from the Civil War to Jim Crow
- ▶ The Civil Rights Movement
- ▶ Discrimination and Classification
- ▶ Affirmative Action
- ▶ Women and Gay Rights

LEARNING OBJECTIVES

When you finish reading this chapter, you will be able to:

1. Cite the significance of the 13th, 14th, and 15th Amendments.
2. List the major events of the Civil Rights Movement.
3. Compare *Plessy v. Ferguson* with *Brown v. Board of Education*.
4. Evaluate pro and anti Affirmative Action positions.
5. Cite four major laws protecting women's rights.
6. Discuss the Supreme Court's position on gay marriage.

HAVE AMERICANS ALWAYS ENJOYED EQUAL RIGHTS?

The American Revolution was fought, in part, for equality. The American colonists demanded that they should enjoy all the rights and privileges of an Englishman as protected under common law and the English bill of rights. But the Crown treated the colonists as second-class citizens and denied them their rights, such as the right of representation in Parliament, the right to approve taxes, and the right to a jury of one's peers. In the Declaration of Independence, Thomas Jefferson protested against the aristocratic society of Britain when he wrote that "We hold these truths to be self-evident, that all men are created equal." Aristocracy is based on the idea that some people are better than others, but equality under the law is a core principle of democracy.

Many provisions in the Constitution imply equality, but the 5th and 14th Amendments most explicitly assert the right of equal treatment. The 5th Amendment states: "No person shall . . . be deprived of life, liberty, or property without due process." The concept of due process implies that the government must follow certain rules and procedures and apply them equally to all people. The 14th Amendment, however, serves as the North Star of equality in US constitutional law. The 14th Amendment says that "*No state shall . . . deny any person within its jurisdiction the equal protection of the laws.*" This is known as the **equal protection clause**. It means that the government must treat everybody and every group equally under the law.

Tragically, American history shows that many groups, including women, Latinos, Native Indians, gays, and others have not been treated equally under the law. The group that experienced the most systematic, long-term mistreatment was African Americans. Indeed, at the time Jefferson wrote that "all men are created equal," he owned about 250 slaves of African origin. In this chapter, we will outline the long struggle of black Americans to win equal rights—a history that all Americans should know. This will provide a historical context for our discussion of civil rights, anti-discrimination laws, and affirmative action.

Civil Rights versus Civil Liberties: Before we continue, it would be useful to define a few related terms. **Civil rights** *refers to the constitutionally protected rights of all persons to due process, the equal protection of the law, and the right not to be discriminated against* by the government based on race, ethnic background, religion, or gender. Sometimes this term is confused with *civil liberties*: the constitutionally protected freedoms of all persons against arbitrary governmental action, such as the freedom of conscience, religion, and expression. Then there is another term students should know. *Legal privileges* are benefits granted by the government, such as a driver's license. Civil liberties and civil rights are considered fundamental human rights, while legal privileges are merely government benefits that can be revoked. Civil rights is the topic of this chapter.

Equal Protection Clause

"No state shall . . . deny any person within its jurisdiction the equal protection of the laws"

Civil Rights

refers to the constitutionally protected rights of all persons to due process, the equal protection of the law, and the right not to be discriminated against

BLACK CIVIL RIGHTS FROM THE CIVIL WAR TO JIM CROW

The Civil War ended the long, terrible history of slavery in America, which began in 1612 when the first African slaves were purchased in Virginia. In 1863, during the second year of the Civil War, Abraham Lincoln issued the Emancipation Proclamation. This war proclamation freed the slaves from Confederate territory, but the document that actually freed all the slaves in America was the 13th Amendment. Signed by Lincoln when it was ratified by Congress in 1865, the **13th Amendment** *states that "Neither slavery nor involuntary servitude shall exist with the United States."* This voided all references to slavery in the Constitution, including the three-fifths clause and the fugitive slave clause. But it took a military victory to make the 13th Amendment a reality. When the northern Union army defeated the southern Confederate army, about 4 million slaves were freed.

Abraham Lincoln was known as the "Great Emancipator" for signing the Emancipation Proclamation and the 13th Amendment.
©Everett Historical/Shutterstock.com

Reconstruction: After the Civil War the former Confederate states refused to grant the freed slaves their political rights. Northern Republicans sought to protect the freed slaves by passing the *Civil Rights Act of 1866*, granting the freedmen all their political rights except the right to vote. After it was vetoed by President Andrew Johnson, who succeeded Lincoln after he was assassinated, Congress overrode his veto with a two-thirds vote. The Civil Rights Act was designed to invalidate the "black codes" passed by the Southern states. *Black codes* were laws passed by local and state governments in the South explicitly citing African Americans as a distinct class with limited rights. Among other things, these laws prohibited blacks from testifying in court, serving on a jury, marrying a white woman, or hanging around the streets without a job (vagrancy laws).

The Fourteenth Amendment (1868): Realizing the Civil Rights Act was being ignored, Northern Republicans sought to strengthen it by imbedding it into the Constitution. They ratified the 14th Amendment, which states that "All persons born or naturalized in the United States of America, and subject to the jurisdiction thereof, are citizens of the United States." This reversed *Dred Scott v. Sanford*, in which the Supreme Court ruled that no black person could be a US citizen. Now the **14th Amendment** *guarantees that all people born in America, even if they were once a slave, are citizens. Furthermore, it prohibits the states from depriving any person within its jurisdiction "the equal protection of the laws."*

13th Amendment

states that "Neither slavery nor involuntary servitude shall exist with the United States"

14th Amendment

guarantees that all people born in America, even if they were once a slave, are citizens. Furthermore, it prohibits the states from depriving any person within its jurisdiction "the equal protection of the laws"

The Fifteenth Amendment (1870): The Southern states continued to deny blacks their political rights, including the right to vote. At this time, the Democratic Party controlled the South. They represented the former slave masters and small farmers who refused to grant black people political and social equality. Working with the Democrats, the Ku Klux Klan used terror tactics to intimidate blacks and white Republicans (who were called scallywags) from voting or running for office. As a result, the North passed the **15th Amendment**, *which states that "The right of citizens of the United States to vote shall not be denied or abridged by the United States or by any State on account of race, color, or previous condition of servitude."* Constitutionally, this expanded to franchise to black Americans.

End of Reconstruction: Tragically, in a series of Supreme Court Cases, most famously the *Slaughterhouse Cases* (1873), the Court interpreted the 14th Amendment in a way that did not protect civil rights. And they struck down parts of the Civil Rights Acts. With these decisions, the Supreme Court tolerated racial discrimination and abetted racism. Seeing a green light, Southern states passed laws restricting black voting rights. They imposed a *poll tax* (a voter registration fee that most blacks could not afford), a literacy *test* (a reading test that most blacks could not pass because slaves were denied an education), and the grandfather clause (a law stating that a citizen could vote only if his grandfather voted, which few blacks could claim because obviously slaves couldn't vote). Sadly, Reconstruction ended in failure. The freed slaves ended up in a caste system, treated as an inferior class of citizens.

Racial Segregation: During Reconstruction, from 1865 to 1877, the Southern states enacted Jim Crow laws (Jim Crow was a derogatory name for black people). **Jim Crow laws** *accomplished two major objectives: they entrenched laws making it more difficult for blacks to vote, and they segregated or separated the black population from the white population.* Black Americans were legally required to live in certain areas of the city. And public spaces were designated as white only, or provided a limited area for "colored people," as signs typically stated. In schools, train cars, parks, restaurants, hotels, theaters, water fountains, and other places, blacks were separated from the rest of the population.

Plessy v. Ferguson **(1896):** When the Supreme Court finally had the opportunity to address the issue of segregation, it failed to apply the principle of equal treatment. In 1892, Homer Plessy, a black man, was arrested

15th Amendment

which states that "The right of citizens of the United States to vote shall not be denied or abridged by the United States or by any State on account of race, color, or previous condition of servitude"

Jim Crow Laws

accomplished two major objectives: they entrenched laws making it more difficult for blacks to vote, and they segregated or separated the black population from the white population

"Jim Crow" was a caricature of African American performers.
©Everett Historical/Shutterstock.com

for sitting in the white car of a Louisiana train. Although only one of Plessy's eight grandparents was black, under the law he was classified as an "octoroon," a mixed-raced person with enough African ancestry to qualify as a black person. When the case was heard at the Supreme Court, Plessy's lawyers argued that segregation violated his constitutional rights, especially the equal protection clause. But the Court ruled against him. *In* Plessy v. Ferguson, *the Supreme Court ruled that as long as cities and states provide separate but equal facilities, segregation doesn't violate the 14th amendment: this became known as* the **separate but equal doctrine**.

With this ruling, the Supreme Court essentially gave its stamp of approval on the racist Jim Crow laws. Ironically, the only justice on the Court that previously owned slaves, Justice John Harlan, was the lone dissenter. In his dissenting opinion, he wrote that the "Constitution is colorblind and neither knows nor tolerates classes among citizens." Harlan also correctly predicted that someday this case would be understood to be egregiously wrong.

THE CIVIL RIGHTS MOVEMENT

It would be some sixty years before the Supreme Court would overturn *Plessy* and declare segregation unconstitutional. Over these six decades, black civil rights activists fought hard but made little progress. The National Association of Colored People (NAACP) was formed in 1909 by a group of Progressive leaders, including W. E. B . Du Bois, to fight the Jim Crow laws. But through World War I, the Great Depression, and World War II, black Americans were told that the country faced bigger problems and civil rights would have to wait. Then after World War II, President Harry Truman desegregated the army by executive order. And his Civil Rights Committee recommended national laws prohibiting election discrimination, segregation, and racial violence. But the real turning point for black civil rights was the landmark Supreme Court case, **Brown v. the Board of Education**, *which overturned Plessy's "separate but equal doctrine" and banned segregated schools in America.*

Brown v. the Board of Education (1954): Linda Brown lived near a white school, but every morning her father had to get up early to drive her across town to attend the designated black school. Thurgood Marshall, a top NAACP lawyer, argued the case for Brown. He asserted that school segregation blatantly violated the 14th Amendment and psychologically harmed black kids by making them feel inferior. The Supreme Court, with its new Chief Justice Earl Warren (who previously was the Republican governor of California), issued a unanimous ruling in favor of Brown, thus overturning *Plessy* and the "separate but equal" doctrine.

Separate but Equal Doctrine

in *Plessy v. Ferguson*, the Supreme Court ruled that as long as cities and states provide separate but equal facilities, segregation doesn't violate the 14th amendment

Brown v. the Board of Education

in this case, the Supreme Court overturned Plessy's "separate but equal doctrine" and banned segregated schools in America

But the Court was afraid to set a concrete deadline that Southern states might ignore, and thus make the Court look weak, and so the Supreme Court said that all public schools must desegregate "in all deliberate speed." This is a meaningless phrase. Some states speedily desegregated their schools, while others deliberated and dragged their feet—some states did not integrate their public schools until the 1970s!

The Beginning of the Civil Rights Movement: Although many states resisted compliance with *Brown*, it gave civil rights leaders new hope that their efforts would now be successful. In 1955, Rosa Parks started a boycott against segregated public buses in Montgomery, Alabama. At that time, blacks had to sit in the back of the bus. And if the bus filled up, a black person was legally required to relinquish her seat to a white person. One day, Parks refused to do this. Soon, a new young preacher in town took a leadership role in the boycott. His name was Martin Luther King, Jr., only 24 years old. After a year, the city gave in and integrated the public buses. King then organized the Southern Christian Leadership Conference (SCLC) and fought to tear down Jim Crow laws all across the South. Soon, other groups also launched protest marches and led sit-ins.

Thurgood Marshall was the first African American Supreme Court Justice.
©catwalker/Shutterstock.com

The Civil Rights Act of 1964: At first President John F. Kennedy was reluctant to engage the civil rights issue. Kennedy very narrowly won the 1960 election, and he needed the Southern vote to win reelection. But throughout 1962 and 1963, the issue kept growing. In April 1963, the country was shocked to see on national TV black women and children fire-hosed and attacked by dogs during a Martin Luther King march in Birmingham, Alabama.

Finally, in June 1963, JFK made a national TV address promising to sponsor new and sweeping civil rights legislation. Two months later, King marched on Washington and gave his famous "I Have a Dream" speech, in which he said that "I have a dream that one day my children will not be judged by the color of their skin but by the content of their character." This was designed to put pressure on the Kennedy administration and Congress to follow through on JFK's promise. Tragically, JFK was assassinated five months later.

Civil Rights Act of 1964

this law made it a federal crime to discriminate in America

Lyndon B. Johnson, JFK's vice president, became the chief executive and pushed the civil rights bill through Congress. The **Civil Rights Act of 1964** *made it a federal crime to discriminate in America.* It entitled all people to enjoy "full and equal enjoyment" of goods, services, and privileges in public places; established the right of equal employment opportunity; strengthened voting rights legislation; created the Equal Employment Opportunity

Martin Luther King, Jr. gave his "I Have a Dream" speech to put pressure on Congress to pass civil rights legislation.
©Atomazul/Shutterstock.com

Commission (EEOC); and ordered national funds be withdrawn if states did not integrate. Some people opposed the Civil Rights Act on the grounds that government cannot stop private acts of discrimination. But it was upheld by the Supreme Court in *Heart of Atlanta Motel v. United States* (1964). Perplexingly, the Court ruled that Congress can pass anti-discrimination laws under the commerce clause, not the equal protection clause.

Voting Rights Act of 1965: In 1964, the 24th Amendment was ratified, banning the poll tax. Then in 1965, LBJ pushed through a landmark voting rights act. The **Voting Rights Act of 1965** *made it a federal crime for state officials to discriminate at the voting booth* and gave the federal government many tools to enforce the act. Among other things, it empowered the attorney general to send voter registration supervisors to areas in which fewer than half the eligible minority voters were being registered. Over the next five years, this act doubled black registration.

It is difficult to overstate the significance of the Civil Rights Act of 1964 and the Voting Rights Act of 1965. It took about a hundred years since the Civil War for the national government to fully enforce the spirit and letter of the 14th and 15th Amendments and protect the civil rights of African Americans. Incidentally, these two laws won bipartisan support: they were sponsored by a Southern Democrat, Lyndon Johnson, and voted for by a majority of Republicans.

Voting Rights Act of 1965

it made it a federal crime for state officials to discriminate at the voting booth and gave the federal government many tools to enforce the act

DISCRIMINATION AND CLASSIFICATION

Now that we have a basic understanding of the struggle black Americans undertook to achieve legal equality, we can better understand the complex issues related to the equal protection clause and discrimination. To fit the concise and brief format of this textbook, we used the history of black Americans to serve as an example of a group that experienced legal discrimination. Certainly, the black experience is an especially important one in American history, but other groups have also been discriminated against as well. So, how does a person of any victimized group prove that he or she has been discriminated against?

Classification of People: To avoid discrimination of any kind, the Constitution forbids the government from making unreasonable classifications of people. A *classification* is when a law designates a group of people to be treated differently. It is unreasonable when there is no relation between the classes it creates and the permissible goals of government. A law prohibiting redheads to vote, for example, is unreasonable and thus impermissible. Thus, a person with red hair could claim that such a law was discriminatory. But a law forbidding people under the age of 18 to vote is reasonable. It is in the public interest that voters be adults who have finished their high school education.

Constitutional Classifications and Tests

The Supreme Court uses three tests to determine if a law that contains classification of people is permissible:

1. **Suspect Classification and the Strict Scrutiny Test:** When the courts review a law that classifies people by race, ethnic origin, or religion, it is automatically suspected of being unconstitutional. This is called *suspect classification*. Laws with suspect classifications undergo the highest degree of judicial inspection and must pass the *strict scrutiny test*: the courts must be persuaded that there is both a "compelling governmental interest" to justify such a classification and no less restrictive way to accomplish this compelling purpose. Classification based on race is always suspect, and it does not make any difference if the laws are designed to help that group. The Court has ruled, for example, that laws giving preference for public employment based on race are subject to strict scrutiny.
2. **Quasi-Suspect Classifications and the Heightened Scrutiny Test:** When a law specifies women as a group, the courts place it in *Quasi-Suspect Classification*, and the law must undergo the *height-*

ened scrutiny test, which is an intermediate level test. To sustain a law under this test, the burden is on the government to show that its classification serves "important governmental objectives." Not until 1971 was any classification based on gender declared unconstitutional. Before that time many laws provided special protection to women. For example, a Michigan law prohibited any woman other than the wife or daughter of a tavern owner to serve as a barmaid. Justice Brennan said such past laws were colored with "romantic paternalism."

3. **The Rational Basis Test:** This is the weakest test. If a law makes a classification based on economic status or age, then the courts will use the rational basis test to judge whether it is discriminatory. Under the *rational basis test*, the government must show that a law makes classifications in order to "achieve a legitimate public interest." For example, the government can pass minimum wage laws to help poor people. And the government can devise programs, such as Medicaid, to help elderly people.

Proving Discrimination: It is important to understand that the 14th Amendment guarantees equal laws, not equal results. This was established in *Washington v. Davis* (1976). In this case a group of black Americans brought a suit against the Washington, DC, police department because whites were passing the recruitment test at a four times greater rate. Two black men who failed the test brought a suit against the mayor, Mr. Washington, on the basis that the test was discriminatory. The test was developed by the Civil Service Commission and tested verbal and other abilities directly related to police activities. The Supreme Court ruled that a law is not discriminatory unless it has the *intent* to discriminate. And it cannot be determined to be discriminatory solely on the basis of outcome or "racially disproportionate impact." Later, Scalia warned that it is almost impossible to discover the "sole discriminatory *intent* of any legislator."

Disparate Impact: The concept of disparate impact seems to contract the ruling in *Washington v. Davis*, but today it is used by many government agencies investigating discrimination. Since the Civil Rights Act of 1964, the government has used the disparate impact rule to penalize institutions for discrimination in employment, housing, and lending. *Disparate impact* is a statistical method used to convict institutions of discrimination without proving intent by merely showing that the minority group in question is significantly lower than in the general population.

AFFIRMATIVE ACTION

In *Plessy v. Ferguson*, as stated above, John Harlan famously said, "Our Constitution is color blind." But as our discussion of the history of black civil rights showed, the government has not always interpreted the Constitution in a color-blind manner. Clearly, blacks were discriminated against, even enslaved, under the Constitution. So, after the Civil Rights Act of 1964, the government sought ways to remedy past discrimination with **affirmative action**: *laws and policies designed to give preference to minority groups in employment and college enrollment.*

Affirmative Action

laws and policies designed to give preference to minority groups in employment and college enrollment

The question is: should society lower standards for minorities in order to make up for past discrimination? Put another way: is the proper remedy for treating people differently under the law in the past to treat people differently under the law today? This has been the subject of protracted debate in America. In general, Democrats support affirmative action and Republicans oppose it.

Pro Affirmative Action Position: Proponents of affirmative action argue that something more pro-active needs to be done to make up for past discrimination. In order to root out institutional racism and to break the cycle of white privilege, minorities and women must be hired in numbers that reflect their proportion in the population. They argue that it is not enough to say, "Okay, now the rules are even." The government must guarantee equal outcome with affirmative action laws. An underlying premise of affirmative

Affirmative action laws seek to create more diversity in the professions.
©iQoncept/Shutterstock.com

action is that the people in charge of selecting college and job applicants are still racists or misogynistic. The only way to counter endemic racism is to set quotas and insure equal outcome. Society will not change until minorities go to college and move into the professions.

Anti Affirmative Action Position: Critics of affirmative action say that the country is clearly not as racist as it was in the 1960s, and so these laws should be phased out. If a college or company is proven to be racist, then they should be severely punished, but the proper remedy is not to continue the unequal application of the law. As Chief Justice John Roberts said, "The way to stop discrimination on the basis of race is to stop discrimination based on race." Critics also make several other points against affirmative action: that it puts a cloud over black achievement (people might assume, for example, that a black Harvard student did not earn her acceptance), that it is actually reverse discrimination because all groups except white males get favorable treatment, and that it unfairly punishes people today for discrimination they never committed. Job placement and employment, they argue, should be based solely on merit.

University of California Regents v. Bakke **(1978):** This case dealt with affirmative action in college applications. In *UC v. Bakke*, the Supreme Court ruled that affirmative action quotas are unconstitutional. Allen Bakke, who was previously a top student at Stanford and a captain in the Marines, was rejected from the UC Davis medical school. The school admitted that of one hundred students they accepted, they set a quota of sixteen slots for minority students. But Bakke's grades and test scores were higher than those of all sixteen minorities accepted.

The Supreme Court ruled that UC Davis's affirmative action program, based on strict numerical quotas, violated the equal protection clause of the 14th Amendment. However, in a signal to future court cases, the Court ruled that the goal of achieving a diverse student body was a legitimate objective of colleges (compelling government interest): students learn important social lessons on a diverse campus, and society benefits from minorities and women going into the professions.

Richmond v. Croson **(1989):** In this case, the Court also ruled against the use of quotas in government contracts. In the 1980s, the city of Richmond passed a law requiring that 30 percent of the budget will go to minority subcontractors to make up for past discrimination. In her majority opinion, Justice Sandra Day O'Conner said such quota programs could only be used as a remedy to correct proven past discrimination. The strict scrutiny test must be applied to affirmative action programs. And remedies for past discrimination must be narrowly tailored, not with the use of indefinite quotas.

California's Proposition 209: In 1996 the voters of California overwhelmingly voted for a proposition that all state agencies—including schools and colleges—are forbidden to discriminate against or grant preferential treatment on the basis of race. Since then, six more states have abandoned affirmative action programs: Texas, Louisiana, Mississippi, Georgia, Florida, and Washington. Texas adopted the "Top 10 Percent" program, automatically accepting to college all high school students that graduated in the top 10 percent of their class. California now accepts the top 4 percent. This type of approach was designed to get more minorities into college without the use of quotas.

University of Michigan Cases (2003): In 2003, the Court heard two related cases concerning University of Michigan's affirmative action program. In *Gratz v. Bollinger*, the Court heard the case of Jennifer Gratz who earned a 3.8 GPA, but was denied admission. The university used a system which allotted 100 points to academic merit, and 20 points for race (out of 150). The Court ruled that this system was unconstitutional because it was essentially a quota system.

But in ***Grutter v. Bollinger* (2003),** *the Supreme Court upheld the law school's affirmative action program because it was not a mechanical point system, rather it made a "special effort" to diversify the campus by evaluating each applicant in a holistic manner.* In 2013, in *Fisher v. University of Texas,* the Supreme Court essentially affirmed its position on affirmative action programs as developed in *Bakke and Grutter:* colleges have a compelling interest to diversify the campus, but they cannot use strict numerical quotas.

WOMEN AND GAY RIGHTS

Besides black Americans, other groups have historically been discriminated against. This chapter will conclude by briefly delineating some of the landmark victories in women and gay rights.

Women Rights: Due in large part to progressive women leaders and groups, such as the National Woman Suffrage Associations (NWSA), women got the right to vote with the ratification of the *19th Amendment* in 1920. But even though women won the franchise, it was common for men to get higher salaries for equal work. In 1963, Congress passed the *Equal Pay Act*, which prohibits employers from discriminating by paying a higher rate to "the opposite sex for equal work on jobs requiring equal skill, effort, and responsibility." And a year later, Congress passed the Civil Rights Act of 1964, which included two sections designed to protect women's rights. **Title IX** *prohibits sex-based discrimination on college campuses that received federal funds.* And *Title VII* guarantees equal employment opportunity for women. The federal agency

Grutter v. Bollinger

the Supreme Court upheld the law school's affirmative action program because it was not a mechanical point system, rather it made a "special effort" to diversify the campus by evaluating each applicant in a holistic manner

Title IX

prohibits sex-based discrimination on college campuses that received federal funds that enforces these laws is the Equal Employment Opportunity Commission (EEOC).

Gay Rights: have been fought on two constitutional grounds, the right to privacy and equal protection. Even by the 1980s, many states had laws on the books prohibiting sodomy, types of sex acts that cannot produce offspring. Often these sex acts were banned by couples of the opposite sex, but the intent of the law also included discouraging homosexuality. In *Bower v. Hardwick* (1986), the Supreme Court upheld the anti-sodomy laws of Georgia and refused to accept that the right of privacy includes the right to engage in sodomy. They ruled that the proper way to get rid of the antiquated laws is for the state legislatures to expunge them. But less than twenty years later, the Court reversed itself. In *Lawrence v. Texas* (2003), the Supreme Court declared anti-sodomy laws unconstitutional on the grounds that they violate an individual's right of privacy.

The 1963 Equal Pay Act ensures a woman's right to equal pay for equal work.
©AVA Bitter/Shutterstock.com

In *Lawrence* the Supreme Court concluded that the only purpose of the anti-sodomy laws was for the majority to impose its morality on a minority group through the penal code, which was wrong. This reasoning would soon be applied to other laws against homosexuals. In 1992, the people of Colorado approved a constitutional amendment to their state constitution that prohibited laws that protected homosexuals. In *Romer v. Evans* (1996), the Supreme Court, in a 6-3 ruling, overturned this amendment on the grounds it violated the equal protection clause. Justice Kennedy, who wrote the majority opinion, said that the only motive for the Colorado amendment was that the majority of the population desired "to harm a politically unpopular group." And using the *rational basis test*, the normal test used when judging equal protection clause cases, Kennedy concluded that there was "no legitimate state interest" in a law that designated a group based on their sexual preference.

Romer v. Evans brings up a complex issue at the heart of a constitutional democracy. In a democracy, the majority have the right to support laws that it believes promotes the common good. On the other hand, under a constitutional system, minority and individual rights are protected. Often, the Supreme Court must decide when the rights of the majority interfere with the rights of the minority.

This is well illustrated with gay marriage. In 2008, the people of California approved *Proposition 8*, a referendum that defined marriage as between one woman and one man. Twenty-three other states passed similar measures. Supporters of Proposition 8 argued that it is in the interest of the community to protect the traditional definition of marriage; and, moreover, states have always had the power to set marriage laws. But the Ninth Circuit Court ruled that Proposition 8 was unconstitutional because it violated the right to privacy and the equal protection rights of gays. In 2015, the Supreme Court agreed with this ruling. In *Obergefell v. Hodges*, the Court ruled that it is unconstitutional for states to ban gay marriage.

FINAL THOUGHTS

In Martin Luther King's famous "I have a Dream" speech, he said that the Constitution and the Declaration of Independence were "promissory notes." "This note" King explained, "was a promise that all men, yes, black men as well as white men, would be guaranteed the 'unalienable rights' of 'Life, Liberty and the pursuit of Happiness.'" As this chapter has demonstrated, America has not always lived up to the promise of equality. But one way to look at the history of the United States is as a struggle to expand equal rights to a growing circle of people. With such landmark achievements as the 15th Amendment, which gave blacks the right to vote, and the 19th Amendment, which expanded the franchise to women, and with the adoption of the many other civil rights laws, the US has worked toward the fulfillment of the promises contained in our founding documents.

NOTES

Erwin Chemerinsky. *The Case against the Supreme Court*. New York: Penguin Books, 2014.

Adam Freedman. *The Naked Constitution*: *What the Founders Said and Why it Still Matters*. New York: Broadside Books, 2012.

Alexander Hamilton, John Jay, and James Madison. *The Federalists*. Indianapolis: Liberty Fund, 2001.

The Heritage Guide to the Constitution: Washington, DC: The Heritage Foundation, 2005.

Alfred H. Kelly et al. *The American Constitution: Its Origins and Developments*. Vol I & II. New York: Norton & Co., 1991.

Michael Les Benedict. The *Blessings of Liberty: A Concise History of the Supreme Court*. Boston: Wadsworth, 2006.

ESSAY QUESTIONS

1. Discuss the significance of the equal protection clause of the 14th Amendment.
2. What were the black codes and Jim Crow laws?
3. Cite the three Civil War/Reconstruction amendments and discuss their significance.
4. Describe the significance of *Brown v. the Board of Education* (1954).
5. How does affirmative action contradict the equal protection clause?
6. Discuss the four major laws protecting women's rights.

TERMS

Affirmative Action: _____

Brown v. the Board of Education (1954): _____

Civil Rights: _____

Civil Rights Act of 1964: _____

Equal Protection Clause: _____

15th Amendment: _____

Grutter v. Bollinger (2003): _____

Jim CrowLaws: _____

Separate but Equal Doctrine: _____

13th Amendment: _____

Title IX: _____

Voting Rights Act of 1965: _____

UNIT THREE

The Three Branches of Government

CHAPTER 11

What Are the President's Constitutional Powers?

TOPICS

► Creating the Presidency
► Three Major Powers of the President
► Other Presidential Powers
► Impeachment and Succession
► Presidential Issues and Controversies

LEARNING OBJECTIVES

When you finish reading this chapter, you will be able to:

1. Describe the significance of "energy in the executive."
2. Outline the three major constitutional powers of the Presidency.
3. Explain how Congress has some ability to check those three powers.
4. Delineate the impeachment process.
5. Compare executive privilege with executive orders.

WHAT ARE THE PRESIDENT'S CONSTITUTIONAL POWERS?

The Framers were afraid of strong centralized leadership, but they knew it was necessary to good government. Americans had long suffered under abusive royal governors, and during the Revolution they had fought against a tyrannical British monarch. So it is understandable that America's first constitution, The Articles of Confederation, had no executive branch at all. But the

Confederation proved to be an ineffectual form of government and it failed. In 1787, the members of the Constitutional Convention faced a great challenge: how do they create a powerful executive with enough power to effectively lead the nation, but without too much power that it might turn into a dictatorship? To accomplish this objective, the Framers invented a new type of executive: the American Presidency.

CREATING THE PRESIDENCY

The Framers of the Constitution created an energetic, independent executive with enough power to protect the nation, but not unlimited power. In some areas these powers are described in vague terms, reflecting the belief of many Framers that it might be dangerous to narrowly proscribe the powers of the presidency, especially in times of crisis. On the other hand, the Framers limited the powers of the Presidency within the context of the three branches of government with checks and balances. So, the Constitution indicates that there are times when the president will lead, as in foreign affairs, and there are times when the president will follow, as in implementing congressional law.

Article II: It is significant that the *second* section of the Constitution describes the presidency. This reflects the Framer's view that Congress—the branch that makes law, controls the budget, and declares war—is the center of government. The Framers envisioned that for the most part, especially in peace time, the president will take a secondary role in government. Article II, Section 3, states that the president "shall take Care that the laws are faithfully executed." The Take Care Clause assigns the creative power to the legislative branch: Congress will make a law, and then the president will execute that law. In other words, the executive branch will implement, enforce, and administer the laws that Congress passed.

Inherent Powers

powers not expressed or implied in the text of the Constitution, but inherent in the function and responsibility of the office

The Executive Vesting Clause: The first sentence of Article II reads: "The executive power shall be vested in the President of the United States of America." What exactly does this mean? It is interesting to note that when comparing this clause to the clauses describing legislative and judicial power, it is not restrictive. Article I says the legislative powers "herein granted," and Article III says "judicial power shall extend to." But the Executive Power Clause is non-restrictive, suggesting that there are **inherent powers** of the presidency: *powers not expressed or implied in the text of the Constitution, but inherent in the function and responsibility of the office*. This remains an area of debate. But several presidents, including Abraham Lincoln, have claimed that the *executive vesting clause* grants broad executive powers, especially to defend and protect the nation.

Single Executive: At the Constitutional Convention, the Framers had conflicting views of the executive branch. Benjamin Franklin, fearful of giving one person too much power, proposed an executive committee consisting of several co-presidents. Alexander Hamilton couldn't imagine anything more ludicrous. In a speech to the Convention lasting several hours, Hamilton argued passionately for a single executive. An executive committee, he asserted, would be crippled by dissention as they blamed each other for failure or tried to take credit for success.

Hamilton convinced the majority of the delegates of the need for "energy in the executive," meaning a single leader that takes full responsibility for the executive branch and that acts quickly in the face of a crisis. Later, in *Federalist #70*, Hamilton wrote, "Energy in the executive is a leading character in the definition of good government," and unity will lead to other executive traits such as "decision, activity, secrecy and dispatch."

Knowing that George Washington would be the first president, the Framers created a stronger Presidency than they otherwise would have.
©Everett Historical/Shutterstock.com

Length of Term: Besides the number of executives, the delegates argued about the length of a presidential term. Many state constitutions limited the governor to a single, one-year term. Hamilton, however, argued that it is essential to achieve more stability in the executive branch, especially to achieve a consistent foreign policy, and this could only be achieved with longer terms. Eventually, the delegates decided to give the president unlimited, four-year terms. Why four years? Well, if we elect a bad president, it is not enough time to do permanent damage to the country. And if we elect a good president, it is enough time to initiate beneficial reforms. But in order to fully implement these reforms, he or she would need popular approval to win a second term.

Term-limits: At the Constitutional Convention, Hamilton argued vigorously for a president elected for life. Most delegates recoiled at this notion, thinking it was too much like selecting a king. But to a large extent, Hamilton got what he wanted. Originally, the Constitution allowed that a president could serve for life, as long as he was reelected every four years. This is essentially what happened with Franklin Roosevelt. FDR was elected four times, serving through the Great Depression and World War II, and died in office in 1945.

Two years after FDR's death, Congress passed the **22nd Amendment**, *limiting the president to two elected terms*. But was this simply a political reaction to the dominance of FDR? Some argue it is better not to have term limits. Term

22nd Amendment

limits the president to two elected terms

limits destine a president to a "lame duck" second term, when his power is so diminished that it is nearly impossible to accomplish anything. Further, if we have a great president, still young and energetic, why can't the majority of the people reelect him or her? This is especially true if we are in the middle of a crisis, such as a world war. On the other hand, few people could handle the stress of the modern presidency for more than eight years. Compare photos of modern presidents at the time they first took office to when they left office eight years later—the increased wrinkles and grey hair reveal how stressful the job is!

Qualifications for President: The Constitution cites three qualifications for the executive office: the president must be at least thirty-five years of age, a natural born citizen, and a resident of the US for fourteen years. In the modern world, where most job postings contain a long list of qualifications, such as years of experience, education, and training, it might strike the reader that these qualifications are rather unusual. But upon further reflection, most people would agree that we would want a president with a certain amount of life experiences and the maturity and wisdom that come with that. By thirty-five, a person's personality and worldview have been developed.

Some students question the idea that the president should be born in America. Indeed, many of the Framers, like Hamilton, were born overseas. The rationale was that the Framers wanted a person who grew up in America and fully internalized American political values. Also, this provision eliminates the possibility that a president may harbor emotional ties to a foreign country, something that would pose grave difficulties if the United States went to war with a president's homeland. So, maturity, patriotism, and undivided loyalty were the key features the Framers were seeking in a president.

Selecting the President: Initially, most of the delegates wanted the president to be selected by Congress. This alarmed James Madison; he wanted a president independent from Congress. At the Convention Madison said, "The executive cannot be independent of the legislature, if dependent on the pleasure of that branch for a re-appointment." This would have made a parliamentary system of government, in which the president and the Parliament are controlled by the same party. The decision by the delegates to create three separate branches, with an independent executive, was a real innovation.

So, even though the delegates came to realize that they did not want the president selected by Congress, they struggled to figure out exactly how the president will be chosen. Gouverneur Morris of Pennsylvania urged for election by popular vote. A direct vote by the people, however, made many delegates nervous, not trusting the knowledge and virtue of the common man. Others wanted the states legislatures to have a role. Eventually they created an election body, the **Electoral College**, *the body that selects the president*, containing elements that gave some power to all three: the people, the states, and Congress.

The Electoral College consists of "electors" from each state, the number of which equals the number of representatives plus the two Senators of each state. Virginia, for example, has nine representative and two senators; therefore, it has eleven electors. This number roughly reflects the population of each state because the census taken every ten years apportions representation in the House based on population. So, the presidential election is actually a state-by-state vote with the winner taking all the elector votes (except in Maine and Nebraska that uses the congressional district method). If no candidate wins a majority of the electoral votes, then the top three candidates have a run-off election in the House of Representatives, each state getting one vote. Surprisingly, this has only happened two times.

John Adams, the first vice president, was bored with the office.
©Everett Historical/Shutterstock.com

The Vice President: Although there was little debate about it, the delegates also created a vice president. The Constitution gives the vice president only two functions: Article II states that if the president is removed from office, dies, resigns, or is unable to carry out his duties, the powers of the office "devolve on the Vice President." And Article I states that the vice president "shall be the President of the Senate, but shall have no vote, unless they be equally divided." These are two rather limited functions: to remain alive and to break a tie in the Senate (which rarely happens). Realizing these limits, John Adams, the nation's first vice president, remarked that it is "the most insignificant office that ever the invention of man contrived or his imagination conceived." Eventually, the office would expand as presidents gave vice presidents more duties and responsibilities.

Oath of Office: Lastly, the delegates decided to have the president make a pledge of allegiance and commitment to the Constitution. Article II states that before taking office, the president must take this oath: "I do solemnly swear (or affirm) that I will faithfully execute the Office of President of the United States, and will to the best of my ability, protect and defend the Constitution of the United States." In one sense the oath has a limiting objective. The president must "faithfully execute" his office and "preserve" or adhere to the Constitution, not going beyond his constitutional limits. On the other hand, the oath seems to once again imply the inherent powers of the office—to "protect and defend" the country.

Electoral College

the body, consisting of 538 electors, that selects the president in state-by-state elections

THREE MAJOR POWERS OF THE PRESIDENCY

The Constitution grants the president three core areas of authority and responsibility: leading the military, conducting foreign affairs, and administrating the law. Yet, the Framers carefully balanced all three areas of executive power with congressional checks, which in essence forced the two branches to share each power. This section will describe the president's major powers and how each is checked by Congress.

Commander in Chief: Article II, Section 2 says the "President shall be the Commander in Chief of the army and navy of the United States, and of the militia of the several States." During war, the president, as Commander in Chief is the functioning head of the military, approving the strategy and picking the generals. Today the US military consists of five branches: Army, Marines, Navy, Air Force, and Coast Guard. And the president is the head of all the US intelligence agencies, including the Central Intelligence Agency (CIA), the Office of Homeland Security, the National Security Council (NSC), and the Federal Bureau of Investigation (FBI). The president, however, would never wear a military uniform. It is a core doctrine of the Constitution that the military is under civilian control.

Congressional Check on the Commander in Chief: Traditionally, it has been understood that the executive's primary responsibility is to protect the

Commander in Chief

the role of the president as the functioning head of the military, approving the strategy and picking the generals

Nixon resumed relations with China in 1973.
©Brendan Howard/Shutterstock.com

nation. But the Constitution gives Congress enormous military responsibility and oversight. This reflects the Framer's fear of executive abuse of the military. As Lincoln once said, the power to declare war could be the most "oppressive of all kingly oppressions." This is why Article I, Section 2 gives Congress several checks on the president's military powers. Not only does Congress have the power to "declare war," but also to raise and maintain the army and navy and to appropriate money to the military budget every two year. So, Congress must take the initiative and declare war, and the president will direct the war once it has begun, but an energetic executive also has the power to defend the country against an attack.

Chief Diplomat: The second major power granted to the executive under the Constitution is that the president will take the lead in foreign policy. Article II, Section 2, gives the president the power to "make treatise" with foreign countries, "appoint Ambassadors," and select ministers in charge of executive departments that deal primarily with foreign affairs. And Article II, Section 3 states that the president will "receive Ambassadors." These three clauses acknowledge the president as head of state and the prime mover in foreign affairs.

Congressional Check on the Chief Diplomat: Although the president is expected to have more leeway in foreign affairs, the Constitution once again grants Congress many powerful checks. The Senate must approve all treatise with a two-thirds vote. This requirement of a supermajority indicates the Framer's deep concern that the president not be allowed to make any agreement with foreign powers that might be contrary to the interests of a major geographic or economic segment of the population. The Senate must also confirm the president's choice of ambassadors and other ministers with foreign policy responsibilities.

Chief Administrator: And the last major power assigned to the president is that of chief administrator. Article II contains three clauses that place the president in charge of executing federal law and administering the executive departments. The Opinion Clause states that the president "may require the Opinion, in writing, of the principle Officer in each of the executive Departments, upon any Subject relating to the Duties of their respected offices." The Appointment Clause states that the president shall appoint ambassadors, public ministers, consuls, and judges. And the Take Care Clause states that the president "shall take Care that the laws are faithfully executed."

These clauses go to the core definition of the president, that he will execute the laws. Moreover, they place the president as head of the personnel of all the executive departments: cabinet members and top federal officials serve at the president's pleasure, meaning he has the sole power to dismiss them.

Congressional Check on Chief Administrator: And, once again, the Constitution gives Congress significant checks on the president as head of the executive department. Technically, the staffing of federal offices is actually a five-step process, and Congress has a significant role: (1) Congress creates all federal departments and offices, (2) the president nominates officers, (3) the Senate confirms or denies nominees, (4) the president appoints officers to their positions, and (5) Congress continues to have the authority to fund and oversee the offices they created. And Congress's oversight powers allow it to order any executive department officer to testify to a Senate or a House committee, under threat of perjury. So, in a conflict between the executive branch and the legislative branch over an administrative issue, Congress has significant leverage.

OTHER PRESIDENTIAL POWERS

Beyond the three core areas of presidential power (military, diplomatic, and administrative), the Constitution also lists several other lesser powers designated to the president. The primary "lesser power" is the president's veto, which gives him substantial legislative responsibility. And the Constitution also grants the president other powers, including the pardon power, the power to convene Congress, and the power to address Congress.

Veto Power: The veto actually allows the president to share in the legislative process, which is a significant presidential power. Hamilton wanted a strong executive with an absolute veto. But the delegates settled on a **qualified veto**: *The president can veto any bill, but a veto can be overridden by two-thirds vote of both chambers of Congress.* Often, a president may threaten to veto a bill if certain changes are not made. Because it is so difficult to override, the mere threat of a veto may cause Congress to change the language of a bill or discard it all together. Technically, the president does not always have to officially veto a bill for it to be considered vetoed. For example, *when Congress is adjourned the president need not sign a veto for it to die within ten days. This is called the* **pocket veto**. But if Congress is in session, the bill will become law if the president signs it or not.

Throughout history, Congress has overridden fewer than 10 percent of vetoes. If Congress is controlled by the opposition party or a coalition of opposition groups, then vetoes are more likely. Franklin Roosevelt made 635 vetoes because a coalition of Republicans and conservative Democrats had a majority in Congress. Reagan made

Qualified Veto

The president can veto any bill, but a veto can be overridden by two-thirds vote of both chambers of Congress.

Pocket Veto

when Congress is adjourned the president need not sign a veto for it to die within ten days

FDR signed a record 635 vetoes.
©catwalker/Shutterstock.com

78 and Clinton 37 vetoes because during their presidencies at least one chamber was controlled by the opposition party.

The Pardon Power: Article II, Section 2, Clause 1 gives the president the "power to grant Reprieves and Pardons . . . except in Cases of Impeachment." This power originates from the traditional authority of kings. The pardon power can be used to lessen sentences or exonerate past convictions. There is no constitutional limit or check on this power, except that it cannot be used to circumvent impeachment proceedings.

Why should a president annul somebody's conviction by a lawful court? Presidential pardons can soften an overly harsh punishment, correct a judicial or jury error, or recognize that an individual has since made positive contributions to society. The vagueness and arbitrariness of this clause, however, has led to some political controversies. On Bill Clinton's last day in office, he pardoned 140 individuals, including March Rich for evading over $48 million in taxes. Later it was learned that Rich's ex-wife contributed $450,000 to the Clinton Library.

Convene Congress: Article II, Section 3, states that the president "may, on extraordinary Occasions, convene both Houses." The British king had the power to both convene and *dissolve* Parliament. On many occasions the king, and royal governors in the colonies, abused this power by dissolving the legislative branch when the executive disagreed with a bill they were deliberating on. Therefore, the Constitution only gives the president the power to convene Congress, which might be necessary in the face of a military or economic crisis, or to complete unfinished business. This power was used to great effect when Lyndon Johnson convened Congress after his 1964 election and ordered it to remain in session until they passed his poverty legislation. More famously, FDR convened Congress the day after the attack on Pearl Harbor, declaring it a "day that will live in infamy."

Power to Address Congress: Lastly, Article II, Section 2 states that the president "shall from time to time give to the Congress Information of the State of the Union." This clause, especially in conjunction with the Recommendation Clause (the president "shall from time to time . . . Recommend to their consideration such measures as he shall judge necessary and expedient") indicates that the Framers wanted to give the president the power to initiative and propose measures, not merely wait for Congress to pass a law so that he can execute it. The State of the Union Address also gives a verbally skilled president the chance to assert political power, the topic of the next chapter.

In modern times, especially since the advent of television, the State of the Union Address has become a major opportunity for the president to address the whole nation. He usually uses this opportunity to list his accomplishments and to make proposals for the future. In the 1980s, Ronald Reagan effectively used the State of the Union Address to rally the nation around his domestic and foreign policy agenda. Reagan also started the practice of inviting an American hero to the address, who sits with the First Lady in the balcony and is introduced to a standing ovation during the speech. This has made the event a more patriotic ceremony.

IMPEACHMENT AND SUCCESSION

The greatest congressional check the Constitution places on the president is impeachment. Congress literally has the power to remove the president from office. The steps of the impeachment process are explained clearly in the original Constitution, but other aspects of the succession process were less clearly defined, necessitating the 25th Amendment to the Constitution.

Bill Clinton was impeached, but not removed from office.
©Everett Collection/Shutterstock.com

Impeachment: The Constitution outlines two steps for the **impeachment process**: *The House must approve the articles of impeachment with a majority vote. And the Senate, with the Chief Justice presiding, must conduct a trial based on those articles, with the president being removed from office with a two-thirds vote.* Article II, Section 4, states that "the President and Vice President . . . shall be removed from Office on Impeachment for, and conviction of, Treason, Bribery, or other High Crimes and Misdemeanors." So, on what grounds can a president be impeached? Treason, Bribery, and even "high Crimes," seemed clear enough. The meaning of "Misdemeanor," however, is more ambiguous. Most constitutional scholars agree that in the eighteenth century misdemeanor meant "misdeed," so this would include any major misconduct or negligence of the president.

Because only a simple majority of the House is needed to impeach the president, it opens up the possibility that the House might be animated by purely political motives. The Senate requirement of a supermajority of two-thirds, however, makes it unlikely that a president will be removed unless he commits obvious and serious wrongdoing. Only two presidents have been impeached: Andrew Johnson in 1867 and Bill Clinton in 1999. Neither was removed from office by the Senate. The Framers understood that the mere threat of impeachment would be a strong deterrent to presidential wrongdoing.

Succession: The Constitution states that if the president is removed from office, can no longer carry out his duties, or dies, the vice president will assume the office. But the brevity of the clause on succession left many unanswered

Impeachment Process

the House must approve the articles of impeachment with a majority vote. And the Senate, with the Chief Justice presiding, must conduct a trial based on those articles, with the president being removed from office with a two-thirds vote questions. The *25th Amendment* (1967) and the Presidential Succession Law (1947) has since clarified these questions:

Questions concerning the consequences of a presidential or vice presidential death are clearly stated now. If the president dies, and the vice president assumes office, is he merely functioning as president until the next election, or is he fully the president? Answer: he is the president. What if the vice president dies or is removed from office? Answer: the president will select a new vice president with confirmation by both houses of Congress. What if both the president and vice president die? Answer: The line of succession is as follows: Speaker of the House, President Pro Tempore of the Senate, Secretary of State, Secretary of Treasure, Secretary of Defense, and down the line through the rest of the cabinet.

And questions concerning a temporary presidential illness are also clear. How is it determined that a president can no longer perform his duties? Answer: If the vice president and a majority of the cabinet or a majority of Congress declares that the president can no longer perform his duties, he can be either temporarily or permanently removed from office. What if the president is going to undergo surgery, for example, and will temporality be unable to serve? He must notify Congress and the vice president will function as president until the president returns.

PRESIDENTIAL ISSUES AND CONTROVERSIES

There are several other issues and controversies related to the president's constitutional powers. Many of these deal with interpreting certain vague clauses or working out complex areas where Congress and the president share power.

War Power: The Constitution divides the war powers between the president and Congress: Article I says Congress has the power to "declare war," and Article II says the president is the "commander in chief." Does this mean that the president needs congressional permission before launching every military action? Thomas Jefferson, a strict constructionist, did not seek permission from Congress when he sent the US Navy to attack the Barbary Pirates. Presidents have since argued that in cases of sudden invasion, or for small military operations, especially when Congress is out of session, the president can, or must, act alone. For major wars, however, a congressional war declaration is necessary. The problem is that in recent decades, Congress has stopped declaring war even for major wars. Of the twenty major wars, and hundreds of smaller military operations, Congress has only officially declared war five times.

The turning point was when Truman did not seek a declaration of war before the invasion of Korea. After Pearl Harbor, Congress dramatically declared war before World War II. But before the Korean War, Congress simply issued a resolution supporting America's joining the United Nations in protecting South Korea. From that point on Congress has not officially declared war, even for major operations such as Vietnam, the first and second war against Iraq, and the invasion of Afghanistan. Why not? It seems that the main reason that Congress has abdicated its constitutional duty to declare war is that members of Congress are afraid of the political consequences of voting for a war that may become unpopular. They seem to simply want to place all the political consequences on the shoulders of the president.

The War Power Resolution: In the last years of the Vietnam War, however, Congress attempted to reassert its war powers by passing the War Powers Resolution. Although Nixon vetoed it, the measure received a two-thirds vote in both chambers of Congress in 1973. The law requires the president to notify Congress within forty-eight hours of committing troops, and forbids those troops from remaining for more than sixty days without a congressional war declaration or authorization. All pres-

The Supreme Court ordered Richard Nixon to release his private tapes, leading to his resignation.
©JStone/Shutterstock.com

idents since 1973, however, have considered this law unconstitutional. Just to name three examples, President Reagan sent troops to Grenada, President Clinton sent troops to Kosovo, and President Obama sent troops to Libya, all without complying with the War Power Resolution.

Executive Privilege: The Supreme Court has recognized the necessity of the president to be able to keep private council and to hold secrets. This is known as **executive privilege**: *the right of the executive to keep communications confidential.* The actual term was first used in the Eisenhower administration, but presidents since Washington have asserted it. Presidents must be able to keep sensitive secrets, especially dealing with international affairs.

But if there is some sort of criminal investigation, or an inquiry of a scandal, presidents cannot claim that they are above the law. Richard Nixon tried to keep his tapes secret, but the Supreme Court, while stating that executive power does indeed exist, ruled that Nixon must comply with the Watergate investigation and release the tapes. Likewise, the Supreme Court denied Bill Clinton's claim of executive privilege and ruled that he had to testify at a sexual harassment lawsuit brought by Paula Jones.

Executive Orders: *Executive branch directives that have the force of law are called* **executive orders.** There is no specific provision in the Constitution

Executive Privilege

the right of the executive to keep communications confidential

Executive Orders

executive branch directives that have the force of law

authorizing the president to make executive orders, but the power is assumed under the authority of the president as head of the executive departments and under the Take Care Clause. Every president since Washington has used executive directives to establish policies for executive departments and agencies, and they have the force of law. But under the Constitution, Congress is supposed to make law, and the president is supposed to execute or carry out the law. So, when does an executive order usurp Congress's constitutional prerogative?

The Supreme Court addressed this question in *Youngstown Sheet & Tube v. Sawyer* (1952) when it struck down President Truman's executive order for the government to seize steel mills during the Koran War. In a concurring opinion, Justice Robert Jackson divided the presidential authority to make executive order in relation to Congress's law-making authority into three categories of descending legitimacy. The president is in a strong position of authority when he acts within the expressed or implied authority of congressional law. The president is in a weaker, but permissible, realm of authority when he acts in an area in which Congress has been silent. And the president acts with little or no authority when defying congressional orders.

This ruling did little to end debate on the topic, and nearly every president has had to deal with controversies related to their executive decisions. This can be illustrated by two famous executive orders, one universally considered good, and the other bad. In 1948, Harry Truman issued an executive order abolishing segregation in the armed services. This order has been praised by historians because it fell squarely under Truman's authority to set policies for the military as commander in chief and it corrected an injustice. On the other hand, President Roosevelt's executive order to deport Japanese Americans to internment camps during World War II has been condemned by historians. This order was bad because it was not related to an internal executive department policy, and any policy that affects hundreds of thousands of citizens should be debated and approved by Congress. Moreover, it patently violated the civil rights and civil liberties of American citizens.

Imperial Presidency

a presidency that is characterized by greater power than the Constitution allows

FINAL THOUGHTS

This discussion of when a president abuses his authority to make executive orders leads us to another concept sometimes used by political scientists and presidential historians, the **imperial presidency**: *A presidency that is characterized by greater power than the Constitution allows, especially by using foreign and domestic administration agencies to carry out actions without congressional approval.* This term was the title to an influential 1973 book by historian Arthur M. Schlesinger, Jr., who was particularly concerned about the abuse of power of Richard Nixon. Schlesinger outlined Nixon's use of government agencies, such as the FBI, CIA, and NSC, to conduct secret military operations and surveillance of Americans citizens without congressional approval. The modern president's ability to use vast executive branch power outside the scope of the Constitution's system of checks and balances, warned Schlesinger, is a troubling problem that seems to grow with each new administration.

Recently, the term imperial presidency has been in the news again. Prominent law professor Jonathan Turley has testified to Congress and written articles describing Barack Obama as an imperial president. Turley has cited several examples of Obama abusing his power, often with the support of his attorney general. These include using the NSA to conduct warrantless surveillance; authorizing drones to assassinate two US citizens without a trial; significantly changing provisions of Obamacare without congressional approval; announcing that the justice department would not enforce certain laws, including the Defense of Marriage Act; and using executive orders to give amnesty to over 5 million illegal aliens. Moreover, it has recently come to light that the Obama administration was conducting surveillance on members of the Trump campaign team before the presidential election, including his campaign chairman and top foreign affairs advisor.

"The danger is quite severe," explains Turley. "The problem with what the president is doing is that he's not simply posing a danger to the constitutional system. He's becoming the very danger the Constitution was designed to avoid. That is the concentration of power in a single branch." This new danger to our constitutional system of checks and balances has come about with the rise of the vast and powerful network of intelligence agencies, which are mostly under the control of the executive branch. Congress needs to come up with a system of checks and balances that does not politicize our national security nor undermine the nation's ability to keep secrets.

NOTES

Alexander Hamilton, John Jay, and James Madison. *The Federalists.* Indianapolis: Liberty Fund, 2001.

Charles O. Jones. *The American Presidency.* Oxford: Oxford University Press, 2007.

James Madison. *Notes of Debates in the Federal Convention of 1787.* New York: Norton & Company, 1966.

Joseph A. Pika et al. *The Politics of the Presidency.* Washington: Congressional Quarterly Press, 2002.

Arthur M. Schlesinger Jr. *The Imperial Presidency.* New York: Mariner Books, Reprint Edition, 2004.

The Heritage Guide to the Constitution: Washington, DC: The Heritage Foundation, 2005.

The Presidency and the Political System. Edited by Michael Nelson. Washington: Congressional Quarterly Press, 2003.

Jonathan Turley. "A Question of Power: The Imperial Presidency." *American Legion Magazine,* June 1, 2014.

ESSAY QUESTIONS

1. What are the qualifications to be president?
2. Describe the president's powers as commander in chief.
3. In what ways can Congress check the president's foreign affairs powers?
4. How does the president share in the legislative process with Congress?
5. How must a president be impeached and forced to leave office?
6. Describe limits the Supreme Court has placed on executive privilege and executive orders.

TERMS

Commander in Chief: _____

Electoral College: _____

Executive Orders: _____

Executive Privilege: _____

Impeachment Process: _____

Imperial Presidency: _____

Inherent Powers: _____

Pocket Veto: _____

Qualified Veto: _____

22nd Amendment: _____

CHAPTER 12

What Are the Keys to a Successful Presidency?

TOPICS
- ► Presidential Leadership
- ► Presidents and the Media
- ► Presidential Party Politics

LEARNING OBJECTIVES

When you finish reading this chapter, you will be able to:

1. Delineate the important leadership traits of successful presidents.
2. Describe the key members of the president's communications team.
3. Explain some of the tactics presidents use to influence the media.
4. Discuss how the structure of Congress, and party politics, make it difficult for a president to pass his agenda.

WHAT ARE THE KEYS TO A SUCCESSFUL PRESIDENCY?

It is hard to imagine a job more difficult than that of president of the United States. Certainly, some presidents handle the challenge better than others: some presidents are defeated by the office, and others transform the office. One mark of a successful president is whether he gets reelected. Surprisingly, since Franklin D. Roosevelt, only two presidents lost their bid for a second term: Jimmy Carter and George H. W. Bush. But even if a president wins reelection, his Presidency can still be deemed a failure. So, what are the keys to a successful presidency? The previous chapter outlined the president's constitutional powers, and this one will focus on the president's political powers, more particularly, the political tools a president needs to be successful.

PRESIDENTIAL LEADERSHIP

In 2005, *The Wall Street Journal* surveyed the top political scientists and historians in the nation, equally balancing liberal and conservative scholars, and asked them to rank the presidents on leadership ability. The top three "Great" presidents, in order, were Washington, Lincoln, and FDR. And the "Near Greats" were Jefferson, Theodore Roosevelt, Reagan, Truman, Eisenhower, Polk, and Jackson.

We may ask, what skills did these men possess that made them successful presidents? Presidential scholars may emphasize different talents and abilities, but certainly a successful president must be able to: (1) manage a crisis, (2) communicate persuasively, (3) possess acute political intelligence, (4) exercise sound management style, (5) provide a moral vision, and (6) demonstrate healthy interpersonal skills.

President as Crisis Managers: The Framers wanted an energetic president who could act with "dispatch" in an emergency. People instinctively turn to the president when faced with a crisis, rallying behind the president regardless of whether they voted for him. In 1991, over 90 percent of Americans approved of George H. W. Bush at the beginning of the first war with Iraq, even though in 1988 only 53 percent of the public voted for him. In a crisis, the president must demonstrate poise and confidence to set the people at ease. If he acts weak or falters, the president may permanently lose the confidence of the public. At the beginning of the Great Depression in 1928, Herbert Hoover looked weak, overwhelmed, and even scared. No matter what actions Hoover took for the rest of his Presidency, he was never able to regain the confidence of the American people.

Persuasive Communication: Richard Neustadt, in his very influential book, *Presidential Power*, concluded that "presidential power is the power to persuade." In other words, the president's real power is political, not constitutional. To get anything done, presidents must be able to persuade groups and individuals. First, to become president you must possess the communications skills needed to persuade people to vote for you. Then once you are president, you will spend most of your time trying to effectively communicate with all sorts of people, including congressmen, reporters, foreign leaders, staffers, interests groups, and the nation. Some presidents are good at persuading individuals and small groups of people, and others excel at mass communication, but the best president have the ability to do both. Lyndon Johnson, for example, possessed legendary persuasive powers when talking one-on-one,

What makes a great president?
©spacaj/Shutterstock.com

but when addressing the nation on television he often looked awkward and hesitant.

In the modern era, two presidents stand out when it comes to effective communication skills: Franklin Roosevelt and Ronald Reagan. Twice a week, FDR brought in group of reporters into the Oval Office and chatted with them about current affairs. His ability to win over the press resulted in better newspaper coverage. At the same time, he used the new medium of radio to his great advantage in his "fireside chats," gaining the personal confidence of people across the nation. Reagan was also very persuasive in small groups and on television. To get his tax bills through Congress, Reagan spent many hours talking with individual congressmen, Republicans and Democrats. And so even though the House was controlled by Democrats, he was able to win bi-partisan support for his reforms. And through his long career on radio, film, and television, Reagan developed excellent mass media communications skills.

Political Intelligence: A successful president will also need to possess a wide range of political skills. Some presidents possess the political intelligence to grasp the details of a particular policy, but they do not possess the political intelligence to understand how Washington, DC, operates and gets their agenda implemented. Bill Clinton understood every detail of his health care bill, but he was not able to get it passed through Congress. On the other hand, FDR was able to get Congress to approve fifteen major bills in his first hundred days in office, but he did not understand the details of each plan, nor did he comprehend that many of his bills were contradictory and actually made the Great Depression worse. The best presidents understand the complexities of policy AND know how to turn a proposed bill into a law.

Likewise, some presidents were lesser skilled politicians, such as senator or governor, and some presidents were great campaigners, but these skills were not enough to make a successful Presidency. Jimmy Carter's 1976 populist campaign was brilliant, but he was less sure-footed as president. And Lyndon Johnson was one of the greatest Senate Majority Leaders of all time, but these skills didn't transfer over to the Presidency.

Great political intelligence seems to be more a talent than a learned skill. Inspiring the nation, skillfully making arguments, dividing the oppositions, building new coalitions, knowing when to compromise, and taking advantage of opportunities, are all skills that are difficult even for life-long politicians to learn. In his book *The Presidential Difference*, Fred I. Greenstein states that Eisenhower was one of the few presidents that possessed all the skills along the political spectrum: from understanding the details of each policy, to successfully working with the powerbrokers of Washington to get his agenda implemented.

Hierarchical Management System

assigns a clear chain of command up the organizational chart, giving each staff member a decision role according to their area of expertise

Organizational Manager: Managing the White House is the least enjoyable aspect of the office for many presidents. Most likely, they got involved with politics because they loved working a crowd or giving an inspirational speech. Few ran for high office because they took pleasure in managing complex organizations. But historians have noted that it is a very important aspect of the job, one that can significantly impact the success of an administration. Jimmy Carter's management style has often been criticized for his micro-management. At first, Carter refused to have a Chief of Staff and managed all aspects of the White House staff himself, even taking it upon himself to write the White House tennis court schedule. This was a waste of his time and energy. And Reagan has been blamed for avoiding face-to-face conflicts with his staff and delegating too much authority to his aides, which helped lead to the Iran-Contra Scandal.

In recent decades, most presidents follow the formalistic or hierarchical style of management first implemented by Dwight Eisenhower, the organizer of D-Day during World War II. Eisenhower's **hierarchical management system** *assigns a clear chain of command up the organizational chart, giving each staff member a decision role according to their area of expertise.* The danger of an overly structured system is that the president will become isolated and not hear a wide range of opinion. Knowing this, Eisenhower deliberately set up a system in which aids would be assigned to present different policy options and Eisenhower would watch as his aids debated. In this way, Eisenhower received a wide range of views on a topic and could choose the best one.

Some presidents have tried a more **collegial style:** *a loose management method that does not follow a strict organizational chart but provides the president with advice from a wider circle of people.* John Kennedy used a collegial style: he relied on a few close aides to help him in a variety of areas, such as Robert Kennedy and Ted Sorenson, but JFK also sought advice outside of his cabinet, conferring with academics, writers, and past presidents. The danger of the collegial style is that it can bog down the decision-making process with too much input. Although different styles may be successful, the best presidential managers achieve the same thing: they get the best people in the right positions, they create a system that allows them to hear a variety of opinions, they encourage subordinates to tell the hard truth, and they inspire deep devotion and loyalty.

Collegial Style

a loose management method that does not follow a strict organizational chart but provides the president with advice from a wider circle of people

Moral Vision: As Chief of State, the president plays a major ceremonial role. Like the British monarch, the president is a symbol of America. The office is capable of provoking deep emotions of patriotism and loyalty. During ceremonies, such as at a State of the Union Message, the president's speeches are expected to express the values and ideals of America and offer a moral vision. The best speeches teach the American people what it means to be American. Kennedy's inaugural address was so eloquent that he inspired a generation. And by articulating patriotic values, presidents can lift the morale of

The best presidents articulate a moral vision that inspires the people.
©Arianna Tonarelli/Shutterstock.com

the country. By the end of the 1970s, morale in America was at a nadir after suffering through the Vietnam War, Watergate, and the energy crisis. In ceremonies like the rededication of the Statue of Liberty, Reagan was able to make people feel patriotic again.

As in other categories of presidential leadership, moral vision has a macro and micro aspect. On the macro level, a president needs to articulate a moral vision to give his presidency legitimacy, honor, and to inspire a nation to support his agenda. Franklin Roosevelt would not have been able to sell the New Deal without appealing to the morality and compassion of the American people. But on the micro level, a president's personal immorality can undermine or even destroy his presidency. Nixon's presidency was destroyed by his personal immorality that resulted in the Watergate scandal. Likewise, when Barack Obama repeatedly broke his word to the American people, his approval ratings dropped. In order to gain support for the Affordable Care Act, Obama said that "if you like your doctor, you will be able to keep your doctor." When this turned out to be untrue, he lost the confidence of many independent voters.

Inter-Personal Skills: Lastly, few individuals possess the interpersonal skills needed to become president of the United States. One must have the unique talent to be able to relate to individuals and large groups in an emotionally satisfying way. The president must forge relationships with other political leaders, including congressmen, governors, foreign leaders, heads of interest groups, CEOs, and union leaders.

In these relationships, the president must know how to handle big egos and negotiate in a way that fosters a spirit of cooperation, even with political enemies. Reagan would occasionally have a beer and swap jokes with Tip O'Neal, the Democratic Speaker of the House. By building a personal relationship, it made it easier for Reagan to get support from congressional Democrats. This principle also applies to foreign leaders. As vice president and president, George H. W. Bush had carefully built personal relationships with leaders around the world. This helped him to build a coalition of over thirty countries to fight in the Gulf War.

On the other hand, personal emotional difficulties can undermine a presidency. After analyzing the leadership abilities of twelve modern presidents, from FDR to George W. Bush, Fred I. Greenstein remarked that there were "an alarmingly large number of chief executives whose emotional flaws impeded the conduct of their responsibilities." Greenstein concludes that of these twelve presidents, four were so "emotionally handicapped" that it injured their presidency, including Johnson, Nixon, Carter, and Clinton. And only four presidents were emotionally healthy: Eisenhower, Ford, George H. W. Bush, and George W. Bush.

Considering the fact that so many recent presidents seem to have had personal emotional problems, one wonders if there is something about the modern Presidency that attracts emotionally perverse people. At the very least, one must possess an outsized ego and colossal ambition to even consider dragging one's family through the torture of a presidential campaign.

THE PRESIDENT AND THE MEDIA

One of the primary political skills a president needs today is to communicate effectively with the American people through the *media*: network TV (ABC, NBC, CBS), cable TV (CNN, MSNBC, Fox), newspapers, talk radio, and the Internet, including social media. If the president can gain approval for his policy, then it is less likely that Congress will oppose it. Gaining popular support is even more critical if the opposition party controls one or both chambers of Congress. Today the Presidency has become the political center of American life. Every day we see the president on TV delivering a speech, engaging in an interview, comforting a family, chatting with celebrities, eating a cheeseburger, or going on vacation. *All* these media events are carefully scripted by the president's political and communication teams in order to gain popularity. The skillful manipulation of the media is essential to presidential success.

Role of the Press: The press plays a fundamental role in a democracy. It's their job to deliver important governmental information to the citizens in

Presidents try to manipulate the press.
©Vlad1988/Shutterstock.com

order for them to intelligently vote. But beyond providing true and important information to the American people, the media is also motivated to increase ratings and attract more readers or viewers. It can do this by exposing White House problems, mistakes, and scandals.

The job of the president's political advisors, on the other hand, is to spin information to the president's advantage in order to gain popularity and to downplay or hide scandals and mistakes. So, there is a natural friction between the White House and the press. In the 1970s, this friction increased dramatically during Watergate when the media exposed the lies and intrigues of Richard Nixon, forcing him to resign. Yet both sides need each other: the press needs information, and the president needs to get his message out to the people.

White House Communications: In recent years, the president's closest advisors usually include communication experts. The rise of the presidential media advisor started with Teddy Roosevelt when he assigned a staff member to provide a daily briefing to reporters. Today the Press Office is housed in the West Wing of the White House, with the Briefing Room directly downstairs. The *Press Secretary* provides the press with routine information in her daily briefings: the president's schedule, appointments, agenda items, and policy. Sometimes these briefings can become heated when the press senses that the Press Secretary is hiding the truth.

The White House Office of Communication was created by Nixon in 1969. This team sets the public agenda and long-term media campaign. Michael Deaver was a top Reagan advisor who orchestrated the president's media strategy. This position is now called the **Communications Director**: *the head of the president's team responsible for crafting the administration's political theme, orchestrating public relations, and articulating policy issues in the most favorable way.* At a time when most Americans got their news from the nightly network news shows, Deaver planned one daily public event for Reagan. This was designed to get at least one favorable photo op and one line of the day to appear on the network nightly news.

Now the communications team routinely set the line of the day, the theme of the week, and gives presidential surrogates their talking points when they go on television. If you pay attention to the news, you will notice that suddenly all the Democrats or all the Republicans are using the same words and phrases. This is because they are working from *talking points*: a list of succinct statements and arguments on a particular topic that are distributed to important political leaders when they make media appearances. The White House communication team will e-mail talking points to their supporters before they make speeches or go on television.

Communications Director

the head of the president's team responsible for crafting the administration's political theme, orchestrating public relations, and articulating policy issues in the most favorable way

**No president has run for president while relentlessly criticizing
the press as Trump did in 2016.**
©stock_photo_world/Shutterstock.com

Another way the White House tries to influence news coverage is through the "leak." A **leak** *is information provided by a government official to a reporter.* A White House official will provide a reporter with exclusive information, giving the reporter a scoop, but the news item will usually benefit the president in some way.

The Press Conference: Through various media events, such as news conferences, speeches, and interviews, the president tries to set the national agenda and control the public debate. Today the president's media advisors have offices in the West Wing, the area closest to the president. Using insights they gleamed from polls and focus groups, media consultants advise the president on what words to use, what arguments to make, and how to frame the debate.

The main presidential media event use to be the **press conference**: *when the president stands before the press corps and answers questions.* On average, Calvin Coolidge and FDR gave over six press conferences a month. Today, presidents might give one or two: George W. Bush averaged 2.18 a month, and in Obama's first term he averaged 1.66 a month. Presidents do not like the press conference because they are dealing with the highly informed White House press corps that will ask difficult questions.

No president, with the possible exception of Richard Nixon, has had such a contentious relationship with the press. In the early months of Trump's presidential campaign, he courageously, and at times recklessly, went on network

Leak

is information provided by a government official to a reporter

Press Conference

when the president stands before the press corps and answers questions

Honeymoon Period

a time of high approval ratings and goodwill that a newly elected president experiences and cable television shows on almost a daily basis. But as his campaign progressed, the political media became more and more antagonistic as they questioned inconsistencies in Trump's statements and focused on rumors and leaks. In the months before and after the election, Trump, to the delight of his supporters, called the press liars and promoters of "fake news." A Harvard University study of press coverage during Trump's first 100 days in office catalogued the contentious nature of the media coverage. It reported that news coverage on CNN and NBC was 93 percent negative and 7 percent positive, while the coverage of Obama during his first 100 days was 60 percent positive and 40 percent negative.

Alternative Media Events: Instead of enduring the pressure of a traditional news conference, recent presidents mostly give speeches to small groups organized by a supportive interest group. For example, a Democratic president might speak to groups of union members or teachers, and a Republican might speak to members of the Chamber of Commerce or a veterans group. At these events the president can control his message and not have to take any difficult questions. Also, presidents like to do events in small towns. The media in a small town, excited and honored by a rare presidential visit, will often ask easy questions and give favorable coverage. Lastly, presidents are making more appearances on *soft media*, such as comedy shows, daytime talk shows, and even sport shows. Obama made regular appearances on comedy shows and daytime talk shows, such as *The View*.

Polls: The media team pays very close attention to the polls. When a new president takes office, he usually enjoys a **honeymoon period**: *a time of high approval ratings and goodwill that a newly elected president experiences.* Since the 1930s, Gallup has been conducting a tracking poll by simply asking: "Do you approve or disapprove of the way the president is handling his job?" With a few exceptions, most presidents start off with high approval ratings and then come down. And once a president becomes unpopular, as each negative story takes its toll, and as the press establishes a narrative of a troubled presidency, a snowball effect can drive the approval rating lower and lower. It is very difficult for presidents to turn this around. Jimmy Carter came in with 90 percent approval, and left with 43 percent; Lyndon Johnson came in with 97 percent, and left with 62 percent.

Going Public: The president's team tries to use polls to the president's advantage by publicizing favorable polls. Another method presidents use to influence public opinion is **going public**: *In order to put pressure on Congress to support the president's proposal, the president will go on a media campaign, sidestepping the press, and directly appeal for public support.* This political tactic was first used by Teddy Roosevelt and Woodrow Wilson. The president will travel around the country explaining why his proposal is so important or

Going Public

in order to put pressure on Congress to support the president's proposal, the president will go on a media campaign, sidestepping the press, and directly appeal for public support

Presidents "go public" and try to get the people to support their agenda.
©Joseph Sohm/Shutterstock.com

explicitly telling the people in television addresses to call their congressmen and tell him to vote for the president's bill. This is why polls are so important. If the president has high approval ratings, and his particular proposal also has high approval ratings, then he can pressure Congress to pass it.

Going public, however, breaks the traditional political practice of working behind the scenes with congressional leaders and forging difficult compromises. Now presidents use their rhetorical skills and media savvy to pressure Congress from a distance. Obama relied almost exclusively on this technique to put pressure on the Republican controlled House to pass his budgets and to raise the debt ceiling. The negative consequence of this tactic is that the public bullying will create resentment by the opposition party in Congress, poisoning any chances of forging personal relationships with individual members of Congress.

Permanent Campaign

when a president maintains a constant media campaign to support his agenda and attack his opponents

The Permanent Campaign: Trying to influence the polls and going public have led to a new aspect of presidential politics, the **permanent campaign**: *when a president maintains a constant media campaign to support his agenda and attack his opponents.* Bill Clinton was the first president to maintain full campaign mode for eight years. Clinton's top political advisor, Dick Morris, created the political strategy of making a new proposal every day, placing the president always on the offensive and forcing the press to broadcast a proactive public image.

The permanent campaign, however, has erased the traditional cycle of campaigning and governing. Campaigns are by nature adversarial. Campaign rhetoric attacks the opponents and makes enemies. The art of governing, however, is to work behind the scenes, build relationships, make coalitions, and forge compromises. Now presidents, using their large and sophisticated communications staff, are constantly making addresses, spinning their agenda, and attacking their foes. This has helped lead to the dysfunction of Washington as Democrats and Republicans are constantly fighting with each other on every topic. The permanent campaign has also led to the omni-present executive, the president who is constantly on television and in our lives.

PRESIDENTIAL PARTY POLITICS

Richard Neustadt said that presidents must constantly be "thinking politically," meaning that within a system of limits and conflicts the president must always be thinking about how he can best influence other institutions to his long-term advantage. This leads to another internal conflict of the presidency. The president is the head of state AND the leader of his political party. As the head of state, the president of the United States is expected to act in a dignified and patriotic manner, doing what is best for the *whole* country. On the other hand, the only real way for the president to pass his agenda is to increase the number of congressmen of his political party in Congress. This means campaigning on their behalf. Yet if he is perceived by the public as being hyper political, bending the truth to his partisan advantage, or making economic and military decisions based on political calculations, he could destroy his presidency.

One president who skillfully balanced the two aspects of the presidency, as head of state and as party leader, was Dwight Eisenhower. In presidential ceremonies, speeches, and press conferences, Eisenhower created a public image as a nationally unifying figure. The public always saw him as cheerful, optimistic, and above party politics. But behind the scenes, Eisenhower instructed his aides to carry out partisan maneuvers. And he left it to administration and cabinet members, such as Vice President Richard Nixon, to make public partisan attacks. This strategy was effective at winning over the majority of the American people, including many independents. Eisenhower enjoyed the highest average approval rating, at 65 percent, than any modern president.

Conflict with Congress: As one of the three branches of government, the president can do very little without congressional support. A large part of the president's job is working with Congress to implement foreign and domestic policy. The two branches, however, are often in conflict. To thwart the immediate impulses of the majority, the Framers deliberately built a system that would work neither quickly nor efficiently: they deliberately built a complex system with internal conflict.

One way the Framers increased conflict was to create executive and legislative branches with different constituents and terms. The president serves a four-year term and represents the whole country. Members of the House serve a two-year term and represent the constituents of their congressional districts. And Senators enjoy a six-year term. Therefore, Representatives may oppose the president because they are constantly thinking of the short term, and Senators may oppose the president because they are thinking about the long term. Indeed, many senators have seen several presidents come and go. So neither chamber of Congress has a strong interest to automatically follow the president.

Divided Government: And conflict between the president and Congress is heightened during periods of divided government. The Framers rejected Britain's parliamentary system wherein the Prime Minister and the majority of the legislative branch represent the same political party. Instead, the Framers created an independent executive, allowing for more conflict, and permitting a situation called **divided government**: *when the executive branch and one or both chambers of Congress are controlled by different political parties.*

Obama's presidency has been dominated by divided government. Only from 2008 to 2010 did the Democrats have a majority in both chambers of Congress. This allowed the president to pass his agenda, such as the Affordable Care Act, without a single Republican vote. Then in 2011, the Republicans gained control of the House. In 2014, the Republicans also gained control of the Senate. This situation of divided government created gridlock and very few bills passed through Congress after 2014. Like Obama, Trump also enjoyed united government as he became president. But to everybody's surprise, Republicans in the Senate were unable to pass Trump's agenda of repealing and replacing Obamacare, even though they had promised to do so for several years.

Surprisingly, the American people seem to like divided government. Over the last forty years, there have only been four two-year periods of united government. Why? The American people seem wary of giving one party too much power. Divided government slows down the passage of an avalanche of unwanted laws, and it controls spending. Since Nixon, the American people are pretty evenly divided between Democrats and Republicans. We will not have united government until one party becomes dominate.

Mandate: One way presidents can gain power over Congress is to claim a **mandate**: *When a president wins an election by a large margin, Congress recognizes that they should implement the president's agenda and comply with the will of the people.* In 1932, FDR had a mandate to pass his legislative agenda

Divided Government

when the executive branch and one or both chambers of Congress are controlled by different political parties

Mandate

is when a president wins an election by a large margin, Congress recognizes that they should implement the president's agenda and comply with the will of the people

Teddy Roosevelt had a mandate to break up monopolies.
©Everett Historical/Shutterstock.com

to deal with the Great Depression. A mandate is strengthened if a president wins a landslide victory and ran explicitly on the agenda item he is urging Congress to pass. After winning a close election in 2004, George W. Bush tried to push Congress into reforming Social Security. Even though Social Security may have been in need of reform, Congress ignored President Bush because he did not have a mandate—Bush did not win a large victory and he did not run on the issue. So presidents must have the political intelligence to understand their mandate and to not overreach.

Realignment: Another way that a president can gain total domination over Congress would be through an election realignment. An **electoral realignment** *is when the majority of voters switch from one party to another and remain loyal to the new party for a generation.* Political scientists have noticed long-term cycles in American history where one party is dominate for about thirty to thirty-five years. There have been about a half dozen electoral realignments since Washington's presidency.

Many times this switch takes place after a charismatic president articulates a new vision for his party, attracting a generation of loyal voters. In 1800, Jefferson articulated a vision of his party based on state's rights and the virtues of the family farmer, making the Democratic Republican Party the dominate part for a generation. In 1828, Andrew Jackson led the Democratic Party to generational dominance. In the 1930s, in a massive realignment, FDR recreated the modern Democratic Party as he gained support for his New Deal

Electoral Realignment

is when the majority of voters switch from one party to another and remain loyal to the new party for a generation initiatives. In 1980, Reagan shifted the country to accept conservative principles of limited government, lower taxes, and a strong defense. For the last several years, we seem to be in a period of balance where neither the Democrats nor the Republicans dominate. When will the next realignment take place?

First and Second Term Patterns: Besides the mega cycles of electoral realignment, political scientists have also recognized smaller political cycles within the president's two terms. The first several months of a new president's term is marked by a *honeymoon period* when the press, Congress, and the American people are willing to give the new executive a chance. Presidents know that this honeymoon period is fleeting, and so they focus very hard on passing major legislation within the first year or so. Then, during the second year of the president's first term, Congress has its mid-term elections. Most of the time the president's party loses seats in the mid-term elections, marking the people's preference for divided government. Usually during a significant portion of the president's eight years, the opposition party controls one or two chambers of Congress.

If the president wins a resounding reelection victory, he may claim a mandate at the beginning of his second term. But the second honeymoon is never as magical as the first honeymoon. Most of the time a second-term president must move to the center and try to work with the opposition party to pass bi-partisan legislation. A good example of this is Bill Clinton. In his second term he was able to work with Republicans to balance the budgets and pass a

Bill Clinton started the presidential practice of the permanent campaign.
©Joseph Sohm/Shutterstock.com

historic welfare reform law. But as a rule, *second terms are always less successful than the first term: this is known as the* **second-term curse.** Second terms are often filled with political difficulties and scandals. This is ironic because after a few years in office the president becomes more skilled at his job. Yet, at the same time he faces more obstacles and opposition.

Incidentally, Donald Trump has been the first president in the modern era to receive no honeymoon period. Remember, a honeymoon is when the media, Congress, and the American people give the new president a chance to establish his administration and set his agenda. But, as we mentioned above, the Harvard study showed that the media ran very few favorable stories on the new president. And the Democrats launched an unprecedented effort to get Republican members of the Electoral College to place their votes for somebody besides Trump, going against the wishes of the voters of the state. Moreover, more than 60 Democrats boycotted Trump's inauguration. Trump was denied a honeymoon because the contest between him and Hillary Clinton was so combative. Also, Trump's aggressive nature and politically incorrect rhetoric often caused deep resentment in enemies.

FINAL THOUGHTS

In the spring of 1947, Harry Truman's advisor, Clark Clifford, warned the president against campaigning until after the national party convention, saying "[the president] must be president of all the people and not merely the leader of a party." Presidents no longer follow this advice. According to Brendan J. Doherty, in his book *The Rise of the President's Permanent Campaign*, presidents are now in permanent campaign mode. In Obama's first term in office, he attended 310 fundraisers. This compares to 173 for W. Bush, 167 for Clinton, and 80 for Reagan. Increasingly, presidents are permanently campaigning because they see themselves as the party leader, and they feel they must raise more money for their party. But is this the best political strategy for a successful presidency?

There are three negative consequences of the permanent presidential campaign. First, nothing is more valuable than a president's time, and if he is spending more time fundraising, this necessarily means he is spending less time thinking about domestic and foreign policy. Second, as mentioned above, the permanent campaign destroys the traditional cycle of campaigning and governing. The more time Obama, for example, spends publically attacking Republicans, the less they will be willing to work with him. This results in a dysfunctional government, where the executive and legislative branches cannot cooperate with each other. And third, the permanent campaign means that the president spends more and more time with hyper-partisan donors

Second-term Curse

second terms are always less successful than the first term

and loses touch with regular Americans. Today people feel angry at the establishment politicians.

It would be refreshing, and more productive, if presidents would listen to Clark Clifford's advice and return to the Eisenhower leadership style of operating above partisan politics and being the president of "all the people."

NOTES

For stats on number of presidential press conferences go to: "The American Presidency Project," Presidential News Conferences: Coolidge–Obama. www.presidency.ucsb.edu.

Brendan J. Doherty, *The Rise of the President's Permanent Campaign*. Kansas: University Press of Kansas, 2012.

Fred I. Greenstein. *The Presidential Difference: Leadership Style from FDR to Barack Obama* (3rd edition). Princeton: Princeton University Press, 2009.

Richard Neustadt, *Presidential Power and the Modern Presidents*. New York: The Free Press, 1990.

Wall Street Journal Online, "Presidential Leadership," Sept 12, 2005.

Eileen Shields-West, *The World Almanac of Presidential Campaigns*. New York: Pharos Books, 1992.

ESSAY QUESTIONS

1. Describe the two presidential management styles and the pros and cons of each.
2. Explain the importance of a president's ability to persuade.
3. Explain the importance of these presidential leadership skills: crisis manager, moral vision, and interpersonal skills.
4. When does the president have the most influence over Congress?
5. What happens in a divided government and why do you think the American people seem to like it?

TERMS

Collegial Management Style: _____

Communications Director: _____

Divided Government: _____

Electoral Realignment: _____

Going Public: _____

Hierarchical Management System: _____

Honeymoon Period: _____

Leak: _____

Mandate: _____

Permanent Campaign: _____

Press Conference: _____

Second-term Curse: _____

CHAPTER 13

What Are the Powers of Congress?

TOPICS

▶ Congressional Constitutional Powers
▶ Structure and Function of Congress
▶ How the House of Representatives Works
▶ How the Senate Works
▶ Congressional Committees

LEARNING OBJECTIVES

When you finish reading this chapter, you will be able to:

1. Outline the core powers of Congress.
2. Discuss how the structure of Congress creates more deliberation.
3. Describe how Congress can check the president.
4. Explain the rules and leadership of each chamber.
5. Understand the important function of the congressional committees.

WHAT ARE THE POWERS OF CONGRESS?

When the Framers wrote Article I of the Constitution, they created America's legislature: the US Congress. Of the three branches of government, Congress is the "people's branch" because it represents the people and it is the only branch in which members are voted into office directly by the people. The two main functions of Congress are making laws and spending revenue. Congress also serves as the most important check on presidential power.

In recent years, polls show that Americans are becoming increasingly frustrated by the way Congress functions. In the modern world we value speed and efficiency, but the Framers deliberately made Congress cumbersome and inefficient. Why? Congress serves as a forum for the American people to work out the problems facing the nation. Each member of Congress represents a relatively small geographical area, filled with people of different economic and ideological interests. It takes an enormous amount of time and debate for all these groups to form a national majority opinion regarding a single issue. But the Framers assumed only the *best* ideas would attract the majority in the long run. This is how Congress is supposed to work.

CONGRESSIONAL CONSTITUTIONAL POWERS

The Constitution grants Congress the power to make law. This is an awesome power. Congress can literally send people to their deaths by drafting them into the army or throw them into prison for not paying their taxes. So the Framers designed Congress carefully, splitting it in half and making it part of a system of three branches, each with checks and balances. Article I, the first and longest article of the Constitution, describes the powers of Congress. The first sentence of Article I states: "All legislative Powers herein granted shall be vested in a Congress of the United States." The legislative vesting clause is limited by the phrase "herein granted," meaning Congress only possesses the powers listed in Article I. Congress has enormous power, but as we will see in this chapter, these powers are carefully limited.

Enumerated Powers: Article I, Section 8 of the Constitution enumerates, or lists one by one, the powers of Congress. These powers can be divided into three broad categories: financial, military, and rules and institutions. Congress is given tremendous financial powers: to collect taxes, to pay debts, to borrow and coin money, and to regulate commerce with foreign nations and among the states. And Congress is granted great military powers: to declare war, to maintain and pay for an army and navy, to punish pirates, and to call forth the militia. Further, Congress can set up certain rules and institutions for various purposes: to establish rules of naturalization and bankruptcy, to erect post offices, to grant copyrights and patents, to constitute a national judiciary, to fix the standards of weights and measures, and to build and run the nation's capital (the District of Columbia).

Necessary and Proper Power: The last sentence of Article I, Section 8 states that Congress shall have the power "to make all laws which shall be necessary and proper for carrying into Execution the foregoing powers (the enumerated powers listed above)." This clause is often referred to as the elastic clause because it stretches the powers of Congress in unclear ways. In *The*

The Capitol building Washington, DC.
©holbox/Shutterstock.com

Federalist #44, Madison argued that the elastic clause prevents the Constitution from becoming a "dead letter." It would have been impossible, argued Madison, to list every power Congress might need to properly address all the nation's present and future concerns. This clause gives Congress the flexibility and agility to address situations the Founders could never foresee.

In the early years of the Republic, Congress argued over how to interpret the elastic clause. In an essay defending the creation of a national bank, Alexander Hamilton wrote: "If the end be clearly comprehended within any of the specified powers, and if the measure have an obvious relation to that end, and is not forbidden by any particular provision in the Constitution, it may be safely deemed to come within the compass of the national authority." In other words, Congress has the power to make laws or establish institutions if the purpose is to execute one of the enumerated powers. Thus Congress created a national bank in order to execute the enumerated powers to collect taxes, coin money, and regulate commerce.

Special Powers of the House and Senate: The Constitution also specifies certain powers to each chamber of Congress. Article I, Section 7 states that "all bills for raising Revenue shall originate in the House." This was part of the English tradition that the power of the purse should lie in the branch closest to the people. The Senate enjoys more substantial independent powers. The Senate has the special power to ratify treaties, with a two-thirds vote, and confirm presidential appointments, with a majority vote.

Power of Impeachment: The Framers gave Congress the ultimate check on the presidency, the power to remove the president from office. The House and the Senate have different roles in the impeachment process. If the president commits certain "high crimes and misdemeanors," the House can write up articles of impeachment, only needing a majority vote. Then a trial is held in the Senate, presided over by the chief justice. After arguments are made for and against the president, the Senate will vote as a jury. If two-thirds or more of the chamber votes for impeachment, then the president will be removed from office. Two presidents have been impeached by the House, Andrew Johnson (1868) and Bill Clinton (1998), but no president has been removed from office. Richard Nixon probably would have been impeached and removed from office, but he resigned before the process started.

STRUCTURE AND FUNCTION OF CONGRESS

By understanding the structure of the legislative branch, one can better understand what function the Framers had in mind for Congress. The structure of Congress was the focus of much debate during the Constitutional Convention. The small states wanted equal representation in the national legislature, but the big states thought that they should be able to send more representatives to Congress. After a great deal of argument, the delegates from the large and small states finally made a compromise. The "Connecticut Compromise" arranged that representation in the House of Representatives would be based

The US House of Representatives during a presidential State of the Union speech.
©Drop of Light/Shutterstock.com

on the population of the state, and representation in the Senate would be equal, each state getting two senators.

The Framers further differentiated the two chambers by giving members of the House and the Senate different terms, constituents, and ways of getting selected. Members of the House of Representatives serve a two-year term and are elected by the people of their relatively small congressional district. Senators serve a six-year term and represent the people of their whole state. This complex arrangement makes lawmaking slow and deliberative, preventing the sudden mood swings of the people to be instantly translated into law. In this way, the Founders rejected direct democracy and established a republic.

A Divided Branch: During the Confederation period (1776–1788), some states experimented with single chamber (unicameral) legislatures, but this proved to be problematic. Jefferson said, "Tyranny of the majority can be just as bad as tyranny of one." By the time of the Constitutional Convention, nearly all delegates concluded that *a two chambered legislature* (**bicameral**) was best. Before becoming law, a bill must pass both chambers of Congress, the House and the Senate, with a majority vote and be signed by the president.

Why did the Framers think a slower bicameral legislature was better than a quicker unicameral legislature? First, because the authority to make law is such an awesome power, it is best to divide the legislative branch for fear that it will overwhelm the other branches. In *The Federalist #51,* Madison said, "in order to control the legislative authority, you must divide it." Second, the Framers divided the legislature in two in order to make lawmaking a more thoughtful process, allowing more time to debate an issue. We have all experienced the feeling of thinking a new idea was absolutely fantastic, only to realize later, perhaps after discussing the idea with friends, that it was actually a poor idea. This is what the Framers were trying to do.

Bicameral

a two chambered legislature

The House of Representatives: The terms, constituents, and manner of selection were designed to make the House of Representatives the "voice of the people." With only a two-year term, representatives must run for election every other year and be responsive to the *present* concerns of the people. And members of the House are voted into office directly by the people. In *The Federalist #10,* Madison said, elections by the people are a fundamental "republican principle." The House was to be the one branch that linked the people to the federal government—originally the Senate was selected by the state legislatures and the president was selected by the Electoral College. Further, members of the House represent a relatively small group of people, originally 30,000 but now about 710,000—still small enough that they can understand the concerns of the people they represent.

The Senate: The terms, constituents, and manner of selection were designed to make the Senate a "council of statesmen" that can focus on the long-term interests of the nation. With a six-year term, senators do not have to worry about the immediate concerns of their constituents. And only one-third of the Senate is up for election at a time, further distancing them from the immediate passions of the people. Originally, senators were selected by the state legislatures, making them ambassadors of their state governments. But with the passage of the 17th Amendment (1912), the people of the state now vote directly for their two senators. The Framers intended to make the Senate the more stable chamber filled with mature and experienced statesmen who, unencumbered by immediate political concerns, would coolly and deliberatively make decisions for the long-term good of the nation.

Checks and Balances: Congress is at the heart of the three-branched structure of checks and balances. The Framers were highly concerned about checking executive power. For nearly every power assigned to the president, Congress has some ability to check it. The president is the commander in chief of the armed forces, but only Congress can declare war and maintain the military. The president makes judicial and executive department appointments, but they must be confirmed by the Senate. The president signs treaties with foreign nations, but the Senate must ratify all treaties with a two-thirds vote. And the president must sign all bills before they become law, but Congress can override a veto with a two-thirds vote. So, the president's success is in the hands of Congress. Congress must pass his legislative agenda, approve his appointments, ratify his treaties, and pass his budget.

Speaker

the presiding officer of the House of Representatives

HOW THE HOUSE OF REPRESENTATIVES WORKS

With 435 members, the House is over four times the size of the Senate and therefore must function under stricture rules and strong leadership. The House is more centralized, hierarchical, and its members more specialized in their area of expertise than the Senate. In the House the majority party runs everything and the minority party is pretty much powerless. Representatives are up for election every two years and so they must be attuned to the concerns of the people in their district. As a result, most representatives work in Washington Monday through Thursday, and then rush home on the weekends to spend time with their families and attend local events.

Speaker of the House: *The presiding officer of the House of Representatives is the* **Speaker.** The Speaker is modeled after the British Speaker of the House of Commons, but unlike the British Speaker, the House Speaker is the primary functioning leader of the House. The Speaker of the House sets the agenda, chooses committee membership, decides what bills move to the floor, and assigns bills to committees and subcommittees. He or she seldom votes or engages in floor debates and never serves on any standing committee, but holds tremendous power behind the scenes. Theoretically, the Speaker is elected by the entire House, but in reality he or she is elected by the majority party. The Speaker is second in line of succession to the president (after the vice president).

Other House Leaders: Besides the Speaker, there are several other important House leadership positions. The *majority leader* is selected by the majority party. As second in command, the majority leader is the right arm of the Speaker, helping plan strategy and shepherd party members to support the Speaker's agenda. He also calls up bills to debate by making the weekly schedule of business. The *minority leader* is the leader of the minority party. If in the next election the minority party wins the majority of the seats in the House, he or she will likely become the Speaker.

Nancy Pelosi, the first woman Speaker of the House, served from 2007 to 2011.
©Ryan Rodrick Beiler/Shutterstock.com

The third most important position is the whip. Working with the top party leadership, the **whip** *prepares summaries of bills, counts the votes, notifies members of the calendar for upcoming votes, and pressures members to vote with the leadership.* The whip has nine deputy whips, representing the different regions of the nation. Speakers do not like to call a vote on a bill unless they know they will win, and it is the whip's job to get those votes. The whip will try to pressure party members to vote for a bill by using a variety of sticks and carrots. This is a difficult position that takes unique skills.

House Rules: As stated above, because the House is so big, it operates under centralized leadership and strict rules. Before any bill goes to the floor for a vote, it must first be granted "a rule" by the powerful *Rules Committee*. Working with the Speaker, the Rules Committee will set the time for the debate and decide if any amendments can be added to the bill. An "*open rule*" allows amendments. A "*closed rule*" prohibits amendments. If the House needs to suspend the rules in order to get something done, it will operate under a "committee of the whole," which only takes a quorum of one hundred members. When representatives finally get the opportunity to vote, it is done by an electronic voting system. The typical floor votes takes about 15–20 minutes.

Whip

an important congressional position that prepares summaries of bills, counts the votes, and pressures members to vote with the leadership

HOW THE SENATE WORKS

With only one hundred members, the Senate is more collegial and informal. There are fewer rules, debate is unlimited, and the leadership is weaker. George Washington supposedly said that just as you pour tea into a saucer to cool it, "we pour legislation into the senatorial saucer to cool it." This expresses the

Framer's vision of how Congress would work: the House would craft most of the legislation based on the demands of the people, and then the Senate would coolly and deliberately decide which laws to pass for the good of the whole country.

An individual senator has more power and responsibility than a representative. A single senator can bring the Senate to a halt with a filibuster or by requesting "unanimous consent." These parliamentary rules allow the minority party to block the will of the majority. Also, senators serve in several committees and thus are more generalists. In addition, with its "advice and consent" powers, senators must ratify all presidential treaties and confirm all presidential appointments. This gives them more leverage over the president in domestic and foreign affairs.

Senate Leaders: The Constitution states that the vice president of the United States is the "President of the Senate." But the only constitutional power he has is to break a tie vote, which seldom happens. So when the vice president is not presiding, which he seldom does, the **president pro tempore** *serves as the official presiding officer of the Senate*. By tradition, the president "pro tem" is the longest serving senator in the chamber.

Although the Constitution assigns the vice president and president pro tem as leaders of the Senate, the real political power lies with the majority and minority leaders. The **Senate majority leader** *is the top leadership position in the US Senate*. He sets the agenda, recommends committee chairs, and he and the minority leader are the first to speak during debate. The Senate majority leader, however, is far less powerful than the Speaker of the House. Since any senator can place a "hold" on a bill or threaten a filibuster, the majority leaders must control the Senate through persuasion, negotiation, and by building relationships. The second most powerful senate position is the *minority leader*, who is the head of the political party that holds the second most seats in the Senate.

Senate Rules: The Senate is smaller and more collegial. In the past, the Senate was conducted according to unwritten but mutually understood rules, almost like a fraternal club. Senators seldom refer to each other by name, but instead as a "friend," such as my "good friend, the distinguished senator from the great state of Georgia." A senator would never insult another senator. A quorum of fifty-one senators is required to do business. There is no rules committee to determine how a bill will be debated. Instead, they rely on a *unanimous consent* agreement. This agreement will set the rules on how long the bill will be debated or if amendments can be added. Sometimes the bill is passed by a unanimous consent without even going to the floor.

President Pro tempore

serves as the official presiding officer of the Senate

Senate Majority Leader

is the top leadership position in the US Senate

Mitch McConnell became the Senate majority leader in 2015.
©Christopher Halloran/Shutterstock.com

It is easy for any senator to delay or stop a vote for a bill. At any time, any senator can stand and say "I object," bringing the whole chamber to a standstill. One delay tactic is to ask the clerk to read the bill three times, which may take several hours. Or a senator can place a "hold" at any time. When this happens, a senator will call his party leaders and say he is placing a hold on a particular bill. The majority leader then will not call up the bill until the hold is rescinded. These parliamentary rules make it very difficult for the leadership to control the chamber.

Filibuster

a long speech delivered by a senator in order to delay a vote on a bill.

The Senate Filibuster: The most well-known senate delay tactic is the **filibuster**: *a long speech delivered by a senator in order to delay a vote on a bill*. In the 1950s and 1960s, Southern Democrats used the filibuster to stop civil rights bills. In 1957 Strom Thurmond, a Democrat from South Carolina, spoke for twenty-four hours and eighteen minutes to delay a voting rights bill. This record still stands. An actual filibuster, however, seldom takes place anymore. In 1917, President Woodrow Wilson suggested that some restrictions be placed on the Senate tradition of unlimited debate. The Senate passed *Cloture Rule 22*, which states that debate will end (*cloture*) with a 60 percent vote. This has fundamentally changed the way the Senate operates. A supermajority of 60 percent is now needed for the majority to conduct business.

Advice and Consent: The Constitution says that "by the advice and consent of the Senate" a majority of senators must confirm presidential appointments and ratify treaties. The Senate confirms the president's appointments to top executive positions. Recognizing that in order to carry out his agenda the president should be allowed to pick his top officials, especially since they will leave office when the president leaves, the Senate gives great deference to presidential appointments. Supreme Court justices, however, receive higher scrutiny. Federal judges are appointed for life, and therefore the Senate examines their background much more carefully. Some judges are rejected purely by their political ideology.

In 2013, Rand Paul filibustered for twelve hours and fifty-two minutes to protest the Obama Administration's use of drones.
©Andrew Cline/Shutterstock.com

Lastly, the Senate must ratify all presidential treaties by a two-thirds vote. This power brings Senators, especially those on the Senate Foreign Relations Committee, into the president's foreign relations process.

CONGRESSIONAL COMMITTEES

The real workhorses of Congress are the committees. Woodrow Wilson said that "Congress in session is Congress on public exhibition, whilst Congress in its committee rooms is Congress at work." Speeches in the chamber are meant for the press or for the constituents back home, but the actual work of crafting legislation is done in committees. There is nothing in the Constitution describing committees, but they were invented in the first years of Congress. Organizationally, committees make a great deal of sense. Committees allow for specialization and expertise. Instead of all members of Congress working on every bill, bills are sent to committees specializing in one area. A farm bill, for example, will be sent to the Agriculture Committee.

Today, party politics plays a major role in committee assignments. The majority party of each chamber gets the chair and a majority of all members of each committee. Especially in the House, this gives the majority party almost total control to pass legislation. At the beginning of each session, the Speaker of the House and the Senate Majority Leader give committee assignments. House members tend to serve on only one committee, giving them greater expertise in that area. Senators tend to serve on several committees, making them generalists.

Types of Committees: Most committees are **standing committees,** *which are permanent committees in session year in and year out.* Ways and Means, Veteran's Affairs, Agriculture, and Homeland Security are Standing Committees. They produce most of the bills. Special or **select committees** *are created for a special purpose, often to conduct an investigation.* Typically, they are given a limited time to produce a report. **Joint committees** *consist of members from both the House and the Senate to oversee something that is of interest to the entire Congress.* And all committees have sub-committees to help them do their work. In 2016, the House and the Senate had forty-two standing committees, five joint committees, and six select committees. Most House committees have about thirty members, and Senate committees have less than twenty-five.

Committee Structure: As stated above, the chair and the majority of the members of each committee are determined by which political party holds the majority in that chamber. This is very important. It allows the majority party to control the legislative agenda. Committee chairs are very powerful. They call and run the meetings, assign the chairs of all subcommittees, and have the power to kill a bill, unless overruled by the chamber leadership. Committee chairs also have a large staff. In the old days, the most senior congressmen were selected as chairs, leading the committees: this is called the *seniority rule.* But since the mid-1970s, junior members have insisted on having more power and now it is more common for freshmen members to get assigned to powerful committees.

Committee Functions: Committees have six broad functions: they authorize, oversee, appropriate, make rules, investigate, and oversee the budget. *Authorizing* committees pass laws that tell the government what they can do. When a law is passed, Congress must either create an agency or tell an agency

Standing Committees

which are permanent committees in session year in and year out

Select Committees

are created for a special purpose, often to conduct an investigation

Joint Committees

consist of members from both the House and the Senate to oversee something that is of interest to the entire Congress to carry out this new function. Committees *oversee* that the agency is carrying out the law properly. *Appropriation* committees determine how much money government is spending on these programs. They decide how much money each bill will get. Rules committees *set the basic rules* for each chamber, for example how many staffers each congressman gets and the rules for debating a bill. Many times, committees *investigate* issues, such as global warming or how to reduce waste. Committees will often hold hearings and people testifying before the committee must swear to tell the truth or face severe penalties. And *budget* committees raise the money set aside by the appropriations committees.

The Most Powerful Committees: There are about a dozen especially powerful committees in Congress. The most powerful House committees are *Appropriations* (all spending bills), *Ways and Means* (all tax, Social Security, and Medicare bills), and *Budget* (helps craft the federal budget). The common denominator of these committees is that they form the core of Congress's "power of the purse." The *House Rules Committee* is also extremely powerful because it sets the rule for how each bill is to be debated.

In the Senate, the most powerful committees deal with money but also with the Senate's power of advice and consent. Appropriations and Budget play the key role in crafting the federal budget. And because the Senate must ratify all foreign treaties, the *Foreign Relations Committee* is very prestigious. Also, the *Senate Judiciary Committee* is very powerful because the Senate must confirm Supreme Court Justices.

The Senate Judiciary Committee holds hearings on Supreme Court appointees.
©Rob Crandall/Shutterstock.com

Conference Committees: Another very important congressional committee is the Conference Committee, which is both a special and joint committee. In order for a bill to become a law, it must pass both chambers of Congress in the *exact same language*. About 80 percent of the time, one chamber accepts the language of the other. But for the other times Congress must create a **conference committee**: *A special type of joint committee with members of both congressional chambers which settle the difference between two bills from each chamber.* Normally, a conference committee is made up of representatives and senators that served on the committee or sub-committee that originally crafted the legislation. Once the reconciled bill is produced by the conference committee, it is sent back to both chambers to be voted on without amendment.

Caucuses: Lastly, members of Congress form another type of group that does not have legislative power but often has political power. **Caucuses** *are informal groups of congressmen that meet on like-minded issues.* Congressional caucuses include the Hispanic Caucus, Woman's Issues Caucus, Pro-Life Caucus, Homelessness Caucus, and the Tea Party Caucus. All kinds of interest groups and issues are the focus of a caucus, which often get media attention. One of the more powerful caucuses is the Congressional Black Caucus, which is made up exclusively of black members and seeks to deal with issues important to African Americans.

Conference Committee

a special type of joint committee with members of both congressional chambers which settle the difference between two bills from each chamber

Caucuses

are informal groups of congressmen that meet on like-minded issues

FINAL THOUGHT

For the Final Thought of this chapter, we will honor a great member of the House of Representatives. One of the heroes in the history of Congress, *John Quincy Adams* was the only man to serve as a president, a US Senator, and a member of the House of Representatives. He was the son of Abigail Adams and John Adams, the second president of the United States. Before John Quincy Adams became president, he was revered as a statesman, having served as ambassador to Russia and Britain, and serving as secretary of state. After losing the 1828 presidential election, Adams won a seat in Congress as a representative of his home district in Massachusetts, serving for seventeen years. Always an opponent of slavery, Adams used his power in Congress, which was enhanced as an ex-president, to fight slavery.

In 1836, Southern members of the House voted in a "gag rule," forbidding any discussion of slavery. This was in response to the thousands of petitions that abolitionists were sending to Congress. Arguing that the right to petition the government was an

John Quincy Adams fought against slavery as a member of the House of Representatives.
©Everett Historical/Shutterstock.com

important 1st Amendment right, Adams ignored the gag rule and introduced an anti-slavery petition to Congress. This earned him the hatred of many of his colleagues.

Southern representatives were so infuriated with Adams's conduct that they censored him. But this attempt to humiliate Adams backfired. According to House rules, Adams was allowed to speak freely in order to defend himself against censorship, and he used that opportunity to make several eloquent and forceful speeches against slavery. In this way Adams became a symbol of integrity and justice. Adams once said, "Always vote for principle, though you may vote alone, and you may cherish the sweetest reflection that your vote is never lost."

NOTES

Alexander Hamilton, John Jay, and James Madison. *The Federalists*. Indianapolis: Liberty Fund, 2001.
For Hamilton's essay defending the national bank, go to "The Avalon Project" at http://avalon.law.yale.edu.
For Thomas Jefferson's comment on the tyranny of the majority, see his letter to J. Sullivan in 1807.
For House committees, go to the official House of Representatives website: www.house.gov.
For Senate committees, go to the official US Senate website: www.senate.gov.

ESSAY QUESTIONS

1. What are the three most important powers of Congress?
2. What are some of the unique features of the House and the Senate?
3. What is a filibuster? How can the Senate stop one?
4. What goals did the Framers wish to achieve with bicameralism?
5. Describe the powers and role of the Speaker of the House, the majority leader, and the whip.

TERMS

Bicameral: _____

Caucus: _____

Conference Committee: _____

Filibuster: _____

Joint Committees: _____

President Pro Tempore: _____

Select Committee: _____

Senate Majority Leader: _____

Speaker of the House: _____

Standing Committee: _____

Whip: _____

CHAPTER 14

How Does a Bill Become a Law?

TOPICS

- ► Running for Congress
- ► Role of the Lawmaker
- ► How a Bill Becomes a Law
- ► What Influences a Lawmaker's Vote?
- ► Problems and Suggested Reforms

LEARNING OBJECTIVES

When you finish reading this chapter, you will be able to:

1. Explain how a representative and senator run for Congress.
2. Compare the trustee and delegate model of representation.
3. Delineate the multiple steps a bill takes to become a law.
4. List the various factors that influence a lawmaker's vote.

HOW DOES A BILL BECOME A LAW?

Otto von Bismarck said, "Laws are like sausages, it is better not to see them being made." This is true. Lawmaking is a complicated, difficult, and messy process. Sometimes lawmakers do not even read the bill they are voting on. Sometimes interest groups write sections of a bill, inserting provisions that financially benefit one particular industry. Sometimes a lawmaker will vote for a bill she disagrees with because party leaders promised to give her money for an upcoming reelection campaign. And sometimes lawmakers insert secret amendments that bring money to their district. All these details are ugly and contribute to the heightened cynicism people feel today toward government. But hopefully, in the majority of cases, the political process works for the common good. And if something is not working, the American people should demand reforms. That too is part of the political process.

RUNNING FOR CONGRESS

The first step in learning how a bill becomes a law is to understand something about how members of Congress get elected. Before a particular bill becomes a law, somebody has to win a seat in Congress in order to propose that bill. And when an individual runs for office, he or she will usually make certain campaign promises, saying, in essence, vote for me and I will support these issues and propose these laws. Also, by understanding how a member of Congress wins her seat, we understand the political obligations the person has to her constituents, party, and interest groups.

Running for the House: Each member of the House of Representatives is up for reelection every two years. As an institution, the House is very aware of the political calendar. And as individuals, House members are almost constantly raising money and preparing for a campaign. There are three constitutional qualifications to run for the House: you must be twenty-five years old, a citizen for seven years, and a resident of the state you are representing.

As a member of Congress, Paul Ryan, Speaker of the House, must run for reelection every two years.
©Seth C Fisher/Shutterstock.com

A representative, however, does not need to live in the district from which she is elected. Congressional districts are relatively small and therefore it is possible for a candidate to meet the people of her district, shake hands, and attend local events. Normally, it takes a few hundred thousand dollars to run for the House.

House Districts: Districts are not required by the Constitution, but the states quickly made congressional districts in order to represent the different geographical areas of the state. Today, each congressional district has over 710,000 people. The larger the state, the more districts it has: South Dakota has one; Virginia has eleven; and California (the largest) has fifty-three districts. The Constitution mandates that every ten years a census be taken to count the residents in each state. *If a state's population increases or decreases by more than the average number of people in a district (today 710,000), then the state will either gain or lose a representative—this is called* **reapportioning**. When this happens, a state must redraw their congressional districts—this is called *redistricting.*

Although some states have tried to make the process less partisan by appointing independent panels, most of the time the political party that dominates that state draws the districts. State political parties try to divide the state in such a way that it creates the highest number of "safe seats," seats either a Democrat or Republican will always win, while at the same time dividing the opposition party. *When a district is drawn in an irregular shape in order to maximize the benefits for one party, it is called* **gerrymandering.** The Supreme Court has ruled that it is illegal to draw a district solely on the basis of race, but otherwise they recognize the redistricting is part of partisan politics.

Reapportioning

if a state's population increases or decreases by more than the average number of people in a district (today 710,000), then the state will either gain or lose a representative

Gerrymandering

when a district is drawn in an irregular shape in order to maximize the benefits for one party

The party that controls a state tries to draw congressional districts in a way that will give members of that party the most "safe seats."
©Kheng Guan Toh/Shutterstock.com

Incumbency Effect: During the last several years, Congress has had extremely low approval ratings, hitting an all-time low of 10 percent in 2012. Yet, even though a high percentage of the public disapproves of the job Congress is doing, representatives win reelection over 95 percent of the time and senators win almost 90 percent of the time. In other words, people hate Congress but they seem to love their individual congressperson. Why do incumbents almost always win? There are several explanations. Gerrymandering has created safe seats that are nearly impossible to lose. In our current media driven culture, incumbents enjoy high name recognition because they are on TV. Members of Congress also get free postage—this is called "franking." Further, and perhaps most importantly, it is much easier for a sitting congressperson to raise money for a campaign than a challenger.

Running for the Senate: Senators must run for reelection every six years, and only one-third of the Senate is up for reelection every two years. Staggered elections were designed to make the Senate less responsive to the emotional fluctuations of the people. Originally, Senators were selected by state legislatures, further distancing them from direct democracy. But since the ratification of the *17th Amendment* in 1913, Senators are elected by the people of their state. There are three qualifications to run for the Senate: you must be thirty years old, a citizen for nine years, and a resident of the state you are representing. Campaigning for the Senate, especially in large states like California or Texas, takes millions of dollars to launch a successful media campaign.

ROLE OF THE LAWMAKER

People have always argued about the proper role of an elected representative. Most people today feel that a representative should vote the way the people of her district or state wish. But the Founders understood that the proper role of an elected representative was to do what was best for the long-term interests of the whole country, regardless of popular sentiments back home. Most members of Congress blend the two. Political scientists call these two views of the role of the lawmaker the *trustee model* and the *delegate model*.

Trustee Model: Edmund Burke (1729–1797), a political philosopher and member of the British Parliament, formulated the trustee model of representation. He said that when a district, Bristol for example, elects a man to serve in the British Parliament, they voted for his judgment, education, and political views. That man is now a Member of Parliament, and so he should not sacrifice his opinions and judgment to merely follow the popular opinions of the people back home. Instead, he should do what he thinks is best for the whole nation. The **trustee model** sees Congress more as a national lawmaking institution, *in which educated and experienced lawmakers craft legislation for*

trustee model

sees Congress more as a national lawmaking institution, in which educated and experienced lawmakers craft legislation for the long-term benefit of the whole nation *the long-term benefit of the whole nation*. The Framers seemed to have created the Senate, with its six-year terms, on the trustee model.

Delegate Model: In the **delegate model**, *the lawmaker votes in accordance with the wishes of the majority of his or her constituents, even if those views are contrary to the lawmaker's*. In this model, the representative acts as a voice of her district or state. And when the representative votes, the primary calculation should be whether the proposed bill helps or hurts her constituents. This perspective sees Congress as a representative assembly, in which lawmakers *represent* the economic, geographical, and political concerns of their constituents in the national government. The House with its two-year terms seems to be especially designed for the delegate model. Lee Hamilton, a long serving member of Congress, said the views of his constituents can aptly be summed up in this quote: "We didn't send you to Washington to make intelligent decisions. We sent you to represent us."

Delegate Model

the lawmaker votes in accordance with the wishes of the majority of his or her constituents, even if those views are contrary to the lawmaker's

HOW A BILL BECOMES A LAW

Now that we understand a little about how a member of Congress gets elected, and the different ways a representative may understand her role, we will discuss exactly how a representative's idea becomes actual, binding law. The process is not easy. In some ways it is similar to the struggle of a baby turtle. A mother sea turtle will lay hundreds of eggs, but only a few baby turtles make

Facing the front of the Capitol, the Senate is on the right, and the House is on the left. A bill must get a majority vote in both chambers to become a bill.
©Orhan Cam/Shutterstock.com

it through all the predators on the seashore—crabs, raccoons, seagulls, fish, and sharks—before it makes it to the safety of the deep ocean. Likewise, most bills die before they become law. In the 111th Congress, 10,000 bills were proposed, but less than 5 percent became law. Each bill must go through several steps, and at each step the bill is likely to die.

1. **Introducing the Bill:** First, a Congressman must have an idea. Perhaps the idea was suggested by a constituent or a staffer or the president, but only a member of Congress can introduce a bill (although several members of Congress can co-sponsor a bill). Most of the time a lawmaker introduces a bill because he or she truly thinks it would solve a problem or make an improvement. Sometimes, however, a congressman might introduce a bill for purely political reasons, knowing that it would never become law. In the upcoming election the representative may say, "I proposed a bill to balance the federal budget, but Congress ignored me."

    The actually drafting of the bill is seldom done by the representative or senator herself. She normally copies a state bill or has the Congressional Research Service (CRS) or a lobbyist draft it for her. Certainly, she relies heavily on her large staff. Then, a member of the House must place a bill in *the hopper* (a mahogany box on the desk at the front of the chamber rostrum), or a member of the Senate must give it to a clerk. Next, the House or Senate clerk assigns a legislative number to the bill, with H. R. for House bills and a S. for Senate bills. Then the Government Printing Office (GPO) prints the bill and distributes copies to each congressperson.

2. **Committee Assignment:** After the law is printed, the House or Senate leadership decides what committee to send it to. If, for example, it is a bill dealing with farming, it will be sent to the Agricultural Committee. Very large and complicated bills may be sent to several committees. Normally the committee then sends it down to the more specialized sub-committees. A sub-committee does the preliminary research and holds hearings. At a hearing, experts are called to give their testimony and are normally given five minutes to speak. As the committee gains more information and as more staffers work on the bill, it will grow. If a majority of the sub-committee members vote to approve the bill, then it is sent back up to the full committee. Most bills never get beyond this point and "die in committee."

3. **Markup and Discharge:** After the study and hearings, and once the committee decides to pass the bill, it will be "marked up." This means the language will be cleaned up and appropriate amend-

ments will be added. "Mark up" refers to the pencil marks covering the bill. Committee members go through the bill line by line. As members of Congress, staffers, and lobbyists assist in marking up the bill, it can grow and change significantly. After this, the full committee votes to recommend or "report" the bill or not. If it is recommended, the bill is ready to be *discharged* to the next step. If it is in a House committee, then it will be sent to the Rules Committee. If it is in a Senate committee, it will be sent to the full chamber. But if the party leadership controlling that chamber does not like the bill, then it will never be discharged.

4.   a)   **Floor Debate in the House:** If a bill gets out of committee, it will be sent before the entire House. If multiple committees worked on the same bill, they will have to rewrite it into one bill. But before it goes to the floor for a vote, it is sent to the Rules Committee. The Rules Committee will issue the "rule" for the debate, providing the regulations, calendar, and length of time for the debate. Representatives can only speak on the bill for a limited time. Sometimes to speed things along, the House meets as a Committee of the Whole, requiring only one hundred members to act. And sometimes the rules will be so restrictive the bill will be voted on with virtually no debate and no amendments. The final vote is done electronically.

Senators talk to each other in an attempt to gain support for their bills. Here Senator Patrick Leahy (D Vermont) is talking with Senator Chuck Schumer (D New York).
©Rob Crandall/Shutterstock.com

b)   **Floor Debate in the Senate:** In the Senate, instead of being sent to the Rules Committee, the bill will be placed on the "business calendar." It must receive "unanimous consent" to go on the floor. Then any senator may put a "hold" on a bill, meaning he or she must be informed before the bill will go to the floor. This usually means she has concerns about the bill, or is simply delaying for some sort of tactical reason. Also, as we learned in Chapter 13, any bill can be delayed with a filibuster.

Most bills die in the Senate Calendar. But if it makes it to the floor for a vote, it is usually passed by a *voice vote*. The presiding officer asks the senators to vote "yea" or "nay," and simply announced which side won. A *roll-call* vote, however, is usually used for more important votes. The name of each senator is called and the Senator must respond "yea" or "nay," and the individual votes are noted for the record. The process takes about fifteen to twenty minutes.

5.   **Pass Both Chambers:** A bill must receive a majority vote to pass the chamber. All along the process the original sponsor or sponsors of the bill must work to get it passed. They do this by talking with as many representatives or senators as they can and make arguments for why the bill must be approved. As the sponsor brings in more supporters, she may have to change the language or add amendments. This is the messy process of political compromise.

6.   **Amendments:** Some members of Congress may vote for a bill only if they can add amendments. In the House, the Rules Committee usually forbids amendments, but the Committee of the Whole can add amendments. In the Senate, riders may be attached to a bill. *Riders* are provisions added to a bill that may or may not be directly related to that bill. Enemies of the bill may add "killer amendments" to make the bill less attractive; supporters of the bill may add "saving amendments" to make the bill more attractive. **Earmarks** *are spending amendments added to an appropriations bill that pay for spending projects for a congressperson's home state.* In recent years, earmarks have become unpopular, but members of Congress defend them as part of their jobs to bring revenue into their state. They say it is better for representatives to make spending decisions rather than the executive department. Since 2000, the number of earmarks has skyrocketed.

7.   **Conference:** If a bill passes one chamber, it must be passed to the other chamber in the exact same language. Most of the time, the second chamber adopts the language of the bill that passed the other chamber. But about 10 percent of the time the language was changed and so it must go to a *Conference Committee*. This is a joint

Earmarks

are spending amendments added to an appropriations bill that pay for spending projects for a congressperson's home state

In this political cartoon, President Arthur is vetoing an immigration bill.
©Everett Historical/Shutterstock.com

committee made up of senators and representatives, normally the lawmakers involved with the bill when it was in committee. Their job is to adjust the differences in two bills to create one new bill. No amendments are allowed. If the conference committee fails to make a compromise, the bill may die there. Sometimes, due to all the deal-making and wrangling, the bill that comes out of the Conference Committee is very different than the bill that went in.

8. **President Signs or Vetoes:** As part of the Framers system of three branches with checks and balances, the president is involved in the bill-making process. James Madison said in *Federalist #47*, the president has a "partial agency" in the legislative process. Perhaps the original bill was proposed by the president and a member of Congress introduced it for him. In this case, or when the president supports any bill, he may campaign across the country trying to get the public to support the bill and put pressure on Congress to pass it. Or perhaps the president likes part of a bill but he wants elements of it changed. He might threaten to veto it unless these changes are made.

Once it reaches the president's desk, he has ten days to do one of four things: (1) He can sign it, and it becomes law. (2) He can veto it, and it will be sent back to Congress. A veto may have a *veto message*, explaining why the president rejected it. (3) If Congress is in session, he can choose not to sign it, but it still will become law.

Presidents might do this if they do not fully like the bill and don't want their name on it. And (4), *If Congress is out of session, then he may not sign it and it will be sent back to Congress.* This is called a **pocket veto**. This bill will also be sent back to Congress when they return to session.

9. **Override:** The Framers did not give the president an absolute veto, meaning once he vetoes a bill it is dead. Instead, they gave the president a **qualified veto**, *meaning Congress can override a veto with a supermajority vote.* Congress can **override** *the president's veto by passing it through both chambers with a two-thirds vote.* This is extremely unlikely, especially in the modern era when neither the Democrats nor the Republicans dominate Congress. In President Obama's nearly two terms, he made nine vetoes of which zero were overridden. In George W. Bush's two terms, he made twelve vetoes of which four were overridden, and Bill Clinton made thirty-seven vetoes of which four were overridden.

WHAT INFLUENCES A LAWMAKER'S VOTE?

Now that we understand the basic mechanics of how a bill becomes a law, we should consider the political forces working on a lawmaker. What factors influence a member of Congress to vote for or against a bill? Below are listed several things that influence a congressperson's vote, but all of these factors are made more complicated by large bills. Most of the times members of Congress are forced to vote for massive bills with hundreds of provisions, some of which they like and some they hate. That being said, the following are the major influences affecting a congressperson's vote:

Personal conviction: Most members of Congress cast their vote based on their *personal convictions*. A liberal member of Congress will vote for a liberal measure, and a conservative will vote for a conservative measure. Originally, a person ran for Congress because he or she held strong political beliefs. They wanted to change the country for the better. So, even though they face all kinds of political pressures, most members of Congress vote in accordance with their core beliefs. Each year a few organizations, such as the *National Journal* and the *American Conservative Union*, publish rankings of how liberal and conservative each member of Congress is based on their voting record. Most members of Congress are consistently liberal or conservative.

Constituents: Members of Congress will certainly consider the wishes of their constituents back home. Usually a liberal or conservative lawmaker is from a liberal or conservative district, so this does not pose a conflict. Usually, the constituents are unaware of what bills are working their way through Congress. So, probably for 90 percent of the votes casted, a lawmaker does not

Pocket Veto

If Congress is out of session, then the president may not sign it and it will be sent back to Congress

Qualified Veto

Congress can override a veto with a supermajority vote

Override

Congress can override the president's veto by passing it through both chambers with a two-thirds vote have to worry about the opinions of his or her constituents. For each issue, however, there is usually a small group of people that are highly concerned about how their representative votes. These people will write letters, send e-mails, and make phone calls to the representative's offices. And this type of pressure can have an effect on the way a lawmaker votes.

Staff: A lawmaker might vote based on the recommendation of his or her staff. Many staff members have been in Washington a lot longer than the lawmaker and have developed a deep understanding of many complex issues. Currently, there are about 25,000 congressional staffers. The average representative has seventeen staffers, and the average Senator has forty! So, a congressperson with little interest or experience in an issue, and who did not have time to study the issue or even read the bill, will often vote based on the advice of her staff. Furthermore, a member of Congress has several very important internal organizations that were created to provide a lawmaker with information, including the Congressional Budget Office (CBO), Government Accountability Office (GAO), the Congressional Research Service (CRS), and the Library of Congress.

interest group

Groups of people that get together to change public policy.

Party: The political party that the lawmaker belongs to will certainly pressure him or her to vote a certain way. But again, most liberal lawmakers are Democrats, and most conservatives are Republicans, and so most of the time voting with their party is consistent with voting according to their personal convictions. In the past, however, it was much more common for members of Congress to cross the aisle and vote with the opposition party. Today, partisanship is much more intense and members of Congress vote with their party over 90 percent of the time. This reflects the fact that the parties have become more ideologically pure. Starting in the 1970s, conservative "blue dog" Democrats have become Republicans. And since the 1980s, moderate "country club Republicans" has been vilified by conservatives and have been unable to get elected.

Interest groups: In our more cynical age, many Americans believe that lawmakers are in the pocket of interest groups. And it is true that interest groups play a major role in the lawmaking process. There are about 13,000 registered lobbyists working in Washington today. But congressmen take money from dozens, if not hundreds, of interest groups, so political scientists have been unable to prove a direct link between financial support of one interest group and individual votes a lawmaker makes. **Interest groups** *are organizations that try to change public policy.* The main way they try to influence the vote of members of Congress is by providing information, often very specialized, technical information. So if a lawmaker

Interest group money buys access to politicians.
©Digital Storm/Shutterstock.com

is about to vote on an education bill, for example, interest groups representing teachers' unions will send him reams of information about that issue.

Colleagues: Sometimes one member of Congress will try to influence another lawmaker's vote. This is especially true if the member of Congress originally proposed the bill or is sponsoring the bill now. It is their job to go around the chamber and ask individual members of Congress to vote for the bill and explain why it is a good bill. Or a member of Congress, who is trying to make up his mind about a vote, may go to a committee member who is an expert in that area. And sometimes a member of Congress may agree to vote for her colleague's bill if the colleague agrees to vote for her measure later— this kind of *vote trading is called* **logrolling.**

Presidential Influence: Lastly, presidents spend a lot of time and effort trying to pressure members of Congress to vote for their measures. If a president is popular, members of Congress will be less likely to vote against him. But if he is unpopular, especially in the last years of his term, most members of Congress will feel unafraid to vote against the president. In a **united government**, *when the majority of seats in both chambers of Congress belong to the same political party as the president*, they will often vote in support of the president's proposals. But during **divided government**, *when one or both chambers of Congress are occupied by a different party as the president*, then it is much more likely that the president's agenda will be blocked. In recent decades, divided government is much more common than united government.

PROBLEMS AND SUGGESTED REFORMS

Of the three branches of government, polls show that the people have the lowest regard for Congress. And yet, as explained above, while Americans complain bitterly about Congress, they typically reelect their own representative or senator. And to be fair, most members of Congress are basically good people that have entered politics to improve the nation. They work very hard and would easily make much more money working in the private sector. The unpopularity of Congress, however, does reflect the fact that there are several problems plaguing Congress that need to be reformed.

National Debt: The Framers gave Congress the "power of the purse," but it has been totally irresponsible in its duty of making the budget. As of 2016, the national debt has reached $20 trillion. How much is $20 trillion? If you stacked 20 trillion dollar bills on top of each other, the pile would go to the moon and back. Five times! How could Congress spend $20 trillion dollars more money than the federal government has? Worse, how can Congress promise to pay or to financially back over $127 trillion in unfunded liabilities, like Social Security, Medicare, federal employees' future retirement benefits?

Logrolling

vote trading

United Government

when the majority of seats in both chambers of Congress belong to the same political party as the president

Divided Government

when one or both chambers of Congress are occupied by a different party as the president

The national debt is a real indictment of Congress. They are burdening the next generation with piles of debt and putting the American economy in danger.

Pork Barrel Spending: Members of Congress often try to add **pork spending** to a bill, *legislation that brings money to their constituents in order to gain political favor*. A fundamental reason for the astronomical national debt is that members of Congress always have a political incentive to spend, but not to cut. When a congressperson is running for reelection, they often say something like, "vote for me because I brought federal money into our district which built that school and that road and that park." But what would happen if somebody ran for Congress by saying, "vote for me because I will cut spending for that school and that road and that park." They would lose the election. This is a fundamental flaw in our political system. Each member of Congress has a strong incentive to spend, but little incentive to cut.

Omnibus Bills: And lastly, another major congressional problem is the practice of *omnibus bills*—massive bills with hundreds of provisions and thousands of pages. Oftentimes, Congress passes giant bills packed with hundreds of amendments and pork. These bills can be thousands of pages long, making it impossible for any congressperson to read, especially when they only have a few hours to vote. In a famous quote, Nancy Pelosi, the then-Speaker of the House, urged her fellow representatives to vote for the 10,000-page Affordable Care Act, saying, "We have to pass the bill so you can find out what is in it." Wouldn't it be more rational for Congress to pass smaller bills, dealing with only one issue at a time, and give each member of Congress time to read and study the bill before casting a vote?

Pork Spending

legislation that brings money to their constituents in order to gain political favor

Senator Henry Clay was called the "Great Compromiser" for his efforts to unite the country.
©Everett Historical/Shutterstock.com

FINAL THOUGHT

In Chapter 13, we used the Final Thought to describe a great congressman, John Quincy Adams. In this Final Thought we will portray another great statesman, orator, and lawmaker, *Henry Clay*. Representing Kentucky, Henry Clay served three times as Speaker of the House of Representatives and four times as a US Senator, and became known as the "Great Compromiser." He earned the nickname of the Great Compromiser because on three different occasions he was able to orchestrate reconciliation between different sections of the country to keep the Union together. In 1820, he put together the

Missouri Compromise, in 1833 he resolved the Nullification Crisis, and at the end of his career he organized the Compromise of 1850. In all of US history, few members of Congress have worked harder to work with the opposition in order to unify the nation.

NOTES

For size of congressional staff, go to Sunlight Foundation: sunlightfoundation.com.

Chris Cillizza. "It wasn't always this bad. The growth of political polarization, in 1 chart." *Washington Post*, June 5, 2013.

Lee Fang. "Where Have all the Lobbyists Gone?" *The Nation*, March 10, 2014.

Vance Ginn. "You think the deficit is bad? Federal Unfunded Liabilities Exceed $127 Trillion," *Forbes*, Jan 17, 2014.

Alexander Hamilton, John Jay, and James Madison. *The Federalists*. Indianapolis: Liberty Fund, 2001.

Lee Hamilton, *How Congress Works*. Bloomington, Indiana: Indiana University Press, 2004.

Joseph A. Pika et al. *The Politics of the Presidency*. Washington: Congressional Quarterly Press, 2002.

Donald A. Ritchie. *The US Congress*. Oxford, Oxford University Press, 2010.

Gregory Gwyn-Williams. "National Debt Stacked in Dollar Bills would Stretch from Earth to Moon Five Times." *CNSnews.com*, July 26, 2013.

ESSAY QUESTIONS

1. Define reapportionment (redistricting) and gerrymandering.
2. What is the incumbency effect?
3. Compare the Trustee and Delegate model of representation.
4. What are the steps a bill must pass through to become a law?
5. What influences a congressman's vote?
6. Explain why the congressional political process tends to work in favor of increasing the national debt.

TERMS

Delegate Model: _____

Divided Government: _____

Earmarks: _____

Gerrymandering: _____

Interest Group: _____

Log-rolling: _____

Override: _____

Pork Spending: _____

Reapportioning: _____

Trustee Model: _____

United Government: _____

CHAPTER 15

What Does the Supreme Court Do?

TOPICS

▸ Constitutional Power of the Supreme Court
▸ Structure of Federal Judiciary
▸ The Political Ideology of the Supreme Court
▸ Judicial Philosophy
▸ The Politics of Appointing Judges
▸ How the Supreme Court Works
▸ Supreme Court Opinions

LEARNING OBJECTIVES

When you finish reading this chapter, you will be able to:

1. Explain how the judicial branch, with judicial review, plays a key role in our three-branch system of government.
2. Understand the constitutional basis of judicial power.
3. Compare liberal judicial philosophy with conservative judicial philosophy.
4. Delineate the steps of appointing a judge to the federal judiciary.
5. Describe the process by which justices write their opinions.

WHAT DOES THE SUPREME COURT DO?

The US Supreme Court wields enormous power. A simple majority of nine judges, often in 5-4 rulings, decide cases dealing with billions of dollars and affecting millions of people. The chief justice presides over presidential impeachments. In 2000, the Supreme Court decided a presidential election. In 1974, they caused a president to resign. In 1858, they helped spark a Civil War. We have come to expect the Supreme Court to decide the most controversial issues facing the nation: slavery, civil rights, national security, free speech, religious freedom, business regulations, abortion, affirmative action, gun control, gay marriage. The Framers would certainly be surprised to learn that the Supreme Court has become so important in deciding such *political* issues, which they assumed the legislature and president would handle.

Upholds the Constitution: How is it that in a democracy nine non-elected judges have the power to decide the most contentious and far-reaching issues facing the nation? Alexis de Tocqueville said in 1835 that "there is hardly any political question in the United States which does not, sooner or later, turn into a judicial one." Tocqueville's statement reflects the fact that America is a constitutional democratic republic (as we learned in Chapter 2). We are not a pure democracy. If we were, then the majority of the people would decide all these issues. Instead, our system must follow the Constitution, which outlines the structure and powers of the three branches of government and lists our individual rights. The Supreme Court must decide important issues based on their interpretation of the Constitution.

The Supreme Court didn't get their own building until 1935.
©fstockfoto/Shutterstock.com

CONSTITUTIONAL POWER OF THE SUPREME COURT

Article III, describing the judicial branch, says, "The judicial power of the United States shall be vested in one Supreme Court, and in such inferior courts as the Congress may from time to time ordain and establish." Article III only contains 500 words. It seems that the delegates at the Constitution Convention were a bit fatigued after spending so much time and energy on Articles I and II, describing Congress and the presidency, and so the section on the judicial branch left many things unresolved: it does not describe the role of the chief justice, it does not mention how many justices should be on the Court, it does not outline the role and structure of the lower courts, and it does not clearly state whether the Court has the power of judicial review. It remained for Congress to actually establish the federal court system, which it did with the *Judiciary Act of 1789* (described below).

Role of the Judiciary: Another reason the Framers spent the least amount of time on Article III is that of the three branches of government they felt the judicial branch possesses the least threat to the Republic. The role of the judiciary is to *interpret the law*. In a dispute between two parties over a statute or legislative act, a judge will interpret the law and decide which party is in the right. So, the act of interpreting the law seemed to be the least threatening to the Framers—if the courts stuck to this role. Alexander Hamilton, in *Federalist #78*, famously said the judiciary is the "least dangerous branch" because it does not have the power of the sword, as the president does, nor does it have the power to make law, as the Congress does. But Hamilton warned, "There can be no liberty, if the power of judging be not separate from the legislative and executive powers."

Independent Judiciary: The great innovation of the Constitution is that it established three independent branches of government with checks and balances. Hamilton said, "independent judges" were needed "to guard the Constitution and the rights of individuals." To make the judiciary independent, the Framers removed it from the political process and gave judges terms for life. The Constitution says federal judges will hold their offices "**during good behavior**," *meaning lifetime terms.*

The president will select a judge, and the Senate will confirm by a simple majority. No longer having to worry about getting elected or raising campaign funds, a federal judge can devote her life to studying the law. The Constitution, however, places two checks on judicial independence. A judge can be impeached with a two-thirds vote by the Senate. And Congress can limit the jurisdiction of the Supreme Court.

Jurisdiction: Article III of the Constitution states that the Supreme Court hears two types of cases. In certain circumstances the Court has *original*

During Good Behavior

the language in the Constitution that means federal judges serve lifetime terms *jurisdiction* and cases go straight to the Supreme Court, such as in cases affecting maritime issues, involving two or more states, dealing with the federal government, or involving ambassadors and other public ministers. And the Supreme Court also has **appellate jurisdiction**, *the power to review decisions from lower courts*. Today the court hears mostly appeals. In deciding to accept appeals, the Supreme Court is less concerned with righting a wrong, but in settling cases that deal with important constitutional issues.

Judicial Review: In the landmark case *Marbury v. Madison* (1803), Chief Justice John Marshall laid out his argument for why the Supreme Court must have the power of **judicial review**: *the power to void congressional acts by declaring them unconstitutional*. With this power, which is only implied in the text of the Constitution, the Supreme Court became a co-equal branch of government with Congress and the Presidency. Today the Supreme Court routinely voids state law, congressional acts, and presidential actions. To read a full description of *Marbury v. Madison*, please read about the case in "Landmark Supreme Court Cases" in the Appendix.

Checks and Balances: How does the Supreme Court function in our system of three branches with checks and balances? Broadly speaking, Congress makes the law, the president executes the law, and the Supreme Court interprets the law. And the Constitution lists specific ways the judiciary can check the other branches, and how the other branches can check the judiciary. The

Appellate Jurisdiction

the power to review decisions from lower courts

Judicial Review

the power of the Supreme Court to declare a congressional act null and void if it is found to be unconstitutional

The East pediment of the Supreme Court building features Moses and the Ten Commandments.
©Gary Blakeley/Shutterstock.com

president selects federal judges, which the Senate confirms with a majority vote. The chief justice presides over presidential impeachments. Congress can impeach a federal judge with a two-thirds vote by the Senate. The Supreme Court, through judicial review, can declare a congressional act or an executive order null and void. If a congressional act is declared unconstitutional, Congress can still make the law by changing the language of the law or by proposing a constitutional amendment, which must be ratified by the states.

STRUCTURE OF FEDERAL JUDICIARY

Article III proclaims that there shall be "one Supreme Court" and as many "inferior courts as the Congress may from time to time ordain." The first major congressional law to establish and arrange the federal court system was the *Judiciary Act of 1789*. The Judiciary Act established a three-tiered court system. At the bottom were the thirteen federal *court districts* with the same boundaries as the thirteen states. Appeals went up to the three *circuit courts*, with jurisdiction over the northern, middle, and southern states. Every two years, Supreme Court justices had to journey from state-to-state to hear the circuit court cases, which was very difficult at the time when travel took place

With the Judiciary Act of 1789 and the Evart Act of 1891, Congress created the federal court system.
©robuart/Shutterstock.com

by horse and buggy. And then appeals from the circuit courts went up to the Supreme Court. The justices hated travelling the circuit, and eventually Congress changed the federal court system.

Structure of the Current Federal Courts: The current system was established with the Evarts Act of 1891. It maintained the three-tiered federal court system, but made many important changes that fit better with the growing nation. At the bottom are the ninety-four *US District Courts*. In a typical year, about 700 judges hear over 300,000 civil and criminal cases. If one of the litigants has a legitimate case for an appeal, then the case will go up to one of the thirteen *US Courts of Appeal*. These are located geographically in eleven areas of the United States, the territories, and the District of Columbia. About 180 appeals judges, in panels of three, review about 70,000 cases a year. And at the top is the US Supreme Court, which hears appeals from the lower courts and other types of cases. This is the "court of last resort."

In America, there are two types of law: criminal and civil. *Criminal law* involves legal codes that protect people and property from behavior that is against public safety and welfare. *Civil law* deals with disputes between individuals or groups of people and defines their legal rights. The Constitution states the US citizens have the right to a jury trial in both criminal (Article III, Section 3) and civil (7th Amendment) courts.

US Department of Justice: The US attorneys prosecute criminal cases and civil cases that involve the national government in the federal courts. The Department of Justice is headed by the US Attorney General, who supervises ninety-four US attorneys, and about 1,200 assistant attorneys. The attorney general and the US attorneys are selected by the president and confirmed by the Senate. President Obama chose Eric Holder as his first attorney general and Loretta Lynch as his second. Although they swear to objectively uphold the law, it is considered a political position and after a president leaves, they are expected to resign. Many US Attorneys run for political office after they leave the Department of Justice. Mayor Rudolph Giuliani was a former US Attorney before he ran for the mayor of New York City.

THE POLITICAL IDEOLOGY OF THE SUPREME COURT

The political ideology of the Supreme Court is so important because the Court resolves so many political disputes in America today. Issues of gay marriage, abortion, guns rights, the death penalty, affirmative action, business regulation, immigration, and many other issues, are decided by the Supreme Court. Liberal judges will decide these issues in a way that will make Democrats happy, and conservative judges will decide these issues in a way that makes Republicans happy. And so, the selection of Supreme Court justices involves a monumental battle between the two political parties. Political ideology, however, does not play a significant role in certain criminal or technical cases, or when the law is clear-cut.

For the last several years, the Court has been closely divided between five conservatives and four liberals, some more moderate or extreme than others. The four liberals are Ruth Baber Ginsburg (nominated by Bill Clinton in 1993), Stephen G. Breyer (Clinton, 1994), Sonia Sotomayor (Obama, 2009), and Elena Kagan (Obama, 2010). The five conservatives include Chief Justice John Roberts (George W. Bush, 2005), Antonin Scalia (Reagan, 1986), Anthony M. Kennedy (Reagan, 1988), Clarence Thomas (George H. W. Bush, 1991) and Samuel Alito (George W. Bush, 2006). In recent years, Kennedy, a moderate conservative, has been the unpredictable swing voter: sometimes voting with the liberals and sometimes voting with the conservatives.

Then, in February of 2016, Antonin Scalia died. Shortly after Scalia's death, Mitch McConnell, the Republican Majority Leader of the Senate, announced that the Senate would not hold hearings to confirm a new justice. He argued that by the time they set up hearings, there would only be about six months until a presidential election. In this unique case, where the political balance of the Supreme Court is at stake, the people ought to vote for the president who picks the next justice. President Obama argued that it is his constitutional right to select a justice and the Senate should confirm or deny by a vote. Filling Scalia's seat did become a major issue of the 2016 presidential election.

Antonin Scalia, the influential conservative Supreme Court Justice, died in 2016, sparking a conflict between the president and the Senate.
©Evan El-Amin/Shutterstock.com

Hillary Clinton promised to nominate the judge that Obama selected, but who was ignored by the Senate. Trump promised to select one of the judges from a list of 20 conservative jurists. After becoming president, Trump chose Niel Gorsuch from that list. So, the ideological balance of the Court did not change because a conservative replaced a conservative.

JUDICIAL PHILOSOPHY

The modern ideological split between liberal and conservative judges began during the Progressive Era with the introduction of the concept of the "living constitution." In Woodrow Wilson's 1912 presidential campaign speech, "What is Progress," he proposed a new way of understanding the Constitution. Wilson said that the nation's laws, including the Declaration of Independence and the Constitution, "have not kept up with the change of economic circumstances in the country." The progressive president went on to say that "the modern idea [is] to leave the past and press on to something new," and so we should "interpret the Constitution according to the Darwinian principle . . . [because] the nation is a living thing and not a machine."

In this speech, Wilson set up the modern debate concerning constitutional interpretation. Liberals feel that for the Constitution to have any relevance in the contemporary world, its principles should be applied using the "evolving standards" of the day. Conservatives, on the other hand, wish to maintain the original structure and intent of the Constitution. These two approaches to constitutional interpretation can be broadly defined as *conservative judicial philosophy*, sometimes called "originalism," and *liberal judicial philosophy*, sometimes called the judicial philosophy of the "living Constitution."

Conservative Judicial Philosophy: In Supreme Court opinions over the last few decades, Antonin Scalia has articulated the three principles of the conservative judicial philosophy: strict construction, original intent, and judicial restraint. First, when deciding a case, judges should first look to see if the law in question violates the clear language of the Constitution. This approach is called **strict construction**: *when interpreting the meaning of the Constitution, judges should primarily focus on the clear, explicit, and literal meaning of the text.* Second, *when interpreting the meaning of the Constitution, judges should understand the original goals and the historical context of the provision written by the Framers*: **original intent**. And third, if the law in question deals with a subject not clearly stated in the Constitution, judges should refuse to accept the case. This is called **judicial restraint**: *Judges should only hear cases that deal with explicit constitutional issues, and allow other issues to be resolved by the political process.*

Conservative justices are primarily concerned with the self-restraint of the Supreme Court. For example, conservative judges are highly critical of *Roe*

Strict Construction

when interpreting the meaning of the Constitution, judges should primarily focus on the clear, explicit, and literal meaning of the text

Original Intent

when interpreting the meaning of the Constitution, judges should understand the original goals and the historical context of the provision written by the Framers

Judicial Restraint

judges should only hear cases that deal with explicit constitutional issues, and allow other issues to be resolved by the political process

**The Supreme Court decides some of our most contentious
political issues, such as immigration.**
©Rena Schild/Shutterstock.com

v. Wade (1973). They assert that in their ruling, the majority of the justices
created a right not found in the text of the Constitution, the right to have an
abortion. The Court should have refused to hear the case and allowed the
people of each state, through the state legislatures, to decide the issue of abortion. And if the nation as a whole felt strongly about the issue, Congress and
the states could have added a pro-choice constitutional amendment.

Conservative justices like Scalia argue that the concept of the "living constitution" essentially renders the Constitution meaningless. The principle of the
rule of law is that fixed rules will establish what is permissible and what is
illegal. But when the majority of justices decide to *reinterpret* the words of the
Constitution, the law becomes subjective and arbitrary. The Supreme Court
should only decide cases affecting explicit constitutional provisions and allow
the democratic process to decide the political issues of the day.

Liberal Judicial Philosophy: Modern liberal judicial philosophy came to
fruition during the New Deal and reached its apex during the Warren Court
(1954–1969) and the early years of the Burger Court (1969–1986). The liberal courts have used a broad interpretation of the Constitution, especially
the commerce clause, to establish a strong national government to protect
civil rights, personal privacy, voting rights, the criminally accused, religious
minorities, freedom of thought, and the separation of church and state. Today
liberal justices, like Stephen G. Breyer, advocate a liberal judicial philosophy

that focuses on three principles: evolving values, loose construction, and protecting minority rights and the democratic process through judicial activism.

Liberals argue that if we only interpret the Constitution by looking at the original intent of the Framers, modern society would be chaining itself to the political values of the eighteenth century, when slavery existed and women were denied the vote. Instead, judges should employ **loose construction**, *broadly interpreting the Constitution.* They should do this by understanding the basic principles of the Constitution and applying them to the *evolving values* of society. In this way the Constitution is a "living document" that is relevant and meaningful to contemporary society. Especially during the Warren Court, liberal judges have employed **judicial activism**: *broadly interpreting the Constitution in order to achieve the values of the judge, and in essence making law.* Liberal judges argued that only an active Court could protect the minority from majority opinion by safeguarding such liberties as freedom of speech and voting rights.

Public Opinion: It must be added that the judicial philosophy of individual justices has always been tempered by public opinion. Throughout American history, the Supreme Court has seldom ventured too far in front of popular belief. The way the Court handled racial segregation illustrates this point. In *Plessy v. Ferguson* (1896), the Supreme Court conformed to the racist views of most Americans at the time and approved segregation. And only after the views of most Americans had become more tolerant, did the Court start the process of ending segregation with *Brown v. the Board of Education* in 1954.

Part of this capitulation to public opinion is due to the fact the Supreme Court has no real power to enforce its ruling, beyond persuasive reason. If the president or Congress refuses to comply with a Court ruling, there is little the Supreme Court can do. This weakness was made abundantly clear when Andrew Jackson refused to abide by John Marshall's ruling in *Worcester v. Georgia*. When Jackson decided to ignore the Supreme Court and go ahead with his popular Indian removal policy, he reputedly said, "John Marshall has made his decision, now let *him* enforce it."

THE POLITICS OF APPOINTING JUDGES

Ever since the controversy of John Adams' "midnight judges" in 1800, the appointment of federal judges has been politically charged. Article II gives the president the power to appoint federal judges with the "advice and consent" of the Senate. In practice, presidents try to get a judge through the Senate whose political philosophy most closely matches his own. It is much easier to do this when the president's party enjoys a majority in the Senate. For example, in 1987 when President Reagan tried to get the conservative jurist Robert Bork

Loose Construction

broadly interpreting the Constitution

Judicial Activism

broadly interpreting the Constitution in order to achieve the values of the judge, and in essence making law

Top row: Associate Justices Elena Kagan, Samuel A. Alito, Sonia Sotomayor, and Neil M. Gorsuch. Bottom row Associate Justices Ruth Baber Ginsburg, Anthony M. Kennedy, Clarence Thomas, and Stephen G. Bryer. Chief Justice John G. Roberts center of bottom row.
©Associated Press

selected to the Supreme Court, he was rejected by the Democratic controlled Senate. Although they admitted Bork was well qualified, Democrats argued that his judicial philosophy was too conservative.

Qualifications: Framers provided no qualifications for justices in the Constitution. They assumed the president would select and the Senate would confirm only qualified people with the proper intellect, temperament, education, and experience. Few people qualify. In *Federalist #78*, Hamilton said, "there can be few men in society who will have sufficient skill in the law to qualify them for the stations of judges. And making the proper deductions for the ordinary depravity of human nature, the number must still be smaller." In the past, presidents tried to appoint some justices with real-life political experience, such as Earl Warren who was the governor of California. But in recent years most appointees come from lower federal courts. Incidentally, in the last few decades, almost all Supreme Court justices have either graduated from Harvard or Yale laws schools.

The President Appoints: The selection process of Supreme Court justices involves a two-step process: the president appoints, and the Senate, by a simple majority, confirms. The president's key advisors on judicial appointments normally include the president's legal councilor and an assistant attorney general in charge of the Office of Legal Policy. They continually work on a list of possible judges in case there is an opening on the Court.

Judge Samuel Alito at his confirmation hearing.
©Rob Crandall/Shutterstock.com

There are also several interest groups that influence the selection process, such as the People for the American Way (a liberal organization) or the Heritage Foundation (a conservative organization). The American Bar Association (ABA) rates nominees on their judicial competence with three ratings: "well qualified," "qualified," and "not qualified." In recent years, however, Republican presidents have stopped using ABA ratings because they believe the American Bar Association leans left.

Senate Confirmation: Presidents have appointed only 160 justices, with 124 (78 percent) being confirmed by the Senate. The normal presumption is that the president should be allowed considerable discretion in selecting federal judges. But because they serve for life, senators believe judges should undergo greater scrutiny than the president's administrative appointees. In recent years, especially after the Bork rejection, the confirmation process has been much more politically intense. Typically, an appointee must submit to an FBI background check, fill out a long questionnaire, and then be interviewed by the Senate Judiciary Committee for two or three days. This is a high-pressure job interview, conducted on live television, with senators and witnesses able to bring up nearly any rumor or make a personal attack—things that wouldn't be allowed in a court of law.

Since Bork, who talked freely about his judicial philosophy, the strategy of nominees to the Supreme Court is to say as little as possible, claiming any comment may jeopardize their appearance of objectivity in future cases. After the Judicial Committee hearing, when the committee will either recommend or reject the nominee, the rest of the Senate will vote. During this time, if the opposition finds that the nominee has committed an ethical breach, made controversial statements, or engaged in an embarrassing peccadillo, it will be publicized in order to derail the confirmation.

In 1991, Clarence Thomas, nominated by Republican George H. W. Bush, experienced one of the most contentious confirmations in recent history. He was accused of sexual harassment by a former subordinate, Anita Hill, who testified in front of the Judicial Committee. Thomas, a black American, denied the charges and accused the Judicial Committee of a "high tech lynching." In the end, Thomas was confirmed by the Senate with forty-one Republicans and eleven Democrats voting for, and forty-six Democrats and two Republicans voting against.

Race, Gender, and Religion: In the past, the Supreme Court was completely dominated by Protestant white men. Since the 1960s, people have argued that in order for the Supreme Court to gain credibility, it should "look like the rest of America." Recent presidents, especially Democrats, have focused more on selecting judges that will add more diversity to the court. Lyndon Johnson appointed the first black justice, Thurgood Marshall. And Reagan appointed the first woman, Sandra Day O'Conner. Today the Court is more diverse, consisting of one African American and three women, including a Latina. Interestingly, for the first time in its history, the Court has no Protestants, but is occupied by three Jews and six Catholics. Actually, Niel Gorsuch was raised Catholic and attended Catholic schools, but in recent years he has been attending an Episcopal church.

HOW THE SUPREME COURT WORKS

The Supreme Court's term runs from the first Monday in October through the end of June, for about nine months. Up to April they listen to arguments, usually scheduled for Monday, Tuesday, and Wednesday morning at 10 a.m. Then for the rest of the term they write their opinions. The Court hears about eighty cases a year. They decide by majority vote, and at least six justices must be present. The Supreme Court is passive in the sense that they do not go out and decide constitutional issues, but instead cases must be brought to the Court. And the Supreme Court will not hear a case unless they have the ability to grant a remedy and the person who brings the suit has *standing*, which means that person was directly harmed by the defendant who broke the law.

Oath of the Office: Upon taking office, each justice must swear or affirm to "administer justice without respect to persons, and do equal right to poor and rich, and that I will faithfully and impartially discharge and perform all the

John Roberts became the seventeenth chief justice in 2005.
©Rob Crandall/Shutterstock.com

duties incumbent upon [me] . . . under the Constitution and the laws of the United States. So help me God." This oath reflects the ideas embodied in "Lady Justice," the traditional statue of the personification of Justice. She is depicted wearing a blindfold, representing the idea that justice should be impartial and objective. And decisions should be made without regard to the wealth, gender, ethnicity, or political persuasion of the defendant and plaintiff.

Powers of the Chief Justice: The chief justice of the United States has no special powers granted by the Constitution, but over the years he has taken on certain duties and traditions. The chief justice is the head of the entire federal judiciary and retains special administrative duties associated with this office by congressional statute: he selects the law books for the Library of Congress, chooses FISA judges, and is a trustee of the Smithsonian Institute.

As one of the nine justices of the Supreme Court, he is only "first among equals." He has one vote just as the other eight justices do. But a good chief justice can shape the Court during his tenure, as exemplified by the unique quality of the "Marshall Court," "Warren Court," and "Rehnquist Court." How do they do this? Some chief justices have the ability to influence the other justices with their intellect and personality. And they strategically assign opinions, writing the most important ones themselves.

What Cases Reach the Supreme Court? Since the time of Chief Justice William Howard Taft and the Judiciary Act of 1925, the Court has had the power to pick which cases it will hear. This power allows the Court to set the legal agenda for the country. In the 2010–2011 term, the Court received 7,857 new petitions and issued seventy-eight opinions, about 1 percent.

So, what kind of cases does the Supreme Court decide to hear? They choose cases that deal with a "substantial federal issue" or an important question concerning the Constitution and the Bill of Rights. Each week the Court receives about 150 formal requests for a *writ of certiorari*: an order accepting a case for decision. The justices have a weekly conference, headed by the chief justice, to review the petitions screened by the law clerks. They discuss and then vote according to seniority. When four justices agree, the case is accepted. This is called the "rule of four."

The Role of Law Clerks: Each justice is allowed four law clerks who are usually recent graduates from leading law schools and who have clerked for a lower court. Each justice picks her own clerks and works closely with them throughout the term, often forming personal relationships. Clerks do legal research, help screen writs of certiorari, write summaries of cases, and assist justices in drafting their opinions. Some say the justices now rely too heavily on the clerks and as a result opinions are getting longer, containing more legal footnotes. As a whole, the Court has a staff of about 400.

Solicitor General: The **solicitor general (SG)** *represents the federal government before the Supreme Court.* Sometimes called the "tenth justice," the solicitor general has an office at the Supreme Court building and argues more cases than any other attorney before the Court each year. Because the federal government is often one of the litigants in impor-tant cases, attorneys in the Department of Justice and from other federal agencies participate in more than two-thirds of the Supreme Court cases. The solicitor general prepares petitions, writes amicus briefs, and files other important papers by the government in the Supreme Court. The solicitor general is an appointee of the president, but she is fairly independent from the White House. SGs are normally career attorneys with very high reputations. Associate Justice Elena Kagan was a former solicitor general.

Solicitor General (SG)

represents the federal government before the Supreme Court

SUPREME COURT OPINIONS

Justices form their opinions based on the written briefs and the oral arguments. Writing a good brief is the most important task of an attorney presenting her case to the Supreme Court. With a 15,000-word limit, the brief is mainly what the justices use to decide the case. Justice Thomas once estimated that oral arguments influence justices only about five or ten percent of the time. But oral arguments are very important, and highly stressful. Each attorney only has only thirty minutes, and the justices can jump in and ask questions on any topic, which they often do. For this reason attorneys may spend months preparing for this brief presentation. Afraid that it would tarnish the mystique and reputation of the Supreme Court, the Court does not allow oral arguments to be televised, but in recent years they have released audio recordings of important cases.

Amicus Briefs: *If somebody has a particular interest in a case or can provide important information, they can file a "friend of the court"* **amicus brief.** Individuals, interest groups, or government agencies often submit amicus briefs to express concerns or to provide more information about a case than would be expressed by the litigants. Special interest groups that are highly concerned about a particular issue might help pay for an attorney, provide research, or even hold mock court sessions to prepare the attorney for oral arguments. Prominent non-profit legal advocacy groups would include the American Civil Liberties Union, the Landmark Legal Foundation, the Pacific Legal foundation, and the American Center for Law and Justice. Indicating that the issue is important, the Court often takes a case when they see many amicus briefs. For example, in *McDonald v. Chicago* (2010), a case about gun control, the Court received thirty-three amicus briefs.

Lawyers only have thirty minutes to make their oral argument before the Supreme Court.
©Katherine Welles/Shutterstock.com

The Conference: During the second half of the Court's term, the justices meet on Wednesday and Friday for *conferences*: meetings presided over by the chief justice to discuss the cases. Having read the briefs and heard the oral arguments, most justices have already made up their minds by the time they attend the conference. The chief justice opens the meeting by delineating the facts of the case, summarizing both arguments, and discussing the constitutional issue in question. Then they go around the table, with each justice giving his or her opinion, in order of seniority. Some chief justices, such as William Rehnquist, were known to run very strict conference, while others, such as John Roberts, run more collegial meetings.

Opinions: Chief Justice John Marshall ended the English practice of *seriatim*, in which each justice issues a separate decision. Instead, Marshall began the practice of the Supreme Court issuing one legally binding majority opinion. Now, the Court issues three types of opinions. The **majority opinion** *is the official, legally binding ruling of the Court, backed by a majority of the justices.* The **dissenting opinion** *is issued by the minority of justices that disagrees with the majority opinion.* And the *concurring opinion* is an opinion written by a

Amicus Brief

if somebody has a particular interest in a case or can provide important information, they can file a "friend of the court" brief

Majority Opinion

is the official, legally binding ruling of the Court, backed by a majority of the justices

Dissenting Opinion

is issued by the minority of justices that disagrees with the majority opinion justice who agrees with the majority, but wishes to make another legal argument. At times the dissenting opinion could be quite scathing, providing an opportunity for the losing judges to criticize the majority. Over the history of the Supreme Court, some dissenting opinions have been the most famous, as in John Marshall Harlan's dissent in *Plessy,* in which he said the "Constitution should be color blind."

Adherence to Precedent: *In order to provide stability, uniformity, and clarity, the Supreme Court tries to abide by the precedents established by previous Courts, this principle is called* **stare decisis.** This is short for a Latin maxim, "to stand by decisions and not disturb the undisturbed." When deciding cases, judges look to past decisions in similar cases and try to adhere to principles that the Court has developed over the centuries. Such principles guide the lower courts and lawmakers. But over time, the Court will reverse itself as it develops a new understanding of an issue. Since 1789, the Supreme Court has reversed itself over 200 times.

Stare Decisis

in order to provide stability, uniformity, and clarity, the Supreme Court tries to abide by the precedents established by previous Courts

FINAL THOUGHTS

John Adams, in Article XXX of the Massachusetts Constitution, wrote that we must be a "government of laws, not men." To make this clear, the Framers placed in the Constitution the requirement that all government officers, including the president, Supreme Court justices, and members of Congress must make a pledge to uphold the Constitution. Yet the job of a judge is not so clear-cut. The Constitution consists of general statements and principles that are often difficult to apply to modern-day, real-life controversies. But even though the American people often disagree with particular Supreme Court rulings, as an institution the Court is highly respected. The people understand that without the Supreme Court upholding the rule of law, the whole system would fall apart.

NOTES

Adam Freedman. *The Naked Constitution: What the Founders Said and Why it Still Matters.* New York: Broadside Books, 2012.

Linda Greenhouse. *The US Supreme Court.* Oxford: Oxford University Press, 2012.

Alexander Hamilton, John Jay, and James Madison. *The Federalists.* Indianapolis: Liberty Fund, 2001.

Mark R. Levin. *Men in Black.* Washington: Regnery Publishing, 2005.

Michael Les Benedict. *The Blessings of Liberty: A Concise History of the Supreme Court.* Boston: Wadsworth, 2006.

The Heritage Guide to the Constitution: Washington, DC: The Heritage Foundation, 2005.

Alexis de Tocqueville. *Democracy in America.* Translated by George Lawrence. New York: Harper Collins, 1969.

Our American Government. Washington: US Government Printing Office, 2003 edition.

ESSAY QUESTIONS

1. How long is a federal judge's term, and how does this create judicial independence?
2. Outline John Marshall's reasoning in support of judicial review in *Marbury v. Madison*.
3. Compare liberal judicial philosophy with conservative judicial philosophy.
4. Describe how the judicial branch functions in the system of checks and balances.
5. Describe the majority opinion, concurring opinion, and dissenting opinion.

TERMS

Amicus Brief: _____

Appellate Jurisdiction: _____

Dissenting Opinion: _____

During Good Behavior: _____

Judicial Activism: _____

Judicial Restraint: _____

Judicial Review: _____

Loose Construction: _____

Majority Opinion: _____

Original Intent: _____

Solicitor General: _____

Stare Decisis: _____

Strict Construction: _____

UNIT FOUR

Political Process

CHAPTER 16

Who Are the American People and What Are Their Political Opinions?

TOPICS

► Demographic Sketch of America
► US Public's Decline in Political Knowledge
► Polling Public Opinion
► Political Socialization
► Red State versus Blue State America

LEARNING OBJECTIVES

When you finish reading this chapter, you will be able to:

1. Cite some basic demographics about Americans.
2. Discuss the elements of scientific polling.
3. List the major influences of political socialization.
4. Delineate the major social factors that indicate whether an individual is likely to vote Democratic or Republican.

WHO ARE THE AMERICAN PEOPLE?

America is a constantly changing and growing landscape. In the first census of 1790, America consisted of thirteen states on the eastern seaboard with a population of 3.9 million people. At that time, most Americans were farmers living in small towns. About 81 percent of the people were white and 19 percent black (of those, 98.5 percent, nearly 700,000, were slaves). A large majority of the white population came from western and northern Europe: mostly from Britain, Germany, Scandinavia, and France. Now America is the third largest country in the world with an extremely diverse population that speaks an estimated 131 languages. The following includes a demographic sketch of America today, and all this information is rife with political implications.

DEMOGRAPHIC SKETCH OF AMERICA

Geography: As of 2017, the US Census reports that the US population is 326,625,000. The six largest states are: California—38 million, Texas—26 million, New York—19.5 million, Florida—19 million, Pennsylvania—12.9 million, and Illinois—12.8 million. The three smallest states are: Vermont—685,000, North Dakota—683,000, and Wyoming—601,000. About 82 percent of the population lives in cities. The largest cities in America are: New York—18.3 million, Los Angeles—12.7 million, Chicago—9.1 million, and Miami—5.7 million.

Who are the American people?
©quinky/Shutterstock.com

Age: According to the *World Factbook*, the average age in America is thirty-seven years old. Twenty percent of the population is between 0–14 years old; 14% of the population is between 15–24; 41% of the population is between 25–54; 12% of the population is between 55–64; and 14% of the population is over 65.

Religion: According to an ABC poll conducted in July of 2017, 83% of Americans identify as Christian. And according to the 2017 Pew Religious Landscape Study, the religious makeup of America is as follows: Protestant—47%, Catholic—21%, Other Christians—3.3%, Jewish—1.9%, Muslim—0.9%, Buddhist—0.7%, Hindu—0.7%, Atheist—3.1%, Agnostic—4.0%, "Nothing in particular"—15.8%. And according to Gallup, 43% of Americans regularly attend church, while only 12% of British and 5% of Swiss people do.

Economy & Income: In 2014, the average household income was nearly $54,000. In 2007, Sociologist Leonard Beeghley divides America into five classes: 1% of Americans are <u>super rich</u> multi-millionaires; 5% are <u>rich</u> with net worths over $1 million; 46% are <u>middle-class</u> with men typically making on average $57,000 and women making 44,000; 40% to 45% are <u>working-class</u> with average incomes for men about $40,000 and for women $26,000; 12% are considered <u>poor</u> with incomes below the poverty line of $18,000 for a household.

Family: In 2010, the median age for marriage for men was 27 and for women was 26. In 2011, the Census Bureau reported married couples represent only 48% of all American households. Indicating the erosion of traditional marriage, this is the first time in American history that married couples were the minority. A more startling indication of the erosion of traditional marriage is the statistics about children born to unwed mothers. In 2014, a study sponsored by the University of Virginia found that 48% of first births are by unwed mothers. About 72% of white mothers are married, and 29% of black mothers are married.

Health: As of 2012, about 33% of the population is obese, 21% smoke, and 11% have diabetes. The average man weighs 195 pounds and is 5 feet 9 inches. The average woman weighs 165 pounds and is 5 feet 4 inches. The average man lives to 76, and the average woman lives to 81.

Education: In 2009, 87% of Americans graduated from High school, 56% attended some college, 39% have a bachelor's degree, 8% have a master's degree, and 3% have a doctorate.

Race & Ethnicity: According to a 2016 US Census report, the racial and ethnic composition of America is as follows: White—77%, Hispanic or Latino—18%, Black—13%, Asian—5.7%, American Indian—1.3%, and Mixed race—2.6%. About 13% of the population is foreign born.

Compared to many other countries, America is ethnically diverse, especially in the cities.
©Daxiao Productions/Shutterstock.com

Gay: In a 2012 Gallup survey of 121,000 people, 3.4% said "yes" when asked to identify as lesbian, bisexual, gay, or transgender (LBGT). This comports with a 2004–2008 study by Gary Gates of the Williams Institute that concluded 3.8% of the American population is LBGT.

US PUBLIC'S DECLINE IN POLITICAL KNOWLEDGE

Since around 1970, the American public has become more ignorant of the basic facts of American government and history. Fewer people read books and newspapers. Reading scores on the SAT have steadily declined since 1973. Ironically, the public's knowledge of history and government has declined just as TV and the personal computer were introduced to the home, two amazing technologies that originally promised to bring a world of knowledge to each youngster. The American public, however, seems to be very knowledgeable about celebrities and popular culture.

But this lack of knowledge about US history and government raises a fundamental question: if the American people are so ignorant, what does this mean for our democracy? This has actually been the subject of debate since the founding of our nation, and there are two main views: one pessimistic and the other optimistic.

Pessimistic View about the Public's Knowledge: Americans are woefully ignorant of US political institutions and history. A 2017 study by the Annenberg Public Policy Center showed that only 25% of Americans can name all three branches of government. And 60% incorrectly think the president can declare war. A 2015 study by the ACTA revealed that college students are not much better than the general public, perhaps worse! Of recent college grads, 80% did not know that James Madison was the primary author of the Constitution, and 80% did not know what the Emancipation Proclamation did. Also, 50% did not know that George Washington led the Continental Army at Yorktown. Polls like these have caused some people to wonder if Americans today are equipped to handle the responsibility to vote.

Radio talk show host Rush Limbaugh routinely calls the American electorate "low information voters." Limbaugh is afraid that the average voter today lacks the intellectual rigor and historical knowledge needed to solve the problems facing the nation today. For example, our national debt is a staggering $20 trillion, but people still vote for more government spending.

Optimistic View: Many of the Framers expressed doubts similar to those expressed by Limbaugh, openly wondering whether the American people have the knowledge and virtue to be responsible voters. James Madison, on the other hand, believed that for the big questions of the day, the public will make the right decisions. Madison believed in the innate wisdom of the majority—that the democratic system will work because in the long run, for

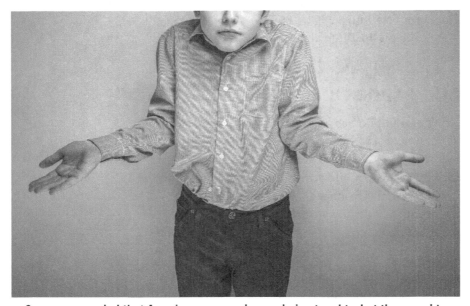

Some are worried that Americans are no longer being taught what they need to know in order to be good citizens and voters.
©maxim ibragimov/Shutterstock.com

the most important questions, the intrinsic genius of the American people will prevail. Even though many Americans do not have a detailed understanding of the issues, they will eventually arrive at the right conclusions. Put another way, the only thing scarier than trusting the "common man" is to trust the educated elites! William F. Buckley once said that he would rather be governed by the first hundred people in the phone book than a hundred Harvard professors. So the debate continues.

POLLING PUBLIC OPINION

In the months leading up to the 2016 election, it seemed that every night newscasters breathlessly reported which candidate was up or down in the polls. Why do polls play such a prominent role in politics today? This is especially troubling when we know how ill-informed the public is. Instead of reporting on the issues and providing the electorate with the necessary information to make an informed vote, the press obsessively provides poll results.

Polling is big business. Collectively, American politicians spend $1 billion a year on polls. There use to be just a few major polling companies, such as Gallup and Harris, but now there are dozens: Pew Research Center, Rasmussen Reports, Mason-Dixon, PPP, Quinnipiac, Ipsos/Reuters, and all the major networks and newspaper companies also conduct polls.

Why are people so interested in polls? A **public opinion poll** *is a scientific survey of public opinion at a point in time.* **Public opinion** *are the views held by the population about issues, individuals, and institutions.* Technically, polls measure public opinion *at that time* the poll is taken. It is simply a snapshot of current views. But the reason people are so interested in polls is that they can help tell the future. Nothing is more intriguing to the human mind than knowledge of the future. If polls show, for example, that Trump is consistently leading in the polls during the months leading up to the election, then this indicates that he will more likely win the election. Of course, anything can happen before an election.

Elements of Scientific Polling: If they follow the correct procedures, opinion polls can be quite accurate. First, they must select the population they are targeting for the survey: the **population** *is the target group of people the poll attempts to gauge.* The population could be one congressional district, registered America voters, or single women who buy perfume. Second, the polling company must select a **random sample** of that population.

Public Opinion Poll

a scientific survey of public opinion at a point in time

Public Opinion

are the views held by the population about issues, individuals, and institutions

Population

is the target group of people the poll attempts to gauge

Random Sample

a sample is truly random only if every person in that population has an equal chance of being selected for an opinion poll

If done properly, polls can accurately reveal what people think about candidates and issues.
©Marish/Shutterstock.com

A sample *is truly random only if every person in that population has an equal chance of being selected*. And third, the polling company must determine what information they need and construct a neutral question. **Neutral questions** *are non-biased and non-leading questions that seek true and honest responses*.

If everything is done correctly, there is still a **margin of error** (or *sampling error*), usually in the range of + or – 3 percent. But sometimes they are off by more than the margin of error. In the midterm elections of 2014, for example, almost all the polls showed that the battleground Senate races were nearly tied between the Democratic and Republican candidates. But on Election Day, the Republicans won by large margins, picking up a historic nine Senate seats. And in 2016, almost all the polls predicted that Hillary Clinton would win the presidency. So it is always wise to cautiously read the opinion polls.

Intensity, Latency, and Salience: A survey that simply reports that a candidate is ahead by five points does not tell the whole story. Skilled pollsters and campaign managers look for subtle changes inside the numbers. They look for *intensity*: what percentage of the population feels strongly about the issue or candidate? They look for *latency*: is public opinion moving in a certain direction that has not yet been made obvious? Good politicians can capitalize on latency and help shape public opinion which has not fully crystallized yet. And they look for *salience*: to what degree do people think this issue is relevant to them? Most people are not concerned with national political issues unless they see it affecting their own lives. So the best pollsters and campaign managers can see slight trends in the polling numbers and this is why their expertise is so valuable to politicians.

Approval Ratings: One poll that has a particular influence on politics is the presidential approval rating, usually revealed in tracking polls. A **tracking poll** *measures public opinion over a long period of time, perhaps even decades*. Gallop was the first to conduct a presidential approval tracking poll by asking the same question every week: "do you approve or disapprove of the job the president is doing." As of October 2017, President Trump's approval rating on the Rasmussen tracking poll is 45 percent. Typically, presidents try to keep their numbers above 50 percent. Another influential tracking poll is the "right direction/wrong direction" poll. For decades polling companies have asked the public: "Do you think the nation is moving in the right direction or wrong direction?" This tracking poll has proven to be a good measure of public optimism. Today, Rasmussen reports that 65 percent of Americans think we are heading in the wrong direction, revealing a high degree of pessimism.

Push Polls: Surveys that attempt to skew public opinion by asking a biased question are called *push polls*. For example, an anti-Obama interest group might pay for a survey that asks people if they "support Obama's health care

Neutral Questions

non-biased and non-leading questions that seek true and honest responses in opinion polls

Margin of Error

the sampling error of an opinion poll

Tracking Poll

a survey that measures public opinion over a long period of time, perhaps even decades

Sometimes polls are used not to discover public opinion but to influence it.
©totallypic/Shutterstock.com

reforms that increase tedious paperwork and fees." This biased question will surely get high negatives. Then the interest group will try to get newspapers to publish the results, perhaps with the headline: "A majority of American oppose Obamacare." And a pro-Obama interest group might survey Americans by asking, "Do you approve of Obama's health care reforms that forbid companies from excluding people with preexisting medical conditions?" This question will probably get high approvals. Then the interest group will try to get newspapers to publish this headline: "A majority of American support the president's plan." So it is important to be aware that partisan groups use polls to try to influence public opinion.

Problems with polls: If you look at the various polls, you will notice that they all report slightly different results. Before the 2012 election, many polls predicted that Romney would win—they were wrong. This demonstrates the difficulties of conducting an accurate poll, especially in a very close election. One problem is the cell phone. About 30 percent of the population no longer uses a land-line phone, yet most polls still rely heavily on traditional phones. Most people have Caller ID and will not pick up a phone unless they know the caller. What time of day the poll is conducted may also skew the results: people at home at 11 a.m. might have different views than people home at 6 p.m.

A further difficulty is that some people do not tell the truth in polls, but instead say only what they think they should say. For example, people always exaggerate how much they give to charity. So, polls about charitable giving are often skewed. Considering the difficulties pollsters face, some political scientists rely only on an average of all major polls, such as the average reported in Real Clear Politics.

POLITICAL SOCIALIZATION

Where do we get our political beliefs? *We develop our political orientation and values as we grow up. This process is called* **political socialization**. Just as we learn other things, like religion, we also get our political beliefs primarily from our parents. Besides our parents, we learn political values from our extended family, neighbors, school, media, and peers. Part of political socialization is *nationalism*—the understanding of the values and history of a country. We learn these things by symbolic and patriotic rituals, such as watching a Fourth of July parade or visiting the Jefferson Memorial. We learn many values and political beliefs as children or adolescents, but political socialization continues over the life span of an individual. Once we form our worldview, each political issue and candidate is filtered through this prism.

Family: The primary influence on political socialization are the parents, but members of the extended family can also have an impact. A grandfather or aunt who likes to talk politics can have a big influence on a youngster. There are several psychological reasons why family is so influential. First, what we learn first about something usually sets the way we think about it. The first

Political Socialization

the process by which people develop their political orientation and values as they grow up

Children learn a lot from their parents, including political values.
©Evgeny Atamanenko/Shutterstock.com

thing we learn about any topic usually sticks with us the longest. Second, children learn by imitating or mirroring their parents. Children automatically pick up many subtle remarks and behaviors from their parents. For example, if a mother talks about a particular president with a strained voice, the child will internalize that that president is bad.

The average American child usually shows political interest by about ten years of age, and by high school he or she may have well developed political beliefs. Just as children learn to identify with one religion or no religion from their parents, children learn to identify with one political party or no party. Political identity is strongest when both parents have the same party identity and when they discuss politics with their children, perhaps at the dinner table. Most young adults share the same party identity as their parents: children of Republicans will vote Republican, and children of Democrats will vote Democratic. Besides political values, children also learn other political *behavior* from their parents. If the parents read newspapers, watch the news, vote, participate in local events, then the child will likely do the same when he or she grows up.

School: The second biggest influence in the socializing of people is school. Part of the purpose of school is to prepare children to be good citizens. And at an early age, schoolchildren absorb the values and attitudes disseminated at school by their teachers and administrators. Some schools have patriotic pledges and assemblies. Children learn about American heroes and the Founding Fathers. From kindergarten to college, most Americans pick up attitudes favorable of American democracy. Compared to other countries, a high percentage of young Americans think their country is the best. Also, things like student elections teach democracy. Beyond internalizing democratic values and patriotism, some students may be influenced by the political beliefs of an influential teacher.

Peers and Popular Culture: As every parent knows, children are highly influenced by their friends. If a kid is ridiculed for his or her political beliefs by other kids, this can have a profound impact. Fortunately, in contemporary America, if a child expresses racist remarks, he or she will probably be censored by their peers. Tolerance and environmentalism are two values that are heavily praised in popular culture today. But other political views are also subtlety and explicitly expressed in the media, including in television, movies, radio, music, and on social media. Over time, these can help shape the political views of the viewer.

RED STATE VERSUS BLUE STATE AMERICA

Since children internalize the political values of their parents, extended family, school, and peers, it is logical that people growing up in different regions of America would have different political views. It is common knowledge that people living in the South or in small towns are more conservative than people living in big cities. But several other factors besides geography contribute to political socialization. Today, political scientists can accurately predict if a person is likely to vote Democratic (more liberal) or Republican (more conservative) by learning just a few details about that person's life. This is Red State/Blue State America. People with certain lifestyles, ethnicities, and incomes vote Democratic (Blue states), and those with different demographics vote Republican (Red States).

Income: Economic status plays a big part in political socialization. On average, people with less money tend to vote for the Democrats, and those that make more money tend to vote for the Republicans. Why? Democrats believe in large government to provide more public services in order to achieve greater social equality. Republicans, on the other hand, tend to believe in reducing federal spending on government programs, lowering taxes, and fostering greater individual responsibility. If somebody has a lot of money, then they use fewer government programs and feel over-taxed. Lower income people do not pay any federal income tax, so they will not resonate with the Republican call for lower taxes. In 2008, 60 percent of people making less than $50,000 a year voted for Obama and only 38 percent for Romney. On the other hand, the wealthiest zip codes in America—the elite cities such as Beverly Hills, San Francisco, and Manhattan—are heavily Democratic.

Education: People with a high school diploma or less tend to vote for Democrats. People with a college degree are more likely to vote Republican. But those with higher degrees, such as a master's or doctor's degree, tend to vote for Democrats. Perhaps this is because colleges tend to be liberal institutions, and so people that spend a lot of time there become more liberal. In 2012, 64 percent of people with no high school voted for Obama, 55 percent of people with postgraduate degrees voted for Obama. In 2016, Trump was able to reverse this trend for Republicans and got the vote of 51 percent of people with a high school degree or less, compared to 46 percent for Clinton.

Region: In America, region plays a powerful role in political socialization. Red States that consistently vote for Republicans are located in the South and Midwest. While Blue States that consistently vote for Democrats are in the Northeast and West coast. In addition, people that live in small towns vote for Republicans, and those that live in big cities for Democrats. Even a Blue State like California is divided. The big California cities along the coast, such as San Francisco, Santa Barbara, Los Angeles, and San Diego vote Democrat. But the small towns in the inland, farming regions, such as Modesto, Fairfield, and Bakersfield, vote Republican. In 2012, 69 percent of people living in a community with over 500,000 people voted for Obama, while 56 percent of people living in communities with under 50,000 voted for Romney. In 2016, Trump was able to attract even more small town voters: 61 percent for Trump, and 34 percent for Clinton.

Race and Ethnicity: Since the 1920s, immigrants, Catholics, Jews, and ethnic minorities have tended to vote for the Democrats, while white Protestants vote for the Republicans. Before the New Deal in the 1930s, blacks voted for the Republicans, the party of Abraham Lincoln. But ever since Franklin Roosevelt created the welfare state, blacks have been the most loyal constituents of the Democratic Party. In 1964, 94 percent of blacks voted for the Democratic candidate Lyndon Johnson. Incidentally, Johnson was the last Democratic presidential candidate to win the majority of the white vote. In 2008, Obama received 95 percent of the black vote; McCain got only 4 percent. In 2012, Romney improved things slightly and got 6 percent of the black vote. In recent years, other ethnic minorities have also voted Democratic. In 2012, 71 percent of Hispanics and 73 percent of Asians voted for Obama. In 2016, Trump did better than McCain and Romney and got 8 percent of the black vote.

Religion: Another factor that influences political socialization is religion. Evangelical Protestants played a strong role in the Reagan Revolution of 1980, and they still vote heavily Republican. In 2012, Protestants who attend church

By knowing a few facts about somebody, such as their race, income, or religion, political scientists can predict if that person is likely to vote Republican or Democratic.
©vectorfusionart/Shutterstock.com

every week accounted for one of Romney's strongest supporters—70 percent. In 2016, 80 percent of white, evangelical Christians voted for Trump.

Traditionally, Catholics tended to vote for the Democrats, especially Irish Catholics. But in recent years they have become evenly split. In 2012, only 50 percent of Catholics voted for Obama, who is strongly pro-choice. Jews in America tend to live in large cities and are very liberal. In 2012, 69 percent of Jews voted for Obama. Some political pundits predicted that because of Obama's lukewarm support for Israel, Obama would lose the Jewish vote, but Jews remain loyal to the Democrats. In general, people that attend church more often vote for Republicans, and secular people vote for Democrats. In 2012, people that attend church more than once a week voted 63 percent for Romney, and people that never attend church voted 69 percent for Obama.

Gender: Women are much more likely to vote for Democratic presidents, especially young, single women. Since the 1980s, about 6 to 7 percent more women vote for Democrats. Women tend to favor more government pro-grams, support affirmative action, oppose military spending, and are against the death penalty—all liberal positions. In 2012, Obama got 55 percent of the women's vote. In 2016, everybody assumed that Hillary Clinton, the first woman to run for president for a major party, would dramatically attract women to her campaign. But this did not happen. Clinton only got 54 percent of the women vote, less than Obama! By the way, the most loyal group to the

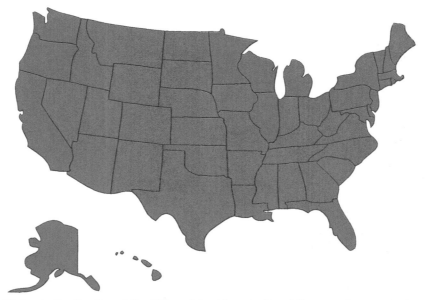

States in the South and the Midwest tend to vote Republican, and states in the Northeast and West coast tend to vote Democratic.

©Adam Tinney/Shutterstock.com

Democratic Party are black women: 89 percent voted for Clinton, and 96 percent voted for Obama.

Other Factors: There are several other factors that influence voting patterns. Young people tend to vote for Democrats. In 2012, Obama won 60 percent of those between eighteen and twenty-nine years of age. But as people grow older, especially in middle age, people vote for Republicans. People who are married with children vote more for Republicans. Gays and lesbians vote heavily for Democrats. People with military backgrounds vote Republican. Government employees and union workers vote heavily for Democrats. And small business owners vote for Republicans.

FINAL THOUGHTS

During the last few presidential elections, pollsters have conducting **exit polls**: *Surveys of voters taken right after they exited the voting booths, collecting data about the voters' opinions and demographics.* The exit polls for the 2012 election are summarized below, reinforcing our Red State/Blue State profiles.

Blue State Profile: *Due to the demographic makeup of the state or region*, **blue states** *consistently vote for Democrats.* Blue state voters tend to be more dependent on the government and have a favorable view of big government. Poor people, single women, young people, government employees, and liberals vote for the Democratic Party. Blacks, other ethnic minorities, recent immigrants, and religious minorities also vote Democratic. Secular people who live in the big cities vote for the Democrats. And union workers, teachers, lawyers, under educated and over educated people vote Democratic.

In 2012, these were Obama's most supportive groups: black women (96%), blacks (93%), people who agreed that "government should do more" (81%), agreed that "abortion should always be legal" (76%), Asian (73%), Latino (71%), Jews (69%), no high school (64%), never attends church (62%), young people (60%), less than $50,000 incomes (60%).

Red State Profile: *Due to the demographic makeup of the state or region*, **red states** *consistently vote for Republicans.* In general, people less dependent on the government and opposed to big government vote Republican. People with high incomes, white males, small business owners, older people, and conservatives are registered Republicans. Religious people living in small towns and in the South vote Republican, especially white Protestants. Married people with children, military vets, and people paying high taxes vote for the Republican Party.

In 2012, these were Romney's most loyal groups: people whose top priority was to reduce the national debt (95%), people who identified as pro-life

Exit Polls

surveys of voters taken right after they exited the voting booths, collecting data about the voters' opinions and demographics

Blue States

due to the demographic makeup of the state or region, blue states consistently vote for Democrats

Red States

due to the demographic makeup of the state or region, red states consistently vote for Republicans

(79%), born-again Christians (78%), people who agreed that "government is doing too much" (74%), white Protestants (69%), white men (62%), white Catholics (59%), older than 65 (56%), making more than $100,000 (54%), and college graduates (51%).

In 2016, Donald Trump ran as an unorthodox Republican, indeed much of the time he was criticizing establishment Republicans, so his poll numbers are slightly different than recent Republicans. The areas where he was strongest were: Conservatives (81%), White evangelicals (80%), those that said he will bring about needed change (80%), White non-college graduates (66%), those that said immigration was their number one issue (64%), served in the military (60%), those that live in a small town (61%), and married men (57%).

NOTES

Most of the demographic information came from 2010 census report: www.census.gov and the World Factbook: www.cia.gov.

The 2012 exit poll information came from: *Barack Obama and the New America: The 2012 Election and the Changing Face of Politics*. Edited by Larry J. Sabato. New York: Rowman & Littlefield Publishers, 2013.

The information about religion in America came from various surveys taken by Pew Research Center: www.pewresearchcenter.org and Gallup: gallup.com.

Some of the information about income came from Tami Luhby. "Household Income is on the rise... finally!" *Money*, Aug 20, 2014; Leonard Beeghley. *The Structure of Social Stratification in the United States*, 5th ed. New York: Pearson, 2007.

The 2016 exit poll information came from the "2016 Election Exit Polls" published by the *Washington Post*.

The information about the ignorance of the American people came from: Devin Dweyer. "United States of Ignorants? Americans Don't Know Constitution, Survey." *ABC News*, March 24, 2011; Survey by the American Council of Trustees and Alumni, "Historical Literacy," Roosevelt Awareness Survey, Sept 2014 and D-Day Awareness Survey, June 2014.

Michael Baron. *The New Americans: How the Melting Pot Can Work Again*. New York: Regnery, 2006.

Andrew Gelman. *Red State, Blue State, Rich State, Poor State*. Princeton: Princeton University Press, 2008.

US Census Bureau report: "Education Attainment in the United States," Jan 29, 2015.

ESSAY QUESTIONS

1. What is the age, religious, and racial makeup of Americans?
2. What are the elements of modern scientific polling?
3. Explain why family and school play such a major part in political socialization.
4. Describe the effect of income, region, and religion on political socialization.
5. Describe what social groups typically vote Democratic (blue state) or Republican (red state).

TERMS

Blue State: _____

Exit Polls: _____

Margin of Error: _____

Neutral Question: _____

Political Socialization: _____

Population: _____

Public Opinion: _____

Public Opinion Polls: _____

Random Sample: _____

Red State: _____

Tracking Poll: _____

CHAPTER 17

How Are American Elections Conducted?

TOPICS

- ▶ Expansion of the Franchise
- ▶ Prominent Features of US Elections
- ▶ Voter Turnout
- ▶ The Electoral College

LEARNING OBJECTIVES

When you finish reading this chapter, you will be able to:

1. Outline the expansion of the right to vote in American history.
2. Compare the primary with the general election.
3. Define turnout and explain several reasons why turnout is low.
4. Describe how the Electoral College selects a president.

HOW ARE ELECTIONS CONDUCTED IN AMERICA?

Elections are the primary characteristic of a democracy: without free, fair, and regular elections, a country cannot claim to be a democracy. America has had a 230-year history of regular elections and peaceful transitions of power. Through elections, the people manifest their will and choose the candidates that they think will implement the best policies. In the past, the political parties asserted more control over the election process, but Americans have always focused on the personality of the individual candidate. In early American history, only white adult males with property could vote. Today, nearly all citizens over the age of eighteen are enfranchised. America conducts nearly twice as many elections as other democracies. But perhaps because there are so many elections, a relatively high percentage of Americans do not vote.

EXPANSION OF THE FRANCHISE

Originally the Constitution left it to the states to determine who can vote. Most states required that a citizen owned land in order to vote. But because land was so cheap and available, America had one of the highest percentages of eligible voters compared to other countries. Still, less than half the population had the franchise, which would not be considered very democratic today. *Suffrage* and *franchise* are terms that mean the right to vote. Throughout American history, more and more people fought for suffrage through the democratic process.

Early Republic: After the Constitution was ratified, almost all the states set a *property qualification* in order to vote, meaning that one had to prove that he owned a certain number of acres of land in order to get the privilege to vote. People believed at the time that only a person with a stake in society should vote. So, for the first forty years of America, mostly white men over the age of twenty-one who owned property could vote. Then during the Jacksonian Era, with its celebration of the "common man," all states got rid of the property qualifications. So by the end of the 1820s white men, rich and poor, gained universal suffrage.

Blacks Get the Franchise: At the time of the adoption of the Constitution, five states granted free black men with property the right to vote. But conditions worsened. By 1858, only two states offered full black suffrage. The Civil War resulted in the emancipation of four million slaves. Ratified in 1870, the **15th Amendment** *prohibited the states from denying people the right to vote on account of race, color, or previous condition of servitude* (if they were previously a slave). But in what became known as the Jim Crow Era, Southern states continued to restrict black voting through several nefarious mechanisms, such as the literacy test, the white primary, and the **poll tax**: a *tax to register to vote designed to discourage the black franchise*. At this time most blacks were poor sharecroppers who could not read or afford to pay a fee to vote.

It took nearly a hundred years after the Civil War for these Jim Crow laws to be eradicated. Southerners said the Democratic Party was a private club and therefore they had the right to deny membership to whomever they wished, including blacks. Initially, the Supreme Court agreed with this, but then in *Smith v. Allwright* (1944) the Court reversed itself and declared the all-white primary unconstitutional. In 1964, the 24th Amendment outlawed the poll tax. The **Voting Rights Act of 1965** *made it a federal crime for state officials to*

15th Amendment

prohibited the states from denying people the right to vote on account of race, color, or previous condition of servitude

Poll Tax

a tax to register to vote designed to discourage the black franchise

Voting Rights Act of 1965

made it a federal crime for state officials to discriminate at the voting booth and gave the federal government many tools to enforce the act

Women won the right to vote with the passage of the 19th Amendment in 1920.
©Everett Historical/Shutterstock.com

discriminate at the voting booth and gave the federal government many tools to enforce the act.

Women and Young People Get the Franchise: In 1869, Wyoming became the first place anywhere in the world to grant women the franchise. After this, several Western states allowed women to vote in state and local elections. But it was not until 1920, with the ratification of the **19th Amendment,** that *women got the right to vote in all the states and in national elections.* During the Vietnam War in the late 1960s and early 1970s, thousands of young people protested the war and the draft. They argued that if an eighteen-year-old could be drafted by the government, then he should have the right to vote. In 1971 the *26th Amendment* was ratified, lowering the voting age to eighteen.

Remaining Restrictions on Voting: Today, nearly all adult Americans can vote, but there are still several restrictions to the franchise. A voter must be a US citizen. Voters must register. Most states require registration thirty days before an election in order to reduce fraud and multiple voting. Yet, this inhibits a certain percentage of people from voting. Felons who have committed serious crimes also lose the right to vote. People in prisons or mental institutions are usually banned from voting. And most states and countries require a citizen to live in the area for at least thirty days before they could vote. Recently, several states require a citizen to show a photo ID when voting. Proponents of a photo ID say that it is needed to reduce fraud and corruption; opponents argue that these laws are designed to reduce black turnout.

19th Amendment

women got the right to vote in all the states and in national elections

PROMINENT FEATURES OF US ELECTIONS

The Constitution says that the states shall decide the time, place, and manner of holding elections for members of Congress and the President, but that Congress retains the right to alter these election laws. At first, the states held elections in a jumble of different times. To reduce the confusion, in 1845 Congress finally stepped in and set elections for the first Tuesday of November in all states.

Why Tuesday? Of course Sunday, the Sabbath, was out. And because of slow transportation in the age of buggies, Saturday and Monday might interfere with the Sabbath. Wednesday was also out because it was the traditional market day for farmers. So, they settled on Tuesday. This also established the tradition of *fixed elections:* In America, elections are conducted according to a fixed or unchanging calendar. No matter what, even in the middle of the Civil War or WWII, America holds presidential and congressional elections every four and two years, respectively.

Primary and General Elections: Elections in America consist of a two-step process. First, in the **primary** *the voters select the candidate to represent the party in the general election.* Second, in the **general election** *the voters select the person who will actually fill the seat of office in the government.* During the Progressive Era, from about 1900 to 1920, political reformers sought to root

Primary

the voters select the candidate to represent the party in the general election

General Election

the voters select the person who will actually fill the seat of office in the government

In the 2016 presidential primaries, thirteen major candidates ran to win the Republican nomination.
©Joseph Sohm/Shutterstock.com

out political corruption by making elections more democratic. They created the primary to take power away from corrupt party bosses.

Closed and Open Primaries: In most countries, party leaders select their candidates to represent the party in the general election. Progressives in America, however, created the primary, giving the people the power to select the party candidate. Today, there are two types of primaries. **Closed primaries** *only allow registered party members to vote for candidates of that party.* **Open primaries** *allow people to vote for any candidate, regardless of what party they are registered as.* Open primaries contradict the original reason for primaries—for party members to select *their* candidate for the general election. But in recent years party loyalty has weakened as more people identify as independents. But an open primary can lead to *crossover voting.* In the 2008 primaries, thousands of Texas Republicans (Texas essentially has an open primary) crossed over and voted for Hillary Clinton as Democrats in order to weaken Barack Obama.

Some states require the winner of the primary to have a majority of the vote, otherwise there will be a *runoff:* the top candidates in a primary must have another election, with the winner getting more than 50 percent of the vote. After the primaries, there are usually two candidates: one representing the Democrats and one representing the Republicans. But in many local elections candidates run as non-partisan (another Progressive reform) and thus the voters do not know the candidate's party affiliation. Also, several third party candidates typically run for office, although they usually get a small percentage of the vote.

Initiative and Recall: Progressives instituted other ways to infuse direct democracy into the American system. Twenty states have the *recall,* making it possible for the people to fire elected officials without waiting for the next election. Surprisingly, this seldom happens. Only two governors in history have been recalled. And twenty-four states have the **initiative,** *a ballot measure which allows citizens the ability to craft their own laws.* In 2012, Colorado through an initiative, legalized marijuana. Usually, 5 to 10 percent of the population must sign a petition to place an initiative on the ballot. Lastly, twenty-three states have the *referendum,* allowing the people to vote on a policy submitted by the elected politicians. Often these are known as a "proposition." They are more popular in the Western states.

Debate on Initiative and Referendum: Rejecting the historic instability of direct democracy, the Framers created a republic. The fundamental idea behind a republic is that because the voters do not possess the knowledge, experience, and virtue to make complicated laws and run the government, the people vote for representatives to do these things. Progressive reforms,

Closed Primaries

only allow registered party members to vote for candidates of that party

Open Primaries

allow people to vote for any candidate, regardless of what party they are registered as

Initiative

a ballot measure which allows citizens the ability to craft their own laws however, allow more direct democracy into our system. People who support the initiative and referendum say it gives the people more say in their government, allowing it to reflect the changing values of society. Opponents say it makes governing more difficult to manage, especially in budgetary matters. For example, they often blame California's budget woes on initiatives that approved government programs without allocating revenue to fund them.

Registration: Another feature of American elections is registration. Registration is designed to reduce voter fraud by making the voter show proper residency papers. It was also designed to reduce multiple voting. In the 1800s each party printed up their own colored ballot and campaigners persuaded people to drop it in a ballot box, often in a saloon under public pressure. During the Progressive era America switched to the **Australian ballot**, *a ballot printed by the state, showing the candidates from both parties, and submitted in a private voting booth.* Today, six states allow same day voting registration. But most other states have a thirty day closing date before the election. Voter registration puts more responsibility on the voter to anticipate the election and take steps to register.

Motor Voter: The so called "motor voter law" made it easier for people to register. In 1993, Democrat president Bill Clinton signed the National Voter Registration Act allowing people to register to vote when they renew their driver's license. This law also allowed welfare offices, schools, and public offices to be used for registration. As a result of this law, registration increased by 5–9 percent, especially for independents. Republicans opposed this law because they assumed it would encourage more young and poor people to vote, groups that tend to vote for the Democrats.

Australian Ballot

a ballot printed by the state, showing the candidates from both parties, and submitted in a private voting booth

Turnout

the percentage of eligible voters who actually cast a ballot in an election

VOTER TURNOUT

In the 1800s, nearly 80 percent of eligible voters came out to vote in presidential elections. But in recent decades, just over half of eligible voters actually cast a ballot on Election Day. Why has voter participation decreased? Is this a sign of some sort of malady in America today? When a high percentage of the population votes, this indicates that the citizens are engaged and feel connected to their country. And when turnout is very low, this indicates that people are alienated from the political process. This section will define voter turnout, provide some historical perspective, and discuss whether turnout in America is at a healthy level.

Turnout: *The percentage of eligible voters who actually cast a ballot in an election is called* **turnout.** For the most part, in America the pool of eligible voters is every citizen eighteen years and older. For the last several years, turnout in America has been rather consistent. For presidential elections, turnout

In the 2016 presidential election, turnout was 60%.
©Brad McPherson/Shutterstock.com

has been between 55% and just over 60%. In 2008 and 2012, Obama's first and second elections, turnout was 62% and 58%, respectively. In 2016, when Trump was elected, turnout was 60%. For the mid-term congressional elections, turnout is usually around 40%. And for local and municipal elections, turnout can be as low as 5% to 15%, meaning local elections can be decided by a few hundred people. And for local and municipal elections, turnout can be as low as 5% to 15%.

Who Votes? Many factors combine to predict higher voter turnout for an individual. If somebody is highly knowledgeable and interested in politics, they will more likely vote. Likewise, people with little knowledge or interest in politics do not vote—which is probably a good thing! Partisanship is another factor. Self-described liberals or conservatives are highly likely to vote, and moderates are less likely to vote.

But several sociological factors also determine turnout. The primary factor is education. The more years of school one completes, the more likely he or she will vote. Regardless of race, ethnicity, income, or age, education is the strongest single factor for turnout. Second, the older a person is, the more likely he or she will vote. Only about 30 percent of young people vote. And people with high incomes vote more than people with low incomes. In the past, for a variety of social and legal reasons, women and blacks voted less than white males. But in recent years women and black turnout have been higher than that of white males. Hispanic turnout, however, is still low. Representing

13 percent of the population, when the Hispanic turnout increases, they will gain tremendous political clout.

Why Don't People Vote? There are many reasons why people do not vote. They are not interested in politics. They do not feel their vote counts. They feel things are basically okay. There are too many elections and feel fatigued by politics. They are interested in other things. They feel that both parties are the same and nothing will ever change. They are too busy. They do not feel a strong connection with either political party. These are all reasons people give for why they do not vote. If people are too busy to vote, then the recent expansion of *early voting* and *mail-in voting* should help. And indeed turnout is slightly up since these new voting methods have been introduced.

Is Low Turnout a Problem? Some say no. They say that it is good that only voters with knowledge and political interest vote. We do not want to force an uninformed voter into the voting booth. And it is a sign of general contentment. If the people were upset, they would come out in large numbers. On the other hand, some argue that low turnout is a serious problem. When so many people express feelings of apathy, disengagement, cynicism, and indifference, it indicates some sort of social malady.

This debate on increasing voter turnout is colored by political considerations. Conservatives tend to say that voting is a civic responsibility. People, out of a sense of patriotic duty, should make the effort to vote. Conservatives say that 60 percent turnout for presidential elections is a high enough number to make our elections legitimate. Democrats, on the other hand, tend to support get-out-the-vote initiatives because the demographics of people that do not vote (young, low income, less educated, minorities) are also the demographics of people who tend to vote for the Democrats. So, Democrats have a direct political motive to increase voter turnout beyond mere social concern.

THE ELECTORAL COLLEGE

On Election Day, the typical voter assumes it is a one-person/one-vote election in which the winner becomes president after he received the most votes in the country. The reality of American presidential elections and the Electoral College is far more complicated. Technically, on Election Day each voter is selecting either a Democratic or Republican slate of electors representing his or her state. Then five weeks after the election, the Electoral College actually votes for the candidate in their respective state capitals and send the results to the US Senate. On January 6, the vice president officially presides over the Senate and counts the Electoral College ballots. This is the day that the winner of the presidential election is officially announced.

The Electoral College: So, what exactly is the Electoral College? *The procedure by which the US president is elected by winning a majority of the 538 electors in a state by state vote is the* **Electoral College**. Each state gets a number of electors equal to the number of their senators and representatives in Congress. All states have two senators, but representatives are apportioned to a state based on the census which counts the state population every ten years. So Texas, a state with a large population, has thirty-eight electors. And Virginia, a state with a smaller population, has thirteen electors. Washington DC, although not a state, also gets three electors. Today there are 538 total electors and 270 are needed to win a majority, and thus the election.

In all states but Nebraska and Maine, *the candidate who wins the plurality of the state's popular vote wins ALL the electors—***winner-take-all**. As we will learn in Chapter 19, the winner-take-all rule in the Electoral College maintains the two-party system. If the states awarded electors based on the *proportion* of the vote (the percentage received by each candidate or each party), then third party candidates would receive more votes. For example, if a Green Party candidate got 10 percent of the vote, then that candidate would get 10 percent of the electors. But because of winner-take-all, either the Democratic or Republican candidate almost always gets all the electors of each state.

History of Electoral College: The Electoral College was the result of a compromise between different groups of delegates at the Constitutional

Electoral College

the body, today consisting of 538 electors, that selects the president in state-by-state elections

winner-take-all

the candidate who wins the plurality of the state's popular vote wins ALL the electors

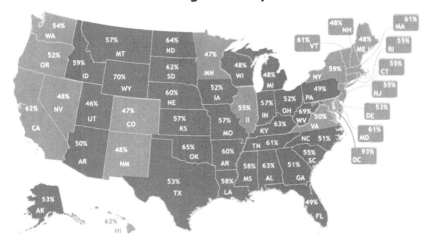

In 2016, Trump won 304 electoral votes from 30 states and part of Maine.
©DNetromphotos/Shutterstock.com

Convention. Many delegates wanted Congress to select the president, some wanted a direct popular vote, and a few delegates wanted the state legislatures to select the president. The Electoral College was a compromise between these three groups: the people vote, but in state units. And if no candidate wins a majority, then there would be a run-off in Congress, each state getting one vote. The Constitution left it to each state how they would select their electors. In early American history, state legislatures usually selected the slate of electors representing their state.

Originally, the system for selecting a president was designed to be non-partisan. The candidate with the most votes would be president, and the candidate with the second most votes would be vice president. But fairly rapidly the two party systems developed in America. In 1796 the leader of the Federalist Party, John Adams, was elected president, while the leader of the Republican Party, Thomas Jefferson, was elected vice president. How could they possibly work together? They didn't; Jefferson went back home to his plantation in Virginia. This situation was remedied with the 12th Amendment, and from then on the president and vice president run as a team.

The rise of the two party systems explains why the congressional run-off is very rare. Indeed, it has only happened twice. In 1800 Thomas Jefferson and Aaron Burr tied and after thirty-six ballots the House declared Jefferson president. And in 1824, none of the four major candidates running received a majority of the Electoral College votes, and so there was a run-off in the House. John Quincy Adams became president even though Andrew Jackson initially won more popular votes. This presents another flaw in the Electoral College. On five occasions the candidate who won the most votes did not become president: 1824 (Jackson won more popular votes than Adams), 1876 (Samuel Tilden won more votes the Rutherford B. Hayes), 1888 (Benjamin Harrison won more votes than Grover Cleveland), 2000 (Al Gore won more votes than George W. Bush), and in 2016 (Hillary Clinton won more votes than Donald Trump). Most of the time when there is a disparity between the electoral vote and the popular vote, it is in an era when the country is evenly divided between two parties.

Should the Electoral College Be Reformed? In recent years, debate has increased between people for and against the Electoral College system.

Reasons against: The biggest flaw of the Electoral College is that five times in history the candidate with the most votes did not become president. This is undemocratic. Another undemocratic element is that electors can actually vote for whomever they want—they are called "faithless electors." But this happens rarely. There are other arguments against the current system. First, it focuses most of the campaign energy on the "battleground states," states with a population that is evenly divided between Democrats and Republicans, such as Ohio or Florida. And second, it discourages voters who belong to the minority party of that state. A Republican in California, for example, would have little motive to vote since 70 percent of the electorate are registered Democrats.

Reasons for: There are several arguments for keeping the current Electoral College system in place. First, the electoral vote usually magnifies the victory, making the outcome more certain and giving more legitimacy to the winner. In 2012, Obama won only 51 percent of the popular vote, but he won 332 to 206 electoral votes. Second, it avoids run-offs, which could be politically destabilizing. Third, it isolates an election problem in one state, like Florida in 2000, rather than bring the whole country into turmoil. Fourth, to become president a candidate must win votes from a majority of states in more than one region, which makes things more balanced geographically. And six, if it were a popular vote, presidential candidates would just run commercials in the big cities and ignore many small states and rural areas in America.

Suggested Reform: Some suggest that we follow the example of Maine and Nebraska. In these states, each elector is chosen based on the plurality vote of each congressional district. And the two senatorial electors are rewarded on the plurality vote of the whole state. To make this clearer, let's look at Nebraska

It is a responsibility of members of a democracy to be informed and vote.
©VectorPic/Shutterstock.com

in 2008. Nebraska has five electoral votes (three congressional and two senatorial). Presidential candidate John McCain won four electors: he won the majority vote in two congressional districts and he won the majority vote for the whole state, thus getting the two senate electors. But Obama got one elector for winning Nebraska's 2nd Congressional Districts. Proponents argue that this change would statistically make the electoral vote more consistent with the popular vote. However, had this system been in place, Nixon would have defeated Kennedy in 1960, and Romney would have defeated Obama in 2012.

FINAL THOUGHT

Voting is the most important responsibility of a citizen in a democracy. By voting, you accomplish at least three very important things: First, you select the best people to run the country. Second, you choose, indirectly, the best policies that will serve your economic and social interests. And third, you hold elected officials accountable—keeping them honest and faithful to their campaign promises. By voting an incumbent out of office, the people are saying, "You did not do a good job and so we will give somebody else a chance." But voting places responsibility on the citizens to be informed and to know how government works. That is the reason why many states like Texas make it mandatory that all college students take a course in US government. The legislators know that democracy will not survive unless the people are informed, engaged, and responsible.

NOTES

For information about voter turnout, go to the Unites States Elections Project at www.electionproject. org

For arguments over the Electoral college go to Prager University (prageru.com) and watch "Do You Understand the Electoral College" and "The Popular Vote vs. the Electoral College."

ESSAY QUESTIONS

1. Why is voting fundamental to a democracy?
2. In the early history of America, who had the right to vote?
3. How does the initiative violate the concept of a republic?
4. What groups are the most likely to vote?
5. How does the Electoral College select the president?
6. What are the arguments for and against the Electoral College?

TERMS

Australian Ballot: _____

Closed Primary: _____

Electoral College: _____

15th Amendment: _____

General Election: _____

Initiative: _____

19th Amendment: _____

Open Primary: _____

Poll Tax: _____

Primary Election: _____

Turnout: _____

Voting Rights Act of 1965: _____

Winner-take-all: _____

CHAPTER 18

How Do You Run for President?

TOPICS

- ▶ Qualifications to Run for President
- ▶ Managing a Presidential Campaign
- ▶ The Three Stages of a Presidential Campaign
- ▶ Voting Choice

LEARNING OBJECTIVES

When you finish reading this chapter, you will be able to:

1. Identify the roles of the top staff of a presidential campaign.
2. Discuss the traditional strategy to win the primary.
3. Explain the objectives of a successful national party convention.
4. Summarize how campaigns try to reach the voter in the general election.
5. Discuss the traditional strategy to win the general election.
6. Delineate the main factors influencing a voter's choice for president.

RUNNING FOR PRESIDENT

No other political event in American life captures the attention of the people and the press as a presidential election. This two-year marathon costs hundreds of millions of dollars, involves tens of thousands of campaign workers, and takes countless hours of television time as pundits discuss every aspect of the candidate's chances for victory. Other countries are amazed at the length and expense of a presidential campaign. The typical election for prime minister in other countries may take about a month. But the president of the United States is the most powerful office in the world, and therefore it makes sense that the vetting process would be arduous. The last thing we would want is to have somebody morally and intellectually unfit for the job. This chapter will describe the arduous gauntlet a candidate must go through to become President of the United States.

QUALIFICATIONS TO RUN FOR PRESIDENT

The constitutional qualifications for president—must be at least thirty-five years old, resided in the country fourteen years, and a natural born citizen—are not the de facto or real-life qualifications to run for president. The actual qualifications are that he or she must have a massive ego and an enormous ambition in order to equip themselves for one of the most grueling contests in the world. Running for president requires an amazingly wide variety of intellectual and emotional skills, extraordinary mental toughness, remarkable physical stamina, and the willingness to open up your personal life history, and the histories of your family members, to the scrutiny of the world press. Every four years only a handful of people meet these requirements.

What Kind of Experience? What kind of job experience and education do you need to run for president? In the last seventy-five years, all presidents have been former vice presidents, governors, or senators. Governors are the most successful because they have executive experience and they can run as a Washington outsider. Senators do the worst because lawmakers must sign a lot of unpopular bills and make many unsavory compromises. This is why it probably helped Barack Obama that he had been a senator for only two years before he ran for president. In the past, military generals have been popular contenders for the presidency, but this is no longer the case. In 1952, Dwight Eisenhower, the famous World War II commander, was the last general to successfully run for president.

Dwight Eisenhower was the last career military leader to become president.

©neftali/Shutterstock.com

Ironically, even though America is the largest economy in the world, and a symbol of free market capitalism, no person has been a successful presidential candidate who ran on their business record alone. In 2012, businessman Mitt Romney ran for president as a Republican, but his wealth seemed to hurt him in the general election and he lost the race. In 2016, the Republicans nominated another businessman, the real estate mogul Donald Trump. Trump as a billionaire was much richer than Romney and had the ability to self-finance his campaign. Also, as a bestselling author of *The Art of the Deal* and a successful television show, *The Apprentice*, Trump had high name recognition."

Trump has boasted that he graduated from the well regarded Wharton business school, but several presidents have never attended college, including George Washington, Andrew Jackson, Abraham Lincoln, and Harry Truman. In recent years, however, most presidents are graduates of America's most prestigious universities. Obama graduated from Harvard Law School. Clinton went to Yale Law School. And George W. Bush earned degrees from Yale (BA in history) and Harvard (MBA). This is because most presidents come from wealthy families that could afford the best schools. Franklin Roosevelt, John Kennedy, and the Bushes were from very rich families. But in the last seventy-five years, a few presidents have come from families of modest means. Lyndon Johnson, Richard Nixon, and Ronald Reagan all came from lower middle class families.

MANAGING A PRESIDENTIAL CAMPAIGN

It takes a lot of money and a large, sophisticated staff to run a modern presidential campaign. In recent years, this effort requires billions of dollars and thousands of people. The management of the campaign and the large campaign staff has become another test for running for president.

Money: As with running for the House or the Senate, a successful candidate must have the ability to raise enormous amounts of money. According to the Center for Responsive Politics, in the 2012 presidential election the Obama campaign spent $683 million, and the Romney campaign spent $433 million. If you include the money spent by the national parties and outside groups, Obama spent $1.1 billion, and Romney spent $1.2 billion. Certainly, each year it is getting more expensive to run for president. But to put these numbers in perspective, in 2010 Americans spent $7.1 billion on potato chips. According to a report by the Federal Elections Commission (FEC), in 2016 Clinton's campaign spent $435 million to Trump's $232 million, about twice as much. And interest groups supporting Clinton spent $204 million to Trump group's $71 million, nearly three times as much.

Campaign Staff: Most of the money spent on campaigns goes to the staff and advertising. The campaign staff is extremely important. They plan strategy, raise funds, allocate money and manpower, write speeches, make TV ads, conduct polls, run focus groups, create a media campaign, send out talking points to surrogates, stage campaign events, respond to controversies, and keep the candidate focuses and prepped. Often, successful campaign managers gain near mystic status in Washington. Lee Atwater headed George H. W.

**George Stephanopoulos, seen here with his wife, helped run
Bill Clinton's successful 1992 presidential campaign.**
©Rena Schild/Shutterstock.com

Bush's 1988 presidential campaign. James Carville and George Stephanopoulos helped Clinton win in 1992. Carl Rove, nicknamed the "the architect" by his boss, won George Bush's 2000 and 2004 elections. And David Plouffe and David Axelrod ran Obama's campaigns. In 2016, Clinton's campaign manager was Robby Mook, who was only 36 years old. Trump's campaign was run by Steve Bannon as campaign chief executive and Kellyanne Conway as campaign manager, the first woman to successfully manage a presidential campaign.

Top Staff Positions: The top staff positions of a presidential campaign are prestigious, well-paying jobs. In recent years, the chief positions include campaign manager, financial chair, and communications director. The **campaign manager** *heads the campaign.* He advises the candidate as he travels with him on the campaign trail, supervises the rest of the staff, devises the long-term strategy, makes the day-to-day campaign decisions, hires and fires top staffers, decides what TV ads to run, and puts out fires—damage control. Perhaps the second most important position is the *financial chair,* who is responsible for raising money, paying expenses, keeping records, and filing the paperwork for the Federal Elections Commission (FEC). The *communications director* develops the campaign theme, supervises speech writers, makes the talking points, decides what words to use and the best way to frame issues,

Campaign Manager

this person heads a political campaign

and directs the media campaign for TV, radio, and the Internet. A key member of the communications team is the *press secretary*, who speaks to the press. One reason that Trump spent much less money than Clinton is he paid for fewer advertisements. Trump believed most people tune-out political ads. Instead he used campaign staff to appear on news shows, such as Kellyanne Conway.

Volunteers and Get-Out-The-Vote: Although the paid staff gets all the glory and money, no presidential campaign could be successful without a large, active volunteer staff. District by district, all across the nation, they make phone calls, knock on doors, hand out bumper sticks and yard signs, and show up at campaign events. Usually their efforts intensify the month or two before the election. On Election Day, they play a very important role in **getting-out-the-vote effort** by *making sure their supporters actually go to the polls*. In recent years this has become a very sophisticated endeavor. In 2008 and 2012, Obama's get-out-the-vote effort was very comprehensive and was a key factor in his victory.

Here a campaign volunteer is trying to get-out-the-vote for Barack Obama.
©Jose Gil/Shutterstock.com

THE THREE STAGES OF PRESIDENTIAL CAMPAIGNS

Running for president is probably the greatest, most grueling, certainly most expensive, contest in the modern world. The Ironman triathlon has three stages: swim 2.4 miles, bike 112 miles, and run 26.2 miles. Running for president also has three stages, and each stage requires a different strategy. First, the nomination: the party chooses its candidate to run in the general election. Second, the national party conventions: although the decision had already been made in the primaries, this is when the parties officially select their candidate. And third, the general election: lasting about twelve weeks, the two candidates come out of the conventions and run against each other in all fifty states. The winner of this stage becomes president.

STAGE ONE—The Nomination

Informally, candidates start running for president years in advance, but the actual primaries start in early January and end in June, taking about six months. Each state has the constitutional power to set the time and rules of their primaries. In recent years many states have moved their primaries up in order to gain more influence. The key to winning the primaries is to appeal to your base and win early.

Pre-Nomination Stage: When does a presidential contest start? It's hard to say. Often, a failed previous presidential campaign serves as the preparation

Getting-out-the-vote Effort

the effort campaigns and political parties make to get people to the polls on Election Day for the current one. Reagan's failed 1976 election earned him greater authority when he ran in 1980. Romney's failed 2008 campaign set him up for 2012. But even if a candidate did not run in a previous presidential campaign, typically there are several things candidates do in preparation for the primaries. They write books. They campaign for other candidates. They travel and meet foreign leaders. They go on talk shows. And they make speeches to interest groups. The important thing is to try to gain some name recognition with the general public and to be seen as a credible candidate with the donor class (the rich, politically motivated people that donate money to campaigns). In 2016, both candidates had tremendous name recognition going into the primaries. Hillary Clinton was the First Lady in the 1990s, and Donald Trump had actually been talking about running for president for a long time, since his 1988 appearance on the *The Oprah Winfrey Show.*

The Presidential Primaries: Since the states have the authority to set their own rules and timetable, every four years the primaries look slightly different. In 2016, with some minor exceptions, the Democrats and Republicans held their primaries on the same dates. Iowa and New Hampshire were first (as always): Iowa was February 1, and New Hampshire was February 9. Most of the time, only one or a few states hold a primary on the same day, but sometimes several states share a date. On March 6, called Super Tuesday, twelve states held primaries. On June 7, six states, including California, held primaries. The last primary was held on June 14 for Washington, DC.

In 2016, Donald Trump won the New Hampshire Republican primary.
©Andrew Cline/Shutterstock.com

Front-Loading: You may have wondered why Iowa and New Hampshire are first. Several decades ago their state legislatures decided they want to be first, so they simply schedule their primaries before the other states. *Jealous of all the electoral influence and media attention Iowa and New Hampshire get, in recent years more and more states have tried to schedule their primaries early. This is called* **front-loading**. Most primaries used to be in March, April, May, and June. Now, many are held in February and March.

What effect has front-loading had on presidential elections? Front-loading gives the early favorite an advantage. The candidate coming into the race with the most money and the highest name recognition can win the whole thing with a series of early victories. In 2016, Trump was able to win many early primaries due to his fame as a reality TV show host, and because as a billionaire he was able to self-finance his primary campaign. Another possible affect of front-loading is that it prolongs the whole presidential campaign, perhaps creating voter fatigue by the time they reach the general election.

Primary Rules: There are two types of primaries: the *primary* (most common) and the *caucus*. The primary works just like a normal election: a voter walks into a booth and fills out a ballot. The caucus is different. They look sort of like a town hall meeting. At the Republican Iowa caucus, for example, party members meet at the local meeting location. Once the meeting starts, people stand up and speak for a particular candidate, and those attending write the name of their favorite candidate on a blank piece of paper and give it to the party leader. Then the party leader tallies the votes and announces the winner for that district.

Front-Loading

in recent decades, more and more states have moved their primaries to an earlier date in order to have more influence on presidential elections

And there are two ways delegates are selected to be sent to the national party convention. In states that use the *Winner-take-all primary*, the candidate who gets the most votes in that state's primary wins ALL the delegates that will go to the national convention. In states that use a *proportional primary*, each candidate gets a portion of the delegates equal to the percentage of the vote they received. For example, if candidate A gets 10 percent of the primary vote, then 10 percent of the state's delegates will go to the national convention representing that candidate. To make things more confusing, some states dictate that the delegates at the convention must only vote for that candidate that won the primary, and other states give the delegates the power to change their minds and vote for any candidate they wish at the national convention.

Primary Strategies: The traditional primary strategy is to win early and appeal to the base. Presidential hopefuls with strong name recognition and credentials seek to raise as much money as they can before the primaries. Then they try to win some early primaries, especially Iowa and New Hampshire. Once a candidate wins an early primary, the press focuses on that individual and, in a snowball effect, the money flows in as people realize that he or she is a serious contender. Only five times in history has a nominee won both the Iowa and the New Hampshire primaries, and each time that candidate won the party's nomination.

The second strategy is to play to the base. Primary voters are the most informed voters, but they also tend to be the most ideologically extreme. Democratic primary voters are very liberal, and Republican primary voters are very conservative. This is why in 2016, liberal/socialist Bernie Sanders did very well in the Democratic primary, and Ted Cruz, the tea party conservative, did very well in the Republican primaries. But the danger is that if a candidate goes too extreme in the primaries, it will be difficult to tack back to the middle for the general election. Few candidates have the rhetorical skills and political talent to appeal to the base in the primary and then a few months later attract moderates in the general election.

STAGE TWO—The Convention

Since 1972, the parties have picked their nominations through the primaries and not at the convention. So if the national party conventions no longer select the candidate for the general election, what does it do? Think of the convention as a multi-million dollar media event designed to portray the party and the party leaders in the best possible light. Each party showcases its talent and ideas, and it reintroduces the candidate to the country. It is the last time all the elements of the campaign come together: the candidates, delegates, staff, volunteers, special interest groups, and elected officials. A successful convention will pump them up and send them off energized.

Beyond the media campaign and the pep rally, three things happen at the conventions: the vice presidential candidate is announced, the party platform is announced, and the party officially chooses its presidential candidate for the general election.

Media Event: The national party conventions normally take place in late summer. In 2016, the Republicans held their national convention July 18- 21, and the Democrats held their convention July 25-28. At the conventions, dozens of party members go on stage and give speeches over a four-day period. In years past, when the conventions actually selected the candidates, the television networks would cover the whole event. But now since there is no read drama, the major networks normally only devote prime time coverage to the last two nights. Of course, the cable shows like CNN or Fox News will cover more of the conventions. The main strategy is to get the most dynamic party members to speak during prime-time and for all speakers to keep to the theme and not make any blunders. Normally, the party leaders pre-approve all speeches.

At the national party conventions, the parties try to highlight their best members and boost the morale of campaign workers.
©Joseph Sohm/Shutterstock.com

Keynote speeches try to do two important things: they attempt to strengthen a perceived weakness of their candidate, and they try to highlight a perceived weakness of the opponent. At the 2012 Democratic convention, Bill Clinton gave the keynote address. Under Obama, the economy had been lackluster, and Romney, as a successful businessman, had promised to turn the economy around. Clinton skillfully went after Romney's perceived strength and said that Romney's economic plan would help the rich and leave the poor behind. In 2016, Ivanka Trump, the daughter of Donald Trump, gave the keynote address. For decades, Trump has been depicted in the tabloids as something of a playboy. Ivanka's job was to depict her father in a new light, as the family man and devoted father.

Party Platform: Wanting to avoid any controversies, today the parties write rather bland platforms. Each party selects a committee that works on the platform for several weeks and presents it on the first night of the convention. The **party platform** *lists the party's positions on the issues and articulates its political values.* The Democratic platform tends to be more liberal, highlighting issues of economic equality, government programs, tolerance, and women's rights. The Republican platform tends to be more conservative, highlighting issues of individualism, economic growth, liberty, low taxes, and less government regulation.

Vice Presidential Nominee: About a week before the convention the presidential nominee announces his vice presidential selection. The act of

party platform

a document released by a political party at the national convention that lists the party's positions on the issue and its political values choosing a good vice presidential running mate may be the first important executive decision the candidate makes. A good pick will highlight the candidate's judgment and infuse the convention with enthusiasm. Most presidential candidates look to "balance the ticket" in a way that makes up for a perceived weakness. Obama was young and inexperienced, and so he selected Joe Biden for vice president, a long serving member of the Senate. And John Kennedy was from New England, and so he picked Lyndon Johnson, a Southerner. Trump chose Mike Pence to shore up his base of Christian Republicans. Trump had been a registered Democrat for most of his life. Furthermore, Trump was not a regular church-goer. By picking Pence as VP, Trump reassured Republicans that he really was an economic and social conservative.

Nomination Speech: On the last night of the convention, the presidential candidate accepts the nomination and makes a speech. This is probably the most important speech he or she has ever made. With tens of millions of people watching, the candidate cannot afford to make a mistake. The primary job of a good acceptance speech is for the candidate to reintroduce himself to the general public. One of the most dramatic acceptance speeches in modern history occurred at the 2008 Democratic National Convention. The Democratic convention was held at the Denver Pepsi Center, but Obama made his acceptance speech at Invesco Field (Mile High Stadium) with 84,000 people in attendance and 38 million people watching on TV. Much of the country wanted to watch the acceptance speech of the first African American man to run for president from a major political party.

The Bounce: One indication if the convention and the acceptance speech were successful is whether the candidate received a post-convention bounce in public opinion surveys. And this may be preceded by a vice presidential bounce. In 2012, Romney got a slight bump in the polls after he announced that Paul Ryan would be his running mate. But after the national convention, his ratings actually dropped a point. That was a bad sign. Obama, on the other hand, enjoyed a two-point bounce, which he held until Election Day. In 1992, Bill Clinton enjoyed one of the biggest convention bounces ever. After the convention, Clinton's poll numbers spiked 16 points. In 2016, CNN reported a 6 point

Mitt Romney, the 2012 Republican presidential candidate, did not get a post-convention bounce.

©Christopher Halloran/Shutterstock.com

bounce for Trump, and a 12 point bounce for Hillary Clinton. But other polls showed different results, so it is not clear what the true bounce was for this last election.

STAGE THREE—The General Election

Traditionally, candidates took a rest between the end of the convention and Labor Day, occurring on the first Monday of September. But now candidates storm right into the general election and campaign hard right up to Election Day, the first Tuesday after the first Monday of November. This gives them about nine weeks. In many ways, in the general election the candidates start all over again. According to FEC rules, candidates are allowed to raise fresh funds and spend new money for the general election period. And the candidates, now that more people are paying attention, attempt to reintroduce themselves to the American people. The strategy in the general election is to not make any blunders, craft an easy to comprehend theme or narrative, energetically make as many campaign events as possible, and appeal to the moderate voter without alienating the base.

Electoral College Strategy: The strategy of a Republican candidate is to win the traditional Republican states, those in the South and the Midwest, and then to pick up a few swing states. Likewise, the strategy of a Democratic candidate is to win the traditional Democratic states, those on the East and West coasts and around the Great Lakes, and then to pick up a few swing states. *The half-dozen or so states that swing back and forth between Democrats and Republicans are called "**swing states**" or "battleground states."* In the last few presidential elections the swing states usually included Ohio, Florida, New Mexico, Colorado, Virginia, North Carolina, Iowa, Pennsylvania, and Nevada. Presidential candidates spend more than 90 percent of their money on swing states. In 2012, Obama won all the traditionally democratic states, plus he held on to the key swing states of Ohio, Pennsylvania, Virginia, and Florida. In 2016, Trump won the election by winning the swing states of Ohio and Florida, and by picking up three Democratic states: Michigan, Wisconsin, and Pennsylvania.

Reaching the Voters: The most difficult challenge for the candidates is to get their message through to the voters. It is very frustrating for a candidate, after giving a well-crafted thirty-minute speech, to see the media pick apart one awkward line on the nightly news. This is a cusp of the campaign/media conflict of a presidential election. The candidate wants to get the most positive message through to the voters, and to do that he or she needs the media, including TV, newspapers, magazines, radio, and the Internet. On the other hand, the average professional reporter doesn't want to be treated as a

Swing States

the states, sometimes called "battleground states," that have populations evenly divided between Democrats and Republicans and that swing back and forth between both parties in presidential elections messenger boy. They want to add their commentary and analysis to the campaign coverage. To increase ratings and to beat the competition, the press is more interested in scooping a scandal, reporting on mistakes and discord within the campaign, and evaluating the candidate's performance.

How Can a Candidate Control His Message? Candidates spend millions of dollars hiring media consultants and communication experts in order to control their message. Traditionally, these experts advise several strategies. First, they try to isolate the candidate from the press, allowing a limited number of interviews in the hope that the rarity of the interview will force the media to broadcast fuller coverage. Second, they carefully choreograph campaign events, hoping that one line or one media image will make it on the nightly news. Third, the communications staff talks with reporters in an attempt to spin each story to their candidate's advantage.

Lastly, they try to circumvent the serious political press by going local or going soft. Local news shows are thrilled to get a presidential candidate, so they tend to offer more positive coverage. And media advisors book their candidate on soft national shows, like *The View*, *Jimmy Fallen*, and *Saturday Night Live*. These shows have millions of viewers and they usually help the candidate look appealing and funny. Trump by-passed the traditional media, which was very hostile to him, by using Twitter and other social media.

Most campaigns run negative ads because they are effective at raising doubts about the opponent.
©Bob Venezia/Shutterstock.com

Advertising: In order to bypass the press and get their message directly to the voter, campaigns spend enormous amounts of money advertising on TV, radio, and the Internet. Generally, there are two types of ads. **Positive ads** *depict the candidate and his family in the most positive light, highlighting the candidate's ideas, accomplishments, and values* while using patriot music and plenty of pictures of the candidate's beautiful family. **Negatives ads**, on the other hand, *attack the opponent, going after his character or some whiff of a scandal.* Candidates usually say they will not use negative ads, but then always use them. They do it because negative ads are so effective. People tend to remember something bad about a person more vividly than something good. Also, many voters are motivated more by voting *against* a candidate rather than voting *for* a candidate.

Growth of the New Media: The news media (the twenty-four-hour cable news shows and the Internet) allow a campaign to respond rapidly to controversies or a new attack. Bill Clinton, in 1992, was the first to use the Internet to raise money. He also used it to send e-mails out to supporters and the press. One of the great features of the Internet for a campaign is its speed. Another idea taken and advanced from the 1992 Clinton campaign is the "war room." The concept is to respond to all attacks within twenty-four hours and thus always be on the offensive. Today, a campaign can produce and disseminate an Internet commercial within one day. And in the last few years, presidential campaigns hire specialists to create a presence on social media, such as Facebook, Twitter, and YouTube.

Election Theme or Narrative: A presidential candidate and his staff work hard crafting a campaign theme or developing a narrative, a story the voters can understand. In 1984, Reagan's theme was "Morning in America," meaning that with Reagan's stewardship of the economy, our best years are ahead. In 2012, Mitt Romney tried to present a straightforward theme: I have the business skill and knowledge to get this country back on a path of economic growth. But Obama's narrative was slightly more effective: "Republican policies like Bush's and Romney's got us into this mess (the 2008 recession), and so my philosophy of government/community partnership is a better, more compassionate approach for the country." Exit polls show that Obama's narrative worked. A high percentage of the voters blamed Bush, not Obama, for the continuing sluggishness of the economy and they said Obama was the more compassionate candidate.

In 2016, Hillary Clinton had difficulty crafting a coherent campaign theme. She seemed to be saying that she would continue to support and expand Obama's policies, plus as the first woman president, she would work for equal pay for women and support women's health issues. Trump, on the other hand, had a simple campaign theme: "Make America Great Again." He coupled the

Positive Ads

the government must provide something to the people, as part of their human rights, such as education, medical support, housing, or welfare

Negatives Ads

campaign commercials that attack the opponent

theme with a platform of stopping illegal immigration, which he said kept blue collar wages down. And he advocated ending the bad international trade deals, which he said was responsible for closing down thousands of American factories. Trump's message resonated with lower class whites, especially in the rust belt. It accounts for why he won such states as Ohio, Pennsylvania, Michigan, and Wisconsin.

Presidential Debates: The last time before Election Day that a candidate has the opportunity to communicate directly with the American people, unfiltered by the press, is at the presidential debates. The first televised presidential debate took place between Richard Nixon and John Kennedy in 1960. But only since the 1980s have they been accepted as a fundamental part of the election. Today, there are three presidential debates and one vice presidential debate. Candidates spend several valuable pre-election days preparing for these debates. They often practice in mock debates on an artificial stage with somebody posing as the opposition candidate. They spend so much time preparing for these debates because they know that if they are behind, this is their last chance to catch up; or if they are ahead, a good performance can cement their lead.

Traditionally, candidates try to accomplish two things during the debates. One, look presidential and demonstrate a grasp of the issues. Two, do not make any mistakes. Any challenger will automatically get the chance to look presidential by being placed on a stage next to a sitting president. Before Reagan's 1980 debate with Carter, people wondered if he had the intellectual skills or moderate temperament to be president. But after standing next to Carter and performing well, in an amiable fashion and demonstrating a grasp of all the issues, the voters thought he could be president. Reagan won in a landslide. Sometimes a simple mistake during a debate can sink the whole campaign. In 1976, President Ford in his debate with Carter said that Poland would never be under the domination of the USSR. Poland was indeed under the domination of the USSR and this blunder probably cost him the election.

November Surprises. Sometimes campaigns release damaging facts about a candidate a few weeks before the Election Day, not allowing the candidate time to respond to the attack and inflicting maximum damage. In 2000,

If a presidential candidate is behind, the debates are his last chance to catch up.
©Aniwhite/Shutterstock.com

three days before the election the Democrats released the fact that George Bush was arrested for drunken driving. His poll numbers dropped and he lost the popular vote (although he won the electoral vote). In 2016, the Trump campaign had to deal with a devastating bombshell. On Oct 7, just before the second debate, an audio tape was released in which Trump used crude language in a private conversation with Billy Bush and said that because he was famous he could have sex with all kinds of women. The audio tape was from a live Mic that was recording Trump just before he went on an episode of *Access Hollywood*. Instantly, dozens of Republicans called for Trump to step down and allow Pence to run for president. Trump, however, issued an apology, calling it locker-room banter, and pledged to continue with the campaign. In the past, this sort of tape would have derailed any presidential campaign, but the normal rules seemed not to affect Trump.

VOTING CHOICE

Politics is so fascinating because of the human element. "Political science" will never be as clear-cut as such sciences as physics or chemistry. When a politician gets on the stage and speaks to the crowd, we are entering the realm of the human mind and heart—murky waters to say the least! It is nearly impossible to explain why some politicians inspire life-long devotion and others provoke intense hatred. One tangible clue as to why people voted for a particular candidate are *exit polls*: This type of poll surveys people right after they voted and asks them a series of questions. After the long campaign, dominated by the commentary of all the pundits, the exit polls reveal what the actual voters were thinking on Election Day. Here are some generalizations about why people vote for a particular candidate:

Party Identification: The number one influence on voter choice is party identification. If you are a life-long Democrat you are going to vote for the Democratic candidate; if you are a life-long Republican, you are going to vote for the Republican candidate—no matter how dull or bad they are. Or, to look at it from another angle, if you are a life-long Democrat, you will vote for any Democrat in order to stop a dreaded Republican from winning. Either way, voter identification is the primary factor. In 2016, 89% of self-described Democrats voted for Hillary Clinton, and 88% of Republicans voted for Trump.

If you look closely at these numbers you will see that Republicans are slightly more loyal than Democrats. This helps explain one puzzling fact. Since 1952, more people are registered as Democrats than Republicans. So why do Republicans win more presidential elections? There are several reasons: (1) Republicans have higher turnout. This is probably due to the demographics. Republicans tend to have the same demographics as high turnout voters:

older, higher income, and higher education. (2) In polls, more people say they are Democrats because in the popular culture the Democrats are seen as being more compassionate and tolerant. But that individual may hold conservative views, so when she is alone in the voting booth, she may vote for the Republican.

Ideology: Party identification is related to voter ideology. Liberal leaning voters will vote for the Democratic candidate. And conservative leaning voters will vote for the Republican candidate. Since the 1970s, the two political parties have become more ideologically pure. Before the 1970s, both conservative Southern farmers and Northern liberal city dwellers would vote for the Democratic Party. But today, liberals vote for Democrats and conservatives vote for Republicans. In 2016, 84% of liberals voted for Clinton, and 81% of conservatives voted for Trump.

Issues: People would like to think they are voting on a rational analysis of the candidate's positions on a set of the issues, but this is not true. They do, however, judge **retrospective issue voting**, that is, *they look at how the candidates actually voted during their whole political career*. And they tend to discount **prospective issue voting**, *issues the candidate says he is for during the campaign*. This is probably wise. Voters tend not to trust candidates' political promises. Some people, however, are single issue voters. They will vote for or against a candidate based primarily on one issue, such as abortion, gun control, or lower taxes.

Retrospective Issue Voting

the actual issues that a candidate supported or voted for over their career

Prospective Issue Voting

issues the candidate says he is for during the campaign

When a person is standing alone in a voting booth, what finally makes them decide who to vote for?
©Burlingham/Shutterstock.com

But there is one more major factor that determines why people vote for a particular candidate, which will be discussed in the Final Thoughts.

FINAL THOUGHTS

After the candidates run for office for several years, spend hundreds of millions of dollars, travel across the country numerous times, and make thousands of speeches, what ultimately determines who wins the campaign? The final deciding factor of who becomes president is usually **candidate appeal**: *the positive feeling a voter gets about an individual candidate*. The voter looks at the whole candidate, including his physical appearance, personality, mannerisms, family, values, and intellect, and basically decides what candidate is most appealing. In other words, the most likable candidate wins. If you look at all the recent presidents, especially in the television era, the candidate with the most likable personality wins. Kennedy was more likable than Nixon. Reagan was more likable than Jimmy Carter and Walter Mondale. Clinton was more likable than Bob Dole. Obama was more likable than McCain. The most likable candidate wins.

Candidate Appeal

the positive feeling a voter gets about an individual candidate

The reason likability plays such a strong influence in the general election is because this is when many moderate, infrequent voters come out and vote. These people are not ideological and do not follow the political issues closely. So they vote on gut. Do I like this person? Does he understand somebody like me? In 2012, 53 percent of people in exit polls said Obama is "more in touch with people like me." 2016 was a different kind of election. Polls showed that a high percentage of people felt personal dislike for both Clinton and Trump. So, why did Trump win if he was not more likable? Over 80% of the people that voted for Trump said he would bring about "needed change." So, they knew there were things about his personality that they did not like, but they thought he would be more able to change Washington than Clinton would. When all is said and done, 2016 was a change election: the American people did not want to continue with business as usual.

NOTES

For money in politics, go to The Center for Responsive Politics: www.opensecrets.org.
For primary schedule, go to www.uspresidentialelectionnews.com.
For 2012 exit polls, go to *Barack Obama and the New America: the 2012 election and the changing Face of Politics.* Edited by Larry Sabato. New York: Rowman & Littlefield Publishers, 2013.
George Will, "The Democratic Vision of Big Brother," *Washington Post*, Oct 17, 2010.

ESSAY QUESTIONS

1. What are the most common professions of people who run for president?
2. What is the traditional strategy to win a presidential primary?
3. What is the traditional strategy to win a presidential general election?
4. What do candidates do to try to win televised presidential debates?
5. What is candidate appeal?

TERMS

Campaign Manager: _____

Candidate Appeal: _____

Front-loading: _____

Getting-out-the-vote: _____

Negative Ads: _____

Party Platform: _____

Positive Ads: _____

Prospective Issue Voting: _____

Retrospective Issue Voting: _____

Swing States: _____

CHAPTER 19

What Do Political Parties Do?

TOPICS

► The Functions of Political Parties
► The Two-Party System
► What Role Do Third Parties Play?
► Party Identification
► Political Parties as Institutions
► Conventional and Unconventional Participation

LEARNING OBJECTIVES

When you finish reading this chapter, you will be able to:

1. Define the functions of political parties.
2. Describe the advantages of the two-party system.
3. Explain how third parties form.
4. Understand how political parties play a major role in running the government.
5. Compare conventional and unconventional political participation.

WHAT DO POLITICAL PARTIES DO?

At the most fundamental level, **political parties**, such as the Democrats and Republicans, *are organized groups of people united by a common political goal.* All the people associated with the party—the voters, volunteers, candidates, paid staff, and government officials—believe they need to get their candidates elected to office in order to implement a political agenda that they think will

Political Parties

organized groups of people united by a common political goal that try to get their candidates elected to office in order to implement a political agenda improve the nation. The Founders, however, feared political parties. Reacting to the historic nastiness of British party politics, and enjoying a brief period of unity during the Revolutionary War, the Founders hoped that Americans would avoid breaking up into groups and fighting with each other. But as we will see, the history of America is closely linked with the history of political parties.

THE FUNCTIONS OF POLITICAL PARTIES

John Adams once said, "There is nothing I dread so much as a division of the republic into two great parties, each arranged under its leader, and concerting measures in opposition to each other." Adams's worst fears came true. Shortly after the establishment of the United States of America, the country divided into two major parties. Ironically, Adams became the leader of one of those parties, the Federalists. But the Founders truly believed that each American should do what was best for the whole nation instead of devoting his or her passions to one group or faction, thus pitting Americans against Americans.

Not all of the Framers dreaded the development of political parties as much as Adams. In *Federalist #10*, James Madison said, "Liberty is to faction like air is to fire," meaning that in a free society people will naturally form their own associations based on common interests. He went on to say that "the causes of faction are sown in the nature of man." It is human nature for people to

**There are many political parties in America, but two parties dominate:
the Republicans and the Democrats.**
©Ryan DeBerardinis/Shutterstock.com

cluster around a charismatic leader. And it is only natural that people would assemble into groups based on their religious, political, or economic interests. Madison concluded that factions pose no danger to the Union as long as one group does not dominate the country. In other words, many groups, competing with each other, with no single group dictating, are natural and healthy for a democracy.

Madison correctly stated that political parties were inevitable in a democracy. Indeed, it is nearly impossible to imagine how our democracy would function without parties. Today it is common for people to disparage the political parties, even members of their own party. In this election cycle, it seems that presidential candidates Donald Trump and Ted Cruz spent more time criticizing "Establishment Republicans" and Washington politics than they did criticizing Democrats. But although parties have always been vilified, there are several vital functions political parties perform in our democratic system:

Organize Political Ideology: Political parties organize candidates into two broad ideology categories. This provides a sort of shorthand for the voter. If a candidate is running as a Democrat, the voter knows that he or she leans toward the left. Liberals believe in a large role for the federal government, focus on social justice and equality, support a woman's choice to have an abortion, and welcome diversity and social change. If a candidate is running as a Republican, he or she leans to the right. Conservatives believe in limited government and lower taxes, support law and order, focus on economic growth, and believe in traditional social norms. This is why it makes sense for many to vote for a "straight party ticket," and select all the Republicans or all the Democrats on the ballot. How confusing would it be to vote if we did not have these ready-made categories?

Recruit and Select Candidates: Parties find people to run for office. Sometimes party leaders go to a prominent citizen, perhaps a successful lawyer or community organizer, and ask her to consider running for city council or for Congress. The national parties have a more elaborate system for selecting candidates for president. In 2012, the sitting president, Barack Obama, decided to run for reelection as a Democrat. On the other side, eleven men and one woman competed for the Republican nomination. After primaries in all fifty states and the territories, and after twenty-seven debates, Mitt Romney was selected to lead the Republican Party in the general election.

Organize the Contest: Think of a political campaign as a courtroom. The voters are the jury, the plaintiff and defendant are the two candidates, and the judge is the Federal Election Commission. Just as easily, we can think of other contests: a boxing fight, a dance competition, or a chess match. Competition can be grueling but it often brings out the best in humans. In politics, the parties organize the contest by recruiting candidates, raising money, registering voters, launching media campaigns, conducting polls, enlisting volunteers, planning the conventions, and organizing the debates. When the voter walks into the booth and casts his ballot, he is voting for the side he thought won the contest.

Make Policy: The goal of political parties is to get their candidates into office so that they can implement their policies. Between 2008 and 2010, the Democrats controlled the White House, the House, and the Senate, and thus were able to implement the Affordable Health Care Act. The Democratic Party achieved a long held goal of nationalizing health care. Party leaders, various party groups, and associated think tanks help formulate policy ideas for the parties, as in this case, health care reform. Also, every four years at the national party conventions, each party presents a *list of the issue positions and political values—this is called the* **party platform**. With the publication of the platform, the party is saying: vote for our candidates and we will implement these policies.

Help Organize Government: Once candidates are elected, the political parties play an important role in organizing state and national governments. Congress is organized along party lines. The party with the most seats in each chamber of Congress chooses the chamber leadership, such as the Speaker of the House and the Senate Majority Leader. They also choose the chairs of each congressional committee and hold the majority of the seats for every committee. This is real power. And whatever party controls the White House also has tremendous power. The president nominates federal judges for life, picks powerful cabinet secretaries, selects thousands of executive department positions, and signs executive orders that may support party constituents. So, today the federal government is structured, to a great extent, around the two-party system.

Party Platform

a document released by a political party at the national convention that lists the party's positions on the issue and its political values

Provide Accountability: Lastly, and perhaps most importantly, political parties hold the other party accountable. It may look ugly, but the job of the party *out* of power is to constantly criticize the party *in* power. Democrats in Congress exposed Reagan's Iran-Contra scandal. Republicans in Congress exposed Obama's IRS interest groups scandal. Members of each party must constantly defend their positions and actions in the face of criticism from the opposition. In polls, Americans express distaste for the nasty partisanship, but without it incompetence and corruption would be exposed less often. This partisanship results in better government.

THE TWO-PARTY SYSTEM

In stark contrast to America's two parties, most other countries have numerous political parties. Italy and Israel, for example, have dozens of active

China is ruled by one political party, the Communist Party. Without an opposition party, who will hold corrupt party leaders accountable?
©windmoon/Shutterstock.com

political parties representing different ideologies and regions. For their governments to function, several parties must combine to form a majority coalition. But in America we have always had two major parties. Perhaps this is because politicians have instinctively sought a political system that brings Americans together. There are so many political and social forces working to divide America: three branches, the federal system with state's rights, individualism, ethnic diversity, freedom of thought, religious liberty. To counteract these many divisive forces, the two-party system works as a glue to bring Americans together into two mainstream camps.

Two Is Better Than One: While America has avoided the excessive factionalism that comes with having many parties, we have also avoided one party rule. In Mexico, for example, the Institutional Revolutionary Party (PRI) dominated the country for seventy-one years, from 1929 to 2000. And since 1947, the Communist Party has monopolized China, making it illegal for any other party to exist. Countries with only one party tend to stagnate because they do not benefit from the new ideas that generate from a competitive political environment. And countries with only one party tend to be corrupt because there is no opposition party to expose wrongdoing. This is especially so if the one controlling party bans a free press, which they usually do.

Two Parties Unify the Electorate: One important feature of the two-party system is that it unifies Americans around two moderate parties. This reduces the harmful effects of people factionalizing into extreme splinter groups or obsessing on one issue. In the two-party system, candidates must articulate general principles and downplay the importance of a single hot-button issue, such as abortion or gay marriage. So, if you are a socialist concerned mainly with labor rights, you will join with the Democrats. And if you are a member of the Tea Party and mostly concerned with gun rights, you will join with the Republicans. The two-party system brings individuals and groups with extreme views into the mainstream.

Divided Government and Incrementalism: Another feature of the American two-party system is that public policy gets implemented in incremental steps. Governments controlled by one party or governments using the parliamentary system (in which one party controls the legislative and executive branches) can rush through a series of reforms with little or no resistance. This is nearly impossible in our two-party system. One party may have a narrow window of opportunity to implement a couple of major reforms, normally during a presidential honeymoon period or during a national crisis. But shortly after this reform period, the people always vote in the opposition party in at least one chamber of Congress, thus creating divided government. It appears that the American people instinctively like to share power between the two parties in order to slow down reform and wait to see if the new laws work before adding on more.

Proportional System

seats in the legislature are allocated according to what percentage of the vote each party receives

How Is the Two-Party System Maintained? The rules of the Electoral College keep the two-party system in place. If America wanted to foster multiple parties, we can do it instantly by instituting proportional representation. A **proportional system,** *like they have in the parliamentary system, means that seats in Parliament are allocated according to what percentage of the vote each party receives.* For example, if 15 percent of the vote went to the Green Party, then 15 percent of the seats in Parliament would go to Green Party members. In the Parliamentary system, the people vote for the party, and the majority party selects the prime minister.

Winner-take-all

a rule of the Electoral College that says the candidate who wins the plurality of the state's popular vote wins ALL the electors

In America, however, we vote for the individual presidential candidate. And according to the *rules of the Electoral College, whatever candidate wins the most votes in a state gets all the electors. This is called* **winner-take-all.** This is the key mechanism that keeps the two-party system intact. It is nearly impossible for a third party to win the most votes of a state.

Potential Negatives of Two-Party System: Some suggest that we should adopt the proportional system and end the domination of the Democrats and Republicans. They argue that the two parties are essentially the same, preventing real reform in America. Others argue that the two-party system suppresses the vote because many people feel that neither of the major parties addresses the issues and concerns that really impact their lives. So they just don't vote. They have become disengaged. These points may or may not be true, but the fact is that the two major parties control the electoral mechanisms that keep the two-party system in place. So, it is highly unlikely it will change.

WHAT ROLE DO THIRD PARTIES PLAY?

There are other parties besides the Democratic and Republican parties. Normally, they are called "third parties." But no third party candidate has ever won the presidency. And since the Civil War, only five third party candidates have won any electoral votes at all. In 1892, Populist James B. Weaver won 22 electoral votes; in 1912, Progressive Teddy Roosevelt won 88; in 1924, Progressive Robert M. LaFollette won 13; in 1948, the State's Rights Democratic Party candidate Strom Thurmond won 39; and in 1968, American Independent Party candidate George Wallace won 46 electoral votes. As explained above, in order to get an electoral vote a candidate must win the most votes in a state, which is hard for a candidate of a new party to do. But regardless of the fact that third parties have never won the Presidency, they have played an important role in US political history.

Types of Third Parties: How are third parties created? Third parties form around an ideology, a single issue, or a personality. In 2012 an ideological third party won the third most popular votes in the nation: The Libertarian

Some third parties are ideological, like the Communist Party,
which won 7,791 votes in the 2012 presidential election.
©Joseph Sohm/Shutterstock.com

Party received 1.3 million votes. In 1920, the Socialist Party candidate, Eugene Debs, won nearly a million votes. Other third parties do not represent an ideology but instead support a single issue: the Green Party (environment), the Prohibition Party (making alcohol illegal), the Liberty Party (abolishing slavery), and the Dixiecrats (maintaining segregation). And some third parties form around a charismatic leader. In 1912, Roosevelt was a charismatic leader who believed in the progressive agenda. Obviously, parties that form around a person tend to be short-lived, but ideological parties can live on for decades.

Bolting: One way third parties form is by *bolting*, marching out of a national convention over a dispute in the platform. In 1860, fifty-one pro-slavery, "fire-eater" Southern Democrats bolted from the National Democratic Convention and held their own convention in Maryland. They created the Southern Democratic Party and elected John C. Breckinridge to run on a "no compromise over slavery" platform. In 1912, progressive Republicans followed Theodore Roosevelt and bolted from the Republican National Convention. Two weeks later they formed the Progressive Party in Chicago and nominated Roosevelt to run for president. In 1948, thirty-five Southern Democrats bolted from the Democratic National Convention in Philadelphia. Announcing that they "stand for the segregation of the races," they formed the State's Rights Democratic Party and Strom Thurmond ran as their presidential candidate.

Influence of Third Parties: Although third parties do not win elections, they still can have a powerful influence on American politics. They mainly do this in two ways: by altering the outcome of an election or by introducing a new issue. Several times in history a third party candidate altered the outcome of an election by *spoiling* the victory of the leading candidate. For example, in 2000, Ralph Nader (Green Party) took thousands of votes away from Al Gore in Florida and New Hampshire, allowing George W. Bush to win. In a more positive way, third parties often bring up issues that the two mainstream parties ignore, but because the third party highlighted the issue, one or both of the mainstream parties eventually accepted it. For example, the Populist Party in 1892 proposed the progressive income tax and recognition of labor unions, something both parties eventually accepted.

Another purpose third parties serve is to allow the electorate to blow off some frustration in a constructive manner. In 1856, The Know Nothing Party won 22 percent of the popular vote. This was an anti-immigration movement that was responding to the biggest wave of immigration in US history. As immigration normalized, the party faded. But by getting people to vote for the Know Nothings, it probably reduced violence directed at immigrants. Likewise, the American Independent Party may have reduced racial violence. In the 1960s, many white Southerners were frustrated that the South was being forced to integrate. In 1968, segregationist George Wallace led the American

Independent Party, winning six Southern states. Perhaps by funneling their frustrations into a conventional political activity, like voting for a third party candidate, racial violence was reduced by some degree.

PARTY IDENTIFICATION

Party Identification: *The personal affiliation that a person has for a political party is called* **party identification**. It is a psychological attachment to or loyalty to one party that is part of a person's self-identity. This is related to political socialization. As we learned in Chapter 16, as a person grows up, he or she internalizes the political values of their family members, teachers, and community. The formation of party identification is part of the political socialization process. Put simply, by the time we reach our teen years, most people have a feeling that one political party is good and the other is bad and that they belong to the good party. But in recent decades, more children are picking up a different message from their parents: I don't care about politics and have no allegiance to any political party. So, party identification has become weaker.

Recent Weakening of Party Identification: In the past, many Americans had very strong party identification. Perhaps in college a young man joined the Young Republicans. And as he reached adulthood, he socialized with fellow Republicans and volunteered or donated money to the party. But today it is less likely that an individual would have a strong, life-long attachment to one political party. More people are disengaging from politics and they would rather call themselves "Independent." This is part of a greater trend. Since the 1950s, less people join groups and organizations of any kind. In the past, it was common for people to be members of many organizations, such as the Lions Club, The Rotary Club, or a philanthropic institution. Today people are more isolated and resist joining civic organizations, including political parties.

Historical Trends of Party Identification: According to the politics of the day, popular culture, and the popularity of the president, party identification in America has fluctuated significantly over the last several decades. According to Pew Research, from 1953 to 1980, a significant majority of Americans identified as Democrats. For example, in 1958, even though Republican president Eisenhower was quite popular, 46% of the voters identified as Democrat, 30% as Republican, and 22% as Independent. This popularity gap reached its greatest point in 1964 (after Democratic president John Kennedy was assassinated): 51% identified as a Democrat, and only 25% as a Republican.

The gap started to close with the election of Reagan in 1980, and by 1985 things equalized: 34% identified as Democrats, 32% as Republicans, and 29%

Party Identification

the personal affiliation that a person has for a political party

Today, fewer people feel devoted to a political party. In 1964, over 50 percent of Americans affiliated with the Democratic Party—today only 34 percent do.
©Gal Amar/Shutterstock.com

as Independent. These numbers remained consistent until about 2004, when Republicans began to lose support during the George W. Bush's unpopular second term. Since then Independents have grown in number as Republicans have shrunk. In 2011, 38% identify as Independent, 32% as Democrat, and only 24% as Republican. But after several years of Barack Obama, as his approval rating remained low, party identification is shifting again. According to a Gallup poll conducted in September of 2017, those that identify as independents have risen to 40%, Republicans have risen to 29%, and Democrats have gone down a couple of points to 30%.

Leaners: As these polls show, more and more people call themselves "independent," but when you look at their actual voting record they voted for the Democrat or Republican candidates their whole lives! Political scientists call these people *leaners*: people who self-identify as an independent, but usually vote for one political party. This is especially true of young people, who resist identifying as belonging to a political party. According to a Gallup poll conducted in May of 2017, Democrats with leaners is 45%, and Republicans with leaners is 38%.

Realignment: Historians have noticed certain mega trends of party identification in US history. These are called **electoral realignments**: *when the majority of voters switch from one party to another and remain loyal to the new party for a generation.* These often occur when a charismatic president

Electoral Realignments

when the majority of voters switch from one party to another and remain loyal to the new party for a generation articulates a new vision and a new set of policies for his party, attracting voters for the remainder of their lives. For example, today there are many people that call themselves "Reagan Republicans," even though Reagan left office over twenty-five years ago.

There have been six great realignments in US history: First, Thomas Jefferson established the Democratic Republicans as the most popular party from 1800 to 1824. Second, Andrew Jackson's populist appeal made the Democratic Party the dominant party from 1828 to 1856. Third, Abraham Lincoln helped create the Republican Party, which dominated from 1860 to 1896. Fourth, William McKinley recreated the pro-business Republican Party, which was in ascendancy from 1896 to 1928. Fifth, after the Great Depression, Democrat Franklin Roosevelt established the New Deal Coalition, lasting from 1932 to 1968. And sixth, after Nixon's stumble, Reagan recreated a conservative Republican Party, which was strong from 1980 to about 2004. Now we seem to be in a transition period where the country is divided between liberals and conservatives with no dominant political party.

Current Partisanship: With no dominant party, the country is currently experiencing a period of heightened partisanship. Senator Orin Hatch, the Republican from Utah who was first elected to Congress in 1976, has said that he has never seen such a partisan atmosphere in Congress. He recalls a time when members of Congress treated each other with more civility and collegiality. Why is partisanship so intense today? It is because the country is so evenly divided between liberals that identify as Democrats and conservatives that identify as Republicans. Liberals and conservatives fundamentally disagree on nearly all the major issues we face today (see Appendix for "Controversial Social and Political Issues"). Not until a large portion of the electorate makes up its mind and moves toward liberalism or conservatism will partisanship subside.

POLITICAL PARTIES AS INSTITUTIONS

Like any large organization, parties have rules, traditions, leadership, and organizational structure. There are three main party groups and functions: (1) *National Party Organization*: The National Republican Committee (RNC) and the National Democratic Committee (DNC) provide leadership on a national level. But under the national organization, each party has state and local organizations. (2) *Party Members in Office:* all the Democratic and Republican executive department officers, congressmen, governors, and state legislatures play an important role in party organization. They promote the agenda, attack the opposition party, orchestrate a media campaign, and build consensus. (3) *Regular Party Members*: the main goal of the parties is to attract more members—voters. In 2012, there were about 72 million registered Democrats and 55 million registered Republicans.

National Party Leadership: Although they may make some media appearances, the national party leaders mostly work behind the scenes. The chair of the Democratic National Party is Tom Perez, the former Secretary of Labor in the Obama administration. And the chair of the Republican Party is Ronna Romney McDaniel, the daughter of the 2012 presidential candidate Mitt Romney. National party chairs develop a political strategy for each election cycle and try to formulate the most positive positions on the major issues. They recruit candidates, raise money, hire pollsters, consult with media advisors, and work with their office holders. But even though Perez and McDaniel are the chairs of their national parties, the de facto leader of the party are the highest ranking office holders of the party. Thus, Donald Trump is the actual leader of the Republican Party.

State and Local Parties: Besides the national organizations, each party also has state, city, and local organizations. Each state has a Republican and Democratic state committee and state chair. And states are further divided into party precincts, often mirroring the congressional district. Obama in 2008 and 2012 was highly successful at getting the vote out at the precinct level.

Associated Groups: Besides the national and state party organizations, each party gets support from numerous associated subgroups. Many of these groups are highlighted on the RNC and DNC websites. The Republican groups include Black Republicans, Hispanic Republicans, Women Republicans, and Young Republicans. Democrats have the National Federation of Democratic Women, College Democrats of America, and many others. And in addition to these official subgroups, there are a constellation of groups outside the RNC and DNC that support the parties in numerous ways. Democrats are helped by unions, pro-choice organizations, teacher unions, organizations of trial lawyers, and black and women groups. Republicans are supported by pro-business groups, the chamber of commerce, low tax advocates, pro-life organizations, and Christian groups. Moreover, there are many liberal and conservative think tanks.

National Conventions: One of the biggest tasks for the party chairmen is to organize the National Party Conventions, which come every four years about three months before the presidential elections. The national conventions are discussed in more detail in Chapter 18. There are four major things the national conventions try to accomplish. (1) They nominate the presidential and vice presidential candidates for the general election. (2) They present the party platform. (3) They enforce party rules for the election cycle. (4) And they orchestrate the public relations theme for the four days of the conventions. Of these four, enforcing party rules probably poses the greatest stress on the party chairs.

Party Rules: In recent years, both parties have had difficulty maintaining their party rules, particularly with three issues. Since the 1984 national convention, 20 percent of the Democratic delegates consist of **superdelegates**, *delegates consisting of party leaders who are not pledged on the basis of primary votes*. Since the disastrous Democratic defeats of George McGovern and Jimmy Carter, the DNC created a system designed to give party leaders the influence to nominate more electable candidates. Superdelegates include Democratic congressmen, governors, mayors, DNC members, and others. In recent years, some party leaders and the media have criticized superdelegates as undemocratic. In 2016, Bernie Sanders was angry that nearly all of the superdelegates pledged support for Hillary Clinton before most of the primaries started.

Superdelegates

delegates consisting of party leaders who are not pledged on the basis of primary votes

Another difficult rule concerns how to allocate primary delegates, proportionally or winner-take-all. In recent decades, the Democrats had more states that allocated delegates proportionally, meaning if a candidate got 30 percent of the primary vote, then he or she would get 30 percent of the state's delegates. Traditionally, Republicans used winner-take-all. But in the last few

Delegates at the 1992 Democratic National Convention.
Some of these are "superdelegates," that were not selected by voters.
©Joseph Sohm/Shutterstock.com

Republican primaries, the early leader with the most name recognition, such as Senators Bob Dole and John McCain, won the nomination without much of a contest. To rectify this, GOP party leaders urged states to adopt proportional representation. Thus, in 2016, most of the Republican primaries allocated their delegates proportionally. The result being an extended primary fight between Donald Trump and Ted Cruz, not exactly what the Republican Party wanted either.

CONVENTIONAL AND UNCONVENTIONAL PARTICIPATION

To conclude this chapter, we will discuss political participation in general. In America, political parties provide the primary way people participate in politics, mostly by voting. This interaction between the people and government is essential to a democracy. A healthy government will provide ways for the people to express themselves and participate in the process. But when a person feels that the system is ignoring a particular problem, they may resort to more extreme ways of seeking social and political change. Political scientists define two ways of political engagement: conventional and unconventional political participation.

Conventional Participation: *The routine and culturally acceptable political activities that citizens use to engage in the political process* are called **conventional political participation**. Many of these activities are associated with party politics: voting, wearing campaign buttons, distributing campaign literature, placing a sign on one's front lawn, or attending a candidate's speech. But there are other conventional ways to participate that are not directly related to party politics: writing a letter to the editor of a newspaper, calling a radio talk show, signing a petition, and even marching on Washington. All these activities are socially acceptable ways to get involved in the political process.

Unconventional Participation: But some political activities cross a line and are considered **unconventional participation**, *political activities that are not socially acceptable, defy social norms, or are illegal.* Unconventional participation would include such things as chaining oneself to a factory, protesting nude, throwing red paint on a politician, rioting, or occupying a government building. Both conventional and unconventional participation have the same goal, they want to change public policy. But unconventional participation tries to accomplish this in more radical or even violent ways. The most extreme form of unconventional participation is **terrorism**, *defined as premeditated, politically motivated violence perpetrated against civilian targets by people who want to bring about a social or political goal.* In America, KKK activity during Reconstruction is an example of domestic terrorism.

Conventional Political Participation

the routine and culturally acceptable political activities that citizens use to engage in the political process

Unconventional Participation

political activities that are not socially acceptable, defy social norms, or are illegal

Terrorism

premeditated, politically motivated violence perpetrated against civilian targets by people who want to bring about a social or political goal

These supporters of PETA (People for the Ethical Treatment of Animals)
are engaging in unconventional political participation.
©s_bukley/Shutterstock.com

FINAL THOUGHTS

In this chapter we have described three ways to participate in politics:
(1) unconventional political participation and (2) conventional political participation (a) in the two-party system or (b) in a third party. Of these three
ways to participate in the political process, which is the most likely to lead to
results? In other words, if you are passionate about an issue, how should you
try to bring about change?

There are many historical examples of when unconventional participation was
effective. In the years before the American Revolution, groups like the Sons
of Liberty, which tarred and feathered tax collectors and destroyed property
(like British tea), were effective at bringing about the political changes they
sought—independence from England. In the late 1950s and early 1960s, Martin Luther King Jr. led civil rights demonstrations through the South. Technically, many of the demonstrations were illegal and thus unconventional
because they did not have a permit. King was certainly successful in bringing
down the Jim Crow laws and achieving greater opportunity for blacks. And in
the late 1960s, many young people protested against the Vietnam War, sometimes illegally occupying college buildings and engaging in violent protests.
The anti-Vietnam war protestors achieved their goal by causing the US government to end the war early.

But other times unconventional participation can backfire because the outrageous behavior can turn the country against the activists. For example, when the Weather Underground (a Marxist group that violently protested the Vietnam War) attacked the Pentagon, most people turned against them. And when Code Pink protested the Iraq War in the Capitol Building, many congressmen, including Democrats, became agitated with their antics. So much of the time it seems that unconventional participation is less than effective.

Historically, third parties have had a limited effect. Most of the time when a person casts her ballot for a third party, the vote is squandered. Let's say that this person is a fierce libertarian who believes in smaller government and lower taxes. If she votes for the Libertarian Party candidate, this essentially takes a vote away from the Republican, to the advantage of the Democrat candidate. If the Democrat wins, this will likely lead to bigger government and higher taxes, the opposite of what the libertarian wanted.

The best thing this libertarian could have done was work within the two-party system and try to push the Republican Party to cut government and lower taxes. Yet it often seems daunting to try to get one of the major parties to adopt a particular policy. Of the three choices—unconventional participation, third party support, or engage in the two-party system—it is probably a more productive use of your time and energy to support one of the two major parties. One of the best ways for a young person to get involved is to volunteer to work for your local party organization during the next election. Almost all politicians, including presidents, have started out that way.

NOTES

For party affiliation trends, go to the Pew Research Center (www.pewresearchcenter.org). "Trends in Party Identification" and Gallup's (www.gallup.com) tracking poll on party affiliation.

For a history of third parties, go to ThisNation.com: American Government & Politcs Online (www.thisnation.com) "What is the history of third parties in the United States."

For the platforms, issue positions, and leadership of the Democratic and Republican Parties, go to their official websites: www.gop.com and www.democrats.org.

Lewis L. Gould. *Grand Old Party: A History of the Republicans*. New York: Random House, 2003.

Alexander Hamilton, John Jay, and James Madison. *The Federalists*. Indianapolis: Liberty Fund, 2001.

Lee Hamilton. *How Congress Works*. Bloomington, Indiana: Indiana University Press, 2004.

L. Sandy Maisel. *American Political Parties and Elections*. Oxford: Oxford University Press, 2007.

Charles Murray. *Coming Apart*. New York: Crown Forum, 2013.

Jules Witcover. *Party of the People: A History of the Democrats*. New York: Random House, 2003.

ESSAY QUESTIONS

1. What are the goals of a political party?
2. How do parties help our democracy function?
3. What are the benefits of the two-party system for our democracy?
4. How do third parties start and what influence can they have?
5. What groups tend to identify with the Democratic and Republican party?
6. Give examples of unconventional political participation.

TERMS

Conventional Political Participation: _____

Electoral Realignment: _____

Party Identification: _____

Party Platform: _____

Political Party: _____

Proportional System: _____

Superdelegates: _____

Terrorism: _____

Unconventional Political Participation: _____

Winner-take-all: _____

CHAPTER 20

What Is the Role of the News Media in Our Democracy?

TOPICS

► The Function of a Free Press in a Democracy
► History of News Media
► Government Regulation of the Media
► Where Do People Get Their News Today?
► The Professional Press
► News Bias

LEARNING OBJECTIVES

When you finish reading this chapter, you will be able to:

1. List the important functions of a free press in a democracy.
2. Outline significant times when the press influenced history.
3. Discuss some FCC rules.
4. Describe the top news sources for Americans today.
5. Explain the practices of the professional press.

WHAT IS THE ROLE OF THE NEWS MEDIA IN OUR DEMOCRACY?

The Founding Generation understood the importance of a free press, which played a vital role during the American Revolution, and so they institutionalized it in the First Amendment. Thomas Jefferson said, "The basis of our government being the opinion of the people, the very first object should be to keep that right." And George Mason called a free press "one of the great bulwarks of liberty." No true democracy could exist without a free press. Indeed, the first thing dictators do is replace the free media with a state controlled propaganda machine. This chapter will explore the reasons why democracies are contingent on the freedom of the press, review the history of the news media in America, and explain the role of professional journalists in the democratic process.

THE FUNCTIONS OF A FREE PRESS IN A DEMOCRACY

In a democratic form of government, the people are the ultimate sovereigns. The government serves the people, and the people express their will through free and open elections. This job is so important that the news media is often described as the "fourth estate," a sort of fourth branch of government. If we analyze the role of the press more closely, we see that they serve several important functions in the democratic process.

The Press Informs the People: In 1995, Saddam Hussein, the dictator of Iraq, won reelection with a stunning 99.9 percent vote. But the world was not impressed. Everybody knew the vote was meaningless not only because the people feared voting against the ruthless dictator, but also because the Iraqi press never gave the people any information except to show how great their leader was. For elections to be authentic, the people must have access to true information. The people need to know about the economy, political issues, the success or failure of government programs, foreign affairs, and many other issues. And if a candidate is running for office, the people must have truthful information about her political record, her personal history, and her associations.

The Press Informs the Government: Every morning the President of the United States is provided with excerpts and summaries of the top newspapers across the country. It is vital for the success of any government official that they understand the state of affairs in their area of their responsibility, be it for the nation, a state, or a district. A free press will also report on the success or failure of a government program. As the Obama administration executed the Affordable Care Act, they have had to make many adjustments based on reports from the media about certain aspects of the law that are

A democracy can't function without a free and independent news media.

©Alexandr III/Shutterstock.com

not working as planned. Moreover, many times the media will actually initiate the reform process. The media might report on a particular problem, outraging the public, and then a lawmaker will step forward to propose a law to fix that problem.

Hold Public Officials Accountable: One of the most important functions of the press is to hold government officials to account. If a politician is incompetent or corrupt, or if his program is not working, the press plays a vital function by exposing their incompetence or dishonesty. The "Fourth Branch" analogy holds because the press is serving as a check on the other three branches of government. *This function of exposing wrongdoing or incompetence of government officials is often referred to as the* **watchdog** *role of the press.* Once the wrongdoing or poor performance is exposed, then the people can decide if the official should be removed from office or if the program should be changed. This will result in better government. Imagine a country in which the government completely controls the press. How would the people know if government officials are doing a bad job?

A Public Forum: *Another way to think of the press is that it serves as a public forum to debate and test ideas. This is called the* **marketplace of ideas**. People can write opinion articles in newspapers and magazines or debate on cable television shows. Journalists can investigate the factual claims of candidates, interest groups, and scholars. All this is done in public, for the people to decide. In modern America, much of this debate is between liberals and conservatives. Who has the best ideas? Supreme Court Justice Oliver Wendell Holmes wrote that "the best test of truth is the power of the thought to get accepted in the competition of the market, and that truth is the only ground upon which their wishes safely can be carried out." In this public contest of ideas, eventually bad ideas will be exposed as faulty and good ideas will prevail as true and right.

Links the Government to the People: Lastly, the news media serves as a connection or conduit between the government and the people. Political scientists call the press a **linkage institution**: *The press links government officials to the people, and it links the people to government officials.* The media provides the necessary information to the people so they can understand what government is doing. And government officials learn the opinions, concerns, and mood of the people through the press. This linkage shows the symbiotic relationship between the politicians and the press. The press needs government information to write stories, and the politicians need the press to get their message out to the people. As we will see in later sections, this symbiotic relationship between the press and politicians is fraught with tension.

Watchdog

this function of exposing wrongdoing or incompetence of government officials is often referred to as the watchdog role of the press

Marketplace of Ideas

another way to think of the press is that it serves as a public forum to debate and test ideas

Linkage Institution

the press links government officials to the people, and it links the people to government officials

HISTORY OF NEWS MEDIA

The news media has played a major role in every important phase in American history. Often the press has influenced events that have had a significant impact on society and the government. This brief history of the American news media will reveal several interesting issues related to media objectivity and influence.

Revolutionary Era: The press played a major role in shaping public opinion during the American Revolution, which was heavily in favor of the patriot cause. During the revolt against Britain, nearly forty newspapers existed in the colonies. One of the most influential voices before the war was Samuel Adams, who published the "Journal of Occurrences." This served as a sort of newswire service distributing hundreds of articles to newspapers all around the colonies describing the misbehavior of the Red Coats that occupied Boston. These stories were often filled with exaggerations and outright lies, which flamed colonial hatred toward the British. This highlights the fact that the press can be used for partisan causes in order to change public opinion, which may distort and bend the truth to achieve a political goal.

Also during the Revolution, pamphlets played a vital role in shaping public opinion. *Pamphlets* were unbound booklets or leaflets, usually under fifty pages long, which made an argument about a single subject. These played an especially important role in turning loyal colonists into revolutionaries as writers and public officials, often writing unanimously, made arguments against the sugar tax, stamp tax, and declaring "no taxation without representation." Of the thousands of pamphlets published during the revolutionary period, by far the most influential pamphlet was Thomas Paine's *Common Sense*, selling over 150,000 copies. Undermining the legitimacy of the divine right of kings, Paine urged Americans to seek independence from Great Britain.

Early Republic: During and after the Revolution, many newspapers were *Broadsides*, news printed on one large sheet of paper, often posted on trees or on tavern walls. Later, most newspapers consisted of one or two large sheets of paper, which, when folded in half, made four or eight pages. The front pages were filled with articles and opinion pieces, and the back pages contained ads. As president, George Washington read several newspapers a day to keep track of public opinion.

As the two-party system developed, the press became highly partisan, supporting one party or the other. The first two political parties in America were the Federalist Party and the Jeffersonian Republican Party. Some newspapers, such as John Fenno's *Gazette of the United States*, supported the Federalist

Party. And other papers, like Philip Freneau's *The National Gazette*, supported the Republican Party. And both parties funneled money to their supporting newspapers by providing them with government-related duties, such as posting government notices.

Jacksonian Era: During the 1830s, an era that celebrated "the common man," the franchise was expanded to include all adult white males regardless of whether they owned property. The press was now seen as an important tool to inform the voting masses. As a result, newspapers adopted a more direct style as they shifted away from elite readers to the barely literate. In 1833, Benjamin Day started selling his paper, the *New York Sun*, for one penny. New technology, mass circulation, and increased revenue from advertising allowed the "penny press" to thrive financially and thus to become more independent from political influence.

The trend toward more objectivity continued in 1848 when the *Associated Press* was established. This was the first wire service in America. The Associated Press provided stories to other newspapers through a new technological breakthrough, the telegraph. Because telegraph companies charge by the word, it forced the Associated Press to adopt a straightforward, succinct style, which became emblematic of newspaper journalism ever after.

Abolitionism: Although it took several decades, the press played an important role in turning public opinion against slavery in the Northern states before

When Andrew Jackson was president, the "penny press"
provided news to the common man.
©Everett Historical/Shutterstock.com

the Civil War. In 1837, Elijah Lovejoy, the publisher of the *Alton Observer*, was shot by a mob and his presses destroyed for speaking out against slavery. At this time, the most famous abolitionist journalist was William Lloyd Garrison, the publisher of the *Liberator*. For thirty-five years Garrison relentlessly advocated for the immediate emancipation of all slaves. Southern states banned his paper and offered a bounty for his head. Even in liberal Boston, he was almost lynched by an angry mob. But slowly more abolitionist papers followed his lead. Garrison closed down the *Liberator* in 1865 after the passage of the 13th Amendment, which abolished slavery in America.

Yellow Journalism: After cartoonist Thomas Nash of *Harper's Weekly* brought down the notorious city boss of New York, William Tweed, journalists realized they had tremendous political clout. By shaping public opinion, they could destroy powerful political machines. Then in the 1890s, newspapers realized they could influence public opinion to support a war. At this time William Randolph Hearst's *New York Journal* was in a circulation war with Joseph Pulitzer's *New York World*. The *Journal* was selling 500,000 copies a day, and the *World* was selling 600,000.

Then Hearst came across a story that would help him sell more papers: the Cuban revolt against Spanish rule. Hearst started publishing sensationalistic stories about Spanish atrocities, such as stories of Spanish soldiers burning priests alive and raping women. When the *USS Main* blew up, probably due to an overheated boiler, Hearst called for war with Spain. Before the conflict started, a journalist in Havana complained that there was nothing to do, and so he wanted to return home. Hearst was said to have replied by telegraph, "Please remain: you supply the pictures and I'll supply the war." During the war he helped to create, Hearst was the first newspaper in America to sell over one million papers in a day.

Muckrakers: During the Progressive Era, from about 1900 to 1920, progressive journalists started writing the *exposé*, an article exposing some sort of evil in society, most often political or business corruption. Often, these stories led to the enactment of new laws. Ida Tarbell, writing for *McClure's Magazine*, exposed the ruthless business practices of John D. Rockefeller, which led to the break-up of Standard Oil. Upton Sinclair's book, *The Jungle*, exposed unhealthful practices of the meatpacking industry, leading to the Meat Inspection Act and the Pure Food and Drug Act. By this time, Hearst became a muckraker and bought *Cosmopolitan Magazine*. He hired David Graham Philips, whose exposé on the corruption of the US Senate, led to the passage of the 17th amendment. The muckrakers established the model of a new type of journalist, the social and political reformer.

Radio: After World War I, when, ironically, many muckrakers were hired by the federal government to propagandize the war effort, radio became the new medium by which Americans got their news. In the 1930s, in radio addresses known as "Fireside Chats," Franklin Roosevelt communicated directly with the American people and explained his New Deal programs. Teddy Roosevelt called this power the "Bully Pulpit," the president's ability to communicate with the American people and set the national agenda.

But much to FDR's chagrin, radio was also used by his political enemies. The most famous of which was Father Charles Coughlin, who relentlessly criticized the New Deal to his 35 million listeners. Eventually Coughlin was driven from the airwaves for his Anti-Semitism and pro-Nazi rhetoric. After the fall of Coughlin, a highly respected radio journalist emerged. During World War II, Edward R. Murrow reported on radio from the front lines in Europe. Working for CBS News, he became the country's most trusted journalist.

Television: In the early 1950s, Murrow was the host of a popular television news magazine called *See it Now*. This was during the Cold War Era when some communist spies, such as Alger Hiss and the Rosenbergs, were exposed in public trials. To gain political popularity, Joe McCarthy, a US Senator from Wisconsin, stirred up fears of a vast communist spy ring. On one occasion, he claimed to have a list of 205 Russian spies that infiltrated the Truman administration. McCarthy recklessly ruined the careers of many people by

Franklin Roosevelt talked to the American people during the Great Depression via the radio in what he called "fireside chats."
©Everett Historical/Shutterstock.com

accusing them of communist sympathy without any proof. On his television show, Murrow showed clips of McCarthy's bullying tactics and called him a villain and a psychopath. Soon, McCarthy self-destructed. Murrow and the McCarthy episode was just a taste of the role television would play in news journalism in the coming decades.

Civil Rights: Television transformed news journalism and became the number one source of news for the American people. With its live images, television was far more vivid, immediate, and visceral than news print. And the power of images seemed to be more effective at influencing public opinion. The civil rights movement, for example, was greatly aided by television. For decades, people had been reading about Jim Crow laws and lynchings in the South, but they had become complacent about it. Now the American people saw with their own eyes live images of peaceful protestors, sometimes women and children, being abused and attacked by locals. This provoked a great emotion response that led to political and social change. By the mid-1960s, Congress passed civil rights legislation that eradicated Jim Crow laws.

Vietnam: Likewise, television journalism turned public opinion against a war. Vietnam was the first war that was broadcast live in American family rooms, complete with all the blood and guts that takes place on the battlefield. By the late 1960s, much of the professional press had become opposed to the war. The turning point of the war was the Tet Offensive. Television and print media characterized the Tet Offensive as a North Vietnam victory, when in fact it was a US victory. By then, Walter Cronkite of CBS news had become American's most respected newsman. When Cronkite announced in a thirty-minute special about Tet that he concluded the war was unwinnable, President Johnson instantly knew this would have a devastating impact. Johnson said, "If I've lost Cronkite, I've lost the war." He was right. Soon public opinion had turned against the war. Four weeks later, LBJ announced he would be reducing troops in Vietnam and that he would not seek re-election.

Watergate: After turning the public against a war, the press would be directly responsible for causing a president to resign from office. Before Richard Nixon's reelection in 1972, operatives working for the Committee to Re-elect the President (CREEP) were caught bugging the Democrat National Headquarters at the Watergate Hotel. The story was reported in the press before the election, but few paid much attention. Then two young reporters, Bob Woodward and Carl Bernstein, were assigned by the *Washington Post* to pursue the story. Due to their persistence and ingenuity, and due to the backing of the editor and publisher of the *Post*, they were able to break a series of stories that exposed the dirty tricks, illegal activities, and unethical behavior of the Nixon Administration. Nixon was forced to resign. Since Watergate, tensions have heightened between the president and the press.

Trump Tweets: As Franklin Roosevelt used radio, and John Kennedy used TV, smart presidents take advantage of the latest technological advancements in media. Donald Trump, for good or for bad, is now associated with online social media, especially Twitter. Like radio and TV for past presidents, Twitter allows Trump to side-step the mainstream media, which is often very critical of him, and talk directly to the American people. During the presidential campaign in 2016, Trump used it to articulate his agenda, but also to attack his opponents, often giving them demeaning nicknames, such as "Crooked Hillary" and "Little Marco." As president, Trump has continued to use Twitter almost on a daily basis, sometimes to announce new policies, and other times to denounce his critics. One of his favorite targets is the news media, which he often calls "fake news." Many

Muckrakers like Ida Tarbell engaged in public advocacy to create greater social justice.
©neftali/Shutterstock.com

of Trumps opponents and followers have asked Trump to stop tweeting, saying it is unpresidential, but if anything Trump has expanded its use. In October of 2017, Trump surpassed the pope and became the world leader with the most Twitter followers, over 40 million. Having direct access to so many people around the world on a daily basis is something past presidents never dreamed of.

Conclusion: This brief history of American journalism from the Revolution to Watergate allows us to draw several conclusions. First, in the early years of journalism, the press was often biased toward one political party or the other. Second, then during the Muckraking era, the press started to claim to be "*objective*," not supporting a political party or agenda. Third, but at the same time, the muckraking press engaged in **public advocacy**, *holding that it is the mission of the news media to enlighten the public in order to achieve greater social justice.* These two roles appear to be somewhat contradictory. Fourth, the news media has had both a negative (Father Coughlin) and positive (William Lloyd Garrison) influence on society. And lastly, the news media has had a major impact on American politics, influencing wars and presidential politics.

GOVERNMENT REGULATION OF THE MEDIA

After the invention of the radio, the government had to regulate the media for practical reasons. Some of the early radio stations had such powerful signals that they would drown out other stations hundreds of miles away. In 1934, Congress created the **Federal Communications Commission (FCC)** *a federal agency that was created to regulate the broadcast media.* Because the radio and television band is limited, the "airwaves" were deemed public property,

Public Advocacy

holding that it is the mission of the news media to enlighten the public in order to achieve greater social justice

Federal Communications Commission (FCC)

a federal agency that was created to regulate the broadcast media and broadcasters were required to get a federal license and were assigned a specific spot on the airwaves band. By requiring that broadcasters receive a license, renewable every five years, the federal government gained leverage over the broadcast media.

Rules of the FCC: Eventually, the FCC established several rules for broadcasters. They deemed that broadcasts must be used for the public good and indecent language was prohibited. The FCC established the *equal time rule,* stating that all stations must provide "equal time" to all political candidates, including advertising time, in order that one candidate or party does not have an unfair advantage.

And they instituted the **fairness doctrine**: *in order to further the "public good," broadcasters were required to provide a "reasonable" amount of time to public policy issues and provide diverse opinions.* For example, if a television station aired a segment on gun control, then they would have to provide another segment on gun rights. But many broadcasters felt this was too controlling and in 1987, as part of the Reagan administration's efforts to deregulate, the fairness doctrine was terminated. Since then, radio talk shows like Rush Limbaugh's can advocate only one ideological opinion without the requirement to balance it with another opinion.

Fairness Doctrine

in order to further the "public good," broadcasters were required to provide a "reasonable" amount of time to public policy issues and provide diverse opinions

WHERE DO PEOPLE GET THEIR NEWS TODAY?

With each technological innovation, the American people have gained more types of news media by which to gain political information. Currently, people get their news from a wide variety of sources. A recent Pew Research Center survey asked, "Where did you get your news yesterday?" The response was: Television—57%, online—38%, radio—25%, and print newspaper—20%. Other polls break these numbers down further. A February 2013 Pew poll shows that for television news, 71% watch local TV news, 65% watch Network TV news (ABC, NBC, CBS national), and 38% watch cable TV news (CNN, MSNBC, Fox). Likewise, for newspapers: of the people who read newspapers, most read local newspapers rather than the national papers (*The New York Times, The Wall Street Journal,* and *USA Today*). This reveals that people tend to follow local news more closely than national news.

Trends in News Media Consumption: Pew polls taken over the last several years reveal several other interesting trends in the way people get their news. In 1991, 68% of people got most of their news from TV, now it is just 55%. Newspaper readership has also plummeted. In 1991, 56% got most of their news from newspapers, but today it is down to 29%. Talk radio is also on the slide: from 54% in 1991, to 33% today. So, where are people going? The Internet is the only media outlet in the ascendency. In 2002, 24% of people got most of their news from the Internet, but today it is 39%. So now newspapers, magazines, and the networks are scrambling to gain an online presence. But currently the biggest growth in online news consumption is on social media. According to recent polls, online readers are getting more news from social media like Facebook and Twitter. The danger of relying on social media for news, rather then outlets with professional editors, is that many news stories on Facebook and Twitter have been identified as fabrications, sometimes by foreign governments.

THE PROFESSIONAL PRESS

Modern media is fragmenting and becoming more personalized. If one goes on the Internet, they have access to hundreds of news outlets all over the world. The Internet also empowers the individual to become a journalist: any person can easily start a blog or go on Twitter and post one's thoughts for the world to see. But while the media world appears to be changing year by year, perhaps even month by month, there is still a professional press that controls the mainstream news. This section will discuss aspects of the professional press.

Media Conglomerates: About a half dozen companies control most of the news media. Comcast owns NBC, Telemundo, MSNBC, CNBC, and 15 TV stations. Disney: ABC, 10 TV stations, and 277 radio stations. News Corp: Fox News, *The Wall Street Journal*, *New York Post*, HarperCollins Publishers, and 27 TV stations. Time/Warner: CNN, and *Time* Magazine. Viacom: Comedy Central, and 10 TV stations. CBS: 30 TV stations. Gannet: 90 daily newspapers, *USA Today*, 1,000 weekly newspapers, and 23 TV stations. The largest American news wire service is the Associated Press, which supplies news stories to thousands of newspapers, radio stations, and TV stations daily. Further, most people get their online news from Yahoo News, Google News, and the Huffington Post. The professional journalists work for these organizations.

Professional Standards: Most professional journalists get a degree in journalism and learn the professional standards of their trade. When writing a story, they are taught to focus on "The Five Ws:" who, what, when, where, and why. Before a story is published, there should be at least two independent sources. And journalists use jargon to describe different types of sources. *On the record* means the journalist can quote and name their source. *Background* means that information can be used, but the name of the source will be vague, usually a "government official." *Deep Background* is used to describe general information, but the name is not even hinted at. *An exclusive* indicates that only one reporter was granted an interview. Most of this information comes through what is called a *leak*, when a government official provides information to a reporter, usually to spin a story to their advantage.

**Who decides what news stories to show on the nightly news?
Why do the network news shows all run the same stories?**
©elder nurkovic/Shutterstock.com

The Gatekeepers: Today there are probably about a hundred prominent editors, producers, and journalists that control much of the content of the mainstream news media. A few decades ago, a handful of news outlets controlled most of the news Americans received: the nightly network news of ABC, NBC, and CBS, *Time* Magazine, *Newsweek*, *The New York Times*, *The Wall Street Journal*, and *The Washington Post*. The editors and producers of these organizations played a decisive role in decided what was news. They were the **gatekeepers**: *the people that decide what news stories to print or broadcast on a daily and weekly news cycle.*

Besides deciding <u>what</u> stories to cover, they often control <u>how</u> a story is to be framed. **Framing** *is when the professional press determines the premise or the questions of an issue.* For example, if the gatekeepers decide they will discuss the Iraq War, the focus may be on how public opinion polls are turning against the war, not the actual military progress of the war. Or when the gatekeepers talk about illegal immigration, they may focus on the hardships the immigrants face, instead of how illegal immigration overburdens the schools and other government services.

Infotainment: Unlike in most other countries (think of Britain and the BBC), in America the news media are privately owned. This means that American news companies are **market driven**: *the media must attract readers and viewers in order to make a profit.* How does this affect the news? Most media conglomerates, such as Comcast, have hard news outlets, such as CNBC, and

gatekeepers

the people that decide what news stories to print or broadcast on a daily and weekly news cycle

Framing

is when the professional press determines the premise or the questions of an issue

Market Driven

the media must attract readers and viewers in order to make a profit entertainment outlets, such as Universal Studios. But in recent decades, the media have learned they can attract large audiences by *mixing news with entertainment to increase ratings: this is called* **infotainment**. Another trend is the *Oprahization* of the news. Referring to the *Oprah Winfrey Show*, this is news that focuses on emotions, personal tragedies, and self-realization. So, news has become more superficial and based on emotions.

A Pew survey showed that 21% of young people get their news from comedy shows. This is disturbing on many levels, but let's first consider whether this is an objective, non-biased source of news. George Mason University conducted a study that covered the opening monologues of four nightly comedy shows, such as *The Tonight Show with Jimmy Fallan*. It compiled all the jokes delivered from September 1 to October 31, just before the 2016 presidential election. The study found that 308 jokes were made about Trump, compared to 107 about Clinton. Furthermore, 71% of the jokes ridiculed personality traits, while only 9% focused on the issues. So, beyond revealing that the comedy shows tend to be biased against Republicans, it shows that the issues are rarely discussed but personality is the fodder of most late night comics. After reading this study, one may ask: Have the comedy shows contributed to the superficiality of news coverage, and have they contributed to the coarsening of political discourse in America?

In general, today more and more people are getting their news from soft news shows like *The View*, the *Today Show*, or comedians like Jimmy Fallon. The fear is that Americans have lost the intellectual rigor that is required to understand the complexities of economic and social policy. This trend has also led to the shrinking of American's attention span. Thirty years ago the average television news bite was forty-two seconds long; today it is eight seconds! This is a by-product of the modern new media. If a TV news show is not entertaining enough, the viewer can instantly click to one of the 250 competing stations. So, as soon as something gets too serious or difficult to understand, click, the viewer is gone.

Infotainment

mixing news with entertainment to increase ratings

NEWS BIAS

In this last segment we will tackle the subject of media bias. When one considers the role the media play in our democracy, as described above, it is vitally important than the news media provide the voters and government officials with accurate and truthful information. In a dictatorship, the news media are merely a propaganda tool used to prop up the government. But in a democracy, the media must be independent and objective, providing truthful information about society, government officials, and government programs. In this way, the news media holds elected officials to account.

On the other hand, if the news media is biased, it poses many dangers to a democratic form of government. If the people feel that the news is not truthful and objective, they will lose faith in the media as an institution. The people may become more open to conspiracy theories and may lose faith in the democratic process, concluding that the "system is rigged." And if the media is biased, the citizens lose out on consuming the full range of political ideas as they search for the best policies that can help improve America. In other words, it will undermine the marketplace of ideas that is so vital to progress and innovation.

Most government textbooks state that the media is not biased, and if they were, the media doesn't sway public opinion. They usually claim that *since most people are aware of their own ideology, they select news outlets that support their beliefs*: this is called **selective viewership**. For example, a conservative viewer will watch Fox News, and a liberal viewer will watch MSNBC. And most textbooks claim that even *if a conservative or a liberal watches a biased news broadcast, he or she will interpret the story to fit their ideology*, this is called **selective perception**. For example, if a liberal were to read an editorial in *The Wall Street Journal*, he or she would recognize that the article is being told from a conservative perspective and not believe the editorial.

Several objective studies, however, have shown that the media is biased to the left and that it does influence public opinion.

Journalists Are Democrats: Several studies confirm that most professional journalists are Democrats. In 1995, Elaine Povich, a fellow at the Media Research Center, conducted a survey of Washington journalists,

Selective Viewership

since most people are aware of their own ideology, they select news outlets that support their beliefs

Selective Perception

if a conservative or a liberal watches a biased news broadcast, he or she will interpret the story to fit their ideology

Do professional journalists tend to be liberal or conservative?
©Paolo Bona/Shutterstock.com

which showed that only 7 percent voted Republican. In 2004, Congressional Quarterly MoneyLine found that 98.9 percent of journalists gave money to Democrat John Kerry. In 2008, William Tate of *Investor's Business Daily* searched campaign contributions of journalists and found that 95.2 percent gave money to Democrat Obama. So, these studies indicate professional journalists are above 95 percent liberal leaning. Indeed, it is very difficult to find any group in America more liberal than journalists. The most liberal congressional district in America is New York's 15th District, which voted 93 percent for Obama in 2008.

Liberal Media Bias: Many other studies demonstrate liberal media bias. In 2004, John Lott and Kevin Hassett conducted a study on how newspapers report hard economic data. For example, if the US Commerce Department releases a report showing unemployment is 6%, do newspaper headlines report this as good news or bad news? Their study concluded that economic data is reported 20 percent to 40 percent more favorable during Democratic administrations than Republican administrations. This study rings true. Over the last seven years the economy has been very sluggish, but in general the news media have not criticized Obama's stewardship of the economy.

And a study conducted by the Media Research Center demonstrated liberal media bias in the way midterm elections are covered. In the weeks before the 2006 midterms, when Republicans under George Bush were expected to lose seats in Congress, the three networks (ABC, CBS, and NBC) reported 159 stories about the election. These stories often reported that the loss of congressional seats showed that George Bush was in trouble. But eight years later, when Obama was president, the networks only ran twenty-five stories about the midterm elections. In 2012, Democrats were expected to lose seats in Congress, but now the news media reported that history shows that members of the president's party often lose seats in a midterm election, protecting Obama from any blame.

Two other studies also objectively showed that the media is biased toward the left. In 2005, Tim Groseclose and Jeff Milyo published a study in the prestigious *Quarterly Journal of Economics*. They measured how often the top twenty news television shows and newspapers cited liberal think tanks and how often they cited conservative think tanks. They showed that in news stories, the press most often cites liberal think tanks. The study concludes that eighteen of twenty news shows and newspapers are more liberal than the average American.

Lastly, two economists at the University of Chicago, Matthew Gentkow and Jesse Shapiro, conducted a study using liberal and conservative catchphrases. For example, liberals tend to use words like "pro-choice" and "gun control," and conservatives tend to use words like "pro-life" and "gun rights." They programmed computers to search news stories, not editorials, in the top US newspapers and found that newspapers more often use liberal catchphrases.

The Media Effect: As stated above, most textbooks say that even if the press is liberal, it has a little or no *media effect*: the influence liberal media has on the public's voting patterns. Some studies, however, show that the media effect is strong. Alan Gerber of Yale University conducted a study in which they randomly selected two groups of people in Virginia. One group was given a free subscription to the liberal *Washington Post,* and the other was given a free subscription to the conservative *Washington Times*. During the next election the *Post* group was 3.8 times more likely to vote for the Democratic candidate than before they got the free liberal newspaper. The percentage 3.8 is enough to change the results of many elections.

Trump Versus the Media: In the above section we cited several academic studies that show that over the last couple of decades, the media have supported Democratic presidents and liberal issues. But the news coverage on Trump has been even more negative. A Harvard University study published in May of 2017 surveyed all the stories of the mainstream media for the first 100 days of the Trump administration. It revealed that 80% of the stories about Trump were negative, compared to 41% of the stories about Obama in his first 100 days. For CNN and MSNBC, 93% of the stories about Trump were negative, compared to 53% by Fox. Moreover, on the issue of immigration, 98% of the stories were negative. A Pew survey published in October of 2017 showed even more negative coverage of Trump. They studied 3,000 stories by 24 news outlets over the first 100 days, and Pew found that only 5% of the stories about Trump were positive, compared to 42% of the stories about Obama. Certainly, Trump made many mistakes that deserved some negative stories, but no president has received such negative coverage in the last 25 years.

FINAL THOUGHTS

It seems that the people sense that the media are biased, and as a result they are losing credibility. A September 17, 2014, Gallup poll shows that media approval is at an all-time low. Only 40 percent of respondents said the media "fully, accurately, and fairly" reports the news. For Democrats, it was 54 percent; and for Republicans, it was 27 percent. So, knowing that the media is biased, how does one find the truth? There are two things you can do to be well informed. First, find good, reliable news sources. The Groseclose/Milyo study concluded that the PBS's *News Hours* and Fox's *Special Report* are very balanced. So, watch credible and balanced shows like these.

Second, you need to read and watch a *variety* of news sources. If you are liberal, don't live in a liberal bubble and only read *The New York Times* and watch MSNBC. And if you are conservative, don't live in a conservative bubble and only read the *Washington Times* and listen to Rush Limbaugh. It is important to get news all along the media spectrum and to carefully draw your own conclusions. Today people have access to hundreds of news outlets all around the country and the world, so make sure to actively seek news from as many different sources as possible. In the end, it is the responsibility of each individual to be well informed.

NOTES

For media conglomeration see: Vanna Le, "Global 2000: The World's Largest Media Companies of 2014," *Forbes*, May 7, 2014; Ashley Lutz, "These 6 Corporations Control 90% of the Media in America," *Business Insider*, Jun 14, 2012.

For studies showing that the media is biased: *Media Research Center*, "Media Bias Basics," at www. mrc.org; David Brooks, *New York Times*, "Ruling Class War," Sept. 11, 2004; William Tate, "Putting Money Where Mouths are: Media donations favor Dems 100-1," *Investor's Business Daily*, July 23, 2009.; Lott-Hassett, "Is Newspaper Coverage of Economic Date Politically Biased?" Revised Oct. 18, 2004 (www.ssrn.com/abstract=588453); Kyle Drennen and Rich Noyes, "TV News Blacks out This Year's Bad Election News for Democrats," *Media Research Center*, Oct. 22, 2014; Tim Groseclose and Jeff Milyo, "A Measure of Media Bias," *Quarterly Journal of Economics* 120, no. 4 (Nov. 2005): Alan S. Gerber and Donald P. Green, "Effects of Canvassing, Telephone Calls, and Direct Mail on Voter Turnout: A Field Experiment" *American Political Science Review* 94, no. 3, (Sept. 2000); Matthew Gentkow and Jesse Shapiro, "What Drives Media Slant," *Econometrica* 78, no. 1 (Jan. 2010).

For recent studies on the media coverage of Trump: Harvard's Shorenstein Center on Media, Politics and Public Policy, "News Coverage of Donald Trump's First 100 Days," May 18, 20017. Pew Research Center, "Covering President Trump in a Polarized Media Environment," October, 2017.

Andrew Beaujon, "Pew: Half of Americans get their news digitally, topping newspaper, radio." *Pew Research Center*, Sept. 27, 2012.

Andrea Caumont, "12 trends shaping digital news," *Pew Research Center*, Oct. 16, 2013.

Tim Groseclose, *Left Turn: How Liberal Media Bias Distorts the American Mind*, New York: St. Martin's Griffin, 2011.

Jan E. Leighley. Mass *Media and Politics: A Social Science Perspective.* New York: Houghton Mifflin, 2004.

Justin McCarthy, "Trust in Mass Media Returns to All-Time Low," *Gallup Poll*, Sept. 17, 2014.

Rodger Streitmatter. *Mightier than the Sword: How the Media Have Shaped American History.* Boulder, Colorado, Westview Press, 2012.

ESSAY QUESTIONS

1. List the major functions that the media play in a democracy.
2. After reading the section on the history of the media, describe a time when you think the press did good for society and describe a time they did harm.
3. Describe the top places Americans get their news and state what sources you think are the best.
4. Knowing that the media might not be 100 percent objective, describe how the media may use its bias as gatekeepers and by framing.
5. Describe infotainment and Oprahization and discuss if you think the news is getting too superficial.
6. How have soft news and the diminishing American attention span affected politics today?

TERMS

Fairness Doctrine: _____

Federal Communications Commission (FCC): _____

Framing: _____

Gatekeeper: _____

Infotainment: _____

Linkage Institution: _____

Market Driven: _____

Marketplace of Ideas: _____

Public Advocacy: _____

Selective Perception: _____

Selective Viewership: _____

Watchdog: _____

UNIT FIVE

Public Policy

CHAPTER 21

What Do Interest Groups Do?

TOPICS

- ▶ Theories about Interest Groups
- ▶ Interest Groups: The Good, the Bad, and the Billionaires
- ▶ Types of Interest Groups
- ▶ Campaign Finance Law
- ▶ How Interest Groups Influence Public Policy

LEARNING OBJECTIVES

When you finish reading this chapter, you will be able to:

1. Compare pluralist theory of interest groups with elite theory.
2. Discuss the beneficial and harmful effects of interest groups.
3. Delineate the different types of interest groups.
4. Identify the major feature of current campaign finance law.
5. Show the different strategies interest groups use to influence public policy.

WHAT DO INTEREST GROUPS DO?

An **interest group** *is a group of people that get together to change public policy.* The Constitution clearly protects this type of activity. The First Amendment protects freedom of speech, the right to assemble, and the right to petition the government for a redress of grievances: all fundamental to the existence, operations, and goals of interest groups.

Interest Group

is a group of people that get together to change public policy.

Although the right to form interest groups is plainly protected by the Constitution, people have always felt anxious about the potential harm interest groups pose to the democratic process. Ironically, people often feel trepidation about *other* interest groups, but they like their own interest group. A teacher who wants to improve public education may belong to the National Education Association (NEA). A student concerned about the environment might belong to the Sierra Club. And a Christian who wants to protect the lives of the unborn may belong to the Christian Coalition. All these people are concerned about a particular issue and want the government to change policies that, in their view, will improve society. But at the same time, they may feel that other groups want to change things for the worse. This negative feeling about interest groups is reflected in the polls. Gallop recently reported that 80 percent of Americans feel interest groups are doing more harm than good.

THEORIES ABOUT INTEREST GROUPS

As the above examples illustrate, many people join groups in order to sway the public and government officials to accept their ideas for the good of the country. But since America's founding, political thinkers have had different theories about how this process should work and whether it is harmful or beneficial to our democracy.

Teachers form interest groups in order to get better pay and benefits.
©Rawpixel.com/Shutterstock.com

James Madison: The Revolutionary Generation was hopeful that "factions," today what we would call political parties and interest groups, would not develop in America. All Americans should do what is best for the country, they argued, not work for the benefit of their particular group. But Madison, in *Federalist #10*, said that factions are inevitable because it is human nature for people with common interest to combine together. And any remedy to restrict interest groups would necessarily violate their rights, making the "remedy . . . worst than the disease." Madison asserted that we need not fear interest groups, especially in a large, diverse country such as America, because the multitude of factions will compete with each other, thus making it impossible for a single faction to dominate.

Pluralistic Theory

the idea that many interest groups representing a wide variety of economic and ideological interests compete with each other

Madison's concept has been called **pluralistic theory**: *many interest groups representing a wide variety of economic and ideological interests, spread over a vast and diversified geography, will compete with each other, but no one group will be able to dominate due to America's tremendous size and decentralized system of government.* In small countries, Madison noted, with a non-diversified economy, one group may be able to control the political process. But in America as a whole, with thousands of different economic interests, no one industry could dominate. Furthermore, in our federalists system, with thousands of local governments, fifty state governments, and one national government divided into three branches, it is impossible for one group to gain leverage over all those lawmakers and bureaucrats.

Alexis de Tocqueville: In the early 1830s, Alexis de Tocqueville, a French aristocrat and intellectual, toured America and wrote *Democracy in America*, one of the most insightful books about American society and politics ever published. One of his keen insights was that America was a "nation of joiners": the American people had a tremendous propensity to form groups or "associations" and that this had a very healthy effect on democracy. In a democracy, Tocqueville explained, all citizens are equal and the individual is free to pursue his or her self interests. But it is harmful for society if each individual only thinks of himself. Associations counterbalance the selfish instinct that is let loose in a democracy. By joining a group, learning to work with others, and trying to bring about change for the common good, the individual not only learns to rise above his selfish pursuits, but learns how democracy works.

Alexis de Tocqueville thought Americans had a great talent to form groups to solve problems.
©Everett Historical/Shutterstock.com

Tocqueville thought of associations very broadly, meaning any group an individual joins, including a town hall meeting, a trade association, or a social movement interest group such as the Temperance Society. Tocqueville said the two most important groups for society are the church and the family. Religion, he said, should be the "first of their political institutions" in a democracy. By teaching virtue and humility, religion tempers the selfish instinct and teaches the individual to open her horizon beyond the self. Likewise with the family. This is especially important for young men. Women civilize men, and the responsibility of raising a family funnels men's energies into more constructive pursuits that work to improve society, such as maintaining a job as a road builder or an accountant.

Social Capital: In 2000, Robert Putnam published the influential book *Bowling Alone: The Collapse and Revival of American Community*. In this book, Putnam asserts that since the 1950s, Americans are less committed to joining small groups and civic organizations. In the past, it was very common for adult men to join organizations such as the Elks Club, the Lions Club, or the Rotary Club that sought to improve the community. People also joined less civic-minded groups such as bowling leagues and sewing clubs. These groups taught people important interpersonal skills and created a sort of matrix that connected the individual to society. Putman called this **social capital** *the interconnection fostered by people joining groups that benefited the society and the individual*. Putman said that it is a mark of an unhealthy society if people remain isolated.

Elite Theory: In the 1970s, Scholars such as E. E. Schattschneider and Theodore J. Lowi critiqued Madison's pluralistic theory, which was advanced again by a group of scholars in the 1950s. America is not a democratic system in which a multitude of groups, representing different economic, geographical, and ideological interests, compete with each other on an equal playing field. Instead, they argue, democracy is a competitive system of winners and losers, and the winners are most often the wealthy elites. **Elite theory** *states that a small group of the wealthy and highly educated elites use interest groups for their own advantage at the expense of the general public*. Schattschneider and Lowi argued that powerful forces in industry, finance, the military, the university, and the media, for example, use interest groups for their advantage, something poor and uninformed people cannot do.

INTEREST GROUPS: THE GOOD, THE BAD, AND THE BILLIONAIRE

Like nearly anything, we can see both good and bad things about interest groups: there are things they do that help our democracy, and there are things they do that harm our democracy. Some fear that the super rich are using interest groups to corrupt politics. In 2016, the main focus of Bernie Sanders's

Social Capital

the interconnection fostered by people joining groups that benefited the society and the individual

Elite Theory

the idea that a small group of the wealthy and highly educated elites use interest groups for their own advantage at the expense of the general public presidential campaign was to take power away from wealthy individuals and groups. In this section, we will analyze the potential benefits and harm interest groups may pose to society and the role of the super rich.

How Interest Groups Help Our Democracy: There are several ways interest groups help the democratic process. First, they encourage civic participation. Say you are concerned about the harmful effects of pesticides, by joining an environmental group you can work to clean the environment. Second, they educate the public and lawmakers. One of the main things interest groups do is provide information. Mothers Against Drunk Drivers (MADD) has been very successful at making the public aware of the dangers of driving while drunk. Third, they aid the election process. Some interest groups encourage people to vote, other groups host debate forums, and other groups provide candidate guides—all these things help the voter. And fourth, interest groups confront difficult issues that the established parties may ignore. For example, in the late 1950s, civil rights groups put pressure on the Democrats and the Republicans to finally pass civil rights legislation.

How Interest Groups Hurt Our Democracy: One danger interest groups pose is political corruption. **Lobbyists** *are hired by interest groups to meet with lawmakers or administrators to persuade them to change a law or policy.* But sometimes lobbyists resort to bribery. One of the most sensational bribery incidents in the modern era was the Tea Pot Dome scandal. In the early 1920s, oil companies gave hundreds of thousands of dollars to Albert B. Fall, the Secretary of Interior, to lease them land with known oil reserves. Fall was found guilty and spent a year in jail. In 2007, congressman William J. Jefferson (D-Louisiana) was convicted of accepting bribes from a high-tech company and was sentenced to thirteen years in jail, the longest sentence ever handed down to a congressman.

Beyond bribery, interest groups pose other dangers. One interesting theory was proposed by Mancur Olson in his book, *The Rise and Decline of Nations.* Olson asserts that when nations are young they experience greater economic growth because their governments are smaller and more flexible. But as a nation matures, more and more interest groups attach themselves to the political process and to the bureaucracy. The nation gets bogged down with endless rules and regulations designed to protect thousands of interest groups. The result is economic stagnation. American history seems to support Olson's thesis. In the 1920s, America enjoyed a 7 percent GDP, which doubled the size of the economy in ten years, raising the standard of living for the whole country. But today our economy is burdened with a myriad of regulations, many inserted by interest groups, and our economy limps along with less than a 2 percent growth rate.

Lobbyists

people hired by interest groups to meet with lawmakers or administrators to persuade them to change a law or policy

The Influence of Billionaires: Today several interest groups are funded by one person with billions of dollars. On the liberal side: International financier George Soros founded Open Society Institute, which funds dozens of liberal organizations. Hedge fund manager Tom Steyer established NextGen Climate Action to support environmental causes. News billionaire Michael Bloomberg uses Independence USA to promote gun control. And Facebook founder Mark Zuckerberg uses his billions to support immigration reform. And between 2001 and 2012, billionaire Warren Buffett has given more than $1.2 billion to abortion organizations. On the conservative side: Billionaires Charles and David Koch spend millions supporting conservative candidates, as does casino magnet Sheldon Adelson.

Billionaire Mark Zuckerberg gives millions of dollars to pro-immigration groups.
©Kobby Dagan/Shutterstock.com

Is it fair that the super rich have the ability to highly influence the political process, while the average person's influence is limited to one vote? When Tocqueville developed his positive understanding of interest groups in the 1830s, interest groups were relatively small organizations created and maintained by ordinary people. Now billionaires can form interest groups to bankroll their pet causes and support their candidates. On the other hand, as Madison noted, any effort to restrict the wealthy from engaging in politics would necessarily violate their First Amendment rights. People's views of wealthy activists normally are linked to their political views. If a rich person is spending money for a "good" cause, then that person is generous and courageous. For example, before the Civil War, millionaires Lewis Tappan and Gerrit Smith bankrolled the abolitionist movement. At the time many thought they were villains, but today they are considered heroes.

TYPES OF INTEREST GROUPS

Today there are more interest groups than ever before. The *Encyclopedia of Associations* lists over 23,000 national organizations in the United States. Broadly speaking, these groups can be placed in two categories: economic interests and social interests. **Economic interest groups** *promote the financial concerns of its members, such as corporations or unions.* Other groups are interested in changing society by promoting an ideology, such as the Cato Institute which promotes libertarianism, or focusing on a single issue, such as People for the Ethical Treatment of Animals (PETA), which protects animals against mistreatment. **Social interest groups** *want to change society for the better, and they include ideological or single issue groups.*

Economic Interest Groups

promote the financial concerns of its members, such as corporations or unions

Social Interest Groups

want to change society for the better, and they include ideological or single issue groups

A. Economic Interest Groups

Corporations: Some of the first interest groups in America represented business. In the early years of the Republic, business interests would meet with lawmakers in order to win charters to build roads and bridges. Industrial and agricultural businesses also lobbied Congress to place high tariffs on their international competition. Later, railroad companies were keen on acquiring congressional land grants. Probably the first presidential election in which corporations were highly involved in was the 1896 election between the pro-business candidate William McKinley and the pro-small farmer candidate William Jennings Bryan. Wealthy capitalists like J. P. Moran and John D. Rockefeller spent hundreds of thousands of dollars supporting McKinley.

Today, all the major corporations spend money on lobbying. Google, Microsoft, Bank of America, Apple, Walmart, defense contractors, the movie industry, the auto industry, the green industry—all have created interest groups with offices in Washington in order to protect their profits.

They also give to presidential campaigns. According to the Center for Responsive Politics, in 2012 the top corporate contributors to Democrat Barack Obama's campaign were Microsoft, Google, Kaiser Permanente, Time Warner, and Disney. The top corporate contributors to Republican Mitt Romney's campaign were Goldman Sachs, Bank of America, Morgan Stanley, JPMorgan, and Wells Fargo—all from the financial sector. Incidentally, in 2008 Goldman Sachs and JPMorgan were top contributors to Obama. This demonstrates that corporations tend to contribute to both Democrats and Republicans, especially incumbents and congressional committee chairmen. Their goal is to gain access to whoever is in power in order to stop laws that might hurt them or promote bills that might help them.

Trade Associations: Professional and trade organization came into being during the Progressive Era. Certain professions wanted to set standards in order to limit access into their profession, thus increasing the status and earnings of members of their group. The government was also interested in protecting the safety of the public, and so state and federal government agencies oversee the issuance of certificates and licenses in many professions. In recent decades, some of the most powerful trade associations are the National Association of Realtors, the National Auto Dealers Association, the American Medical Association (AMA), National Association of Home Builders, and the American Bar Association (ABA). Like corporations, they tend to be neutral politically, giving money to whoever is in power in order to gain access.

Private Sector Unions: Since Franklin Roosevelt's New Deal and the passage of the Wagner Act (1935), which protected the rights of union workers

**Labor unions are very active in the political process,
most often contributing to Democrats.**
©a katz/Shutterstock.com

and legalized collective bargaining, labor unions have been loyal to the Democratic Party. In the 1950s, unions such as the Teamsters and the AFL-CIO were major supporters of the Democrats. According to *The Wall Street Journal*, from 2005 to 2010, unions have spent $4.4 billion on politics, by far the most of any type of interest group. Nearly all of these contributions went to Democratic candidates. The Center for Responsive Politics' published a report titled "Heavy Hitters: Top All-Time Donors, 1989–2014." Unions dominated this list. Some of the top donors included the International Brotherhood of Electrical Workers, United Auto Workers, Carpenters & Joiners Union, Laborers Union, and Communications Workers of America.

In recent years, the Service Employees International Union (SEIU), representing nearly 2 million health care workers, local and state employees, and janitorial and food service personnel, has been one of the most politically active unions in America. In 2008, the SEIU provided $60 million in money and manpower to the Obama campaign. After Obama won the presidency, Andrew Stern, the head of the SEIU, visited the White House twenty-two times, making him the most frequent visitor. This demonstrates how campaign contributions buy access to power.

Public Sector Unions: While private sector unions have played a major role of money in politics, *public sector* unions, representing government workers, have had even a larger impact in recent decades. In the Center for Responsive

Teacher's unions are some of the biggest campaign contributors in America.
©Atomazul/Shutterstock.com

Politics' list of "Heavy Hitters," four of the top twelve biggest donors of all time were public sector unions: American Federation of State, County & Municipal Employees (AFSCME), The National Education Associations (NEA), The American Federation of Teachers (AFT), and the SEIU, which represents both private and public sector workers. All these groups give primarily to Democrats. With 3.2 million members, and an operating budget of $376 million, the NEA is one of the most powerful unions in America. After they supported Jimmy Carter in 1976, Carter created a new cabinet position: the Department of Education.

Until the 1960s, government unions were banned because they pose a unique threat to the democratic process. Franklin Roosevelt was a big supporter of private sector unions, but he opposed public sector unions. FDR said: "Meticulous attention should be paid to the special relations and obligations of public servants to the public itself and to the government . . . The process of collective bargaining, as usually understood, cannot be transported into the public service."

What he meant was that unions representing government workers can help elect lawmakers, and these lawmakers can turn around and give government workers raises and increase their benefits *with taxpayer's money*, something private sector unions cannot do. As a result of the powerful political influence of public sector unions, today federal employees now earn an average of $123,049 in pay and benefits, twice the average annual compensation for private sector workers. And the generous healthcare and pension benefits provided to city and state employees are resulting in massive deficits for local and federal government.

B. Social Interest Groups

Christian Groups: Starting in the Second Great Awakening (about 1790 to 1840), Christian groups have sought to change aspects of American society. The American Bible Society was formed in 1816 to distribute free Bibles. The Female Missionary Society sought to convert people to Christianity. Christians were behind the Temperance Society, formed in 1826 to eradicate alcohol from American society. And Christians filled the ranks of the leading abolitionist societies before the Civil War.

After the Progressive Era, Christian groups were less active in American politics until 1973, the year the Supreme Court ruled that states cannot ban abortions in *Roe v. Wade*. In order to fight back against the secular and leftist groups that dominated in the 1960s and 1970s, Christian groups returned to prominence. During the 1980s, the Moral Majority, led by Jerry Farwell, was a big supporter of Ronald Reagan and the Republicans. The Christian Coalition was founded by Pat Roberts, who ran for president in 1988. And Focus on the Family, which also rose to prominence during the 1980s, was led by James Dobson. In general, these groups sought to highlight the importance of the traditional family, opposed abortion, and tried to promote Christian values. They mostly supported Republicans.

Environmental Groups: In the 1970s, when pollution was becoming an obvious problem in many major cities in America, dozens of environmental groups were formed. They focused on several goals: to improve the quality of the air and water, to promote recycling, to encourage people to pick up trash, to fight dangerous pesticides, and to protect endangered species. These groups were very successful at getting the federal government to pass laws to protect the environment. In 1973, Congress created the Environmental Protection Agency (EPA), which enforced thousands of regulations on industry in order to reduce pollution. In recent decades environmental groups are focusing on transitioning our economy away from dependence on fossil fuels to renewable energy. They argue that Global Warming is a result of fossil fuels.

Some of the wealthiest, most powerful interest groups in America are environmental groups, including the Wildlife Conservation Society, the Conservation Fund, Climate Works, the National Audubon Society, and the Sierra Club. National Conservancy is the biggest with $4.9 billion in assets and $925 million in revenues in 2010. By one account, American environmental groups have a combined net worth of $9.3 billion with $3.6 billion in annual revenues. These groups mostly give to Democrats. They have been very successful at influencing federal agencies to achieve their goals.

Women's Groups: Women played a prominent leadership role during the Progressive Era (1900–1920), leading many influential interest groups, such as the Women's Christian Temperance Union, the General Federation of Women's Clubs, and the National American Suffrage Association. Ironically, once women won the vote with the passage of the 19th Amendment in 1920, they became less prominent in politics. Then in the late 1960s, with the rise of the modern feminist movement, interest groups led by women returned to prominence. In the late 1970s and 1980s, the League of Women Voters sponsored all the presidential debates. Today, the two most powerful women's groups are EMILY's LIST and the National Organization for Women (NOW). Both are very liberal. EMILY's LIST is a pro-abortion group that since 1998 has donated over $240 million to Democratic candidates.

Political Groups: Lastly, in every election cycle hundreds of groups form to help Democratic and Republican candidates. Political groups tend to have shorter life spans than the single issue groups such as the National Rifle Association (NRA), which was formed in 1871. During the 2012 election cycle, some of the most powerful liberal interest groups that gave money to Democrats were Priorities USA Action, led by former Clinton advisor Harold Ickes, Majority PAC, and House Majority PAC. In 2012, the top conservative groups that gave money to Republicans were Restore Our Future, led by many people from the financial sector, American Crossroads, and FreedomWorks for America. The largest political donor in America is ActBlue, which, according to *The New York Times*, has given over $430 million to Democrats as of November 2013.

CAMPAIGN FINANCE LAW

All the interest groups listed above must comply with US campaign finance and tax laws. The Tillman Act of 1907 was the first campaign finance law passed by Congress. It banned corporations from making campaign contributions to people running for federal office. The Taft-Hartley Act of 1947 extended the ban to unions. To get around this ban, the Congress of Industrial Organizations (CIO) created the first Political Action Committee (PAC). Technically not a union, it allowed union members to voluntarily contribute money that was donated to candidates through the PAC. Soon corporations adopted the

The NRA is one of the most effective interest groups in America.
©digitalreflections/Shutterstock.com

PAC. This demonstrates the general pattern of campaign finance laws: Congress will pass a law to restrict money in politics, and interest groups will figure out a way to get around the law. The following will outline the basic structure of current laws which apply to interest groups:

The Federal Elections Commission: Created in 1975, the **Federal Elections Commission (FEC)** *is a federal regulatory agency that oversees all federal elections and enforces federal election laws.* It consists of six members appointed by the president, split evenly between Democrats and Republicans. All candidates are required to file reports to the FEC, disclosing all of the campaign's contributions and spending. When people file their taxes, they have the option to donate $1 to finance presidential campaigns. In recent years, however, presidential candidates have refused this money because they do not wish to abide by the FEC spending limits.

The Bipartisan Campaign Reform Act of 2002 (BCRA): This law was introduced by John McCain, a Republican, and Russ Feingold, a Democrat, and thus is often referred to as the McCain-Feingold Act. The law was designed to limit the influence of money in politics. It placed limitations on how much money individuals can give to political parties, called soft money, which before 2002 was unlimited. Today, an individual can contribute up to $30,800 to a national political party. BCRA also limited the amount of money interest groups could spend on advertising, but this provision was overturned by the Supreme Court in *Citizens United v. FEC* (see below). BCRA has established the current spending limits, which are enforced by the FEC. Today, individuals, PACs, and political parties can only contribute up $5,000 to each candidate.

Citizens United v. FEC **(2010):** In 2008, an interest group, Citizens United, sought to air a thirty-minute documentary critical of Hillary Clinton on DirecTV. The FEC banned the film because they said it violated a provision of BCRA that prohibited advertising of interest groups thirty days before a primary and sixty days before a general election. The Supreme Court overturned this provision of BCRA, ruling that it violated the free speech rights of interest groups. As a result of this ruling, today all interest groups, including unions and corporations, can run advertisements expressing their political concerns or advocacy. Before this ruling they could only fund such activities through their PACs.

Political Action Committees (PACS): As stated above, this type of organization was designed to circumvent the campaign contribution limits established in the Taft-Hartley Act. **PACs** *are entities formed by interest groups to give money directly to candidates.* All types of interest groups form PACs, including corporations, trade associations, unions, and social interests groups. For

Federal Elections
Commission (FEC)

is a federal regulatory agency that oversees all federal elections and enforces federal election laws

PACs

are entities formed by interest groups to give money directly to candidates.

John McCain, the Republican senator from Arizona, co-sponsored the McCain-Feingold Act to limit money in politics.
©Drop of Light/Shutterstock.com

example, the Sierra Club is an environmental interest group, but they also have a PAC that contributes money to candidates that they support. Individuals can only give $5,000 to a PAC. And PACs can only contribute $5,000 to each candidate. The money they give to candidates can be used for any purpose.

527 Groups: This type of organization was created to circumvent the campaign contribution limits of the McCain-Feingold Act. They are named for section 527 of the US Tax Code which describes tax-exempt organizations. 527 Groups are tax-exempt organizations that can spend unlimited money for political advertisements, but the contributions have to be reported and they must remain independent from the candidates. One of the most famous 527 Groups was Swift Boat Veterans for Truth. In 2004, they aired ads critical of presidential candidate John Kerry's Vietnam War record, which contributions to his defeat by George W. Bush.

501 (c) 4 Groups: These nonprofit groups can participate in some lobbying and election politics, as long as they are primarily engaged in civic and social welfare. 501 (c) 4 Groups are not required to disclose donors, but contributors are not tax deductible. They can endorse candidates and causes. Currently there is an IRS scandal involving 501 (c) 4 Groups. In 2013, the IRS admitted that before the 2012 election groups with "Tea Party" or "patriot" in their titles underwent higher scrutiny when applying for non-profit status.

Investigations further revealed that dozens of conservative groups were rejected, while only a few liberal leaning groups were denied non-profit status. Obviously, this caused a firestorm of controversy because the idea that the IRS helps one political party, the Democrats, is very troubling.

Super PACs: *Groups that must report their contributions to the FEC, but can raise money from any source without limits are called* **Super PACs**. One individual can contribute millions of dollars to these organizations. Super PACS, however, can only engage in "independent expenditures," meaning they cannot coordinate their advertising campaigns with candidates. And they cannot contribute directly to candidates. These groups came about after *Citizens United v. FEC* and played a big role in the 2012 election. They mostly spend their money producing political ads.

Bundling: Since the McCain-Feingold Act limited the amount of money interest groups can give a candidate, interest groups started bundling. **Bundling** *is the process by which individuals give a limited amount of money to a fundraiser, and that fundraiser gives all the money (in a bundle) to a candidate.* This practice adheres to the law by limiting individual donations to the $5,000, but it allows the bundler to make a large impression on the candidate, and thus gain more influence. According to the Center for Responsive Politics, Obama's top three bundlers in 2012 were Jeffrey Katzenberg of DreamWorks Animation ($1.8 million), Barry and Wendy Meyer of Warner

Super PACs

groups that must report their contributions to the FEC, but can raise money from any source without limits

Bundling

is the process by which individuals give a limited amount of money to a fundraiser, and that fundraiser gives all the money (in a bundle) to a candidate

Jeffery Katzenberg, CEO of DreamWorks Animation, raises millions of dollars for the Democratic Party.
©drserg/Shutterstock.com

Brothers ($1.6 million), and Elizabeth Bagley of the US Department of State ($1.4 million). The top three Romney bundlers were Bill Graves of the American Trucking Assn ($1.8 million), David Beightol of Dutko Grayling ($1.6 million), and Dirk Van Dongen of the National Assn of Wholesale Distributors ($1.4 million).

HOW INTEREST GROUPS INFLUENCE PUBLIC POLICY

Interest groups engage in the political process in order to influence government and change public policy. Many groups do this by aligning with the political parties. Small business groups, Christian groups, the Chamber of Commerce, and veteran groups, to name a few, support the Republican Party. Teachers' unions, trial lawyers, pro-choice groups, ethnic groups, and public and private sector unions, for example, support the Democratic Party. Broadly speaking, beyond supporting the political parties, interest groups have learned to assert pressure on the political process by implementing two strategies: an election strategy and a legislative strategy.

A.   Election Strategy

Election Strategy is the political strategy of electing individuals to public office that support the goals of the interest group.

EMILY's list is one of the most powerful pro-choice interest groups in America.
©a katz/Shutterstock.com

Give money: Interest groups, mostly through their PACs, give money to candidates they support in order to get as many people into elected office as possible with the hope that they will support legislation favored by that interest group. It is easiest for incumbents and chairpersons of congressional committees to raise money because interest groups want to have access to these powerful lawmakers. For several decades, the American Israel Public Affairs Committee (AIPAC) has been considered one of the most effective interest groups in America. They support candidates they believe will support diplomatic and military initiatives that will protect Israel. EMILY's list has also been a very powerful force. They give millions of dollars, mostly to Democrats, which promote pro-choice legislation.

Recruit candidates: Some interest groups find, train, and promote individuals to run for office. This most often happens at the local level. If an interest group can get a candidate elected to city council or the state legislature, then perhaps one day that person may become a US Senator. The AFL-CIO runs several training candidates schools and has successfully placed hundreds of candidates in elected office. With the goal of getting more women into public office, the National Women's Political Caucus (NWPC) has been training women candidates since the early 1990s. Other groups, like the National Rifle Association (NRA) don't run training schools but provide candidates with multi-media materials showing how to make the most effective gun rights arguments when running for office.

Endorse candidates: Each election cycle, candidates seek the endorsement of several powerful interest groups. Liberal candidates seek the endorsement of the AFL-CIO, EMILY'S LIST, or the NAACP. Conservatives seek the endorsement of the NRA or Tea Party. These endorsements can help sway voters. With so many elections in America, voters often rely on interest group *voter guides* to help decide what candidates to vote for. Another way that interest groups try to inform and influence voters is by publishing candidate *scorecards* based on a lawmaker's voting record. The Americans for Democratic Action (ADA) issues a liberal scorecard, and the American Conservative Union (ACU) issues a conservative scorecard. Proud liberal or conservative lawmakers will often cite their scores in public speeches and advertisements.

Mobilize Voters: Lastly, some interest groups concentrate on getting people to the polls. This is called *voter mobilization*, and because it is considered a civil enterprise, many groups that do this can qualify for non-profit status. These groups recruit thousands of volunteers to make phone calls, go door-to-door, pass out flyers, or even drive voters to the polls on Election Day. In recent years, groups supporting the Democrats have been more effective in voter mobilization. In 2008, ACORN and America Votes (a coalition of dozens of unions), spent millions of dollars and recruited tens of thousands of volunteers to get people to the polls to vote for Obama. This was an important part of Obama's victories in 2008 and 2012.

B.   Legislative Strategy

Legislative strategy focuses on influencing sitting lawmakers and government officials to support laws that benefit an interest group.

Direct lobbying: Interest groups will hire a *lobbyist* to contact lawmakers, staffers, or administrators in order to attempt to persuade them to make a change in a law or policy. The lobbyist does this by providing expert information. Lobbyists will either schedule an appointment with a lawmaker or attempt to "button-hole" a congressman in the lobby (which is how the term came about). Lawmakers will often come to rely on lobbyists to provide specialized information and may even seek their assistance in crafting legislation. Lobbyists are often lawyers or previous lawmakers, staffers, or administrators with connections. They are well paid and many of them have offices on K Street in Washington, DC.

Think Tanks

are organizations that hire scholars to perform research and public education on issues in order to influence public policy

Grassroots mobilization: One of the most important jobs of a lobbyist is to watch Congress carefully and know what bills are working their way through committees. Sometimes, if a lobbyist learns that a particular bill is about to move to the floor for a vote, then the lobbyist's interest group will try to mobilize its members to influence the vote. For example, if the US Congress were about to vote for a bill banning oil drilling off the US coast, environmental groups may urge their members to call, e-mail, or fax their congressmen and urge them to vote for the bill. Or sometimes interest groups will hold demonstrations outside of Congress or the White House in order to influence policy.

Public Education and Think Tanks: Interest groups know that lawmakers follow public opinion closely. Congressmen will often introduce legislation on issues that polls show that the people strongly favor. Interest groups, therefore, try to influence public opinion by trying to educate the people about their issue. To counter bad press after the Gulf Coast oil spill, petroleum companies like BP have spent millions of dollars on advertisements to show the benefits of the oil industry. Interest groups also try to educate the public through academic institutions. **Think tanks** *are organizations that hire scholars to perform research and public education on issues in order to influence public policy*. The Center on Budget and Policy Priorities and the Center for American Progress are prominent liberal think tanks. The American Enterprise Institute, the Heritage Foundation, and the Hoover Institute are prominent conservative think tanks.

LGBT interest groups have been very effective at getting the courts to support gay marriage.
©Kobby Dagan/Shutterstock.com

Litigation: Lastly, some groups have realized that the best way to change the law is through the courts. Probably the most successful group to use this strategy has been the National Association for the Advancement of Colored People (NAACP). In 1954, NAACP lawyer Thurgood Marshall convinced the Supreme Court, in *Brown v. Board of Education*, to end school segregation in America. Environmental groups have also won thousands of cases against polluters. And in recent years, gay groups have been successful at overturning state constitutional amendments and getting the Supreme Court to legalize gay marriage.

FINAL THOUGHTS

What do you think is the biggest, most powerful interest group in America? Big oil? Big finance? No, the largest interest group in America, with over 37 million members, is the American Association of Retired Persons (AARP). AARP is involved in issues that affect people over the age of fifty. With such a large membership, they are able to raise immense revenues. In 2006, the AARP had about $1 billion in revenue and spend $23 million on lobbying. Beyond its large membership and budget, another reason why AARP is so influential is that its members vote. A high percentage of older people vote and engage in the political process, such as sending e-mails and donating money. In 2008, AARP was instrumental in supporting Obama's Affordable Care Act.

NOTES

For all aspects of interest groups and money, go to the Center for Responsive Politics at www.open secret.org, and of special importance is their article "Heavy Hitters: Top All-time Donors," 1989–2014.

Dennis Cauchon, "Federal Workers Earning Double their Private Counterparts," *USA Today*, 8/13/2010.

Alexander Hamilton, John Jay, and James Madison. *The Federalists*. Indianapolis: Liberty Fund, 2001.

David Horowitz. *The New Leviathan*. New York: Crown Forum, 2012.

Theodore J. Lowe. *The Politics of Disorder*. New York: Norton, 1974.

Mancur Olson. *The Rise and Decline of Nations*. New Haven: Yale University Press, 1984.

Robert Putnam. *Bowling Alone: the Collapse and Revival of American Community*. New York: Touchstone Books, 2001.

Mark J. Rozell, Clyde Wilcox, and Michael M. Franz. *Interest Groups in American Campaigns: The New Face of Electioneering*. Third Edition. Oxford: Oxford University Press, 2012.

E. E. Schattschneider. *The Semi-Sovereign People: A Realist's View of Democracy in America*. New York: Wadsworth, 1975.

Alexis de Tocqueville, *Democracy in America*. Translated by George Lawrence. New York: Harper Collins, 1969.

WSJ, "Political Spending by Unions Far Exceeds Direct Donations," July 10, 2012.

Leon Watson, "'Sage of Omaha' Warren Buffett Has Donated $1.2 Billion to Planned Parenthood and Pro-Choice Groups in Past Decade." *Daily Mail.com*, May 14, 2014.

ESSAY QUESTIONS

1. Describe Madison's pluralistic theory and the elite theory. Which do you think is correct?
2. How do interest groups help the democratic process?
3. List and describe the top economic interest groups in America today.
4. What does a PAC do and when did they come into existence?
5. What strategies do interest groups employ to change public policy?

TERMS

Bundling: _____

Elite Theory: _____

Interest Group: _____

Pluralistic Theory: _____

Economic Interest Groups: _____

Federal Elections Commission (FEC): _____

Lobbyists: _____

Political Action Committee (PAC): _____

Social Capital: _____

Social Interest Groups: _____

Super PACs: _____

Think Tanks: _____

CHAPTER 22

How Is Public Policy Made
and Implemented?

TOPICS

► What Is Public Policy?
► The Public Policy Process
► Flaws in the Public Policy Process
► How Does the Bureaucracy Make Law?
► The Size of the Current Federal Bureaucracy
► Problems with the Large Federal Bureaucracy
► Reforming Bureaucracies

LEARNING OBJECTIVES

When you finish reading this chapter, you will be able to:

1. Describe the five steps of agenda making.
2. Analyze some of the common flaws in the agenda making process.
3. Outline the major federal departments and agencies.
4. Discuss some of the problems with large federal bureaucracies.
5. And list reforms that have been used to control government agencies.

HOW IS PUBLIC POLICY MADE AND IMPLEMENTED?

The Framers of the U.S. Constitution created a decentralized government; therefore, many entities make public policy. The primary task of the legislative branch is to make law. Thus, Congress is responsible for making most federal policies. The president, however, can initiate policies and get Congress to pass legislation he supports. And every year the President signs dozens of executive orders. Therefore, the president has a role in making policy.

After Congress passes a law, the federal bureaucracy implements it. In implementing the law, the administrative agencies must make the specific rules and regulations that actually carry out the law. Therefore, to a degree, the administration also makes policy. Moreover, the courts, in their rulings, sometimes make policy. For example, in *Roe v. Wade*, the Supreme Court ruled that states cannot ban abortions. So, in fact, the legislative, executive, administrative, and executive branches all play a role in making policy. And in our federal system, all this is replicated for each state.

LEGISLATIVE

EXECUTIVE

JUDICIAL

Although Congress is the lawmaking branch, each branch of government plays a role in making public policy.

©JPL Designs/Shutterstock.com

WHAT IS PUBLIC POLICY?

All the laws, rules, regulations, codes, programs, and recommendations of government are **public policy**. Really, everything a government does or does not do is public policy. It is how government addresses such issues as education, health care, energy, the environment, defense, welfare, public safety, and economic issues. The government's policies or lack of policies on public issues reflects the values and priorities of that society. For example, if a country imposed a $1,000 fine for littering, we could assume that nation places a high priority on keeping the public places free of litter. But if we come across a country that has no fines for littering, and the streets and parks are filled with trash, then we would assume that that country places a low priority on keeping things clean.

There could be another reason why that country is filled with trash. That nation may be so poor or dysfunctional that it does not have the administrative capacity to implement and enforce prohibitions against littering. This brings us to the second topic of this chapter: the bureaucracy. An administration or bureaucracy is needed to carry out and enforce public policy. A government can pass all the laws it likes, but if it does not have the ability to put them into effect, then nothing will happen. Thus, the lawmaking entities make policy, and the administration executes and enforces policy. Both are needed.

THE PUBLIC POLICY PROCESS

Policy-making is a complicated, and often messy, process that includes several entities operating at different times with different agendas. To help visualize this complicated procedure, political scientists have developed the Public Policy Model that divides the process into five steps: (1) Agenda Setting, (2) Policy Formulation, (3) Policy Adoption, (4) Policy Implementation, and (5) Policy Evaluation. If, after time, the policy is considered to be ineffective, the process will start all over again from step one, agenda setting. So, this is a circular, ongoing process.

Agenda Setting: *The process by which government decides that a problem exists and that it needs an imminent solution is called* **agenda setting**. Normally, before this can happen the citizens need to reach a consensus that a problem exists, that it needs to be addressed now, and that it can be solved by government. For example, there does not seem to be a strong consensus that the national debt needs to be addressed today, and so the national government has not enacted serious reforms to reduce the debt.

Public Policy

all the laws, rules, regulations, codes, programs, and recommendations of government

Agenda Setting

the process by which government decides that a problem exists and that it needs an imminent solution

Public Policy Model

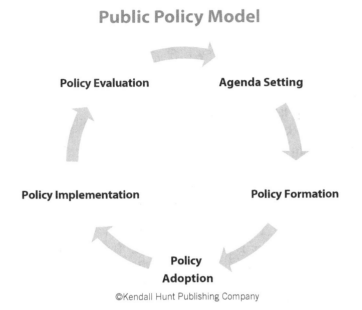

©Kendall Hunt Publishing Company

The media also plays a prominent role in agenda setting by focusing the public attention on a problem and creating a sense of urgency that this problem needs to be addressed soon. Many groups, including politicians, interest groups, and think tanks, compete for the public attention, which is limited and fleeting. Oftentimes it takes a crisis or disaster for people to decide to fix a problem—but by then the problem is more difficult to solve.

Policy Formation: Once it is decided that a problem needs to be addressed, officials devise a government solution to this problem, this is called *policy formulation*. Much of the time they are formulating adjustments to current policy, but sometimes they create whole new policies. Barack Obama's Affordable Care Act, for instance, was a whole new policy designed to increase access to affordable health care. Many entities are involved in this step. Congressional committees hold hearings and listen to the testimony of experts. Bureaucrats in Congress or in the executive department provide their expertise. Think tanks and universities publish papers analyzing the history of an issue and offering their solutions. Also, any good policy formulation will include a cost-benefit analysis. By law, many bills require that the Congressional Budget Office (CBO) provide a cost analysis before the bill is brought to a floor vote.

Policy Adoption: When a government entity or entities in charge of public policy approve a proposal and makes it legally binding, this is called *policy adoption*. For example, when an act passes both chambers of Congress and is signed by the President, the policy has been adopted. Likewise, when the president signs an executive order, the policy has been adopted. Normally, the adoption of a policy could not be achieved unless it won the support of a significant percentage of the public. There is usually a brief window of political opportunity to pass a law. When President Obama was first elected and both chambers of Congress were controlled by the Democrats, the president knew this would probably be the only time he could adopt sweeping health care reform.

Policy Implementation: *The process of setting up and carrying out the actual reform is called* **policy implementation**. The bureaucracy plays the leading role in this step by crafting the often complex rules and regulations that people and businesses must follow. This step gets little notice from the media. The implementation of the Affordable Care Act, however, was an exception to the rule. After five years and hundreds of millions of dollars, the Obama Administration finally opened the website, healthcare.gov, through which people could purchase health insurance on the government managed exchanges. In the first several weeks the website constantly crashed and users complained of a rash of difficulties. Eventually, the government was able to fix these problems, but this was one of the rare occasions when the public was aware of the complexity of policy implementation.

Policy Evaluation: After a policy has been implemented for a number of years, it is logical to check to see if it is actually working. *Policy evaluation* is the process of assessing whether a policy is successfully achieving its intended objective. Many government and non-government entities are involved in evaluation, including congressional committees, presidential task forces, the press, and bureaucratic agencies. For example, the Office of Inspector General (OIG) evaluates government agencies, especially accusations of wrongdoing or the misuse of funds. And The Government Accountability Office (GAO) is a federal agency whose job is to conduct studies to evaluate the cost efficiency of government programs. Sadly, in 2012, the General Services Administration (GSA), an agency charged with minimizing costs of government programs, was involved in a scandal in which it spent nearly a million dollars on a Las Vegas conference and provided nearly $440,000 of free iPods for employees!

Policy Implementation

the process of setting up and carrying out the actual reform

If the government or the public decide a policy is not working, then the whole process will start from the beginning with agenda setting and formulation. The Public Policy Model is a circular process with no real beginning or end.

FLAWS IN THE PUBLIC POLICY PROCESS

Many laws are properly implemented and truly improve the quality of life for the citizens. By criticizing the policy making process, we do not mean to imply that all laws are inherently irrational and counterproductive. The point of this section is to highlight the difficulties of crafting and executing good policy. But politics is a human endeavor which entails some irrational elements, and therefore public policy is not a perfect science. Sometimes politicians propose reforms to get elected, knowing that they will never actually implement them. A recent example of this is John McCain. When he ran for reelection to the US Senate, he pledged to "repeal and replace Obamacare." But when the time came to actually do this, he voted no. At other times, politicians will avoid unpopular issues that actually need reform. The following are some additional mistakes that public policy officials often make:

One-Stage Thinking: Many of the policy process flaws are a result of what Thomas Sowell, the Hoover Institute economist, calls "one-stage thinking." Politicians love to make a public display of compassion and pass a law to help a particular group, but they fail to think of the second and third stage economic consequences of the new policy. For example, Congress passed a law that required 10 percent of gasoline to contain ethanol, produced mostly from corn. This was designed to help small American farmers. But lawmakers failed to understand secondary problems: ethanol damaged many types of engines, corn became too expensive for poor families, and expensive corn harmed livestock farmers that feed hogs and other animals corn. Policy makers should remember to study a reform carefully and think through all the economic consequences.

Lawmakers seldom take the time to think beyond the first stage of policy implementation and understand the far-reaching consequences of a new law.
©Visual Generation/Shutterstock.com

Responding to a Crisis: Many policies are enacted in a time of crisis. Suddenly the media and the people are demanding that "something must be done" and it must be done "now." Sometimes, however, doing nothing is the best thing to do in a particular situation. In crisis mode, lawmakers do not have enough time to properly think through a complex law or to study how other countries have dealt with a similar problem. When the Great Depression hit in 1928, there was a general call to do something. Congress passed the Smoot-Haley Act, dramatically increasing tariffs on imported goods in an effort to protect American jobs. The consequence of the act is that it provoked other countries to increase tariffs on American goods, thus bringing to a halt overseas trade and international economic activity. So, a policy that was designed to correct the Great Depression actually made it worse.

The Law of Unintended Consequences: The Smoot-Haley Act is an example of unintended consequences—instead of reducing unemployment, the law actually increased unemployment. Because Congress seldom has the time to deeply research and evaluate a proposed policy, either because they are in crisis mode or because a brief window of political opportunity presents itself, *lawmakers sometimes pass a law intending to solve one problem but it ends up making other problems worse: this is called* **the law of unintended consequences**. Prohibition is probably the most infamous example of unintended consequences. Lawmakers were concerned about the ill effects of excessive alcohol consumption. Consequently, they passed the 18th Amendment prohibiting the manufacture, transportation, and sale of alcohol. True, the law did reduce alcohol consumption in American. But it also created a multi-million dollar black market, by which gangsters like Al Capone became rich.

Laws Change the Environment: Lawmakers often think that the policies they make will go into effect in a static environment and do not realize that laws change human behavior. For example, to help young Americans go to college, Congress created the Pell Grant, which gives low interest loans and grants to college students. But since this law was enacted, the cost of a college education has increased five times the rate of inflation. When parents had to pay for tuition and textbooks with hard-earned savings, it forced colleges to keep prices down. But now that a third party, the government, pays the bills, prices have skyrocketed.

Likewise, welfare programs have also changed the human environment. In the 1960s, many welfare programs were enacted to help poor families. This seemed like the compassionate thing to do. But there were unintended consequences that lawmakers did not foresee. When single mothers became eligible

The Law of Unintended
Consequences

lawmakers sometimes pass
a law intending to solve one
problem but it ends up making
other problems worse

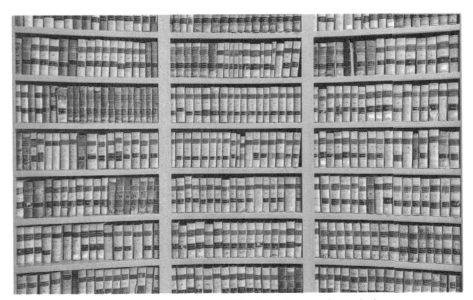

**Who can possibly keep up with all the laws and regulations
created by modern government?**
©Nagel Photography/Shutterstock.com

for government hand-outs, they no longer needed the father. This helped lead to fatherless families, which consequently led to greater poverty and other social problems.

Too Many Laws: Lastly, lawmakers feel that they must constantly be making new laws or they will be accused of being a "do-nothing Congress." But it is relatively easy for Congress to pass a law. The difficulty is in *implementing laws*, which means creating new bureaucracies, and *enforcing laws*, which means creating new regulatory agencies and law enforcement organizations.

According to a 2014 Heritage Foundation study, the number of criminal offenses in the United States Criminal Code increased from 3,000 in the early 1980s, to over 4,450 by 2008. Besides criminal laws, people can be punished for violating regulations. In his book, *Overcriminalization*, Douglas Husak asserts that there are at least 300,000 federal regulations that are enforced by federal agencies with the power to wield criminal punishment. Husak estimates that about 70 percent of Americans have unwittingly committed felonies for which they could be imprisoned. So Congress and government agencies keep making so many laws that the police and the people can no longer keep up with them.

HOW DOES THE BUREAUCRACY MAKE LAW?

Most people assume that the legislature, the lawmaking branch, makes public policy. And many also know that the president plays a major role in policy making by proposing reforms and by making executive orders. Few, however, know that to a large degree the bureaucracy makes law. This occurs at two steps on the Public Policy Model: policy formation and policy implementation.

Policy Formation: When making law, members of Congress rely heavily on the expertise of career bureaucrats. When formulating law, bureaucrats may testify at congressional hearings but most of the time they work behind the scenes. When a bill is actually being crafted, the bureaucrats will do the difficult work of writing, line-by-line, complex legislation. Often, lawyers working for interest groups will provide information to these bureaucrats in an attempt to insert favorable provisions into the laws. Beyond congressional bureaucrats, members of Congress use several federal agencies to help them formulate bills, such as the Congressional Research Service (CRS) and the Congressional Budget Office (CBO), which provides a cost analysis to proposed bills. And with regard to executive orders, bureaucrats in several administrative agencies help formulate the president's executive directives.

Administrative Discretion: The biggest impact the bureaucrats have on policy making is in the implementation stage and it involves two influential

Congress makes general laws, but the government bureaucrats make the specific rules and regulations that people and businesses must follow.
©Nirat.pix/Shutterstock.com

powers: administrative discretion and rule making. *The authority of bureaucrats to make reasonable judgments or choices when implementing congressional law or executive orders is called* **administrative discretion**. Congress passes laws which are broad and generalized. It is the job of the agency bureaucrats to make the day-to-day decisions on how best to carry out the laws. For example, Congress might pass a law that individuals making $100,000 per year must pay a 36 percent income tax. But individual IRS agents must review each tax return and make a judgment call. If an IRS agent reads a tax return that seems to have a mistake, the agent can either send a notice to the taxpayer to correct the error or launch a full audit. This is up to the IRS agent's discretion.

Rule Making. Related to administrative discretion is the bureaucrat's power of *rule making*: the bureaucrat's authority to make the specific rules, regulations, and codes when carrying out and enforcing a general policy. Again, Congress will pass a general law. After the law passes, it is up to the administrative agencies to actually implement the law and create the detailed regulations to make the law work. In 1971, Congress passed the Clean Water Act. But it is up to the bureaucrats in the Environmental Protection Agency (EPA) to set the precise regulations and establish the fines. For example, if a lake contains 300 parts per million of a certain chemical, the local sewage plant could be fined $500,000. The bureaucrat's authority to make rules is a semi-legislative power that is legally binding and has a tremendous impact on the country.

Administrative
Discretion

the authority of bureaucrats to make reasonable judgments or choices when implementing congressional law or executive orders

THE SIZE OF THE CURRENT FEDERAL BUREAUCRACY

Every year the federal government keeps growing and growing. In 1791, George Washington had five cabinet members: secretary of state, secretary of treasury, secretary of war, attorney general, and postmaster general. The department with the most federal employees was the post office. Today there are fifteen federal departments consisting of over 1,100 agencies with over four million federal non-military and military bureaucrats. Another way to calculate the growth of the federal bureaucracy is to look at total federal spending. In 1796, total spending for the US government was $6 million; in 1940, $20 billion; and today it is over $6 trillion. Yet another way to understand the growth of the federal bureaucracy is by the number of pages of the *Federal Register*, a government publication that lists all the current federal regulations. In 1936 the Federal Register had only 2,620 pages, and by 2012, it had 78,961 pages! Who can keep track of all those regulations?

Federal Departments: Currently, there are fifteen cabinet departments: Defense (civilian, active military, and reserve employees 3 million), Veterans Affairs (312,000), Homeland Security (240,000), Treasury (134,000), Justice (115,000), Agriculture (107,000), Transportation (59,000), Interior (70,000), Health & Human Services (76,000), Commerce (44,000), State (50,000), Labor (18,000), Energy (16,000), Housing & Urban Development (11,000), Education (5,000). Each of the massive departments has many sub-divisions and agencies. Also, these figures do not indicate the number of contracted employees, which is significant.

Independent Agencies: For various reasons, when Congress creates certain agencies, it decides not to place them in one of the existing departments, so they become independent agencies. It was decided, for example, that the CIA would not be part of the state or defense department because of the controversial nature of the CIA's function. Other agencies are independent because of their regulatory nature. The Security and Exchange Commission (SEC) is an independent agency that regulates the stock market. Other federal independent agencies include the Environmental Protection Agency (EPA), the Federal Communications Commission (FCC), the Federal Trade Commission (FTC), the Smithsonian Institute, and NASA.

Government Corporations: *Independent agencies that are owned by the federal government and operate by charging a fee for a service are called* **government corporations.** Government corporations include Fannie Mae (buys and sells home mortgages), the Tennessee Valley Authority (a utility company), and Farm Credit Banks (lends money to farmers and ranchers).

Government Corporations

independent agencies that are owned by the federal government and operate by charging a fee for a service

**Amtrak is a government corporation that seldom makes enough
profit to survive without taxpayer bailouts.**
©Richard Thornton/Shutterstock.com

If government corporations do not make enough profit to cover their expenses, the taxpayer must pay to keep the government corporation afloat. The largest government corporation in America is the US Postal Service, which has 630,000 employees (the largest non-military government agency). In recent years, the US Postal Service has been losing money. In 2010 it had an annual deficit of $8.5 billion, and in 2011 it had a deficit of $3 billion. Another government corporation that runs annual deficits is Amtrak, a government run railroad company. In the last several years Amtrak has needed about $1.5 billion in federal grants to maintain operations.

PROBLEMS WITH THE LARGE FEDERAL BUREAUCRACY

Dealing with bureaucrats is a frustrating experience. We have all had to wait in long lines at the DMV to renew our driver's license or have been placed on hold for over an hour trying to talk with somebody at the IRS. Or perhaps you incorrectly filled out Form 23140B-26 when you applied for a city permit? The world of a federal bureaucracy is a world of tedious forms, complex systems, long lines, and uncompassionate bureaucrats. Besides the poor customer service and long waits, the ever increasing size of the US federal bureaucracy poses some real dangers to our system of government. This section will list some of the dangers and inconveniences large government bureaucracies pose.

Bureaucracy Violates Three Branches: The modern federal bureaucracy was unforeseen by the Framers of the Constitution and does not fit squarely into the three-branch system. The bureaucracy has executive, legislative, and judicial functions. Take, for example, the National Labor Relations Board (NLRB). Created by Congress in 1933 to enforce federal labor laws, the NLRB is an "independent agency." Asserting enormous power over all US businesses, the NLRB issues regulations, investigates violations, prosecutes offenders, and sits in judgment over its own rulings. In essence, it has the power of lawmaker, police officer, judge, and jury. In a democracy, the people are the sovereigns. But by placing much of the bureaucracy outside of the three-branch system with checks and balances, federal agencies are unaccountable to the people.

Surprisingly, the president, the head of the executive department, doesn't even have control over many bureaucrats. In a lawsuit over the Federal Trade Commission, the Supreme Court ruled in *Humphrey's Executor v. United States* (1935), that the president does not have the power to remove officials from independent agencies because they are "quasi-legislative," "quasi-judicial" bodies. This seems to violate Article II of the Constitution, placing a single, independent executive at the head of the federal administration. The Framers created one president vested with the responsibility to "take care that the laws be faithfully executed." Independent agencies, beyond the control of the presidency, are contrary to the concept of an independent Presidency vested with the power to administer the law.

When dealing with a bureaucrat, sometimes it is nearly impossible to figure out the maze of forms and procedures to comply with.
©Golden Sikorka/Shutterstock.com

Poor Customer Service: Perhaps not as serious as violating the three-branch structure of the Constitution, bureaucracies can be tedious due to their poor customer service. Unlike a for-profit business, where the customer is king and service is expected to be excellent, government agencies often treat the customer poorly. Why is this? Bureaucrats don't need to be nice to the customer because the customer is not paying the bill, the taxpayers are. Also, bureaucrats get into trouble by not following the rules of the organization, not due to slow or rude service. Thus, government workers often do their work by rote: automatically following routine, avoiding responsibility, and not making commonsense decisions.

Tendency toward Growth: Another problem with government bureaucracies is that they tend to automatically grow. This is because the employees of a government agency or department want that agency to continue to grow more powerful and influential. Each year, they tend to push for more staff and bigger budgets. If a new president floats the idea of cutting the budget of a particular program, leaders of that agency will go to the press or Congress to complain about the cuts by citing all the important work they do and all the people they help. Soon, the president will back off. This is one of the problems that have contributed to the $20 trillion national debt. It is nearly impossible to cut a government program.

Crony Capitalism: In contrast to free market capitalism, **crony capitalism** *is a system in which business success is enhanced by connections to government officials, knowledge of legal loopholes (and tax breaks), and by government favoritism.* In a free market, business success is a result of hard work and innovation, and competition takes place in an equal playing field established by the rule of law. But in a system based on crony capitalism, business success is a result of acquiring favorable government permits, contracts, tax breaks, and legal loopholes. Crony capitalism is more prevalent in countries with large bureaucratic systems. This is because giant corporations that can afford a large staff of lawyers to review all the government rules and regulations have a great advantage over smaller companies. And corporations that can afford expensive lobbyists who insert favorable provisions into multi-page bills, which few people read, give that corporation a financial advantage.

Crony Capitalism

is a system in which business success is enhanced by connections to government officials, knowledge of legal loopholes (and tax breaks), and by government favoritism

Slow Economic Growth: When businesses are forced to spend more time and money understanding and complying with the many complex government rules and regulations, this reduces their ability to make a profit. And when it becomes too difficult to start a new business due to the endless regulations produced by the bureaucracy, then that is a lost opportunity for new jobs. Today America is one of the most regulated nations in the world. According to a report by Clyde Crews, published in the National Center for Policy Analysis, in 2013 Americans spent $1.863 trillion complying with federal regulations. Crews also estimated that for every law Congress passes, the bureaucracies make fifty-one new rules. All of these rules are a drag on the economy.

A Partisan Bureaucracy: A bureaucracy should be politically neutral, serving the administrations of both parties with equal dedication. In 1939, Congress passed the Hatch Act, limiting the ability of federal government employees to engage in political activity. This law was passed after news reports accused employees of the Works Progress Administration of electioneering for local Democrats. And in 1935, the Wagner Act excluded government workers from the ability to form unions, fearing they would elect politicians that would give government union workers raises with taxpayer's money. Both these laws recognized the dangers of a partisan government bureaucracy. But since the 1960s, these policies have been reversed and government workers are now allowed to unionize. Today some of the most politically active unions in America are government unions: the American Federation of State, County & Municipal Employees (AFSCME), the National Education Association (NEA), and the Service Employees International Union (SEIU).

And in 1993, the Hatch Act was further liberalized to allow more political activity of government workers. They can now assist in voter registration drives, contribute money to political organizations, attend political rallies and fundraisers, and campaign for candidates. Since most government workers tend to identify with one party, the Democrats, some have raised questions about the dangers of a partisan bureaucracy. Before the 2012 presidential elections, the IRS was involved in a scandal involving political favoritism. IRS officials denied most conservative Tea Party groups tax exempt status, shutting them out of the campaign. In recent years career government bureaucrats have been accused of helping the Obama administration by manipulating data about unemployment, inflation, government spying, and the Affordable Care Act. Obviously, a politically biased bureaucracy poses many dangers to our democracy.

Bureaucratic red tape makes it more difficult for companies to prosper or for people to start new businesses.
©jorgen mcleman/Shutterstock.com

REFORMING BUREAUCRACIES

Most bureaucrats are conscientious, hard-working public servants. Today, we need uniform rules crafted by skilled bureaucrats to regulate life in a complex world. Professional bureaucrats make the government function, help the poor and needy, and keep people safe. They do very important work. But this brings us to a fundamental dilemma of modern government. The federal government created bureaucracies to better serve the people, but as bureaucracies grow, they became less efficient. Hence, one of the biggest challenges of modern government is how to make bureaucracies more efficient, less expensive, and better able to serve the people. The following are several ways the US government has tried to reform the bureaucracies:

Pendleton Act: In the 1800s, *elected public officials would distribute government jobs to loyal members of their political party, this is called the* **spoil system**. For example, a person might get a job in the post office if he gave money to a successful Republican presidential candidate. But the spoil system was phased out in 1883 after a disgruntled job seeker shot President James Garfield. The *Pendleton Act* replaced the spoil system with the civil service system. Now civil servants (professional bureaucrats) must pass a test in order to get a government job, and he or she cannot lose their position simply because a new political party takes over government. The modern bureaucracy is based on merit, not political connections. This has greatly reduced corruption and increased competency.

Performance Standards and Codes of Conduct: Government bureaucrats, in order to enhance good public service and reduce corruption, must follow established *codes of behavior*. In 1992, the Office of Government Ethics published a comprehensive ethical code that all national government employees must abide by. Another attempt to improve bureaucratic service was the establishment of *performance standards*. In 1993, Congress passed the Government Performance and Results Act, mandating that each agency must develop a five-year plan to reach certain goals and prepare annual performance reports reviewing the agency's success at achieving those goals. These reports must be made public on the agency's websites.

Whistle-blower Laws: Another way to reduce corruption and mismanagement is by protecting **whistle-blowers**: *government employees that report acts of waste, corruption, and mismanagement*. The Civil Service Reform Act of 1978 protects whistle-blowers from retribution from superiors, such as demotions or firing. In 2014, many whistle-blowers stepped forward to report gross neglect of sick and injured veterans at the Veterans Hospitals, which are owned and operated by the federal government. Whistle-blowers revealed that the VA Hospitals kept fake waiting lists in order to show that veterans were treated in a timely manner, while dozens of actual veterans died waiting to see a doctor.

Spoil System

elected public officials would distribute government jobs to loyal members of their political party

whistle-blowers

government employees that report acts of waste, corruption, and mismanagement

Privatization: Starting in the 1970s and accelerating in the 1980s, there have been several attempts to reform the bureaucracy by contracting private sector organizations to do many tasks previously done by government agencies. This is called **privatization**: *transferring management of a government agency to a private company.*

Related to this idea is **deregulation**: *ending or reducing government regulation of an industry to create more competition.* In the 1980s, for example, the Reagan administration deregulated the telephone and airline industry. The concept is based on the assumption that private companies would compete for government contracts and run things cheaper and more efficiently than government bureaucracies, which are essentially a monopoly. Today, the federal government outsources thousands of functions to private companies, doing such things as collecting revenue, providing security, managing prisons, and feeding soldiers.

Whistle-blower laws protect government employees that publicize government mistakes and corruption.
©Elnur/Shutterstock.com

Trump Deregulation: When Donald Trump ran for president, he said, "We are going to be cutting regulations massively." Trump said that business leaders have told him that even more than tax cuts regulatory reform would bolster the economy and allow businesses to thrive. In Trump's first year in office he signed several executive orders that cut federal regulations. First, he rescinded 860 recent Obama regulations. The American Action Forum, a conservative think tank, estimated that this alone saved American businesses $21 billion. Second, Trump created the Two-for-One Policy: for every new regulation, an agency must cut two older regulations. Third, Trump ordered every federal agency to create a Regulatory Reform Task Force to review all existing regulations and to make suggestions for cuts. Also, he terminated Obama's Clean Power Plan, which Trump said was designed to kill the coal industry. As proof that regulatory reductions have stimulated economic growth, Trump points to the fact that US GDP grew by 3.2 % in spring of 2017, the highest in five years.

Sunset and Sunshine Laws: Lastly, Congress has attempted to hold the government agencies accountable by placing time limits on legislation and making bureaucratic records public. Some laws include a *sunset clause*, which sets a termination date on a government program unless Congress renews it. This will force Congress to evaluate the program. And if they discover that the program is not working, Congress can end or reform it. The Patriot Act, for example, has a sunset clause, forcing Congress to review the controversial surveillance law every four years. Another way to force accountability is by

privatization

transferring management of a government agency to a private company

deregulation

ending or reducing government regulation of an industry to create more competition making records public. *Sunshine laws* require that government agencies make meetings, records, votes, and official actions public. This allows the press, interest groups, and individuals to investigate public institutions and make sure they are doing their job properly.

FINAL THOUGHTS

In *Democracy in America* (1835), Alexis de Tocqueville warned America about the dangers of the ever increasing government bureaucracy, which some have called the **bureaucratic state**: *A government dominated by non-elected officials that create a complex maze of rules and regulations that burdens the economy and crushes freedom and innovation.* The bureaucratic state "covers the surface of society with a network of small complicated rules," asserted Tocqueville, "which the most original minds and energetic characters cannot penetrate."

Tocqueville was worried that one day a large government bureaucracy would sap America's energetic spirit. He said that under the bureaucratic state, "The will of man is not shattered but softened." And eventually the bureaucracy "enervates, extinguishes, and stupefies the people, till each nation is reduced to nothing better than a flock of timid and industrious animals, of which the government is the shepherd." Do you agree with Tocqueville? Have Americans become nothing more than timid rule followers who comply with the government?

Bureaucratic State

a government dominated by non-elected officials that create a complex maze of rules and regulations that burdens the economy and crushes freedom and innovation

NOTES

For government spending, go to US Government Spending at www.usgovernmentspending.com.

Jeffrey M. Berry and Clyde Wilcox. *The Interest Group Society*. New York: Pearson, 2009.

Clyde Crew, "The Cost of Ever-Increasing Federal Regulations," *National Center for Policy Analysis*, May 21, 2012.

Wayne Crews and Ryan Young, "The Towering Federal Register," *The Daily Caller*, May 21, 2013.

Adam Freedman. *The Naked Constitution: What the Founders Said and Why it Still Matters*. New York: Broadside Books, 2012.

Steven M. Gillon, *That's Not What We Meant to Do: Reform and Its Unintended Consequences in the Twentieth Century*. New York: W.W. Norton & Company, 2000.

Douglas Husak. *Overcriminalization: The Limits of the Criminal Law*. Oxford: Oxford University Press, 2009.

John Malcolm and Paul Larkin, "Overcriminalization," *Heritage Foundation Report*, 2014.

Thomas Sowell, "One Stage Thinking," in *The Thomas Sowell Reader*, New York: Basic Books, 2011.

Courtney Subramanian, "GSA Scandal." *Time*, April 18, 2012.

Alexis de Tocqueville. *Democracy in America*. Translated by George Lawrence. New York: Harper Collins, 1969.

James Q. Wilson. *Bureaucracy*. New York: Basic Books, 1989.

James Q. Wilson et el. *American Government: Institutions and Policies*. New York: Wadsworth Publishing, 12th ed., 2015.

ESSAY QUESTIONS

1. What is public policy and who makes it?
2. What are the five steps of the Public Policy Model?
3. Name and describe three problems produced by the large federal bureaucracy.
4. Do you agree with Tocqueville's characterization of the bureaucratic state?
5. Name and describe three efforts to reform bureaucracies.

TERMS

Administrative Discretion: _____

Agenda Setting: _____

Bureaucratic State: _____

Crony Capitalism: _____

Deregulation: _____

Government Corporations: _____

Law of Unintended Consequences: _____

Policy Implementation: _____

Privatization: _____

Public Policy: _____

Spoil System: _____

Whistle-blowers: _____

CHAPTER 23

What Is the
US Economic Policy?

TOPICS

- ► Economic Terms
- ► Laissez-Faire versus a Controlled Economy
- ► Monetary Policy
- ► Supply-Side Economics
- ► The Triumph of Keynesian Economics

LEARNING OBJECTIVES

When you finish reading this chapter, you will be able to:

1. Define basic economic and personal finance terms.
2. Compare laissez-faire economics with Keynesian Economics.
3. Describe monetary and fiscal policy.
4. Explain how America turned from supply-side economics to Keynesian Economics.

ECONOMIC TERMS

Before we start our discussion on US economic policy, it would be helpful to go over some basic economic terms. Recent polls have shown that people today know very little about economics. The National Council on Economic Education created a survey based on twenty-four questions to assess the public's knowledge of economics and personal finance. The results of the survey were less than stellar: adults earned a C and high school students earned an F. By reading this section, your economic IQ will get a quick boost, and you will soon know more about economics and finance than most Americans.

Supply and Demand: The *supply* of something refers to the number of items of it in production or in storage (inventory) that the consumer can buy. *Demand* refers to a consumer's desire to buy an item, reflected by how much money that person is willing to pay. If the supply of something goes down, then the price will go up. For example, if the supply of eggs drops, then people will pay more for eggs. Consequently, as farmers see the price of eggs rise, they will make more chicken coops and produce more eggs, thus increasing supply again. But if there are too many eggs on the market, then the price will drop, and farmers might switch to raising something else, perhaps cattle. In this way supply and demand automatically allocates resources.

Entrepreneur: *A person who is willing to risk his or her money and time to start a business.* An entrepreneur may have a brand new idea, or she may take over an existing business with the idea of running it better. Entrepreneurs are the real engines of growth and innovation in our economy. Some famous American entrepreneurs would include Bill Gates (the founder of Microsoft), Steve Jobs (Apple Computer), Sam Walton (Walmart), Ray Kroc (McDonalds), Walt Disney (Disney Studios & Disneyland), and Henry Ford (Ford Auto Company), just to name a few. Throughout history, American culture has celebrated the risk-taking, innovation, and hard work that enable entrepreneurialism.

Gross National Product (GNP): **GNP** *is the total market value of all the goods and services produced within a country in one year*. According to a 2017 report by the International Monetary Fund, the US has a GNP of $19.4 trillion, the

Entrepreneur

A person who is willing to risk his or her money and time to start a business.

GNP

is the total market value of all the goods and services produced within a country in one year

An entrepreneur is somebody who takes a risk to start a business. They are the engines of growth and innovation in the economy.
©mavo/Shutterstock.com

largest in the world. The following six countries are: China ($11.8 trillion), Japan (11.8 trillion), Germany ($3.4 trillion), United Kingdom ($2.6 trillion), India ($2.5 trillion), and France ($2.4 trillion).

Economic Growth: The economic growth of a country is normally measured by the GNP Growth Rate, the percentage increase of the production of all goods and services year after year. In the decade of the 1950s, the US had an average GNP Growth Rate of 4.7 percent. In the last ten years, the US had a rate of only 1.8 percent. This reflects the fact that in recent years America has implemented economic and social policies that have resulted in slow economic growth. But a nation gains many benefits from strong economic growth, including job creation, a higher standard of living, new innovations, and more tax revenue.

Inflation: *The rate at which prices rise for goods and services.* In periods of high inflation, the prices of everything goes up—gas, milk, eggs, autos, movies, a haircut—and consequently, your purchasing power decreases. The most common way that inflation is measured is by the Consumer Price Index (CPI), which measures the change in the price of a "basket of goods and services" each month. These goods and services include select items of food, fuel, clothing, housing, transportation, and medical services. In 2013, the CPI was about 1.5 percent, which is in line with the long-term average of about between 1 to 3% percent. When the economy is slow and unemployment is high, as it has been in recent years, inflation tends to be low because the population as a whole has less money to spend. When the economy is booming and when the government prints lots of money, inflation tends to go up.

Inflation

The rate at which prices rise for goods and services.

Unemployment Rate: The US calculates the unemployment rate by estimating the number of people over the age of seventeen without jobs *and* actively looking for work within the last four weeks. As of April 2016, the official unemployment rate was 5 percent, which is good. This is down from a 10 percent unemployment rate at the end of 2009. However, if you calculate unemployed people who have given up trying to find a job and people who have a part-time job but want a full-time job, then the "real unemployment" rate is about 14 percent. The *Labor Force Participation Rate* is the percentage of people in the economy who are employed or unemployed but looking for work. Usually it is around 68 percent, but today the Labor Force Participation is 63 percent, the lowest it has been since the 1970s. Currently, some 94 million adults are out of the labor force.

Business Cycle: The economy is never static but always expanding and contracting. Periods of accelerated economic growth are called "booms," and periods of sudden economic collapse are called "busts." Often the president gets the blame or credit for the economy, but most of the time he just happens to be in office during a boom or bust cycle. But if a president actually implements policies that stimulated or hindered economic growth, then, of course, the president should get the credit or blame.

Recession and Depression: The definition of a recession is two consecutive quarters (six months) of negative economic growth. An economic depression, as in the Great Depression of the 1930s, is marked by a significant drop in the GNP, a high rate of business failures, and sustained high unemployment. Ronald Reagan said, "A recession is when your neighbor loses his job. Depression is when you lose yours." So, everything is relative, and recessions and depressions can affect different segments of the economy and different geographical areas of the country.

Investing: Most people invest in stocks and bonds, although some buy precious metals like gold and silver. A *stock* is a share in a particular company. The price of one share of Apple Computer stock in 2007 was $200, and in 2013 it was $400. So an investor could have doubled her money. But this is unusual. Over the last fifty years, the average return on stocks is about 9 percent. *Bonds* are assets issued by governments or companies that pay a fixed amount every month or year. When you buy a bond, you are lending institution money, which they will pay back with interest. Bonds are safer than stocks but give you less money. The return on a total bond market mutual fund over the last ten years was about 4 percent. As people grow older and get closer to retirement, they should own more bonds and fewer stocks.

Through the miracle of compounded interest, anyone can be a millionaire if you invest every month.
©pathdoc/Shutterstock.com

How to Make a Million Dollars: The key to successful investing is to start early and to put a little money into investments every month. You can arrange to have your company automatically transfer a percentage of your paycheck each month into an investment account. If you invest early in your life, you can easily have a million dollars by the time you retire. This is due to the miracle of **compounded interest**: *interest paid on the original amount of money, plus the interest paid on the interest already earned.* Einstein called compounded interest the "greatest mathematical discovery of all time." Here is how it can work for you. If you invest $208 a month in the stock market, starting at the age of twenty, by the time you reach sixty you will have $1,000,000. The easiest way to do this is to buy a S&P 500 fund (SPY), which gives you a share of the top 500 companies in America. So get started!

LAISSEZ-FAIRE VERSUS A CONTROLLED ECONOMY

For most of American history, free market capitalism reigned supreme, and America became the richest country in the world. But starting in the 1930s, the national government adopted policies that asserted more central control over the economy. This policy is known as Keynesian Economics. It promised to reduce the boom-and-bust cycle of the economy, but people like Frederick Hayek warned that it could lead to other problems.

Laissez-Faire: A French term, laissez-faire means "to leave alone." *Economies run by free market capitalism with little or no government regulation are called* **laissez-faire**. From its founding to the 1930s, America had essentially a laissez-faire economy. During the period after the Civil War to the 1920s, the US experienced one of the greatest economic booms in world history, in which America became the wealthiest country in the world with the highest standard of living. During this industrial revolution, American society experienced amazing technological advancement. For example, in the decade of the 1850s, the US Patent Office issues fewer than 2,000 patents. But by the 1890s, it issues 200,000 patents! And modern capitalism transformed the lives of Americans in countless ways. Before the Civil War, most Americans lived on small, isolated farms, travelled by animal, and made most of their own food and clothing. By the 1920s, American homes had electricity, people travelled by auto, and consumers could buy tens of thousands of items from the Sears catalog.

The rapid modernization of society and the widespread reduction of poverty was a result of free enterprise or **capitalism**: *an economic system characterized by private property by which the allocation of labor and recourses is determined by competition in free markets.* One of the first to write about free enterprise was Adam Smith in his landmark book the *Wealth of Nations* (1776). In this book, Smith criticized British mercantilism, a system in which

Compounded Interest

interest paid on the original amount of money, plus the interest paid on the interest already earned

Laissez-Faire

economies run by free market capitalism with little or no government regulation

Capitalism

an economic system characterized by private property by which the allocation of labor and recourses is determined by competition in free markets

**In the history of the world, no system has lifted
more people out of poverty than capitalism.**
©Travel Stock/Shutterstock.com

the government highly regulated business and trade and granted monopolies. Smith said that the economy would be more efficient and productive without government interference. In a free enterprise system, Smith argued, an "invisible hand" of supply and demand automatically guides the economy as each person pursues his own interests.

By the turn of the century, free market capitalism came under attack from the Progressives. They argued that capitalism increased **income disparity**: *the unequal distribution of individual or household income, often measured by comparing the incomes of the bottom 20 percent of the population with the top 20 percent.* Progressives also argued that capitalism exploited the worker with low wages, harmed the environment with pollution, and endangered the consumer with unsafe products. Progressive presidents, such as Theodore Roosevelt and Woodrow Wilson, began controlling the economy by breaking up monopolies, setting railroad rates, creating a progressive income tax, establishing the Federal Reserve, and regulating business. During the Wilson administration alone, from 1913 to 1921, the size of the government increased 171 percent.

Income Disparity

the unequal distribution of individual or household income in society

The Great Depression and the New Deal: Conservatives during the industrial revolution argued that poverty was a result of laziness and other poor character traits. But during the Great Depression, when unemployment reached 30 percent, people realized that forces beyond the control of the individual could create poverty. By the 1930s a majority of the American people accepted the policies of Franklin Roosevelt when he argued that the economy needed more regulation and that the people needed government protection. With the Social Security Act of 1935, FDR created a "safety net" to protect the poor and elderly from economic turbulence. Social Security provided unemployment insurance for people who lost their job, an old age pension for all people over sixty-five, and welfare for poor families and the handicapped.

Keynesian Economics: Beyond creating this basic economic support for each American citizen, FDR started using the federal government as a tool to influence the business cycle. He did this by adopting the policies advocated by the British economist John Maynard Keynes. In 1936, Keynes published *The General Theory of Employment, Interest and Money*, one of the most influential books written in the twentieth century. In this book, Keynes said recessions happen when *aggregate demand* (the total income available to consumers, businesses, and government to spend on goods and services) is less than *productive capacity* (the total value of goods and services produced by the economy at full capacity).

John Maynard Keynes argued that governments can use fiscal policy to reduce the severity of the economic cycle.
© Bettmann/Getty Images

Keynes argued that governments can correct recessions through its **fiscal policy**: *a government's spending and taxing policies*. During a recession, the government could boost aggregate demand by increasing spending and creating public works projects to give unemployed people jobs. Now that they have more money, the employed people will buy goods and services and this money will ripple through the economy stimulating growth. This is called the *multiplier effect*. For example, if a person gets a government job, then she will have money to buy a car. Then the car salesman will have more money to buy shoes, and so on.

Governments can also stimulate the economy by reducing taxes, which will give people more money to spend on goods and services, but Keynesians preferred public works projects. During recessions, Keynesian economics recommends that government use **deficit spending**, *which is when government spending exceeds tax revenues*. Keynes argued that once the economy starts to grow again, governments should increase taxes and reduce spending to restore a balanced budget.

Friedrich Hayek: Although they were friends, Friedrich Hayek was the intellectual rival of Keynes. In *The Road to Serfdom* (1944), Hayek attacks planned

Fiscal Policy

a government's spending and taxing policies

Deficit Spending

when government spending exceeds tax revenues

economies as advocated by Keynes. Hayek argued that governments should provide a basic safety net for the poor and construct laws that correct market failures, but within this framework, governments should allow free markets to operate. Why? Put simply, markets work and government don't. Free markets set the appropriate prices for goods and services, which sends the proper signal to producers and consumers. Free markets are the most efficient way to allocate labor and recourses. Planned economies, on the other hand, set goals based on ideas of social justice that are divorced from economic reality. True, free markets fluctuate as they work through the business cycle, but the best way to handle a recession is leave the economy alone and allow it to correct itself.

A fundamental idea of Hayek's is that it is impossible to maintain individual freedom without economic freedom. Planned economies give the government too much power. And too much government power destroys liberty and turns people into serfs or slaves, thus paving the "road to serfdom." A planned economy is based on the preposition that a few elites could guide the lives, goals, and aspirations of hundreds of millions of people. A planned economy, said Hayek, is the first step toward totalitarianism. And for the government to plan the economy it necessitates propaganda to convince the masses that the goals set by a few government officials justifies the economic inefficiency and loss of individual freedom of the rest of the population.

In recent decades, however, many people have accepted planned economies because of the promise of greater economic security. In response to this, Hayek quotes Ben Franklin, who said, "Those who give up essential liberty, to purchase a little temporary safety, deserve neither Liberty nor Safety."

Friedrich Hayek argued that as government control over the economy grows, individual liberty shrinks.
©Apic/Hulton Archive/Getty Images

MONETARY POLICY

In the 1960s, Milton Friedman, who started out as a Keynesian but ended up as a follower of Hayek, advocated for the use of monetary policy to control inflation and encourage economic growth. *Government control of the money supply and interest rates through a central bank is called* **monetary policy**. According to the tenants of monetarism, during a recession the government should lower interest rates and increase the money supply. Lower interest rates make it cheaper for businesses and people to borrow money to buy expensive items. This will foster economic growth. Also, by increasing the

Monetary Policy

government control of the money supply and interest rates through a central bank money supply, people will have more money to spend on goods and services. But when the government prints too much money it leads to inflation. So once the economy starts to grow again, then the government should slowly decrease the money supply and increase interest rates.

The Federal Reserve System: *In the US, the central bank is called the Federal Reserve, created by Congress in 1913 to set monetary policy.* The "Fed" is mandated to control inflation and maximize employment and is controlled by the *Board of Governors*. To reduce political influence, the seven members of the Board are selected by the president and confirmed by the Senate to serve a single fouteen-year term. The Board of Governors sets monetary policy and oversees the twelve regional *Federal Reserve Banks*. The *Chair of the Federal Reserve*, one of the most powerful offices in the world, is appointed by the president for a four-year term, which runs from the mid-point of one administration to the midterm of the next, guaranteeing that the Fed Chair will serve at least two presidents. The Fed Chair can be reappointed to unlimited terms, but most have served only one or two terms.

By law, the Fed Chair is required to provide a report to Congress at least two times a year. Markets around the world often fall or rise in response to a single word by the Fed Chair, and so he or she must craft their reports very carefully. Allan Greenspan, who served as Fed Chair for four presidents, was famous for giving opaque congressional reports. Greenspan once said, "I know you think you understand what you thought I said, but I'm not sure you realize that what you heard isn't what I meant."

Federal Reserve

in the US, the central bank is called the Federal Reserve, created by Congress in 1913 to set monetary policy

In 2014, Janet Yellen became chair of the Federal Reserve.
©GongTo/Shutterstock.com

How the Fed Influences Interest Rates and the Money Supply: The Fed Chair establishes monetary policy at meetings of the Federal Open Market Committee (FOMC), which meets eight times a year. The Fed has several tools by which it sets monetary policy and stimulates the economy. It controls interest rates by setting the *discount rate*: the interest rate the Fed lends money to member banks. If the discount rate is lowered, banks will borrow more money from the Fed and lend it to customers at lower interest rates. And the Fed controls the money supply by setting the *reserve requirements*: the amount of cash banks are mandated to keep in their vaults. If the Fed decreases reserve requirements, then this will expand the money supply.

The Fed also controls the money supply and interest rates through *open market operations*: the selling and buying of short-term government bonds by the Federal Reserve. When the Fed buys bonds from member banks, it provides the banks with more money. This should decrease interest rates and expand the money supply.

But during the Great Recession, the normal tools of the Federal Reserve failed to stimulate the economy, even though discount rate was nearly zero. So the Fed has engaged in innovative open market operations called *quantitative easing*: the Fed buys riskier financial assets from commercial banks and other private institutions, which should also lower interest rates and increase the money supply. Economists are unsure about the impact of quantitative easing. Some say that it has led to the rise in the stock market, which gives people more money to spend on consumer items. Others have warned that this policy could produce inflation and create a stock market bubble.

SUPPLY-SIDE ECONOMICS

Ronald Reagan, a follower of Hayek and Freidman, rejected Keynesian economics, which had become standard policy in the US and other industrialized nations around the world. Reagan said that government officials are fond of Keynesian economics because it gives them more power and control, but it has two main flaws. First, the use of public works projects to stimulate the economy is too slow and cumbersome. By the time government creates a government program and the bureaucracy to implement it, the recession is past its peak. As President Obama famously said about the public works projects he created, "Shovel-ready jobs were not as shovel-ready as we expected." Second, elected officials are always eager to spend money to stimulate the economy, but they never follow Keynes' recommendation to balance the budget during periods of economic growth. As a result, Keynesian economics has led to enormous government debt around the world. According to NationalDebtClocks.org, worldwide debt is over $60 trillion.

**Ronald Reagan used supply-side economics to reduce poverty
and create tens of millions of jobs.**
©Joseph Sohm/Shutterstock.com

During the 1980s, the Reagan administration engaged in **supply-side economics**: *the government's attempt to stimulate long-term economic growth by bolstering the supply of goods and services through policies of lower taxes, less government regulations, and less government spending*. Supply-side theorists argue that more government spending crowds out private sector spending. Government regulations burden businesses as they have to spend more of their time and labor dealing with complex regulations rather than increasing sales.

And steep progressive taxes hinder economic growth in several ways. If people know they will be taxed more if they earn more money, they will not take on extra work. Thus, lower taxes increase the incentive to work hard and start additional businesses. And if people pay less in taxes, then they will have more money to buy goods and services. Further, if businesses pay lower domestic taxes, then they will open more factories in America, rather than go overseas.

Supply-side policies worked in the 1980s and beyond. During the recession of 1981–1982, unemployment peaked at 10.8 percent, inflation and interest rates were at record highs, and the poverty rate was 15.2 percent, another record high. Then Reagan drastically cut taxes and simplified the tax code. When Reagan came into office there were several income tax brackets, the highest being 70 percent. When he left office there were only two brackets: 28 percent and 15 percent. He cut government spending, especially non-military spending. And he reduced government regulations and ended price controls. As a result, the economy quickly rebounded. By 1984, the economy was growing

Supply-side Economics

the government's attempt to stimulate long-term economic growth by bolstering the supply of goods and services through policies of lower taxes, less government regulations, and less government spending by 7 percent, a fifty-year record. By the time Reagan left office in 1988, the economy had grown one-third its original size, unemployment dropped to 5.3 percent, per capita incomes rose 18 percent, and the poverty level went down to 13 percent.

Laffer Curve: Contrary to most predictions, government revenues actually doubled after the Reagan tax cuts were implemented. How could this be? Well, if taxes are low, people will actually pay the tax, rather than find ways to avoid it. And lower taxes stimulates the whole economy, creating more jobs and increasing incomes, so more people pay taxes even at lower rates. This relationship between taxes and revenues is illustrated by the Laffer Curve, developed by Arthur Laffer, one of Reagan's economic advisors. The **Laffer Curve** *is a graph that illustrates how higher taxes reduces government revenues.* At the left side of curve is a 1 percent tax rate, which almost 100 percent of people will pay. On the other end of the curve is a 100 percent income tax, which nobody will pay. So, what is the tax rate which will bring in the most revenue? A recent study by Christina Romer, an Obama economic advisor, concluded that a tax rate of about 33 percent, would bring in the maximum revenue.

THE TRIUMPH OF KEYNESIAN ECONOMICS

Despite the strong record of supply-side economics, its principles were slowly abandoned. After 1990, taxes, government spending, and regulations slowly crept up again. And to deal with recessions, both Republican and Democratic administrations used Keynesian economics. In response to the economic slowdown in 2007, the George Bush administration implemented a $160 billion stimulus package and every taxpayer received a government check for $600. This did little to stimulate the economy and by 2008 about 2.6 million people had lost their jobs.

Then in 2008, there was a panic in the financial industry due to the collapse of securities based on subprime mortgages. During the past two decades, the government has encouraged people with poor credit and low incomes to buy mortgages. It was believed that home ownership would have positive social consequences. These mortgages were bundled and sold as investment vehicles. When these investments began to falter, it threatened to bring down some of the biggest banks and investment houses in America. To prevent a total financial collapse, the government spent $700 billion on the Troubled Asset Relief Program (TARP), which used taxpayer's money to buy assets and lend money to financial institutions. Then in 2009, the Obama administration spent about $790 billion on another stimulus program, called the American Recovery and Investment Act. Although progress has been very slow and

Laffer Curve

a graph that illustrates how higher taxes reduces government revenues

GNP remains low, the economy has recovered and the unemployment rate is gradually going down.

So, Keynesian economics won out over Hayek's proscription that recessions be allowed to correct themselves. Politically, Keynesian economics was more attractive. During a recession, people are scared and they want the government to do something, even if in reality it may create a slower recovery. It is politically impossible for the president to tell the American people to just wait for the economy to correct itself. The last president to do that during a major recession was Grover Cleveland in 1892. He received so many death threats that security guards had to surround the White House. Today nearly all major industrial governments use Keynesian economics in response to a recession.

Trump's Economic Plan: Trump's political and economic agenda has been called "nationalistic populism," meaning he wants to do what is best for America (America first) and the working class people (the forgotten man). His economic plan is mostly conservative, but it also contains elements of traditional liberal economics. Following the Supply-siders, Trump wants to lower taxes and simplify the tax code. He proposes reducing the number of tax brackets from six to four: 0%, 12%, 25%, and 35%. He wants to eliminate tax deductions except for home mortgages and charitable giving. Trump is seeking to lower the corporate tax rate from 35% to 20%, which would make it slightly lower than the average industrialized countries. He also proposes a one-time repatriation tax of 10%. After the last couple of decades, because

Arthur Brooks argues that greater freedom leads to greater prosperity, which leads to more jobs.
©Creativa Images/Shutterstock.com

US corporate taxes are the highest in the world, many countries have moved assets overseas. It is estimated that the repatriation tax could bring $3 trillion back to the US. And Trump is not only following Reagan by lowering taxes, but he is also drastically cutting federal regulations.

On the other hand, Trump's economic agenda contains some elements normally popular with Democrats. Reminiscent of Franklin Roosevelt's public works projects, Trump wants to launch a massive effort to rebuild American roads and infrastructure. Another major aspect in Trump's agenda is to renegotiate the international trade agreements, such as NAFTA. Trump argues that they have hurt American manufacturing and closed down thousands of factories. In the past, the Democrats have opposed free trade because they wanted to protect union jobs. So, Trump may be able to pick up some support from Democrats in Congress on these two proposals.

FINAL THOUGHTS

Even though Keynesian economics won acceptance by most economists and government officials, the debate between liberal and conservative economists continues.

Today, liberal economists, such as the Nobel prize-winning economist and *New York Times* columnist Paul Krugman, advocate a set of economic policies that focus on reducing income inequality. Using northern European countries such as Denmark as the model, mainstream liberal economists support a redistributive tax policy, which includes a steep tax on high income earners, corporations, and large asset owners. Tax revenues will go to form a wide array of government programs to provide an expansive social safety net. And they also support a high minimum wage. Liberal economists argue that the government needs to regulate business to protect workers, consumers, and the environment. A primary social responsibility, they argue, is to guide the economy away from fossils fuels that are causing global warming and to provide subsidies and tax breaks for eco-friendly energy companies.

Instead of looking to northern Europe as an economic model, conservative economists such as Arthur Brooks, president of the American Enterprise Institute, suggest we use the freest nations in the world as our model. Each year the Fraser Institute publishes its "Economic Freedom Index," which ranks countries by its level of personal freedom. Brooks points out that in the top fifth freest nations, the income is eight times that of the lowest fifth or least free nations. In *The Road to Freedom*, Brooks argues that not only do free-market economic systems reduce poverty and create more jobs, they are more ethical. A system that rewards merit and hard work is more fair than a system that gives money to people the government thinks deserves it. When you allow people the freedom to *earn their success*, argues Brooks, individuals feel a deep sense of personal satisfaction. But a system that gives things to people for doing nothing only fosters dependency and dissatisfaction.

It is clear that the liberal, redistributive model and the conservative, pro-growth model are based on different worldviews. The liberal model focuses on safety and comfort. It provides cradle to grave government programs, such as government provided health care and long mandatory vacations. In exchange for these programs, however, individuals give up their freedom and the economy usually experiences low GNP and higher unemployment. The conservative model is more dynamic. It rewards hard work and innovation, thus increasing GNP and lowing unemployment, but it demands more individual responsibility and risk. So it comes down to this: Do you want greater safety but more government dependence or do you want more prosperity but greater individual responsibility?

NOTES

For international economic data, go to United Nations, Statistics Division (unstats.un.org/unsd/default.htm) and World Factbook (www.cia.gov).

For Reagan supply-side economics, see William A. Niskanen and Stephen Moore, "Supply-side Tax Cuts and the Truth about the Reagan Economic Record," *Cato Institute Policy Analysis No. 26*; Peter Ferrara, "Reaganomics vs. Obamanomics: Facts and Figures," *Forbes, May 2011*; Peter B. Sperry, "The Real Reagan Economic Record: Responsible and Successful Fiscal Policy," *Heritage Foundation Report, March 1, 2001.*

Arthur C. Brooks. *The Road to Freedom*. New York: Basic Books, 2012.

Friedrich Hayek. *Road to Serfdom*. Chicago: University of Chicago Press, 1994.

John Maynard Keynes. *The General Theory of Employment, Interest and Money*. New York: Macmillion & Co., 1964.

Dana Markow and Kelly Bagnaschi, "What American Teens & Adults Know About Economics," *National Council on Economic Education*, April 26, 2005.

Adam Smith. *Wealth of Nations*. Washington: Regnery Publishing, 1998.

Lawrence H. White. *The Clash of Economic Ideas: The Great Policy Debates and Experiments of the Last Hundred Years*. Cambridge: Cambridge University Press, 2012.

ESSAY QUESTIONS

1. Describe the success of laissez-faire economics in America and the Progressive critique.
2. How does Keynesian economics use fiscal policy to stimulate the economy?
3. How does the Federal Reserve Board use monetary policy to stimulate the economy?
4. Define the tenants of supply-side economics.
5. Why have governments around the world turned to Keynesian economics?

TERMS

Capitalism: _____

Compounded Interest: _____

Deficit Spending: _____

Entrepeneur: _____

Federal Reserve: _____

Fiscal Policy: _____

GNP: _____

Income Disparity: _____

Inflation: _____

Laffer Curve: _____

Laissez-faire: _____

Monetary Policy: _____

Supply-side Economics: _____

CHAPTER 24

How Does the Government Make the Budget?

TOPICS

▶ The Budget Process
▶ Types of Taxes
▶ Tax Issues
▶ Government Spending
▶ The Debt Problem

LEARNING OBJECTIVES

When you finish reading this chapter, you will be able to:

1. Cite the four steps of the modern budget process.
2. List the major sources of revenue for the federal government.
3. Compare progressive and regressive taxes.
4. Describe the difference between mandatory and discretionary spending.
5. Explain how annual deficits have led to a tremendous national debt.

HOW DOES THE GOVERNMENT MAKE THE BUDGET?

The Constitution gives Congress tremendous taxing and spending powers. Considering America's long fight with Britain over unjust taxes, the Revolutionary Generation was very trepidatious about granting the national government strong tax powers, powers which can be so easily abused. In America's first constitution, the Article of Confederation, the national government had very limited tax authority. Indeed, it was so limited that it made it nearly impossible to conduct the Revolutionary War. After several years of budgetary crisis when the US struggled to pay its war debts, the Founders realized that Congress must have strong taxing and spending powers in order to defend the nation and provide for the general welfare. But in recent decades, the taxing and spending process has not worked so well, and the nation's debts keep mounting.

This chapter is a bit technical in nature, and for that reason it is the shortest chapter in the book. But although the chapter is brief, it deals with an important subject: how the national government spends our money. In the pages below, we will outline the budget process as conducted by Congress and the president and how the process has broken down in recent years. Because of flaws in the budgetary process, America has taken on enormous debt. The chapter will conclude by suggesting a solution to this problem.

THE BUDGET PROCESS

The current federal budget process was shaped by two major laws. During World War I, when the executive branch oversaw the very expensive war effort, many realized that the president needed to participate in the budget process

Making the annual budget is a complicated process, but in recent years the normal process has broken down as Democrats and Republicans fight over spending and taxing priorities.

©pedrosek/Shutterstock.com

with Congress. Up to this time, Congress, as the branch with the constitutionally mandated power of the purse, was in sole control of the federal budget. The *Budget and Accounting Act of 1921* required that the president submit a proposed budget to Congress each year. Then in 1974, after the struggles over spending between Congress and the Richard Nixon Administration, Congress passed the *Congressional Budget and Impounding Control Act,* which established the formal system by which the executive and legislative branches formulate the budget today. There are four major steps of the budget process, which operates on the fiscal year, from October 1 to September 30.

Step One—The President Submits a Budget Request: Near the beginning of the year, usually the first week of February, the president submits to Congress his proposed budget for the coming fiscal year, which starts on October 1. Over the previous year, every detail of this budget was reviewed by the president's budget director and the **Office of Management and Budget (OMB)**, *the largest office of the Executive Office of the President. The OMB reviews the spending requests of each department and agency of the executive branch and provides detailed reports on the OMB website.* The president's budget constitutes his proposed tax and spending plans for the following year, which outlines the president's domestic and foreign policy priorities. In this way, the president's budget proposal is a political document.

Step Two—The House and Senate Pass Budget Resolutions: The president's budget is then sent to House and Senate budget committees. During this time, the **Congressional Budget Office (CBO)**, *an independent government agency staffed by professional economists, examines the budget and conducts a cost analysis for Congress.* In March the CBO will publish an analysis of the president's budget proposal, including a ten-year projection of the costs. This is published on the CBO website. The House and Senate then must pass a *budget resolution*, which consists of general spending and revenue targets for the following year. Then the House and Senate resolutions must be reconciled in a conference committee and voted on again by each chamber. This is supposed to be completed by April 15.

Step Three—The House and Senate Pass Appropriation Bills: The House and Senate resolutions are broken up into thirteen parts and sent to thirteen subcommittees, where they are written up as thirteen appropriation bills. Each subcommittee holds hearings and mark up the bills, which are sent to the House and Senate floor for a vote. Before the floor vote, members seek to add amendments that bring money to their home district. Then each House and Senate bill must be sent to a conference committee to be reconciled, which provides another opportunity to add pork and special interest provisions to the bill. After that, the bills are sent to each chamber again to be voted on in the exact same language.

Office of Management and Budget (OMB)

the largest office of the Executive Office of the President. The OMB reviews the spending requests of each department and agency of the executive branch and provides detailed reports on the OMB website

Congressional Budget Office (CBO)

an independent government agency staffed by professional economists, examines the budget and conducts a cost analysis for Congress

Step Four—The President Signs the Budget Bill: Then the separate appropriation bills are sent to the president, which are supposed to be signed by September 1. If Congress and the president are unable to complete this process by the end of September, then Congress must pass a *continuing resolution*, which temporarily funds the government until a budget is signed. Often at this point, all the remaining appropriations bills are rolled into one "omnibus" spending bill, usually consisting of thousands of pages. This massive omnibus spending bill, which few have time to actually read, must be signed by the president before the beginning of the fiscal year. If it is not signed by October 1, then the government could shut down, which happened in 1995 and 2013. Shutdowns are very unpopular with the American people, and both parties have vowed not to do it again.

The Broken Process: In recent years the budget process has not followed the normal steps or met the proscribed deadlines. Since 2010, when the Republicans took control of the House and the presidency was controlled by Barack Obama, a Democrat, divided government has made it much more difficult to pass a budget. Before 2015, the Senate was dominated by Democrats and they did not pass a budget resolution in 2011, 2012, and 2013. In these cases, the 2010 budget (passed by the Democratic Congress) remained in force. And in 2014, the president didn't submit his budget until April, some three months late.

It should not be surprising that in times of *divided government*, when the Republicans control one branch of Congress or the presidency and the Democrats control another branch of Congress or the presidency, the normal budget process breaks down. Republicans and Democrats have very different tax and spending policies, and these fundamental differences cannot be easily worked out.

In Trump's first year in office, he enjoys united government, with Republicans holding majorities in the House and Senate. Yet, several Republican senators have voiced criticism of Trump over various economic issues, so at this point it is unclear if Trump will be able to get his first budget through Congress.

TYPES OF TAXES

The federal budget, like any budget, is an estimate of the revenue (taxes) and expenses (spending) over a specified period of time, normally one year. Let's first look at the revenue side of the ledger. According to National Priorities Project (a left-leaning, non-profit think tank which explains the budget process and its impact on social policy), President Obama's budget request for 2015 estimates that the federal government will bring in $3.3 trillion in revenue. This revenue comes from four major sources: income taxes, payroll taxes, corporate taxes, and excise taxes.

The main way the national government gets money is by the personal income tax.
©mathom/Shutterstock.com

Individual Income Tax (46 percent): By far most federal tax revenue, 46 percent, comes from individual income taxes. **Individual income tax** *is a direct tax on the income an individual earns in one year*. By law, all citizens must file a personal income tax statement. Today more than 100 million Americans (or 53 percent of working age adults) pay federal income taxes, which is automatically deducted from a worker's paycheck. Most of the time, more money is deducted from an individual's paycheck than he or she will be required to pay in income taxes at the end of the year. So after people submit their tax returns, which are due by April 15, the Internal Revenue Service (IRS) sends out a refund check to make up the difference.

Payroll Tax (32 percent): About 32 percent of revenues come from **payroll taxes**, *a tax paid jointly by employers and employees out of a worker's paycheck*. On your pay stub, these deductions are labeled as "FICA," for Federal Insurance Contributions Act. This revenue is designated to go into the federal "trust fund," meaning it is mandated to be spent only for certain entitlements, mainly Social Security and Medicare.

Corporate Taxes (13 percent): Corporations also pay taxes, which account for 13 percent of federal revenues. At 35 percent, America has one of the highest corporate tax rates in the world. The corporate tax rate of France is 33 percent, Germany 30 percent, Britain's 24 percent, Russia 20 percent, Finland 20 percent, Hong Kong 17 percent, and Canada 15 percent. Advocates of a high corporate tax say it helps create more equality through income distribution. Opponents say corporations pay for taxes by increasing prices and

Individual Income Tax

a direct tax on the income an individual earns in one year

Payroll Taxes

a tax paid jointly by employers and employees out of a worker's paycheck lowering wages, which hurts America consumers and workers. Also, high corporate taxes forces countries to move operations overseas, which also hurts American workers. In Trump's tax plan, he is proposing that the US lower its corporate tax to 20%.

Excise Tax (3 percent): Making up just 3 percent of revenues, **excise taxes** *are taxes on luxury consumer items, such as cigarettes, liquor, and gasoline.*

Capital Gains Tax: Lastly, there is another type of tax, called the *capital gains tax*: a tax on profits from a sale of capital goods such as stocks, bonds, precious metals, or property. In America, short-term capital gains are taxed at a higher rate than long-term gains, capital held for more than a year. Again, America has one of the highest capital gains taxes in the world. And like other taxes, the capital gains tax is the subject of political debate. Conservatives argue that a low capital gains tax stimulates the economy because it frees up money to be invested in new opportunities, financing innovation and making the economy more dynamic. Liberals, on the other hand, want high capital gains taxes in order to tax the wealthy, which often do not earn regular incomes but live off their investments.

TAX ISSUES

Currently, the US Federal Tax Code is 73,954 pages long! By contrast, in 1970 it was less than 17,000 pages long. This means individuals and corporations spend an enormous amount of time and money preparing their tax returns. An estimated 1.2 million people work as tax preparers in America. These thousands of pages of codes are filled with special interest loopholes that benefit certain industries, such as tax credits for electric cars, racehorses, private jets, yachts, and for writing songs. The best way to get rid of crony capitalism and to make our economy more efficient would be to simplify the tax code. *Crony capitalism* is a system in which business success is enhanced by connections to government officials, knowledge of legal loopholes (and tax breaks), and by government favoritism. Trump's tax plan promises to simplify taxes so that a family can do their taxes on one page.

Regressive Taxes: *Taxes in which poor people pay a higher percentage of their income in taxes are called* **regressive taxes**. For example, sales, gasoline, and cigarette taxes are regressive because poor people spend a higher percentage of their income on these items than do rich people. Local governments rely heavily on these types of taxes. Politically, is easiest to raise taxes on things like cigarettes and alcohol, often called "sin taxes," because these are not necessities and they are thought to be harmful indulgences.

Progressive Taxes: *Taxes in which wealthy people pay a higher percentage of their income are called* **progressive taxes**. America has an income tax system

Excise Taxes

are taxes on luxury consumer items, such as cigarettes, liquor, and gasoline

Regressive Taxes

taxes in which poor people pay a higher percentage of their income in taxes

Progressive Taxes

taxes in which wealthy people pay a higher percentage of their income

The US has one of the most progressive tax systems in the world.
The top 10 percent of earners pay 68 percent of the all taxes in America.
©Stuart Miles/Shutterstock.com

consisting of six brackets, from 10 percent to 39.6 percent. If you make, for example, between $8,925 and $36,250 a year, you are in the 15 percent tax bracket. And if you make over $400,000, you are in the 39.6 percent tax bracket. America has a very progressive income tax system: the rich pay most of the taxes and the poor pay little taxes. The top 10 percent of earners pay 78 percent of all federal income taxes. And due to the earned income tax credit (EITC), the federal government actually pays money to low income families through a "tax refund." Because of the EITC, 43 percent of US households paid no federal income taxes in 2013.

The Politics of Taxes: Liberal Democrats and conservative Republicans have different views on taxes. Liberals advocate higher taxes on the wealthy to distribute the wealth and achieve greater income equality. A key theme of Obama's 2008 and 2012 presidential campaigns were to raise taxes on the wealthy. Conservatives, on the other hand, advocate lower taxes. The most conservative president in recent history was Ronald Reagan and tax cuts were central to his platform. Reagan argued that tax cuts allow greater freedom, reduce the size of government, and stimulate economic growth. Incidentally, both liberals and conservatives say that their tax policy will help the poor. Liberals say high taxes on the rich finance welfare programs, which help the poor. And conservatives say that lowering taxes creates more jobs, reduces the poverty rate, and stimulates the *whole* economy—as John Kennedy once said, "a rising tide raises all boats," rich and poor.

Suggested Tax Reforms: Critics highlight a number of problems with the current American tax code. First, its complexity (as stated above, the US Tax Code is nearly 74,000 pages long). This drains time and energy out of the economy as people and corporations spend too much time preparing their taxes. Second, the steep progressive nature of the tax code punishes the most productive citizens and discourages them from making more money because they would be pushed into a higher tax bracket. Third, the punitive corporate taxes encourage American companies to relocate overseas, taking away American jobs. And fourth, critics claim that it is unhealthy for a society that nearly half of the population does not pay any federal income taxes. As a civil duty, we all benefit from living in America, and so we should all contribute something.

With these criticisms in mind, two tax reforms are gaining popularity: a flat tax and a consumption tax. A *flat tax* is a system that applies the same tax rate to every taxpayer, regardless of income, and offers no deductions or exemptions. Advocates contend that it greatly simplify the process of calculating taxes, thus freeing up resources for more productive endeavors. And the flat tax would provide an incentive to work harder and make more money. In the 2016, two Republican presidential candidates, Ben Carson and Ted Cruz, proposed a flat tax. Over forty countries have a flat tax, including Russia which has 13 percent flat tax rate.

And advocates of a consumption tax also argue that it would stimulate the economy and greatly simplify the tax process. A *consumption tax* is a tax on spending on certain goods and services. A 20 percent consumption tax, with basic groceries exempt, would provide the needed revenue to the government without anybody having to file a tax return. A consumption tax would encourage savings, broaden the tax base, and eliminate unfair tax loopholes and crony capitalism. And the tax is more efficient, as it eliminates the need to file a tax return or hire an expensive accountant. One critique of the flat tax and consumption tax is that it would eliminate deductions for charitable giving and home ownership, two activities that are beneficial to society.

GOVERNMENT SPENDING

Governments take the tax revenues and spend it on the things Americans want and need. Throughout American history, as the role of the federal government has expanded, the US government spends more and more money. In 1900, federal spending equaled less than 7 percent of GDP. Then after the spike in spending during WWII, spending came down to 21 percent of GDP in the 1950s. In the last few decades, the government has maintained spending at about 36 percent of GDP. According to the National Priorities Project, the following are the percentages of mandatory and discretionary spending for the 2015 budget.

65 percent of federal spending goes to mandatory entitlement programs like Medicare.
©zimmytws/Shutterstock.com

Mandatory Spending (65 percent): About 65 percent of the budget consists of **mandatory spending**: *spending on entitlement programs such as Social Security and Medicare that require no congressional authorization but are automatically paid for according to a formula.* For Obama's 2015 budget, the federal government spent $2.56 trillion on mandatory spending.

Discretionary Spending (29 percent): Only about a third of the budget consists of **discretionary spending**: *non-entitlement spending that is up to the "discretion" of Congress and the president to spend each year.* For Obama's 2015 budget, discretionary spending was $1.16 trillion.

Interest on the Federal Debt (6 percent): Every year the federal government borrows billions of dollars in order to keep the government running. Interest payments on that debt account for about 6 percent of annual spending. Fortunately, interest rates have been extremely low in recent years. When interest rates rise, the percentage of the budget that goes to paying interest on debt will increase, taking money away from more useful things, such as food stamps and road construction.

Total Spending: According to the website usgovernmentspending.com, government spending for 2013 totaled $3.5 trillion: 25 percent pensions, 25 percent health, 24 percent defense, 12 percent welfare, and 15 percent miscellaneous (debt payments, transportation, science, environment).

Mandatory Spending

spending on entitlement programs such as Social Security and Medicare that require no congressional authorization but are automatically paid for according to a formula

Discretionary Spending

non-entitlement spending that is up to the "discretion" of Congress and the president to spend each year

THE DEBT PROBLEM

Debt results when somebody spends more money than they make. America has a big debt problem. Many American citizens and the American government spend much more money than they make. According to a 2014 Federal Reserve Bank of New York report, Americans own $8.2 trillion in mortgage debt, $1.1 trillion in student loan debt, $875 billion in automobile debt, and $659 billion in credit card debt, for a total of $11.7 trillion in all debt! Piling up a lot of debt puts strain on household finances, but the strain on the US government due to debt can have serious consequences for the whole nation. This section will outline our national debt problem.

Annual Deficits: *When annual government spending exceeds annual tax revenue, the result is a budget* **annual deficit.** For the last five years, the US government has run up massive deficits: In 2013 it was $680 billion; in 2012 it was $1.1 trillion; in 2011 it was $1.3 trillion; in 2010 it was $1.3 trillion; and in 2009 it was $1.4 trillion. In 2013, for example, the federal government spent about $3.5 trillion, but total tax revenue was only about $2.8 trillion, so the government spent $680 billion more than it made. How do governments spend money they do not have? They sell bonds. When a government sells bonds, it takes in cash from the individuals, corporations, or foreign countries that buy US bonds, and promises to pay it back with interest. As stated above, about 6 percent of federal spending goes to pay the interest on these bonds.

Annual Deficit

when annual government spending exceeds annual tax revenue, the result is a budget annal deficit

National Debt: *The accumulated annual deficits result in the* **national debt.** For example, if we add up the annual deficits from 2009 to 2013, it comes to a national debt of $5.78 trillion, which is added to the previous debt. As of 2017, the national debt is over $20 trillion, which comes to about $56,000 per person. In 2000, the national debt was just less than $6 trillion. So, in fourteen short years, over the George W. Bush and Barack Obama administrations, the national debt has grown threefold: from $6 trillion to nearly $18 trillion!

National Debt

the accumulated annual deficits

History of National Debt: Due to inflation, the best way to understand national debt is to compare it to the size of the total US economy, the Gross Domestic Product (GDP). In 1900, before the Progressive Era, the national debt as a percentage of GDP was only 10 percent. During the New Deal of the 1930s, it jumped to 40 percent. During World War II, it spiked at 120 percent, but by the 1970s, it had gone down to 35 percent. In the 1980s, with Reagan's defense build-up, the national debt went up to 50 percent. In 2006, before the Great Recession, the national debt was about 62 percent of GDP. By the end of 2014, it has reached 100 percent of GDP! Economists consider national debt/GDP at 100 percent a dangerous number. Many countries that have debts equaling the size of their economy, find it very difficult to pay it down, resulting in default. If America were to default on its debts, it would trigger a global financial crisis.

**The president and Congress have irresponsibly put the nation in tremendous debt.
As of 2016, the national debt is $19 trillion.**
©razihusin/Shutterstock.com

Why Is America Building up Debt? Put simply, Congress and the president are spending more money than they should. There are two fundamental reasons the national government spends too much money. First, entitlements, such as Social Security, Medicare, and welfare, keep growing as the population ages and people become more accustomed to government programs. And Congress has relinquished responsibility for spending on entitlements. As we learned above, entitlement spending, which accounts for two-thirds of the budget, is mandatory and automatic. This leaves Congress with control of only one-third of the budget.

Second, there is no political incentive to cut spending. Let's imagine two people who are running for Congress: Mr. Santa Clause and Mr. Austerity. Mr. Santa Clause runs for office by promising to build a senior citizens' center, to support a bridge project, to strengthen our national defense, and to increase food stamps. Mr. Austerity, on the other hand, runs for office by promising to spend less money than his predecessor. Who do you think will be more likely to win office? So, the bottom line is that the people are ultimately to blame for the national debt. They want more and more government programs without paying for it. In reality, the current generation is enjoying the government freebies and passing the bill on to the next generation, who will have to eventually pay the bill. Young people are going to feel the pain of the actions of the previous generations—which is unfair.

FINAL THOUGHTS

How is the national government going to fix its spending problem, which potentially could have disastrous consequences for the country? We suggest two possible solutions. Almost all states have some sort of *balanced budget amendment* in their constitution. This has helped these states keep their debt low. Some have suggested that the federal government also adopt a balanced budget amendment. This would force lawmakers to live within their means and not spend more money than we have. But some congressional members fear this might hamstring the government when we face a national crisis that requires additional spending, such as a world war or a financial collapse. To deal with this contingency, a balanced budget amendment could contain a supermajority vote to temporarily spend more money during a crisis.

There is another plan that is winning more support: the "*one cent solution.*" This plan is attractive due to its simplicity. If the government could cut one cent out of every dollar of total spending each year for five years, we would have a balanced budget! Then continue the one cent cuts until overall federal spending is 18 percent of GDP, a sustainable ratio. This plan gives Congress flexibility because they can leave important programs alone as long as total spending decreases by 1 percent a year. Today there are seventy-two congress-persons that have pledged support for a "one cent solution" bill. But whatever the plan is, our elected officials must do something now to correct this serious problem. Instead, they keep kicking the can down the road.

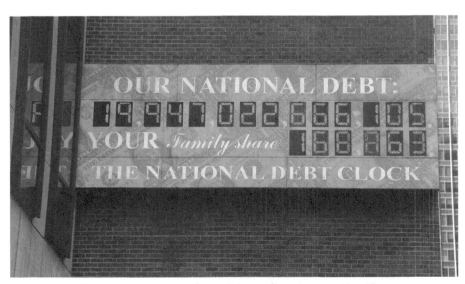

Every second our national debt goes up. National leaders must find a way to stop this before it creates a financial crisis.
©Leonard Zhukovsky/Shutterstock.com

NOTES

For tax and spending and for steps of the budget process: "Budget Process: Federal Budget 101," National Priorities Project (www.nationalpriorities.org); and "Policy Basics: Introduction to the Federal Budget Process," Center on Policy on Budget and Policy Priorities (www.cbpp.org).

For facts about federal taxes go to the Tax Foundation (www.taxfoundation.org).

For information about the "one cent solution" go to www.onecentsolution.org.

For a comparison of the flat tax and consumption tax read J. D. Foster, "The New Flat Tax: Easy as One, Two, Three," *The Heritage Foundation Backgrounder #2631*, Dec. 13, 2011; Alan S. Blinder, "The Folly of the Flat Tax Consumption Tax," *WSL*, Nov. 14, 2011; and Len Burman and William G. Gale, "The Pros and Cons of a Consumption Tax," *Brookings Institute*, March 3, 2005.

For information about personal debt go to Federal Reserve Bank of New York (www.newyorkfed.org) and read "Report on Personal Debt, 2015."

ESSAY QUESTIONS

1. What does the Office of Management and Budget do?
2. What are the advantages and disadvantages of a high corporate tax rate?
3. Explain how a more complicated tax code fosters crony capitalism.
4. What is the difference between the deficit and the national debt?
5. Explain why the national debt keeps growing.

TERMS

Annual Deficit: _____

Congressional Budget Office (CBO): _____

Discretionary Spending: _____

Excise Taxes: _____

Individual Income Tax: _____

Mandatory Spending: _____

National Debt: _____

Office of Management and Budget (OMB): _____

Payroll Taxes: _____

Progressive Taxes: _____

Regressive Taxes: _____

CHAPTER 25

What Is America's Foreign and Defense Policy?

TOPICS

▶ Tools in Foreign Policy
▶ The Constitution and Foreign Policy
▶ Two Foreign Policy Approaches
▶ Early American Foreign Policy
▶ Modern US Foreign Policy

LEARNING OBJECTIVES

When you finish reading this chapter, you will be able to:

1. Discuss the various ways countries try to influence each other.
2. Describe the powers granted to the legislative and executive branches in the fields of foreign affairs and war.
3. Compare the two main foreign policy approaches.
4. Explain the key features of the history of American foreign policy.

WHAT IS AMERICA'S FOREIGN AND DEFENSE POLICY?

Foreign policy, simply put, *is a nation's set of policies and objectives in dealing with other nations*. A sub-category of foreign policy is *defense policy*, defined as a nation's military policies and objectives, including its arrangement of military assets and personnel, designed to protect the nation from military threats. In this chapter, we will discuss the tools countries use when engaging

Foreign Policy

a nation's set of policies and objectives in dealing with other nations in foreign policy, examine how the Constitution allocates foreign policy powers, and outline the history of US foreign policy. Perhaps it is fitting that this final chapter will demonstrate the growth of the American republic as a global power. In the last hundred years America has been a great force for freedom around the globe, but this has not been without its burdens. Today most Americans feel fatigued and wonder why America has to be the "policemen of the world." This chapter will help explain how we arrived at this position.

TOOLS IN FOREIGN POLICY

Another way to define foreign policy is that it is how one country tries to influence the behavior of other countries. As every parent or spouse knows, it is very difficult to influence the behavior of even one individual let alone a nation of millions. So, how can America expect to influence other countries? Traditionally, there have been several foreign policy tools that have been practiced ever since nations first started trying to interact with each other. Obviously, these tools are more effective when a country is large and powerful, rather than small and weak. A large country like Russia will have more influence on global affairs than a tiny country such as Belize or Senegal. But all countries, large and small, engage in some degree of foreign policy.

Diplomacy

when countries use diplomats or other public officials to negotiate with the leaders of other countries to try to influence them

Diplomacy: First, a nation may try to influence another nation by talking to its leaders. *When countries use diplomats or other public officials to negotiate with the leaders of other countries to try to influence them it is called* **diplomacy**. The US Department of State, headed by the Secretary of State, conducts diplomatic missions for the United States. It currently employs 15,000 Foreign Service professionals that work in nearly 300 US embassies and consulates around the world. Sometimes diplomacy is conducted by lower level state department officials, and other times the leaders of countries talk directly with each other. During the Cold War, American presidents would meet and talk with the leaders of the Soviet Union in what the press called "summits." These meetings reduced tensions and misunderstandings between the two superpowers and may have helped divert World War III.

World Organizations and Alliances: A nation will often have more success at influencing another country if it is part of a group or coalition of countries working together or if it is operating within an international organization. For example, America is a member of the North Atlantic Treaty Organization (NATO). Formed in 1949, this organization consists of dozens of nations from Western Europe, Canada, and America that formed a military alliance in order to deter a military invasion of Europe by the Soviet Union. Even though the Soviet Union no longer exists, NATO continues because these countries still believe it is beneficial for them to keep this arrangement of mutual defense.

America is also a member of the **United Nations (UN)**: *co-founded by the United States in 1945, the UN is an intergovernmental organization consisting of 193 member nations whose objective is to foster international peace*. The UN has two primary bodies. The *General Assembly* is composed of all member states and decides most issues by majority vote. And the *Security Council*, which consists of five permanent members (the US, Russia, China, Britain, and France) and has veto power over General Assembly resolutions. The UN is led by the Security General, currently Ban Ki-moon of South Korea, who is recommended by the Security Council and elected by the General Assembly. The UN provides a useful forum by which the nations of the world can communicate with each other.

Economic Sanctions: If diplomacy doesn't work, a nation may try to influence another nation by imposing *economic sanctions*: not buying products from that country or cutting off all economic activity, including banking and investments. Before the Revolution, America used a boycott to influence Britain's tax policy. Boycotts work better if several countries join. In the 1980s, the boycott movement in the United States and Europe is credited with precipitating the fall of apartheid, the system of racial segregation enforced by the government of South Africa. Before President Obama lifted them, America led a coalition of countries to impose an economic boycott against Iran in an attempt to halt its effort to build nuclear weapons.

United Nations (UN)

co-founded by the United States in 1945, the UN is an intergovernmental organization consisting of 193 member nations whose objective is to foster international peace

The United Nations creates a forum for 193 nations to communicate with each other, hopefully to reduce the likelihood of war.
©Drop of Light/Shutterstock.com

Covert Operations: Nations have always used spies and other secret means to influence other countries. The CIA was created after World War II in order to spy on the Soviet Union, to assist in the containment policy (see below), to prevent countries from spying on us, and to protect the nation. Today, the Director of National Intelligence serves as the head of the US intelligence community, which now includes nineteen separate agencies. Besides the CIA, some of these other agencies include the FBI, Homeland Security Investigations (HIS), the National Geospatial Intelligence Agency (NGA), US Cyber Command (CYBERCOM), and the National Security Agency (NSA). According to the 2012 federal budget, the US intelligence budget was $54 billion.

In recent years, the NSA has been the focus of controversy. The NSA uses a sophisticated network of supercomputers to read global communications for foreign intelligence purposes. It is also charged with protecting US government communication and information systems. The computers red-flag certain words or phone numbers associated with terrorists or other threats. Before a NSA agent is allowed to investigate further, they must get approval from a judge from the FISC (Federal Intelligence Surveillance Court). But recently the NSA has been accused of eavesdropping on American civilians and friendly foreign leaders.

Limited War: If diplomacy fails, countries will use their military to try to influence other countries. But this does not always mean that countries will launch a full-scale war. Often countries engage in *limited war*, a war with limited military objectives that uses less than the nation's total military recourses. America has conducted many limited wars, sometimes referred to as quasi wars or undeclared wars. From 1798 to 1800, America fought a quasi war against France in order to protect American merchant vessels sailing to Europe. Actually, all US wars conducted since World War II has been limited wars because America chose not to use its full military capacity, including its nuclear arsenal.

War: If everything else fails, including diplomacy, economic sanctions, covert actions, and limited war, a country will use war to influence another country. And just as with diplomacy or economic sanctions, war can be more effective if a coalition of armies fights against another country. In 1990, a coalition of thirty-four nations, led by the United States, attacked Iraq after it invaded and annexed Kuwait. In World War I, over two dozen countries attacked Germany after it invaded France. World War I is an example of **total war**: *a war that uses all of a nation's recourses to target any of another nation's recourses, including military installations, crops, factories, and civilian population centers.*

In America, the defense department runs the military. The Secretary of Defense, whose office is in the Pentagon, which happens to be the largest

Total War

a war that uses all of a nation's recourses to target any of another nation's recourses, including military installations, crops, factories, and civilian population centers

World War I is a devastating example of total war, when military and civilian centers are targeted.
©Everett Historical/Shutterstock.com

office building in the world, is the chief executive officer of the Department of Defense. The United States Armed Forces consists of five branches: the Army, Navy, Marines, Air Force, and Coast Guard. The defense department consists of about 720,000 civilians, 1.5 million active duty, and 1 million reserves. In 2010, its annual budget was $553 billion, which represents 24 percent of the federal budget. As a percentage of America's GNP this is 4.35 percent, which ranks the US ninth in the world, but in total dollars is ranked number one. America maintains between 700 and 800 military bases in sixty-three countries.

Just and Unjust Wars: In the 1970s, it was common to see the bumper sticker "War is Always Wrong." Is this true, are *all* wars by definition wrong? Certainly war is tragic. It is always awful when innocent people die and suffer as they do in all wars. But this does not mean that no good comes from war. America won its independence as a result of the Revolutionary War. Four million slaves were freed as a result of the Civil War. Dozens of countries were liberated from Nazi and Imperial Japanese occupation as a result of World War II.

In the thirteenth century, Thomas Aquinas, the great Catholic philosopher and theologian, defined a *just war* as having three components: First, a just war must be conducted by a legitimate state authority. Two, it must be carried

The philosopher Thomas Aquinas said some wars are just if the ultimate goal is peace.
©CkyBe/Shutterstock.com

out for a good purpose (defending oneself or helping an ally) and not for an evil end (gaining territory or power). And third, peace must be the ultimate goal of the temporary violence.

THE CONSTITUTION AND FOREIGN POLICY

The core principle of the US Constitution is separation of powers; and the Framers faced an especially difficult task in balancing responsibilities of the executive and legislative branches in foreign affairs and war. They knew in the past that kings sometimes started wars for petty reasons, and so they wanted to check this power. In a 1798 letter to Jefferson, Madison said that "the Constitution supposes, what the History of all Governments demonstrates, that the Executive is the branch of power most interested in war, & most prone to it. It has accordingly with studied care, vested the question of war with the Legislature." Thus, the Constitution lays out a mixed system that provides significant power to <u>Congress</u> in the matters of war and international relations.

On the other hand, the Founders wanted to create an energetic presidency. In *Federalist #70*, Alexander Hamilton said, "energy in the executive is a leading character in the definition of good government." The Federalist Papers reveal that the Founders wished to create an executive with "decision, activity, secrecy and dispatch." The creation of a strong president, independent from Congress, was vital for national security.

In framing the Constitution, the Founders had the exceedingly difficult task of giving the president enough power and flexibility to defend the country and carry out the complexities of foreign affairs, while granting Congress enough power to prevent the president from making any decisions that might be contrary to the interest of the majority of the citizens—for there are always small groups that want war. So, the Framers made war a two-branch enterprise. As James Wilson said at the Pennsylvania Ratification Convention, it will not be "in the power of a single man" to "hurry us into war."

Congressional Foreign Affairs and War Powers: If one were to read the Constitution for the first time, it would appear that the legislative branch was given a near monopoly in war powers. Article I, Section 8 states that only Congress can "declare war," raise and support the army and navy, approve the military budget every two years, organize the militia, and punish piracy. Congress is not only given the power to declare full-scale war, but to also engage in limited warfare. The Constitution says that Congress can "make the rules concerning captures on land and sea" as well to "grants letters of marque and reprisal," which is when the government authorizes the owner of a private ship to attack and capture an enemy vessel.

**The Constitution says only Congress can declare war,
but Congress has not officially declared war since World War II.**
©Drop of Light/Shutterstock.com

Presidential Foreign Affairs and War Powers: Yet, the Constitution clearly gives the president primary power in foreign affairs. Article II states that the executive shall "receive ambassadors and other public ministers," make treaties (provided two-thirds of the Senate approves), and appoint ambassadors and executive branch ministers in charge of foreign policy (provided a majority of the Senate approves). The Framers understood that the president would take the lead in foreign affairs, but that his policies and appointments would be checked by the Senate.

Most importantly, the Constitution says the president "shall be commander in chief." The president's role as commander in chief was elucidated at the Constitutional Convention when delegates debated the language of Congress's war powers. On August 17, James Madison and Eldridge Gerry made a motion to change the language of an early draft of the Constitution by inserting "declare" and striking out "make" war; "leaving the Executive the power to repel sudden attack." And earlier at the Convention, Hamilton proposed that the Senate have the "sole power of declaring war" and the president have power of "directing the war once authorized or begun."

So, it seems clear that Framers intended to vest the president with the power to defend the country from surprise attack and order military operations to protect Americans, but that before the country goes into a major war, Congress must debate and approve it. And once the war has begun, the president will lead it.

The Imperial Presidency: Seeing that America was quickly becoming a vast and wealthy country, in 1832 Alexis de Tocqueville predicted that in the future the American presidency may become more powerful than the Framers intended. In *Democracy in America*, Tocqueville said, "it is chiefly in its foreign relations, that the executive power of the nation finds occasion to exert its skill and strength. If the existence of the American union will perpetually be threatened, if his chief interests were daily connected with those of powerful nations, the executive would assume increased importance."

In many ways, this is what has happened. Since World War I, the president's powers in foreign affairs and war had grown beyond the Framer's carefully balanced system of shared powers. This was due in large part because America, as a global super power, has constantly been involved in dangerous conflicts that require secrecy and dispatch. During prolonged conflicts, such as World War II, the Cold War, or the War on Terror, the president often finds it advantageous to operate outside of congressional oversight. In these operations, it is up to the president and his advisors to act prudently, but there is a danger of the presidential miscalculation.

TWO FOREIGN POLICY APPROACHES

Compared to other nations, the history of American foreign and defense policy is quite unique. Think about some of the great nations in world history, such as Rome, Spain, France, Great Britain, Russia, Japan, and Germany. When they were at the height of their military power, they amassed empires by conquering other nations and taking their land. The term **empire** *refers to when one nation takes over other nations and maintains military and political control over the conquered nation for economic and geo-political advantage.* For example, the French Colonial Empire established colonies in Africa, North America, the Middle East, India, and Asia covering an estimated 4.8 million square miles. The Empire of Japan covered about 7.4 million square miles.

America, on the other hand, never established an empire. When America rose to superpower status in the twentieth century, America went to war to liberate dozens of countries not subjugate them. At the beginning of the Iraq War in 2003, Secretary of State Colin Powell attended a conference in England. He was asked by the Archbishop of Canterbury if America's objective in Iraq was to build an empire. Powell responded by saying that "Over the years, the United States has sent many of its fine young men and women into great peril to fight for freedom beyond our borders. The only amount of land we have ever asked for in return is enough to bury those that did not return."

Two Approaches to Foreign Policy: Broadly speaking, nations adopt two types of foreign policy approaches, realistic and idealistic. **Realpolitik** *is a diplomatic approach based on the practical calculations of power, material gain, and other realistic factors of international relationships.* This is in contrast to countries that adopt an idealistic, religious, or moral approach to foreign policy. Although America takes into consideration *realpolitiks*, it is primarily motivated by ideology and morality. America was founded on the ideals of liberty and freedom, and thus the American people will often support **wars for liberation**: *wars primarily intended to bring freedom or liberation to a people subjugated by a colonial power or a dictator.* Although wars for liberation are animated by good intentions, they are not without burdens, including the loss of American lives and treasure.

EARLY AMERICAN FOREIGN POLICY

In the early years of the Republic, American foreign policy was dominated by two concerns: Great Britain and westward expansion. America fought the Revolution to win its independence from the British. The leader of the victorious American army, George Washington, became the first president of the United States. Difficulties with the mother country, however, did not end with the Revolution. When Great Britain and France, instigated by Napoleon,

Empire

refers to when one nation takes over other nations and maintains military and political control over the conquered nations for economic and geo-political advantage

Realpolitik

is a diplomatic approach based on the practical calculations of power, material gain, and other realistic factors of international relationships

Wars for Liberation

wars primarily intended to bring freedom or liberation to a people subjugated by a colonial power or a dictator

The Spanish America War was the US's first war for liberation, freeing the Cuban people from 400 years of Spanish rule.
©Everett Historical/Shutterstock.com

fought a multi-decade war, America declared neutrality and asserted its right to trade non-military goods to both sides. But eventually America was drawn into the war, first with France in the so called "Quasi War," and then in a full-scale war with Britain, called the War of 1812. This war produced another hero who would become president, Andrew Jackson, and it also marked the last war between Britain and America.

The other major concern of America during these early years was westward expansion. Since colonial times, Americans have always believed they were destined to occupy the whole North American continent. This relentless push to the Pacific Ocean is called *Manifest Destiny*: the widespread belief that America, due to its special virtues and democratic institutions, had an almost divine mission to expand westward and settle the whole continent. This enterprise resulted in thousands of conflicts between the American settlers and Native Indians.

Three major foreign policy events secured the land that accomplished the goals of Manifest Destiny, one orchestrated by President Thomas Jefferson and two by President James K. Polk. Jefferson purchased the Louisiana Territory from France in 1808, thus doubling the size of the United States. Polk negotiated the possession of the Oregon Territory from Britain in 1846. And by winning the Mexican-American War, Polk secured the Southwest Territory, what eventually became Texas, New Mexico, Arizona, Nevada, and California. With these actions, Polk again doubled the size of the United States and expanded America from the Atlantic to the Pacific Ocean.

The Monroe Doctrine: Not long after the conflict between France and Britain ended, the European powers began colonizing the rest of the world. But in the 1810s and 1820s, several Latin American countries won their independence from Spain. This is when America announced that it would protect Latin America from European encroachment. In his state of the union address in 1823, James Monroe proclaimed that "the American continents, by the free and independent condition which they have assumed and maintain, are henceforth not to be considered as subjects for future colonization by any European powers." The policy to protect the newly won freedom of the Latin American countries became known as the "Monroe Doctrine."

This marks the first time America would commit itself to protecting the liberty of other nations. What we might call the "liberty agenda" would become the hallmark of American foreign policy. As Washington said in his Farewell Address, "The sacred fire of liberty and the destiny of the republican model of government are . . . entrusted in the American people." True enough, as with the Monroe Doctrine, the America people have always felt a duty to protect other democratic governments around the world.

Spanish-American War: America's first war for liberation was the Spanish-American War. In 1895 the Cuban people revolted against Spanish rule. The New York newspapers led the "Cuba Libre" movement as they published sensationalized stories of Spanish brutality. President William McKinley was reluctant to go to war and tried to negotiate with Spain, but when the *USS Maine* blew up in the Havana Harbor (probably from a boiler room accident) he finally urged Congress to declare war. To make it abundantly clear that this was a war for liberation and not a territorial grab, Congress attached to the war declaration the Teller Amendment, which said "the people of the island of Cuba are of right to be free and independent" and when the war is over America will "leave the government and control of the Island to the [Cuban] people."

Another domestic faction, however, wanted to use the war with Spain to enter the colonization race with Europe. This faction was led by Theodore Roosevelt, who romanticized war. By 1898, when the war with Spain started, the European powers had divided up the whole continent of Africa and had a growing presence in Asia and the Middle East. Roosevelt felt that America had to join the race before it was too late. The *realpolitik* faction especially had an eye on the Philippines, a Spanish possession strategically located not far from China and Japan. When the war ended, there was a big debate in America about

In the Monroe Doctrine, America promised to protect Latin America from European colonization.
©Olga Popova/Shutterstock.com

whether America should claim the Philippines. The industrialist Andrew Carnegie vociferously opposed it, but in the end McKinley decided America should temporarily annex the Philippines. America occupied the Philippines for forty-six years, until the end of World War II.

MODERN US FOREIGN POLICY

At the beginning of the twentieth century, America was an economic powerhouse. Led by such names as Edison, Carnegie, Rockefeller, Morgan, and Ford, America was the manufacturing, commercial, and transportation leader of the world; and so when World War I started, the US was capable of building a massive army in a couple of years and win the conflict. For the rest of the century, America ascended to superpower status. But it should always be remembered, America's military power, and thus diplomatic and geopolitical power, was built on the foundation of a strong economy, especially a powerful manufacturing base.

World War I: World War I, at the time called the Great War, started in 1914 when Germany attacked France through Belgium. After the unification of Germany by Bismarck in the second half of the nineteenth century, Germany felt emboldened as it found itself the most powerful country in continental Europe. The war was really the culmination of decades of growing nationalism and empire building by the European powers. When the Great War first started, America declared neutrality and tried to ship goods to both sides. But after German submarines sank US merchant ships and several passenger liners, most notably the Lusitania, America entered the war in 1917 on the side of the Allies (Britain, France, Italy, and Russia). When the war ended in 1919, America emerged victorious with its economy intact and recognized as the new leader of the world.

After the war, President Woodrow Wilson proposed a lasting peace based on his Fourteen Points Plan, but the allied powers largely ignored him and the *Treaty of Versailles* was highly flawed. At Versailles, the Allies punished Germany for starting the war by taking away some of its land and making it pay $32 billion in reparations (this would be over $442 billion in 2015 dollars). This only caused the German economy to collapse, eventually helping to trigger the Great Depression. It also created a generation of German resentment, which led to the rise of Adolph Hitler.

World War II: World War II started on September 1, 1939, when the Germans invaded Poland. A year earlier, the Allies, led by British Prime Minister Neville Chamberlain, tried to appease Hitler at the *Munich Conference*. Hitler signed a paper promising that if the allies allowed him to take a portion of Czechoslovakia, he would renounce all further territorial ambitions. Met with a roaring crowd at the airport, Chamberlain breathlessly waved the agreement in the air, announcing that he had achieved "peace in our time." Six months later Hitler's armies took over the rest of Czechoslovakia, a peaceful democracy. Soon Europe would suffer more Nazi barbarity. During World War II, the Nazis constructed a series of concentration camps, the most famous of which is Dachau, in order to get rid of the "undesirable" elements in the population, including Jews, gypsies, slaves, homosexuals, and the physically and mentally handicapped. Nearly six million Jews were exterminated.

Before World War II, about 80 percent of Americans believed in **isolationism**: *The belief that America should not be involved with other countries and should not go to war unless attacked.* The American people saw Hitler taking over Europe in the West and Imperial Japan attacking China and Southeast Asia in

Isolationism

the belief that America should not be involved with other countries and should not go to war unless attacked

**In World War II, America liberated dozens of countries
from Nazi and Imperial Japanese occupation.**
©multitel/Shutterstock.com

the East, and they wanted no part of it. All this changed on December 7, 1941, when the Japanese attacked Pearl Harbor, America's naval base in Hawaii. Calling it a "day that will live in infamy," FDR urged Congress to declare war on Japan. Shortly after, Hitler declared war on America because Germany had an alliance with Japan. In one of the greatest accomplishments in world history, due to the tremendous industrial and technological base of the American economy, in four short years the United States built an army with more armaments than Japan and Germany combined and won World War II.

Miraculously, America ended the war early by developing a new weapon, the atom bomb. When World War II was over, with the strongest economy, largest military, and in possession of nuclear technology, America secured its position as the world's supreme power. And by liberating dozens of countries from Nazi and Japanese occupation, the US stood as the symbol of freedom and a force for good around the world. World War II, however, wasn't followed by a period of world peace. A new conflict developed, this time between America and Russia, which became known as the Cold War.

Cold War: After World War I, the Russian czar and his family were murdered and the communists took over the government, renaming it the Soviet Union. In 1939, Hitler made a pact with Joseph Stalin, the leader of the Soviet Union. The treaty stipulated that neither party would go to war with each other or aid the enemy of the other party. There was also a secret part of the treaty which divided up Eastern Europe between Germany and the Soviets. But in 1941, Hitler broke the treaty and attacked Russia, and thus the Soviets joined the Allies. Although the Allies welcomed the Soviet's help in defeating the Nazis, they were uneasy about working with the ruthless Joseph Stalin. Historians estimate that before World War II, Stalin was responsible for killing between 20 and 30 million Russian people.

At the heart of the Cold War was a conflict between two countries with diametrically opposite belief systems. America is based on the ideas of individual freedom, equality under the law, economic liberty, religious freedom, and the idea that there are certain God-given rights that governments cannot violate. The Soviet Union, however, was based on communism or *Marxism*, which believes in the abolition of private property in order to achieve equality. Marxists assert that the communist government must be granted total power to eradicate capitalistic impulses and enforce material equality. To this end, they centrally manage the economy and take away freedom of speech, freedom of religion, and freedom to travel.

In the twentieth century, horrendous mass murder was committed in the name of communism. As mentioned above, communist Russia (the Soviet Union) killed up to 30 million people. In China, under Mao Zedong, 65 million people were killed. And in Cambodia, under the communist Khmer Rouge, 2 million people were killed—nearly a quarter of the country's population.

Containment Policy: When World War II ended, the Soviet Red Army occupied parts of Germany and several countries in Eastern Europe, including Poland, Czechoslovakia, Hungary, Romania, and Bulgaria. At the Yalta Conference in 1945, Stalin promised Roosevelt and Winston Churchill that he would allow free elections in areas the Red Army occupied after the war. But Stalin failed to honor his promise. A year later in a speech at Westminster College in Missouri, Churchill said that all these countries under the domination of the Soviet Union lay behind an "Iron Curtain."

Then in 1947, communist forces tried to take over the governments of Greece and Turkey. In response, President Harry Truman addressed Congress, saying that "I believe that it must be the policy of the United States to support free people who are resisting attempted subjugation by armed minorities or by outside pressure." This became known as the "Truman Doctrine" or the **Containment Policy**: *America was committed to stopping the spread of communism around the globe.*

The containment policy was a major shift in US foreign policy. Before World War II, Americans were isolationists, a tradition going back to Washington's Farewell Address, in which he warned Americans about entangling alliances and being drawn into foreign conflicts. But now in 1947, the President of the United States announced that he is committed to protecting free countries around the globe.

This shift in policy reflects a new understanding of America's position in the world. Before World War II, America shrank back and disengaged from the world, allowing the bad guys to take over. After World War II, Americans realized that they must remain engaged in global affairs and try to be a force for good. To this end, the Truman administration proposed the "*Marshall Plan*," named after Secretary of State George Marshall. It distributed $15 billion in loans and grants to sixteen European nations liberated by America in order to help rebuild their economies and protect their independence.

Korean War: With Soviet backing, in 1949 Mao Zedong and the communists won the Chinese Civil War and took over China. America had backed Chiange Kai-shek, the president of the Republic of China, who was defeated and fled to Taiwan. At home, Republicans were highly critical of President Truman for "losing China."

Then in June of 1950, the communist leader of North Korea, Kim Il-sung, invaded South Korea, which had been supported by the US. Before the invasion, Kim had a secret meeting with Stalin and Mao, and Stalin backed the

Containment Policy

America was committed to stopping the spread of communism around the globe plan. By this time, the Soviets had detonated their first atom bomb (after stealing American secrets) and US troops had fully withdrawn from Korea, so Stalin did not think the US would fight for South Korea, especially after the US did not do much to fight Mao in China. But Stalin was wrong. Truman was furious and with UN backing he sent the US military to defend South Korea against the communist invasion.

American troops, lead by Douglas MacArthur, fought the communist North Korean army all the way to the Chinese border, which sparked a massive Chinese invasion. Not believing in limited warfare, MacArthur wanted to take the fight to the Chinese and even publically suggested that the US use tactical nuclear weapons. Preserving the principle that only the president, as commander in chief, has the authority to make military policy, Truman called MacArthur home. Truman did not want to risk sparking World War III.

Subsequently, US troops were pushed back to the 38th parallel, the line that divided North and South Korea. The result of the war was that America was successful at protecting South Korea, which today is one of the most prosperous democracies in the world. In stark contrast, North Korea remains a communist country and under the totalitarian control of the Kim family. North Korea is so poor that they cannot even feed their people without food donations from other countries.

During the Korean War America protected South Korea from an invasion by communist North Korea. As a result, today South Korea is one of the most prosperous countries in the world, while North Korea remains one of the poorest.
©Sean Pavone/Shutterstock.com

Vietnam: The Korean War haunted the thinking of US military and political leaders during the Vietnam War. Like Korea, communist North Vietnam, led by Ho Chi Minh, invaded democratic South Vietnam with the military backing of the Soviet Union and China. And like the Korean War, the president was afraid of sparking World War III and fought a limited war. President Lyndon Johnson sent over 500,000 troops to South Vietnam, but they were never permitted to launch a ground offensive in North Vietnam.

Instead, US troops had to fight an extremely difficult and confusing defensive war against Vietcong guerrillas and the North Vietnam army in the dense jungles of Southeast Asia. Johnson heavily bombed North Vietnam, but because they got their weapons from Russia and China, there were few industrial targets to bomb. It is a military axiom that bombing alone does not win wars; it must be followed up by boots on the ground. In Vietnam, America violated this axiom.

Certainly Johnson faced more difficulties than Truman did during the Korean War. Many of the Vietnamese people did not trust the motives of the US, thinking that America intended to colonize Vietnam as the French had done. And the South Vietnamese government was incompetent and unstable.

Johnson failed to win the Vietnam War for two reasons: (1) He failed to adjust his tactics and find a winning military strategy; and (2) Johnson withered under the growing anti-war sentiment at home, led by radical college students, Leftists, the press, and members of the Democratic Party. Johnson refused to run for reelection in 1968 and Richard Nixon, a Republican, was elected president. After Nixon ordered intense bombings of Hanoi, North Vietnam's capital, and Haiphong, its port city, the North Vietnamese signed the Paris Peace Accords in January of 1973. But the Democratically controlled Congress later refused to aid the South Vietnamese government as stipulated in the treaty, and as a result South Vietnam was eventually taken over by the communists.

Détente: During the Vietnam War, Nixon, assisted by his National Security Advisor, Henry Kissinger, implemented *a foreign policy initiative to improve relations with the Soviet Union, called* **détente**, which means relaxing of tensions in French. Nixon knew that a rift had developed between Mao and the Soviet leaders, and he exploited this to his advantage. In 1972 Nixon travelled to China and renewed diplomatic relations. Then Nixon negotiated a series of nuclear arms control negotiations with Russia, called the Strategic Arms Limitations Treaties (SALT). The two superpowers agreed to freeze the production of intercontinental ballistic missiles, which both sides had enough of to blow up the world several times over. Nixon's successors, presidents Gerald Ford and Jimmy Carter, continued the policy of détente. Carter signed

Détente

a foreign policy initiative to improve relations with the Soviet Union

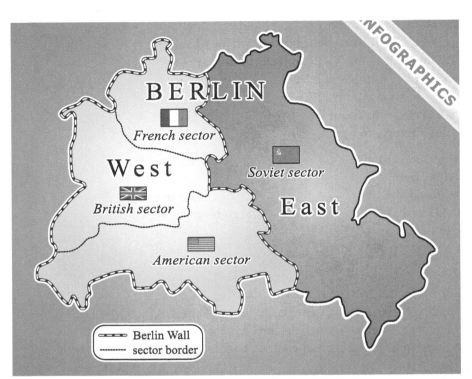

During the Cold War, the Soviets built the Berlin Wall, which was torn down in 1989.
©Peteri/Shutterstock.com

SALT II, designed to further reduce the production of nuclear missiles, but Carter broke off relations with the Soviets after they invaded Afghanistan in December of 1979.

End of the Cold War: While visiting Moscow, Ronald Reagan was asked what his Cold War strategy was, and he said: "We win, they lose." Becoming president in 1981, Reagan reversed détente: instead of easing tension with Russia, he purposefully increased tensions. He knew that the Soviet Union was a paper tiger that on the surface looked like a strong military power, but on the inside its communist economy was hollow. Every day millions of Russians waited in long lines to buy basic foodstuffs such as bread and cheese. Reagan was a conservative who ideologically opposed communism. So, in order to force a collapse, Reagan aggressively challenged the Soviet Union around the world by ridiculing Marxist doctrines, supporting freedom fighters around the world, and building up US military might.

Reagan rebuilt the US military, which had decayed during the 1970s, and constructed more modern nuclear weapons. He sent arms to Afghanistan to support the Mujahedeen against the Soviets. The stinger missile was especially effective and the Soviets withdrew in 1989. Reagan also deployed intermediate missiles in Europe in 1984. And he exposed Russia's human rights violations, calling the Soviet Union the "Evil Empire."

Faced with trying to keep up with an arms race with America, the new Soviet Leader, Mikhail Gorbachev, initiated reforms known as glasnost (openness) and perestroika (economic restructuring). Reagan challenged Gorbachev to keep going. He made a speech at the Berlin Wall and said, "Mr. Gorbachev, tear down this wall." As the long oppressed people were given a little freedom, they wanted more. By 1991 the Soviet Union collapsed, the Berlin wall was torn down, and Eastern Europe was liberated. America won the Cold War.

War on Terror: When the Soviet Union collapsed and the Cold War ended, there was great sense of relief in America. Many hoped that America could turn from world affairs and spend more energy and money solving domestic issues. Indeed the 1990s was a period of political reform and prosperity: the welfare system was improved, the budget was balanced, and the economy prospered as America enjoyed the "peace dividend."

The terrorist attacks on 9/11 was the deadliest attack since Pearl Harbor.
©Ken Tannenbaum/Shutterstock.com

Then everything changed on 9/11/2001. On this date, nineteen hijackers took over four commercial airlines and crashed them into the World Trade Center, the Pentagon, and the fourth plane, probably headed to the Capitol building or the White House, crashed into an open field in Pennsylvania because the passengers rushed the cockpit. Over 3,000 Americans died that day. This was the worst attack on America since Pearl Harbor. The hijackers were members of the Islamist terrorist organization called al Qaeda, headed by Osama bin Laden.

Who Are the Terrorists? So, what is this "war on terror" and how do we fight it? Actually, "war on terror" is a poor label. Terror is a tactic, not an enemy. **Terrorism** *is premeditated, politically motivated violence perpetrated against civilian targets by people who want to bring about political or social change.* America is actually fighting radical <u>Islamist</u> (not Islamic) groups that use terror tactics. Extreme or **radical Islamists** *believe that all of mankind should be converted to Islam, by violent means if necessary, and that all Muslims should be governed by Sharia, a law code derived from the Koran which is administered by Islamic leaders (a caliphate).*

Terrorism

is premeditated, politically motivated violence perpetrated against civilian targets by people who want to bring about political or social change

Radical Islamists

believe that all of mankind should be converted to Islam, by violent means if necessary, and that all Muslims should be governed by Sharia, a law code derived from the Koran which is administered by Islamic leaders (a caliphate)

This has been the goal of such groups as al Qaeda, the Taliban, the Islamic State in Syria (ISIS), and Boko Haram. In Nigeria, Boko Haram has slaughtered the residents of whole towns and committed mass rape on girls as young as ten years old. In Syria and Iraq, ISIS has taken over vast regions of land and has shocked the world by producing videos of beheadings and burning alive people they have captured. Isis is also killing the remaining Christians that live in the region and calling for the destruction of the state of Israel.

Bush and Obama Foreign Policy: After 9/11, President George W. Bush invaded Afghanistan, the country controlled by the Taliban that harbored Osama bin Laden and al Qaeda. Bush then developed the *Bush Doctrine*: make no distinction between terrorist and the nations that harbor them, take the fight to the terrorist overseas before they can attack us at home, confront threats preemptively before they fully materialize, and promote liberty and democracy abroad (the liberty agenda). As part of the Bush Doctrine, he ordered the invasion of Iraq, which was ruled by the dictator Saddam Hussein.

As a coalition of dozens of countries, Bush launched the war on Iraq because Hussein was supporting terrorism and violating United Nations sanctions imposed on him after he invaded Kuwait. Also, the international intelligence community advised Bush and the leaders of other countries that Hussein had weapons of mass destruction (WMDs), such as poison gas, which he had used before on civilians. It was feared that Hussein would give WMDs to terrorists, who might use them on Americans. In October of 2002, the US Senate authorized the war, and many Democratic senators such as Hillary Clinton and John Kerry voted to invade Iraq. Bush eventually won the war and achieved his objectives: Hussein was deposed and the Iraqi people implemented self government. But the war was much more difficult than military experts predicted and only a small amount of WMDs were found, which led to Bush becoming very unpopular.

President Barack H. Obama continued the war in Afghanistan, as well as Bush's drone attacks on terrorists, but he withdrew all the US troops stationed in Iraq. Just as US troops continue to be stationed in South Korea, Japan, and Germany, these troops were meant to keep the peace by protecting Iraq's fragile democracy. Shortly after American troops left Iraq, ISIS conquered many of the Iraqi cities that US troops fought so hard to liberate during the war.

Obama changed other aspects of Bush's War on Terror as well. Sensitive to the fact that Muslims may experience bigotry and hate crimes, the Obama administration refused to use the words "radical Islamic terrorism." Obama did slowly allow some troops back into Iraq, mostly to train Iraqi soldiers, but he fought ISIS very carefully. Obama, for example, refused to permit the US Air Force to bomb ISIS oil trucks for fear that civilians may die. In the tradition of America's liberty agenda, Obama joined a coalition of European forces that deposited the long-time dictator of Libya, Omar Khadafy. But the coalition failed to erect and support a new government and now ISIS is taking over large segments of Libya. As the War on Terror stands today, ISIS seems to be taking over more territory in Iraq, war-torn Syria, and Libya, but Obama has been successful at preventing another major terrorist attack on American territory.

Trump Foreign Policy: In many ways, Trump's foreign policy has been a reversal of Obama's. Trump, never one to use politically correct speech, uses the term "radical Islamist terrorism." In Trump's first year in office, he has given wide latitude to his generals to fight ISIS more aggressively. And they have had success at pushing ISIS out of Iraq. Going on its sixteenth year (the longest war in American history), the war in Afghanistan continues. Trump has reestablished warm ties to Israel, which had cooled during the Obama years. Also, after Obama had been drawing down military spending, Trump is building it

American soldiers fought to free other countries, not conquer other countries.
©Stuart Monk/Shutterstock.com

up again, including modernizing the US nuclear arsenal. Currently, the biggest challenge to the Trump administration is North Korea's aggressive missile testing. Trump has said that North Korea needs to be dealt with, but no good solution seems available.

One last interesting thing must be said about the Trump administration. Although Trump has had a business background, he seems to feel very comfortable with military leaders. No other administration in history had had so many generals in executive department positions, including General James Mattis as secretary of defense, Lieutenant General H R McMaster as national security advisor, and General John Kelly as the White House chief of staff.

FINAL THOUGHTS

In his inaugural address, John F. Kennedy said, America will "pay any price, bear any burden, meet any hardship, support any friend, oppose any foe, in order to assure the survival and success of liberty." Critics of America's foreign policy, at home and abroad, often accuse the United States of using its military for economic gain or for empire building. America fought World

War I and World War II, freeing dozens of countries from occupation, without acquiring any land. America fought the Cold War, stopping the spread of communism, without acquiring any land. And Americans fought in Iraq and Afghanistan to liberate its people, without acquiring any land. Today, America is fighting Islamist terrorists—who kill, torture, and frighten people in an attempt to take away their freedom—all around the world.

Americans should be exceedingly proud of its legacy. What act is nobler than risking one's life or dying in order to give another person his or her freedom? This is what the US military does every day.

NOTES

For the size of the state department go to state department's website: www.state.gov.

For size of defense and intelligence departments go to the defense department (www.defense.gov), the US intelligence community (www.intelligence.gov), the CIA's World Factbook (www.cia.gov), the Department of Defense Base Structure Report (search "Base Structure Report" at www.defense.gov/News/Publicans), and read "The World's Biggest Military Bases" at armytechnology.com, 4 Sept 2013.

Thomas Aquinas, *The Summa Theologica*, Part II, Question 40 (dhspriory.org/Thomas/summa/)

Stephane Courtois et al. *The Black Book of Communism*. Cambridge, MA: Harvard University Press, 1999.

Alexander Hamilton, John Jay, and James Madison. *The Federalists*. Indianapolis: Liberty Fund, 2001.

James Madison. *Notes of Debates in the Federal Convention of 1787*. New York: Norton & Company, 1966.

Arthur Schlesinger Jr. *The Imperial Presidency*. New York: Mariner Books, Reprint Edition, 2004. Introduction.

Alexis de Tocqueville, *Democracy in America*. Translated by George Lawrence. New York: Harper Collins, 1969.

ESSAY QUESTIONS

1. Describe the foreign policy tools a country will try before declaring war.
2. Describe the powers the Constitution gives Congress in foreign policy and war.
3. Why does America fight wars for liberation? List at least three examples.
4. Compare America's foreign policy before World War II (isolationism) to our foreign policy during the Cold War (containment). Why did America change its policy?
5. What are the objectives and tactics of violent, radical Islamists?

TERMS

Containment Policy: _____

Détente: _____

Diplomacy: _____

Empire: _____

Foreign Policy: _____

Isolationism: _____

Realpolitik: _____

Terrorism: _____

Total War: _____

Radical Islamists: _____

United Nations: _____

Wars for Liberation: _____

APPENDIX A

Controversial Social and Political Issues

This chapter explores the top social and political controversies that are often the focus of debate today between liberals and conservatives. Each controversial topic is introduced by providing some basic background information and then listing the most common liberal and conservative arguments "for" or "against" the issue.

This chapter may be utilized in several different ways: Students can read this chapter to gain an overview of contemporary American political and social issues. Students can read this chapter to get started on writing a paper on one of these issues. And students can read this chapter for preparation for a classroom debate. This chapter can also be used as a reference guide.

Abortion: In its landmark case, *Roe v. Wade* (1973), the Supreme Court prohibited states from banning abortions during the first two trimesters but allowed states to restrict or ban later term abortions when the fetus is viable. In accordance to *Roe* and other Court decisions, the fifty states have developed a wide range of policies. Today, eighteen states prohibit abortions after twenty weeks. Other states require that a late term abortion may be performed if a physician agrees that the mental or physical health of the woman may be harmed. It has been estimated that about 1.2 million abortions are performed a year and that since 1973 there has been over 56 million abortions performed in America. Democratic states, such as California, have the most liberal abortion laws, and Republican states have stricter abortion laws. A new Texas law requires a woman to view a sonogram of the fetus twenty-four hours before she can get an abortion.

Nobody can run for president on the Democratic ticket unless they take a pro-choice stance. Pro-choice advocates say that the decision to have an abortion must be made solely by the mother—it's her body and her choice. The government cannot force a woman to have a baby or she will seek a dangerous back-alley abortion. And pro-choice advocates say that abortions are the best tool to fight against poverty and unwanted children. On the other hand, pro-life advocates say that the pro-choice position makes no sense: if the mother wants the fetus it is called a living baby but if she does not want the fetus it is called a lump of cells. Pro-life advocates say that each God-created life is precious and must be protected. They say that abortion on demand, when a mother can get an abortion because pregnancy is merely inconvenient, is profoundly immoral. Nobody can run for president on the Republican ticket unless they take a pro-life stance.

Affirmative Action in College: "Affirmative action" originated in the US by executive actions signed by John F. Kennedy and Lyndon B. Johnson in the 1960s. Affirmative action lowers acceptance standards for minority groups and women so that they can gain access to college and thus promote equality in job opportunities. The Supreme Court, in *Grutter v. Bollinger* (2003), ruled that affirmative action policies violate the equal protection clause if they use strict quotas, but if the policies holistically evaluate each student, affirmative action policies are constitutional because they have valid objectives: to promote student diversity and to foster equality in the professions. Proponents of affirmative action assert that affirmative action is still needed to overcome white privilege and institutional racism. Without these policies, they argue, white males would still dominate the elite college campuses and maintain control of the professions of wealth, prestige, and power.

Thomas Sowell, the conservative black economist, has criticized affirmative action in his book, *Affirmative Action Around the World*, and in numerous articles. Sowell argues that affirmative action violates a fundamental constitutional principle that all citizens, regardless of race, be treated equally under the law. By giving blacks and other minority groups (except Asians) privileges, colleges only prolong racial identity and racial tension in America. Affirmative action hurts black students by undermining their achievement (people will question whether they really deserved their degree) and by placing them in a college above their academic level and setting them up for failure (a high percentage of black students who received affirmative action drop out of college). Lastly, Sowell argues that affirmative action results in a net loss for society as a whole because it mostly helps middle- and upper-class blacks, but it hurts poor blacks, poor whites, and Asians. Sowell says that if we keep standards high for everybody, blacks will rise to meet the challenge.

Get Money out of Politics: Liberals tend to favor strict campaign finance laws, and so they were especially upset at the Supreme Court's ruling in *Citizens United* (2010). In this case, the Court held that the 1st Amendment prohibits the government from restricting political expenditures by corporations, unions, and nonprofit groups. In his 2010 State of the Union Address, President Obama scolded the Supreme Court justices by saying that "The Supreme Court . . . opened the floodgates for special interests." He went on to say, "I don't think elections should be bankrolled by America's most powerful interests . . . [but] Should be decided by the American people." To get around *Citizens United*, in February 2015 congressional Democrats introduced a constitutional amendment to ban all campaign contributions except those given by individuals in races they can vote in. Every Senate Democrat voted for the amendment and every Republican voted against it, but it did not get the required two-thirds vote.

Conservatives agree with the Supreme Court that the Constitution protects campaign spending. The 1st Amendment states that "Congress shall make no law . . . abridging the freedom of speech . . . or the right of the people peaceably to assemble, and petition the government." Clearly, groups of people, in profit or nonprofit associations, have the right to participate in politics. And the only way to participate in politics today is by spending money. Conservative columnist George Will has long been a proponent of deregulation of political campaigns. Will says that relative to the size of the American economy, not much money is spent on politics. The 2012 presidential election cost the same amount that Americans spend on Easter candy—$2 billion. George Will also points out that strict campaign laws allow media corporations to endorse candidates, so why not other corporations? Lastly, Will says the main beneficiary of campaign finance laws are incumbents who always have an easier time raising money than challengers.

Death Penalty: Currently, thirty-two states have the death penalty. But since 2007, six states have abolished it. This reflects a shift in popular sentiment. According to Pew, 78 percent of Americans approved of the death penalty in 1993, but today only 55 percent do. This shift in opinion is probably a result of several high profile cases in which people convicted of crimes have been exonerated due to new DNA evidence. According to the Innocent Project, 316 people have been exonerated in the US after they were convicted of serious crimes, including eighteen on death row. Opponents of the death penalty say that it should be abolished because it is irreversible. If it is later discovered that the convict was innocent, then there is no way to exonerate him. In general, opponents of the death penalty argue that it is barbaric, that the state should not kill in the name of justice, and that life in prison is a worse punishment than death.

The debate on the death penalty goes to another core difference between liberals and conservatives. Conservatives believe there is evil in the world and evil acts must be punished. Liberals, on the other hand, feel that evil is an antiquated concept and often ridicule conservative presidents who use the term, such as when Ronald Reagan called the Soviet Union an "Evil Empire." Liberals argue that crime is a result of poverty or a bad childhood or other social and biological factors and thus should not be punished harshly. Conservatives think that evil acts deserve harsh penalties, and that the only fitting punishment for premeditated murder, the most evil act, is death. Moreover, conservatives argue that a lifetime prison sentence is not a proportional punishment because murderers could still enjoy many of the pleasures of life that their victims could no longer enjoy, such as friendship, eating delicious foods, sex, watching movies, and enjoying a sunset.

Gay Marriage: In recent years gay marriage has gained wide acceptance. According to a 2016 Pew poll, 54 percent of Americans now approve of gay marriage. A few short years ago, gay marriage wasn't legal in any state. Then by early 2015, thirty-six states allowed gay marriage: three by popular vote, eight by legislative action, and twenty-five by court order. By the end of 2015, the Supreme Court, in *Oberfell v. Hodges*, ruled that all states must grant gay marriage certificates. All this shows that gay marriage advocates have been very successful, especially in the courts. Their success has been based on appealing to American's basic tolerance of alternative lifestyles and on a few basic arguments. They argue that all Americans should have an equal right to marry whomever they wish. They argue that the only reason people oppose gay marriage is due to bigotry, just as people used to oppose marriage between blacks and whites. And they argue that people ought to marry whomever they love, which is none of the government's business.

While libertarian conservatives tend to support gay marriage, social conservatives opposed it. They argue that legal protections could be provided to gay couples through a "civil union" or "domestic partnership," which would give gay couples the right to such things as inheritance and hospital visitation. Social conservatives, however, say that the term "marriage" should be reserved for a union between one man and one woman. They argue that Western civilization has been based on the institution for over two thousand years, and it should not be overturned lightly. Married parents of the opposite sex, they maintain, is the best arrangement in which to raise children. Lastly, they argue that if you say that people should be able to marry "whomever they love," soon people will seek marriage between multiple people or pets or something else outlandish. All this undermines the traditional family, which, they argue, is the foundation of society.

Global Warming: The Obama administration has implemented an aggressive environmental policy justified, in large part, on the premise of man-made *global warming,* the theory that carbon dioxide and other gases released by carbon-based fuels are causing the planet's temperature to rise. Since becoming president, Obama has authorized billions of dollars in subsidies to green energy companies. He has also granted generous tax credits to homeowners and businesses that make energy efficient improvements. In 2015, Obama vetoed plans to build the Keystone XL pipeline that would have pumped oil from Canada to refineries in Texas. Obama has also authorized the Environmental Protection Agency (EPA) to enforce higher standards for emissions, including "greenhouse gases" which includes water vapor. "Climate change is a fact," said Obama shortly after the release of his National Climate Assessment report, "It's causing hardship now. It's affecting every sector of our economy and our society—more severe floods, more violent wildfires."

Climate change skeptics make several arguments. They say that it is ridiculous to assume that if it were not for human industrialization that the climate would remain constant. To the contrary, the climate is always changing. During the Middle Ages the earth experienced a global warming period and there was a mini ice age in the mid-1700s—both before industrialization. Further, over the last few decades all the computer models predicting global warming have failed. The assessment by the Intergovernmental Panel on Climate Change (IPCC), which advocates the global warming theory, reported that global temperatures have risen over the last one hundred years by only 0.8 degrees Celsius. Skeptics argue that it is absurd to implement policies that may not work and that would drastically slow down economic growth, including in the Third World-poverty stricken areas, because temperatures have risen less than one degree.

Equal Pay for Equal Work for Women: Liberals and feminist argue that cultural sexism and gender bias make it more difficult for women to earn as much money as men do or obtain upper-level positions. To support this contention, liberals often cite the 2012 Census Bureau Statistics that says that, on the whole, women earn 77 cents for every dollar that men earn. In President Obama's 2014 State of the Union Address, he said "You know, today, women make up about half our workforce, but they still make 77 cents for every dollar a man earns. That is wrong, and in 2014, it's an embarrassment. Women deserve equal pay for equal work." Feminist groups such as the National Organization for Women (NOW) say that the gender pay gap is due to workplace discrimination and societal stereotypes of women that guide them into lower paying careers.

Conservatives debunk the statistic of 77 cents and deny that sexism is a major force in society today. A 2009 US Department of Labor study found that after controlling for education and job differences the gender pay gap was actually 96 percent. Conservatives say that the remaining gender pay gap reflects fundamental differences in men and women and the career choices they make. Women often decide to take a leave of absence or work part-time or refuse a more demanding job in order take care of their children. This decision may result in less pay but that does not mean that it is less rewarding or less important. Also, in college women tend to pick majors in the social sciences and men pick majors in math and science, which can lead to more lucrative jobs, such as in computer science or engineering. Lastly, men more often choose dangerous occupations that pay well, such as firefighters and police.

Good and Bad Luck: You might think it strange that a subject like "luck" would be included in a list of political issues, but it goes to a core difference in the way liberals and conservatives think about the individual and her place in society. Take poverty, for example. Liberals tend to think of people in poverty as deserving of public assistance because most people are poor due to bad luck: a person may have been unlucky enough to have been born to an alcoholic single parent or born with learning disabilities or born in a crime-ridden neighborhood with horrible schools. None of this is that person's fault, and so they deserve welfare programs. Likewise, wealthy people were mostly lucky and do not deserve to keep all their money. A wealthy person was likely born in fortunate circumstances: had two involved parents, went to private schools, had relatives that lent them money to start a business. And so, since they did not deserve their wealth, they have an obligation to pay higher taxes.

At their 2012 national convention, Republicans ridiculed one of Obama's speeches in which he said: "If you have been successful, you didn't get there on your own." They scoffed at this quote because conservatives emphasize self-determination and free will. Conservatives think that in the long run, you make your own luck; that where you end up in life is a result of all the decisions you have made. If you work hard, stay out of trouble, and educate yourself, then you will do well in life. Sure, almost all people have experienced some hard times or misfortune, but these are learning experiences. Each individual must struggle to overcome obstacles in life. Thus, conservatives think fewer people are deserving of long-term welfare because individuals have the power to transform their lives and get out of poverty on their own.

Government Shouldn't Legislate Morality: Like good and bad luck, this is another issue that goes to a core difference between liberals and conservatives. Liberals often say that "you cannot legislate morality." Liberals are for social freedom, permissiveness, and progressivism—breaking the chains of traditional customs and moralities. When discussing such issues as legalization of marijuana, gay marriage, birth control, or abortion, liberals will often say that conservatives "should get out of the bedroom" and let people make their own choices. Liberals often claim that conservative laws are remnants of America's strict "puritan heritage."

Conservatives reply that all laws by their very nature "legislate morality." If a society thinks murder or rape, for example, is morally wrong, then they will make it a crime. Conservatives go on to assert that when liberals are in control of government they also impose morality; it is just a different type of morality. Liberals value tolerance, environmentalism, public health, multiculturalism, animal rights, and sexual equality. And so when liberals control a state or a city or a college campus, they make laws that enforce their morality. Examples of liberal laws that legislate liberal morality would include banning large sodas, forbidding Christmas trees, forcing people to recycle, making college speech codes, banning wood-burning fireplaces, eradicating secondhand smoke, forcing schools to provide free condoms, and forcing schools to allow kids to use the bathroom of their choice. The truth is that when any group, liberal or conservative, is in power they legislate their value system.

Gun Control: Liberals support more gun control in order to reduce violent crime. They interpret the 2nd Amendment as guaranteeing a group right by emphasizing the first phrase of the amendment: "A well regulated militia, being necessary to the security of a free state." In the wake of several mass shootings in America, including the killing of twenty children and six adults at Sandy Hook Elementary School in 2012, President Obama signed twenty-three executive orders regarding gun control. And he has urged Congress to ban assault weapons, limit the ammunition magazines to ten rounds, impose a background check for all gun sales, and increase penalties for gun traffickers. Michael Bloomberg, the billionaire former mayor of New York, created a special interest group with $50 million to support gun control legislation in cities and states across the nation. Bloomberg said that the reason violent crime has gone down in New York is due to its very strict gun control laws.

Conservatives say that right to bear arms is an essential constitutional right and that it prevents crime. They interpret the 2nd Amendment as guaranteeing an individual the right by focusing on the second half of the sentence: "the right of the people to keep and bear arms, shall not be infringed." In *McDonald v. Chicago* (2010), the Supreme Court ruled that the 2nd Amendment does indeed protect an individual's right to possess and carry a firearm for traditional lawful purposes, such as self-defense. According to the National Rifle Association (NRA), one of the most powerful interest groups in the country, as gun ownership has risen in America over the last few decades, crime has decreased. The NRA estimates that there are about 300 million privately owned firearms in the US. And according to studies conducted by criminologist Gary Kleck and the US Justice Department, guns are used between 1.2 and 2.5 million times a year in self-defense.

High Taxes on the Rich: Liberals advocate high taxes on the rich to achieve greater income equality and fairness. President Obama, in a 2012 speech at the University of Florida, justified higher tax rates on the rich by saying that "we are better off when everybody gets a fair shot, and everybody does a fair share." Senator Elizabeth Warren, a rising star in the Democratic Party, argues that lowering taxes on the rich merely "helps the rich and powerful get more rich and powerful while it cuts the legs out from under America's middle class." And Bernie Sanders, the socialist who ran for president as a Democrat in 2016, placed high taxes and "income equality" at the center of his plank. Sanders suggests that a 90 percent tax on the rich is needed because "the top one-tenth of 1 percent owns as much as the bottom 90 percent." Sanders says the rich "are so greedy . . . they think they own the world . . . I'm sorry to tell them that they are going to have to pay their fair share."

Conservatives argue that lower taxes on the rich results in greater economic growth for the whole economy, which helps create jobs for everybody. Conservatives say this is not theory; one merely needs to look at recent history to see that this is true. When Kennedy and Reagan lowered taxes on the rich, the GDP sky-rocketed and tens of millions of jobs were created. And when countries like Venezuela implement punitive taxes on the rich, the whole economy fell apart and the poor suffered. Conservatives argue that high taxes on the rich take away the incentive to work hard and start another business. They argue that it is better to allow wealthy people to spend their money on goods, services, and investments, which creates jobs. And conservatives argue that America already has one of the steepest progressive tax rates in the world, higher than Sweden's. Today, the top 10 percent of income earners pay 71 percent of all federal taxes. In conclusion, the only reason why liberals want to punish the rich is due to resentment and envy, which is no proper way to make public policy.

Illegal Immigration: According to the Pew Research Center, the estimated illegal population in the US in 2013 was 11.3 million, about half coming from Mexico. Most of the illegal immigrants live in the Southwestern states of California, Arizona, New Mexico, and Texas, but other states have significant unauthorized populations, including Florida, New York, New Jersey, and Illinois. In general, liberals favor not enforcing strict immigration laws and granting amnesty for the illegal immigrants that already live here. Many liberal cities, such as San Francisco, Los Angeles, Denver, Chicago, Baltimore, and New York, are "sanctuary cities" that do not enforce federal immigration laws. Advocates of loose immigration laws argue that we must show compassion for hardworking immigrant families who merely seek a better life. America has always been a land of immigrants, but now Latino immigrants are being discriminated against due to the bigotry of the native, white population.

While some traditional conservatives oppose strict enforcement of immigration laws due to the reliance of certain businesses on cheap labor—such as agriculture, hotels, and restaurants—social conservatives strongly advocate strict border enforcement. Social conservatives, like columnist Pat Buchanan, argue that mass illegal immigration hurts America in several ways. First, they point out that in the past immigrants came from all over the world to live in America with the objective of becoming American by assimilating the language and culture. But today it is different. People from a neighboring region and country (Mexico) are seeping into the Southwestern states and retaining their original language and culture. Eventually, they warn, this will tear America apart. Second, illegal immigration is straining our schools, prisons, and welfare and health care systems. Third, porous borders pose a security threat by easily allowing terrorists and criminals to get into America. And fourth, illegal immigration pushes down wages and hurts blue-collar workers, especially African Americans.

Institutional Racism in America: Liberals tend to believe that institutional racism is perpetuating racial inequality in American and that it is the root cause of black poverty and other social problems, such as the high crime rate. Institutional racism, they assert, is prevalent in education (with standardized testing and IQ tests that are culturally biased), in colleges (who fail to employ black professors), in bank loans and mortgages (which penalize blacks based on their zip codes), and criminal convictions (with racial profiling). In a 2009 interview with *Essence* magazine, President Obama articulated his view of institutional racism: "I don't believe it is possible to transcend race in this country. Race is a factor in this society. The legacy of Jim Crow and slavery has not gone away. It is not an accident that African-Americans experience high crime rates, are poor, and have less wealth. It is a direct result of our racial history."

While recognizing the historical fact of racism in the United States, conservatives assert that America provides any black person with the opportunity for success. Conservatives argue that liberal programs designed to help blacks have actually been harmful. This is the theme of Jason Riley's book titled *Please Stop Helping Us: How Liberals Make it Harder for Blacks to Succeed*. Riley shows that programs such as minimum wage have hurt black teenagers because it makes their labor too expensive. Today black teenage unemployment ranged from 20 to 50 percent, but before the establishment of minimum wage laws young blacks were actually employed more than young whites. And welfare programs penalized marriage and rewarded single parenting. The resulting fatherless families have been devastating to black youth. Studies show that kids without a father have a much greater likelihood to abuse drugs, become pregnant, drop out of high school, and get arrested. Riley says that "having a black man in the Oval Office is less important than having one in home."

Legalization of Marijuana: Since 1990, nineteen states have passed laws allowing people with certain medical conditions to smoke marijuana. In 2012, voters in Colorado and Washington State passed initiatives making recreational marijuana legal for adults over the age of twenty-one. And in 2014, the voters of Washington, DC, the nation's capital, voted to legalize marijuana. The Obama administration, under Attorney General Eric Holder, has indicated that they would not aggressively enforce federal marijuana laws for small-time offenders.

Some say that all the states should go ahead and legalize marijuana for recreational use. They claim that it is no more harmful than alcohol, which is legal. They argue that it is ridiculous for people to go to jail for marijuana possession, which hurts nobody. And they say that if it were legalized, then it could be regulated and taxed, helping to reduce budget deficits. Opponents to marijuana assert that the drug is anything but harmless. Most people that get addicted to hard drugs started with marijuana. The Office of National Drug Control Policy cites medical studies that show long-term use of marijuana linked to memory loss, lack of concentration, slower reaction time, increase in schizophrenia in some vulnerable individuals, and a lowering of IQ by as much as 8 points. Also, nearly 10 percent of marijuana users get addicted. Opponents argue that the last thing America needs is something that makes people lazier and more stupid.

Marriage in Society: The institution of marriage is in decline in America. In 1960, only 8% of adults had never been married, but today it is 20%. And this trend is more pronounced for men and minorities. In 2012, 23% of adult men had never been married, and 36% of blacks had never been married. Likewise, today more women are raising children by themselves. In 1960, only 8% of children lived in a mother-only household, while now it is 24%. And more women are having babies out of wedlock: 70% of all black births are to unmarried women and 35% of white births are to unmarried women. Several social factors account for this trend. Since the late 1960s, people tend to focus more on themselves and feel fewer obligations to follow traditional social norms. The sexual revolution, feminism, no-fault divorce, and celebrity culture have also contributed to the decline in marriage.

America is politically divided over the issue of the importance of marriage in society, and this is reflected in voting patterns. In 2012, 67% of single women voted for the Democrat presidential candidate, but only 46% of married women did. In general, secular liberals are less concerned about the decline in marriage than social conservatives, and feel that marriage is fundamental to the health of society. Social conservatives argue that the rise of single mothers accounts for much of the poverty in America. Today just 8% of children raised by married couples live in poverty, compared to 40% raised by single mothers. And social conservatives cite dozens of studies that show that children raised in a home with fathers are much better off: they get better grades in school, commit less crime, suffer less illness and injury, and are less likely to drop out of school. Teenage girls raised without a father have lower self-esteem and are eight times more likely to get pregnant.

Minimum Wage: In 1938, Congress enacted the Fair Labor Standards Act, establishing a minimum wage of 25 cents per hour. Unlike other government programs, it is not automatically linked to inflation but must be raised by an act of Congress. In 2007, the national minimum wage was increased from $5.15 to $7.25 an hour. States can enact minimum wages higher than the national one. In 2014, President Obama signed an executive order requiring all companies getting federal contracts to pay their workers at least $10.10 an hour, and he called on Congress to increase the federal minimum wage to the same amount. In a speech supporting the bill, the President said that each worker should receive a *living wage*, which would provide enough money for a full-time worker to keep out of poverty and enjoy a basic living. Obama said it is better for a person to work their way out of poverty than to give them welfare.

Opponents of a minimum wage say whenever you artificially raise the price of something, in this case low-skilled labor, the demand for it will decrease, resulting in high unemployment. Minimum wage jobs are entry-level jobs meant to give young people entering the job market their first work experience. According to Pew, only 2.8% of all wage and salary workers get minimum wage, but that represents 51% of people between the ages of 16–24. If minimum wage goes too high, businesses will not hire these young people but will get more work out of their existing workers or perhaps turn to automation. In 2013, Germany, which has no minimum wage, had a youth unemployment rate of 8%, while France, which has a high minimum wage, had a youth unemployment of 26%. In America the youth unemployment is high, especially for African Americans (36%). Opponents of minimum wage say that if it is abolished it will help young African Americans get entry-level jobs and build up their resumes.

Multiculturalism: Many liberals believe in multiculturalism, the idea that ethnic and cultural differences should be celebrated and preserved. Supporting this idea is that all cultures are equally important and that a person's ethnic and racial background is a primary element in their self-identity. Multiculturalism has become an important movement in the public schools and in the universities, which have many multicultural programs and clubs. For example, UCLA sponsors dozens of clubs based on the student's race and ethnicity: the "Association of Chinese Americans," "United Arab Society," and "Social Welfare Black Caucus." And the curriculum in these schools has moved away from teaching traditional American history and Western civilization. At UCLA, which is representative of many elite colleges, it is possible to get a degree in English literature without taking a single class in Shakespeare (arguably the greatest writer of the English language), but it is mandatory to take courses in Gender, Race, Ethnicity, Disability, or Sexuality Studies.

The preeminent American historian Arthur M. Schlesinger, Jr. warned against the dangers of multiculturalism in *The Disuniting of America.* He wrote that the great genius of the United States was that for over two hundred years it has been able to attract people from all over the world who "yearned to become American. Their goals were escape, deliverance, and assimilation." This idea is captured in the American motto *E pluribus unum*, "one out of many." One of the main tools of unifying all these diverse people into one American identity was the public schools, which taught the American Creed— the ideas on which America is based. But now, said Schlesinger, the "militants of ethnicity" contend that the "main objective of public education should be the protection . . . and perpetuation of ethnic origins and identities." Schlesinger warned that "If the separatist tendencies go unchecked, the result can only be fragmentation, re-segregation, and tribalization of American life."

The Profit Motive: Liberals often demonize the profit motive and the capitalistic system on which it is based. Liberal politicians, such as Elizabeth Warren, decry corporate greed and Wall Street ruthlessness. They argue that capitalism makes people too materialistic, creates powerful big businesses that exploit their workers, and leads to gross inequality. Michael Moore, the famous liberal filmmaker, said: "Capitalism is an organized system to guarantee that greed becomes the primary force of our economic system and allows the few at the top to get very wealthy and the rest of us riding around thinking we can be that way, too—if we just work hard enough, sell enough Tupperware and Amway products, we can get a pink Cadillac." Cornel West, liberal college professor, said, "I defend the fundamental claim of Marxist theory: there must be countervailing forces that defend people's needs against the brutality of profit driven capitalism."

Conservative Arthur Brooks, in his book *The Road to Freedom*, defends capitalism by showing how free enterprise (based on the profit motive, private property, and free labor) has lifted billions of people out of poverty like no other system in world history. It is hard to imagine how the modern world would function if people did not expect to make a profit. Would somebody cut your hair, make you a car, or invent your cell phone if they did not expect to make a profit? Actually, conservatives like Georg Gilder point out that capitalism is not based on greed but instead it is based on concern for others. No business would be successful unless it cared about their customers. Conservatives, however, think of "profit" more broadly than making money. The free enterprise system allows people to build their world and pursue their own happiness. Communism, which eradicates the profit motive, takes away freedom and always results in poverty and misery.

School Choice: Americans spend more money on education than any other country. According to a 2013 report by the Organization for Economic Cooperation and Development, the US spends an average of $11,500 per K–12 student, more than any other developed country in the world. But we aren't getting much for our money. In 2013, the Program for International Student Assessment (PISA) recorded that twenty-nine countries beat America in math and twenty-two countries beat America in science. There is another troubling aspect of the American education system. Students are assigned a school based on where they live. So, if the local assigned school is horrible, families have no choice but to send their children there. This situation has caused some school districts to allow school choice in the form of *charter schools*: These are semi-public schools, founded by universities, corporations, or other groups, that take public and private money to establish a school that does not need to follow the normal rules for public school. Today, there are 6,000 charter schools serving 2 million students in forty-two states.

One of the first to advocate school choice was the Nobel prize-winning economist Martin Friedman. He argued for an *education voucher*: each family will receive a government certificate or voucher to be used to send their children to the private or public school of their choice. Friedman argued that be it in sports or business, competition brings out the best in people and institutions. We ought to force local schools to compete for students, just as colleges do. The current system is a monopoly—which has been banned in American business since the 1800s because it offers no accountability. The school choice concept has gained some acceptance in America. Vouchers are currently used in four states: Wisconsin, Florida, Ohio, and Georgia. A majority of states currently have charter school programs. And nearly all states allow *home schooling*, where parents teach their own children at home but must follow state directives in curriculum.

Liberals, such as Hillary Clinton (who recently came out against charter schools), oppose the school choice movement and support the traditional public school system. In recent years, those that support the status quo have gained a strong advocate in the imminent education historian, Diane Ravitch. In her book, *Reign of Error*, Ravitch says that public schools are doing a fine job and there is no need for reform. The underperforming schools are doing poorly not because of bad teachers, but due to poverty, out of wedlock births, diversity, and recent immigrants. And American students do not perform well on the standardized tests that PISA measures because they don't take these tests seriously. "Public education," asserts Ravitch, "is the backbone of our democracy, and we cannot turn it over to privateers," such as charter and private schools.

Religion in Society: According to a 2012 Gallup survey, 82.5% of Americans identify with a religion, with 77% as Christian. This is much higher than European countries, but secularism is increasing in

America. In 2012, nearly 16% identified with no religion, up from just 4% in 1970. Religion marks one of the key differences between Democrats and Republicans. In 2012, 70% of people with no religious affiliation voted for Obama, while only 26% voted for Romney. Secular liberals, such as Phil Zuckerman, author of *Living the Secular Life*, contend that modern people can live moral, connected lives without religion. They can form social groups and make moral decisions based on "listening to one's own moral compass." Other secularists such as Christopher Hitchens, author of *God is not Great*, argue that organized religion is nothing that needs to be emulated because it is the source of "violence, irrationalism, intolerance, and racism" in the world.

Social conservative Dennis Prager, in his book *Still the Best Hope* and in numerous articles, makes the case for why religion based on Judeo-Christian values is an irreplaceable force for good. Liberals tend to believe that people are basically good, but conservatives think people are naturally neither good nor bad but mostly selfish. Therefore, humans need institutions such as the church to teach them to be good. And there is "no better system than the God-based Ten Commandments," says Prager, "for making a better world." Prager states that without God, all moral judgments are simply subjective opinion. God is needed to make morality objective, and God is needed to make moral demands on individuals to do good. Moreover, God is needed to make individual rights objective. If governments are the source of our rights, then governments can take them away. In America, which was founded on "In God We Trust," our liberty and human rights come from God and thus limit the power of government.

Lastly, Prager disagrees with Hitchens that religion is the source of most of the wars and violence in the world. True, Christians have been responsible for tens of thousands of deaths in the Crusades and the Inquisition and other religious wars between Catholics and Protestants, but secular ideologies were responsible for tens of millions of deaths in the twentieth century. The Nazis and the communists in Russia, China, and Cambodia killed well over a 100 million people. These were secular ideologies that were led by intelligent, well-educated people. But without a morality imposed by a Judeo-Christian ethic, the Nazis and communists invented justifications for mass murder. In the name of doing what was best for the nation, they denied individuals their human rights, which Prager argues are "sacred" only in a God-based moral system.

Truman's Decision to Drop the Atom Bomb on Japan: In August of 1945, President Harry Truman made the decision to drop two newly developed atom bombs on the industrial and military cities of Hiroshima and Nagasaki, thus ending the war with Japan. Within four months of the bombings, it is estimated that between 90,000 and 166,000 died in Hiroshima and between 39,000 and 80,000 died in Nagasaki. Today, it is probably the mainstream view taught on the college campuses that dropping the atom bomb was morally wrong. Four reasons are often offered: Japan was ready to surrender due to the intense conventional bombings of Japanese cities and the naval blockade maintained by the US navy. The target cities contained mostly civilian populations. The atom bombs were actually dropped to scare off the Soviets. And dropping the atom bomb on the Japanese was racist, reflecting the popular view in America at the time that Asians were inferior.

Many historians, including Professor Wilson Miscamble, author of *The Most Controversial Decision: Truman, the Atomic Bombs, and the Defeat of Japan*, argue that Truman's decision was morally correct. These historians say that Japan was preparing for an all-out defense of the homeland, even training women and children. It is estimated that a conventional invasion of Japan would have cost over

1 million American and Japanese lives. Proof that Japan was not on the verge of surrendering is that even after the US dropped two atom bombs, the military and political leaders of Japan refused to quit. Emperor Hirohito had to step in and call for surrender. Also, if it was learned that Truman had this weapon available but called for a conventional invasion of Japan anyway, he would have had to explain to hundreds of thousands of parents why he sent their sons into an unnecessary bloodbath. That would have been a morally untenable position to be in.

Voter ID Laws: In 1970, Hawaii and South Carolina were the first states to request that somebody show some kind of identification at the polls. By 2000, fourteen states had voter ID laws. Five years later, the bipartisan Commission on Federal Election Reform recommended that all states pass voter ID laws. As of 2014, most states request some form of identification when voting, but ten states have strict ID laws that require identification before voting, these include Arizona, North Dakota, Kansas, Texas, Mississippi, Indiana, Tennessee, Georgia, Ohio, and Virginia. The Obama administration has called these laws racist in intent, designed to suppress the black vote. Attorney General Eric Holder said that "photo identification can be used to disenfranchise particular groups, either by racial designation or ethnic origin for partisan reasons." In 2011, Holder sued Texas after it passed a strict photo ID law, but the Supreme Court lifted the injunction before the 2014 election.

Conservatives say that in order to reduce fraud and maintain the integrity of American elections, requiring a photo ID when voting is reasonable. Nearly all countries require identification to vote, as recommended by Jimmy Carter's Democracy Program, which monitors elections around the world. In America, the press routinely reports examples of voter fraud, whether it is people voting several times or that the names of dead people are on registrations rolls. In America today, photo IDs are required to cash a check, go to an airport, enter a federal building, or to check out a library book. So IDs should be required for the very important act of voting. Lastly, some conservatives, like writer Dennis Prager, asserts that assuming that blacks are incapable of getting a photo ID is a racist assumption. This notion should be insulting to blacks. Indeed, in recent elections black turnout has been higher than white turnout.

War on Poverty: In his 1964 State of the Union Address, Lyndon Johnson declared "unconditional war on poverty in America." Johnson explained that "our aim is not only to relieve the symptoms of poverty, but to cure it." The weapons in this war were dozens of government programs which drastically expanded the welfare state, including Head Start, food stamps, government housing, job training, Medicare, Medicaid, and the expansion of Aid to Children with Dependent Families. In a speech commemorating the 50th Anniversary of the War on Poverty, Barack Obama said that the War on Poverty "reaffirmed that we live in a great country." He went on to say that "If we hadn't declared 'unconditional war on poverty,' millions more Americans would be living in poverty today." Liberals consider the War on Poverty to be one of the greatest successes of the twentieth century because it expanded government in order to help the poor.

Conservatives think the War on Poverty was a failure because it made people dependent on government, undermined personal responsibility, sabotaged the work ethic, and helped undo the family. In a Heritage Foundation report, "The War on Poverty after 50 Years," a graph shows the poverty rate during three dates: in 1950 the poverty rate was 35 percent, in 1967 (when the program was being implemented) it was 14 percent, and in 2014 it was 15 percent. So, *before* the War on Poverty, the poverty rate was rapidly declining, but since its implementation poverty has remained steady. And this is after spending over $22 trillion!

Walter Williams, a conservative economist, argues that the cause of poverty is bad decisions by individuals, and government can do little to stop people from making bad decisions. Williams says that poverty statistics reveal that poverty in America can be avoided by doing four simple things: (1) graduate from high school, (2) get married before you have children and stay married, (3) avoid criminal behavior, and (4) get a job and keep the job even if it pays minimum wage. If a person does these four things, they will not be poor.

NOTES

The author recommends **Prager University** (www.prageru.com) as a research tool to learn more about various political and social issues.

Abortion: Guttmacher Institute report, "State Policies in Brief: State Policies on Later Abortions," Feb. 1, 2015; LifeNews.com, "56,662,169 Abortions in America Since Roe vs. Wade in 1973," Jan. 12, 2014.

Affirmative Action: Thomas Sowell. *Affirmative Action Around the World: An Empirical Study*. Princeton: Yale University Press, 2005; Thomas Sowell. *The Thomas Sowell Reader*. New York: Basic Books, 2011.

Atom Bomb: Wilson Miscamble. *The Most Controversial Decision: Truman, the Atomic Bombs, and the Defeat of Japan*. Cambridge: Cambridge University Press, 2012; Wilson Miscamble, "Was it Wrong to Drop the Bomb?" *Prager University Course*.

Death Penalty: Michael Lipka, "Support for Death Penalty Drops among Americans," *Pew*, Feb. 12, 2014; Innocence Project website.

Equal Pay: Obama, 2014 State of the Union Address; Glenn Kessler, "Fact Checker: President Obama's persistent '77-cents' claim on the wage gap gets a new Pinocchio rating," *Washington Post*, April 9, 2014. National Organization for Woman, "Economic Justice" (now.org/issues/)

Gay Marriage: Jocelyn Kiley, "61% of young Republicans favor same-sex marriage," *Pew*, March 10, 2014; ProCon.org, "37 states with legal gay marriage and 13 states with same sex marriage bans." *Pew Research Center*, "Changing Attitudes on Gay Marriage," May 12, 2016.

Get Money out of Politics: George Will, "Money in Politics: What's the Problem?" Prager University Course, Oct. 6, 2014.

Global Warning: Obama, 2014 State of the Union Address; Nigel Lawson, "A wicked Orthodoxy," *National Review Online*, May 5, 2014.

Gun Control: *Reuters*, "Former New York Mayor Bloomberg to spend $50 million on gun control," April 16, 2014. Obama, 2013 State of the Union Address; *Gun Owners of America* (GOA), "Gun control Fact-sheet 2004; *NRA.org*, "Fact sheet."

High Taxes on the Rich: Ewen MacAskill, "Obama Targets Millionaires and Romney in Speech at Florida University," *The Guardian*, April 10, 2012; Elizabeth Warren, Speech to AFL-CIO, Jan. 7, 2015; *Peter Ferrara. "Reaganomics vs. Obamanomics: Facts and figures, Forbes, May 2011;*

Lee Ohanian, "Do the Rich Pay their Fair Share?" Prager University Course; Tim Groseclose, "Lower Taxes, Higher Revenue," Prager University Course; Bernie Sanders interview on NBC News, May 26, 2015; Stephen Moore, "Why Tax Rate Cuts Work," *Washington Times*, May 15, 2016.

Immigration: Jens Manuel Krogstad and Jeffrey S. Passel, "5 facts about illegal immigration in the US," *Pew*, November 18, 2014. Pat Buchanan. *State of Emergency: The Third World Invasion and Conquest of America*. New York: St. Martin's Griffin, paperback edition, 2007.

Institutional Racism: Obama interview, *Essence* Magazine, 2009; Jason Riley. *Please Stop Helping Us: How Liberals Make it Harder for Blacks to Succeed*. New York: Encounter Books, 2014. Walter Williams, "Please Stop Helping Us," *TownHall.com*, Feb. 28, 2015.

Legalization of Marijuana: Whitehouse.gov, Office of National Drug Control Policy, "Answers to Frequently Asked Questions about Marijuana."

Marriage in Society: Charles Murray. *Coming Apart: the State of White America, 1960–2010*. New York: Crown Forum, 2012; D.C. McAllister, "Yes, Katy Perry, Babies Need Daddies," *The Federalist*, Aug. 15, 2014; Wendy Wang, "Record Share of Americans Have Never Married," Pew, Sept. 24, 2014.

Minimum Wage: Obama, 2014 State of the Union Address. Thomas Sowell. *The Thomas Sowell Reader*. New York: Basic Books, 2011, chapter "Minimum Wage Law." Thomas Sowell, "Ruinous 'Compassion,'" *Townhall.com*, March 18, 2015; David Henderson, "What's the Right Minimum Wage?" *Prager University Course*.

Multiculturalism: Arthur M. Schlesinger, Jr. *The Disuniting of America: Reflections on a Multicultural Society*. New York: WW Norton, 1991. Heather MacDonald, "Who Killed the Liberal Arts?" *Prager University Course*, Oct. 26, 2015.

Profit Motive: Arthur Brooks. *The Road to Freedom*. New York: Basic Brooks, 2012. George Gilder, "What Creates Wealth?" and "Why Capitalism Works," *Prager University Courses*.

Religion in Society: Frank Newport, "Percentage of Christians in US Drifting Down, but Still High," Gallup, Dec. 24, 2015. Phil Zuckerman. *Living the Secular Life*. London: Penguin Press, 2014. Christopher Hitchens. *God is not Great*. New York: Twelve Books, 2009. Dennis Prager. *Still the Best Hope*. New York: Broadside Books, 2012.

School Choice: NEA.org, "Vouchers"; www.oecd.org, "Education at a glance." www.oecd.org. "PISA 2013 Results." Milton Freidman. *Free to Choose*. Chapter 6, "What's Wrong with our Schools?" New York: Harvest Books, 1979; American Federation for Children, "Facts." Alain Jehlen, "Ravitch Blasts 'So-Called Reforms,'" NEA website, June 6, 2016; Nina Reese, "Unfair Attack on Education Reform, *US News & World Report*, Sept. 23, 2013.

Voter ID: National Conference of State Legislatures (NCSL), Dennis Prager, "Accusation that Voter ID is Racist Demeans Blacks," June 7, 2011.

War on Poverty: Barack Obama "Statement by the President on the 50th Anniversary of the War on Poverty," *White House website*, Jan 8, 2014; Heritage Foundation report #2955, "The War on Poverty after 50 Years," Sept. 15, 2014; Walter Williams, "How not to be Poor," *Townhall.com*, May 11, 2005.

APPENDIX B

Landmark
Supreme Court Cases

This "bonus" chapter can serve several functions. First, it can be used as a reference. Whenever a Supreme Court case is mentioned in the text, the student can look here to get a fuller explanation of the case. Second, an instructor may wish to assign this chapter to provide the student with a brief overview of the history of US constitutional law. And third, this chapter can be used for research on a paper.

Whatever the specific purpose, it is very useful for the student of American politics and government to have a list of the most important Supreme Court cases, because they have influenced millions of people and changed the structure and policies of the US government. Because of its paramount importance, several paragraphs are devoted to *Marbury v. Madison*. Most of the other thirty cases, however, are described in one or two paragraphs.

Marbury v. Madison (1803): In this case, the Supreme Court claimed for itself the power of *judicial review*: the power of the Supreme Court to rule congressional acts unconstitutional and thus null and void. This case dealt with a controversial presidential appointment. In the last days, even hours, of the lame duck session of Congress controlled by the Federalist Party, John Adams appointed dozens of national judges with Federalist sympathies, known as the "midnight judges." Adams signed and the secretary of state John Marshal sealed and delivered these commissions. But because time ran out, the commission for William Marbury was not delivered but instead languished on a desk in the White House.

The incoming president, Thomas Jefferson, found Marbury's undelivered commission and ordered the new secretary of state, James Madison, to ignore it because he opposed Adams and the Federalist Party's court packing scheme. Madison and Jefferson were leaders of the opposition party, the Republican Party. Consequently, Marbury sued the secretary of the state for not delivering his commission. Marbury understood that the Judicial Act of 1789 gave the Supreme Court the power to order a *writ of mandamus*, a court order directing officials to do something. And because this case dealt with the secretary of state, he took his case directly to the Supreme Court, which had original jurisdiction in cases involving federal officials.

Adams appointed his former secretary of state, John Marshall, to Chief Justice of the Supreme Court (1801–1835), who was ratified by the Federalist dominated Senate. (Never mind that Marshall should have recused himself from the case because he was directly involved!) This case offered several thorny issues for the new chief justice. How should he rule? If Marshall ordered a writ and Jefferson ignored it this would destroy the prestige of the young Court. And if he gave into Jefferson, this too would be a sign of institutional weakness. Marshall demonstrated great political and judicial ingenuity by forging a third course.

On February 24, 1803, Marshall issued his opinion containing three conclusions: (1) Marbury had a right to his commission and Madison should have delivered it. (2) US law does provide a legal remedy for Marbury. However, (3) contrary to what the Judicial Act of 1789 states, the Supreme Court does not have the power to issue a writ of mandamus in this case. Marshall wrote that Section 13 of Congress's Judicial Act states that the Supreme Court can issue a writ in areas of original jurisdiction. But Article III of the Constitution says nothing about granting the Court the power of issuing a writ of mandamus in original jurisdiction cases. Therefore, Congress unconstitutionally expanded the Court's powers. Then, using some of Alexander Hamilton's arguments from *Federalist #78*, Marshall asserted that it is the role of the judiciary to interpret the law and if congressional law is contrary to the Constitution it must be ruled invalid. And thus Marshall declared Section 13 of the Judiciary Act null and void.

With this case, the Court established its power of judicial review, which eventually gave the Supreme Court co-equal powers with the executive and legislative branches. Marshall accepted a short-term political loss (his Federalist judge was not appointed) for a long-term institutional gain (the Supreme Court could nullify congressional and presidential acts if deemed unconstitutional).

Summary of Marshall's Argument for Judicial Review in *Marbury v. Madison*: Because the Supreme Court's claim of judicial review has had such a monumental impact on the history of the United States, this section will summarize John Marshall's argument for judicial review.

The Constitution, ratified by the people, is "fundamental" law. This document organizes the government and assigns certain powers. Most significantly, "it establishes certain limits not to be transcended." America is either a limited government or not, there is no middle ground. The Constitution is either superior or it is on a level with ordinary legislative acts, and Congress can change it at any time. If the Constitution is superior, fundamental law, then when Congress passes a law repugnant to the Constitution, it must be voided, otherwise the Constitution is absurd. To make it clear that the Constitution is fundamental law, the Framers instructed all judges, executive branch officials, and members of Congress, to swear an oath to uphold the Constitution.

Article III, Section 1, grants the Supreme Court "the judicial power of the United States." It is emphatically the province and duty of the judicial department to say what the law is. If two laws are in conflict, the courts must decide the operation of each. And Section 2 says "the judicial power extends to all cases . . . arising under this constitution." Further, Article VI says "the Constitution . . . is the supreme law of the land." Thus, if a law is in conflict with the Constitution, then the Supreme Court must decide in favor of the Constitution. Let's look at an example. The Constitution declares that Congress cannot pass a bill of attainder. If Congress went ahead and passed a bill of attainder, then soon the Constitution would be meaningless and our country would be ruled by "legislative supremacy," a concept the Founder's emphatically rejected. Thus, the phraseology of the Constitution and the principles of a limited government confirm that a law repugnant to the Constitution must be declared void by the US Supreme Court.

Dartmouth College v. Woodward (1819): A New Hampshire law converted Dartmouth from a private college to a public one under state control because it resented the religious elites that ran the college. The famous constitutional lawyer Daniel Webster represented the trustees of Dartmouth. Marshall invalidated this law citing the contract clause. He said that when the state created the charter to establish Dartmouth College this was a binding contract that could not be broken.

This case represented a political struggle between the Federalist Party and the Republican Party. In the eighteenth century, states created corporations to build things like bridges, roads, and colleges. In exchange for the construction, the corporation would be granted a monopoly to reap the profits for an extended period of time. By the early nineteenth century, many people in the Republican Party, which represented the "common man," came to perceive these charters as a legislative gift to well connected special interests. But many Federalists, like Marshall, abhorred state laws that took private property away from one group to give to other groups, such as the indebted poor. The Marshall Court used the contract clause to protect corporations from this type of populous legislation.

McCulloch v. Maryland (1819): Many consider this John Marshall's greatest case, laying out his vision of implied powers, national supremacy, and modern commerce. Again, this case must be understood within the political context of the times. The Republicans who controlled the state of Maryland opposed the Bank of the United States (BUS), the nation's central bank, and passed a law levying a $15,000 tax on all banks not incorporated in Maryland. Federalists, like Marshall, supported the national bank, which was established by secretary of treasure Alexander Hamilton during the Washington administration.

In his unanimous opinion, Marshall established the means-ends doctrine of implied powers. Quoting from Hamilton's essay defending the BUS, Marshall said that if the national government's end is necessary and legitimate and if it is "within the scope of the Constitution," then the means are valid. In this case, a national bank is the proper means for carrying out the enumerated powers of Congress, and thus it is constitutional. Next, he established the supremacy doctrine. "The power to tax can be used as a power to destroy," and the state of Maryland cannot use a tax to destroy congressional law. When in conflict, if the national law is valid, then national law is supreme to state law under the "supremacy clause." This case protected the institution of the BUS, which Marshall thought was vital for encouraging national economic growth by financing construction of much needed infrastructure and by providing loans to businesses and farms.

Gibbons v. Ogden (1824): This was John Marshall's last great case. And it was the first case dealing with the commerce clause. New York had rewarded Robert Fulton, the innovator of steam-powered ships, with a shipping monopoly on all New York waterways. Aaron Ogden, a franchisee of Fulton's, ran a line from Manhattan to New Jersey. When Thomas Gibbons, who possessed a US congressional coastal license, started running ships on the same route, Ogden sued.

In a unanimous decision, Marshall sided with Ogden. Under the commerce clause of Article I, Section 8, the national government has complete authority "to regulate Commerce . . . among the several States." Marshall said the commerce clause was "complete in itself, may be exercise to its utmost extent, and acknowledges no limitations, other than are prescribed by the Constitution." New York can grant charters within its borders, but not to businesses conducting commerce between two or more states. If states would have been allowed to grant monopolies to businesses conducting commerce between two or more states, American economic activity would have been strangled.

Marshall's ruling in *Gibbons* defined the commerce clause as it applied to the powers of the national and state governments for generations. But certain comments he made in his opinion established the foundation for a broader interpretation of the commerce which Progressives would use a hundred years later. Marshall said that "commerce" means any "economic intercourse" that may "affect other states." This very broad interpretation of commerce contradicted the understanding of the word as the Framers used it, meaning "trade." Marshall's broader interpretation of commerce would eventually be used by the Supreme Court to affirm congressional laws regulating all types of activity, including manufacturing, banking, farming, and labor.

Charles River Bridge v. Warren Bridge **(1837):** This was the first case of Chief Justice Roger Taney, who had just been selected by Andrew Jackson. In 1785, the Massachusetts legislature granted the Charles River Bridge Company a charter to construct a bridge over the Charles River, thus connecting Boston with Charleston. For constructing the bridge, the company was granted the exclusive rights to collect tolls for forty years, later extended seventy more years.

In 1828, Massachusetts chartered another company, the Warren Bridge Company, to build a new bridge adjacent to the Charles River Bridge. This charter granted exclusive rights to the Warren Bridge Company to collect tolls for only six years, after which the bridge would be free to the public. The Charles River Bridge company sued, hiring Daniel Webster. Webster, citing the Dartmouth case, said the state legislature violated the contract clause when it chartered the new bridge, which will certainly destroy the Charles River Bridge's business.

Taney, however, upheld Massachusetts's new charter. Taney said that in circumstances such as this a charter must be interpreted narrowly. The original charter did not promise perpetual exclusivity. Private property and the obligation of contracts are fundamental rights, but they must be weighed against the good of the community. Boston was a booming city and it needed more bridges. These old charters cannot be used to stop progress and economic development. Under the Marshall Court, the contract clause had been used to allow corporations to foster economic growth and to protect them from "leveling" legislative acts. Now the Taney Court would more broadly interpret contracts in order to prevent the old charters from strangling economic progress.

Dred Scott v. Sanford **(1857):** In an attempt to resolve the issue of slavery in the territories, Roger Taney exercised judicial review for only the second time in the Court's history by declaring a congressional act (the Missouri Compromise) unconstitutional. The question at stake was essentially a political one and the Court never should have taken this case. At the time, the Republican Party took the position that slavery must be contained in the Southern states, where it would eventually become extinct, and that slavery should be prohibited in the territories. The Democrats, led by John C. Calhoun, argued that slaves were private property and that the national government should have no authority to neither regulate labor in the states nor prohibit slavery in the territories. Instead of allowing these questions to be resolved through the political process, the Taney Court essentially took the Democratic position.

This case involved a slave, Dred Scott, who had resided with his master for several years in the free territory of Wisconsin and the free state of Illinois before returning home to the slave state of Missouri. After his master died, he sued for his freedom on the grounds that he had lived outside of a slave state for many years. This is considered one of the worst decisions in the history of the Supreme Court. In ***Dred Scott v. Sanford*** (1857), Taney not only denied Scott his freedom, but ruled that no black man could set foot in a federal court because they were a perpetual slave race that could never retain US citizenship. Taney cited the Fifth Amendment, which prohibits the federal government from depriving people of their "life, liberty, or property, without due process." And since slaves are private property, argued Taney, any congressional act that prohibited slavery in the territories was unconstitutional.

Taney's ruling was filled with all sorts of factual errors and logical inconsistencies. He said blacks could never be citizens because at the time of the framing of the Constitution, no blacks were citizens. This is not true. By 1787, five of the thirteen states had either freed their slaves or started the process of gradual emancipation. And he ignores the clear meaning of Article IV, vesting Congress with the power to "make all needful rules and regulations" respecting the territories. Roger Taney's activist opinion, which radically misinterpreted the text of the Constitution in order to further his own political agenda, caused a firestorm of protest. In his attempt to maintain state's rights, he went too far and denied the national government a power enumerated in the Constitution (that it could regulate the territories) and implied that any state that prohibited slavery violated the Constitution. Instead of resolving the slave issue, the Supreme Court actually helped precipitate the Civil War.

Slaughter House Cases (1873): During Reconstruction, the 14th Amendment was added to the Constitution in order to protect the rights of the freed slaves. It says that no state can abridge the *privileges and immunities* of citizens or deny them *due process of the law* or the *equal protection of the laws*. In 1869, in order to improve the safety of the meatpacking industry and reduce contamination of the Mississippi River, the state of Louisiana created a butcher monopoly, called the Grand Slaughterhouse, which the state could strictly regulate. The independent butchers who lost their jobs filed a suit. They claiming the law abridged their privileges and immunities, which traditionally under common law included the right to "labor freely in an honest vocation."

In the *Slaughter House Cases*, the Court would make an unusual interpretation of the 14th amendment, which would have long-lasting implications. First, they said the 14th Amendment's *privileges and immunities* clause only protects the rights of national citizenship, not state citizenship. Day-to-day activities like employment and work regulations fall under the rights of state citizenship, so the state can regulate the butcher industry under its police powers. Second, the Court very narrowly interpreted the *due process* and the *equal protection* clauses of the 14th amendment, saying they only applied to the national government not the state governments—even though the 14th Amendment clearly said that they apply to "the states." As a result, this ruling made it nearly impossible for the federal government to enforce civil rights laws meant to protect African Americans.

The reason that the Supreme Court made such a strange ruling in the *Slaughter House Cases* is that it saw the implications of the 14th Amendment and shrank back. The 14th Amendment did something new: it prohibited the states from violating the rights of its citizens. The Court knew that if it broadly interpreted the 14th Amendment, then any citizen who felt a state law violated his rights could seek redress from the Supreme Court. The justices were right. Eventually the due process and equal protection clause of the 14th Amendment would radically alter federalism and give the federal government nearly unlimited power over the states.

Plessy v. Ferguson **(1896):** In 1890, the state legislature of Louisiana passed a law requiring separate railway cars for black and white passengers. A group of civil rights activists persuaded Homer Plessy, who was born free and was an "octoroon" (a person of one-eighth black descent), to buy a first-class ticket for a white car in order to challenge this law. Plessy was arrested and the case went to the Supreme Court, just as planned. Plessy's lawyers argued that the Louisiana law clearly violated the equal protection clause of the 14th amendment.

Writing for the majority, Justice Henry Brown wrote that forced segregation of the two races in no way implies "a badge of inferiority" to blacks. He further stated that "social prejudices" cannot be "overcome by legislation." In this case, the Court established the "separate but equal doctrine," which states that as long as state and local governments provide separate but equal facilities to whites and blacks, then they do not violate the equal protection clause of the 14th amendment. In a scathing dissent, Justice John Harlan wrote that the Constitution should be "colorblind" and that one day this case would be as infamous as the *Dred Scott*. Harlan was right. Now this case is recognized for causing great harm by giving the green light for Southern states to pass Jim Crow Laws that maintained segregation and restricted the voting rights of Black Americans.

***US v. E. C. Knight* (1895):** Responding to the rise of big business conglomerations, in 1890 Congress passed the Sherman Anti-trust Act, essentially making monopolies illegal. *Monopolies* have several detrimental effects on the economy: they restrict the employment options for workers, lower wages, reduce competition, and raise prices. In 1892, President Grover Cleveland, in an effort to enforce the Sherman Anti-trust Act, ordered the justice department to break up E. C. Knight Company, which controlled about 98 percent of the American sugar refining industry. In this case, however, the Supreme Court ruled in favor of E. C. Knight. Taking a narrow interpretation of the commerce clause, the Court said commerce traditionally meant "trade," and therefore Congress did not have the authority to regulate *manufacturing* inside a state, even if it indirectly affects other states.

***Lochner v. New York* (1905):** During the Progressive Era, from about 1900 to 1920, state legislatures started passing laws designed to protect workers and regulate local business. The New York legislature passed the "Bakeshop Act," limiting bakers from working over ten hours a day or sixty hours a week. Joseph Lochner, an owner of a local bakery, sued the state. The Supreme Court ruled in his favor and voided the New York law applying a new concept to the due process clause of the 14th Amendment.

Traditionally, due process referred to procedures the government had to follow when arresting a person or taking away his property, such as the right to a jury. In *Lochner*, the Supreme Court developed the concept of "substantive due process rights," meaning the due process clause contained substantial rights, in this case the right of private property and liberty of contracts. By broadly interpreting the due process clause, the Supreme Court sought to block Progressive laws which they thought violated an individual right to private property. *Lochner v. New York* has always been the object of great scorn from progressive lawyers and academics because they say that the Supreme Court tried to defend laissez-faire economics, the doctrine that the government should not interfere with free market capitalism.

***Muller v. Oregon* (1907):** In many ways *Muller v. Oregon* represents the beginning of the Progressive Supreme Court. It was in this case that the Court accepted a new judicial philosophy, called *progressive pragmatism*. Instead of holding to the text and original intent of the Constitution, Supreme Court justices would now look at the real-life social implications of their rulings.

In this case, the Court overturned *Lochner* and upheld an Oregon law that limited women to working ten hours in a laundry. Louis Brandies, the lawyer representing Oregon, submitted a brief that only contained two pages of legal arguments but dozens of pages of sociological data. Since *Muller,* federal judges started to accept the notion that the government could impose regulations on the economy. Today the ruling is seen as paternalistic due to the fact that the reason the Supreme Court ruled that women could not work over ten hours is that it would strain their delicate reproductive systems.

Standard Oil v. US (1911): Theodore Roosevelt was the first progressive president. He believed that some corporations or trusts were good (those that produced beneficial goods and services and treated workers fairly), but that other trusts were bad (monopolies). Using the Sherman Anti-trust Act of 1890, Roosevelt busted a dozen trusts, including John D. Rockefeller's Standard Oil. In a series of opinions, starting with *Northern Securities Co. v. US* **(1904)** and *Swift & Co v. US* **(1904),** the Supreme Court reversed its ruling in *Knight* and rejected the distinction between commerce and manufacturing. Now the Court supported a broad interpretation of the commerce clause and ruled that it was constitutional for the federal government to break up monopolies if it can "reasonably" demonstrate that a corporation restricted trade.

Schenck v. US (1919): In an effort to garner full public support for the war, during World War I Congress passed the Espionage and Sedition acts. These laws authorized government officials to censor any anti-war or radical material transported through the US mail, made it illegal to do, say, or write anything that was against the war effort, or to use any "disloyal, profane or abusive language" to describe the government or government officials. In the past, judges had used the *Bad Tendency Test* to limit any speech that had the tendency to corrupt public morals or lead to criminal acts. In this ruling, the Supreme Court limited free speech during war.

Charles Schenck, a leader of the US Socialist Party, was arrested under the Sedition Act for distributing anti-war leaflets to people standing in a draft line. Schenck argued that the arrest violated his First Amendment rights of free speech. In a 9-0 ruling, Oliver Wendall Holmes wrote that protest speech, especially speech that interfered with a government war action such as organizing a draft, presented a "clear and present danger" and therefore could be limited. Speech that could put people in harm, such as yelling "fire" in a crowded theater, must be limited.

Helvering v. Davis (1937): After Franklin Roosevelt was elected president in 1932, he pushed dozens of laws through Congress in order to combat the Great Depression. But the Supreme Court, consisting of justices selected by previous, more conservative presidents, declared some of these laws unconstitutional. In 1935, Congress passed FDR's landmark legislation, the Social Security Act, providing unemployment insurance, old pensions, and relief for poor families and the handicapped. Afraid that the Court would also declare Social Security unconstitutional, after FDR was reelected in 1936 he tried to implement a scheme to pack the Court with liberal judges. Realizing this would break the constitutional principle of three independent branches of government, Congress rejected this scheme. But by 1937, with the appointment of some new justices and the conversion of some old justice, the Supreme Court began upholding New Deal legislation by broadly interpreting the general welfare clause and the commerce clause.

In *Helvering v. Davis*, and in the opinions of **Steward Machine** and **Southern Coal & Coke,** the Supreme Court upheld the constitutionality of the Social Security Act by broadly interpreting the general welfare clause. In his opinion, Justice Benjamin N. Cardozo admitted that the "general welfare clause" had been traditionally interpreted to mean that Congress should provide for the "general" good of the country, not for particular interest. "The concept of 'general welfare' is not static," he continued, "but adapts itself to the crisis and necessities of the times." Now the country is facing a crisis in which millions of people are unemployment and millions of elderly are destitute. Therefore, concluded Cardozo, Congress must interpret the general welfare clause in a way that will enable it to help the general problems facing the nation. This case opened the way for the modern welfare state.

National Labor Relations Board v. Jones and Laughlin Steel Corporation **(1937):** In this case, the Supreme Court upheld the Wagner Act, which protected the rights of workers to form unions and collectively bargain for higher wages and better work conditions. Using a broad interpretation of the commerce clause, the Court said Congress has the full authority to regulate labor conditions in American, even in manufacturing plants within a state. This case set the stage for massive federal control over the marketplace.

Wickard v. Filburn **(1942):** After the first Agricultural Adjustment Act (AAA) was declared unconstitutional, Congress passed a second AAA in 1938, which limited wheat production based on the acreage of a farm. Under the new AAA law, an Ohio farmer, Roscoe Filburn, was fined for growing grain that was not sold but used to feed his family and livestock. In an unanimous ruling, the Court said, "homegrown wheat in this sense competes with wheat in commerce." So, because Filburn does not have to buy wheat at the market (since he grew it himself), his decision impacts the interstate commerce of wheat, and therefore Congress can regulate wheat used for personal consumption under the interstate commerce clause. *Wickard* exemplifies how the New Deal Court used a very broad interpretation of the commerce clause to establish the power of the national government to regulate the economy.

Korematsu v. US **(1944):** During World War II, Franklin Roosevelt signed Executive Order 9066, relocating about 110,000 Americans with Japanese ancestry into internment camps. This order clearly violated the Fifth Amendment, which states that "no person shall be . . . deprived of life, liberty, or property without due process." Fred Korematsu was arrested for defying this order. Hugo Black, writing for the majority, said that any law that singles out a particular race must be reviewed by the Court using *strict scrutiny*, the highest standard. But in this case, the Court ruled that the law was necessary in order to enforce the Espionage Act and to defend the nation against a potential Japanese invasion of the West Coast.

Youngstown Sheet & Tube Co. v. Sawyer **(1952):** President Truman ordered the government to take over the nation's steel mills to preempt a threatened labor strike, which he claimed interfered with the government ability to fight the Korean War. During World War I, President Woodrow Wilson had taken over the railroads, which was upheld by the Court in **Northern Pacific Railway co. v. North Dakota (1919).** But in this case the Court ruled against the president. Hugo L. Black wrote the opinion and rejected Truman's claim of inherent executive power.

Robert H. Jackson's concurring opinion is most often cited today because it outlined the limits of executive orders. He said US presidents act in three zones of authority: (1) Within the explicit realm of congressional authorization, the president has maximum power. (2) Within the realm where Congress has not authorized, the president has some "twilight power" depending on the circumstances. (3) But in an area where Congress prohibited action, the president has no power. In this case, Jackson said that Truman was acting outside of the law.

Brown v. the Board of Education Topeka, Kansas **(1954):** In 1953, President Dwight Eisenhower, a Republican, selected the Republican governor of California, Earl Warren, to be the next Chief Justice of the Supreme Court. To Eisenhower's dismay, instead of guiding the Court back to a moderate conservative path, Warren led the Supreme Court in its most liberal period in history. Representing a triumph of liberalism, the Warren Court accomplished several achievements: (1) it expanded free speech, (2) it opposed government efforts to impose a moral code or promote religion, (3) it protected civil rights by using the equal protection clause, (4) it equalized voting rights, and (5) it protected the rights of the criminally accused. *Brown v. the Board of Education* was the first major case of the Warren Court, marking the shift to liberal jurisprudence that would last for decades.

Oliver Brown sued because his daughter was forced to go to the segregated black school across town rather than the much closer white school. His lawyer, Thurgood Marshall, argued that this violated the "equal protection clause" of the 14th Amendment and caused psychological damage to young black students who were made to feel inferior to whites. In this landmark case, the Court overturned *Plessy* and its "separate but equal doctrine." In a manner reminiscent of John Marshall, Warren was able to get a unanimous ruling, even though some justices resisted. In his opinion, Warren wrote that "separate educational facilities are inherently unequal." And he agreed with the recent research that showed segregation made black children feel inferior. But enforcement was the difficult part. In ***Brown II*** **(1955)**, the Court said that the states must end school segregation "in all deliberate speed." Because of this vague deadline, many Southern states resisted segregating the public schools for decades.

Mapp v. Ohio **(1961):** Police got a tip that Dollree Mapp was harboring a bombing suspect and entered her house waving a fake search warrant. They did not find the bomber, but instead discovered child pornography and arrested her for that. The case went to the Supreme Court, where Mapp claimed that her 4th Amendment right against a warrantless search and seizure had been violated. The Court agreed. In this case the Warren Court established the *exclusionary rule*, wherein if police find evidence without a warrant or beyond the permissible scope of the warrant, then it will not be allowed into court. This case also exemplifies the Warren Court's efforts to *selectively incorporate* provisions of the Bill of Rights as applying to the states through the 14th Amendment.

Engel v. Vitale **(1962):** In a major victory for advocates of the separation of church and state, the Warren Court ruled that public school teachers could not lead students in prayer because it violated the establishment clause of the 1st Amendment.

Heart of Atlanta v. US **(1964):** The Heart of Atlanta was a 216-room hotel in Atlanta, Georgia, which only allowed white patrons. The owner of the hotel, Moreton Rolleston, refused to comply with a provision of the Civil Rights Act of 1964 that banned racial discrimination in public facilities. Rolleston argued that in no way did his hotel conduct interstate commerce and that the law was an overreach of Congress's commerce clause powers. Instead of relying on the equal protection clause, the Court upheld the Civil Rights Act based on the commerce clause citing that 75 percent of the hotel's clients were from out-of-state.

Griswold v. Connecticut (1965): Estelle Griswold, the executive director of Planned Parenthood in Connecticut, opened up a birth control clinic in New Haven, violating an 1879 state law banning contraceptives. In a controversial opinion, Justice William O. Douglas overturned the state law for violating married couple's "*right of privacy,*" a right not explicitly stated in the Constitution.

Douglas argued that several provisions of the Bill of Rights combine to form a "penumbra" or zone of privacy. These provisions include the 1st Amendment right of association, the 3rd Amendment ban against quartering military troops in private homes, the 4th Amendment safeguarding against unreasonable search and seizure, the 5th Amendment protection against self-incrimination, and the 9th Amendment assurance that all unenumerated rights are reserved to the people. In a famous dissent, Hugo Black warned the Warren Court not to be too activistic. The way to overturn bad laws is through the democratic process, not by the Court creating new rights.

Miranda v. Arizona (1966): Ernesto Miranda was arrested for kidnapping, raping, and robbing an 18-year-old mentally handicapped girl, based on a tip by the victim's brother. After two hours of interrogation, Miranda signed a statement confessing to the crime and stating that the confession had not been coerced. In the opinion written by Warren, the Court ruled that all police interrogations are coercive in nature if a suspect is not informed of his 5th Amendment right against self-incrimination and 6th Amendment right to an attorney. As a result of this ruling, police are now required to read a suspect the *Miranda Warning* before they are interrogated.

Loving v. Virginia (1967): In 1958, Mildred Jeter, a black woman, married Richard Loving, a white man, in violation of Virginia's law forbidding interracial marriage. Based on an anonymous tip, the police raided their home at night and found them in bed together, where they were arrested. In his opinion, Chief Justice Warren wrote that all laws banning interracial marriage are racist in nature and that they are unconstitutional because they violate the due process and equal protection clause of the 14th amendment.

Brandenburg v. Ohio (1969): Clarence Brandenburg, a Ku Klux Klan leader, was filmed by a local television station making a racist speech against blacks and Jews while holding a gun. He was arrested for advocating violence. The majority sided with Brandenburg and declared that his free speech rights had been violated. Modifying the "clear and present danger" doctrine established in *Schenck*, the Court now said that only speech that directly leads to "imminent lawless action" can be limited. Brandenburg's speech was racist and reprehensible, but it did not place anybody in immediate danger. This case greatly expanded free speech associated with political activism.

Lemon v. Kurtzman (1971): This case was typical of the new Court led by Chief Justice Warren E. Berger, which did not extend the liberties established under the Warren Court, but instead tried to organize and rationalize the underlying principles of the previous Court. In this case, the Court overturned a Pennsylvania law that used public funds to help support religious schools. The Pennsylvania legislature tried to comply with the establishment clause by proscribing that the funds only be used to pay for the salaries of teachers who taught secular material, for secular textbooks, and for secular classroom materials.

The Court's decision, written by Berger, overturned the law and established the "Lemon Test": government action must have a secular purpose, its primary effect must not advance or inhibit religion, and it must not "excessively entangle" government with religion. The vagueness of the Lemon Test, and its inconsistent application, however, has not helped the Court establish a coherent doctrine with regard to the establishment clause.

New York Times v. US **(1971):** During the Vietnam War, *The New York Times* published a classified defense department document that analyzed the government's decision-making process over the history of the war. President Richard Nixon sought an immediate injunction to stop further publication of the so-called "Pentagon Papers" on his executive authority to maintain secret information.

The Court ruled against Nixon, refusing to violate the long held prohibition of *prior restraint*: government cannot censor material *before* it is published, but publishers can be held accountable to libel and slander suits after publication. In this case, the Court established a rule for prior restraint. The government "caries a heavy burden" when requesting that the courts violate prior restraint in order to censor material. It must demonstrate exceptionally strong justifications, perhaps a threat to national security. In the case of the Pentagon Papers, the Court concluded that the information was merely embarrassing and not an actual threat to national security.

Roe v. Wade **(1973):** In a 7-2 ruling, the newly seated associate justice Harry Blackmun wrote the ruling striking down a Texas law outlawing abortion. He ruled that during the first two trimesters the mother's right to privacy (established in *Griswold*) outweighed the fetus's 5th Amendment right to life. But states can limit abortions in the third trimester when the fetus can live outside the mother's body and so can claim a right to life. This ruling continued the Warren Court's efforts to protect reproductive privacy and prevent the government from imposing a moral code. But critics say this is an example of liberal judicial activism. The Court should have allowed the abortion issue to work its way out in the elected branches of government.

If Roe were ever overturned, then each state would be allowed to craft its own abortion laws. In the 1990s, after Republican presidents were able to appoint several conservative justices, creating a majority block, the Court heard another case dealing with abortion, ***Casey v. Planned Parenthood*** **(1992).** Many conservatives anticipated that the Court would finally overturn Roe, but they were disappointed. Sandra Day O'Connor, the first female Supreme Court Justice (who was appointed by Ronald Reagan), wrote the opinion. Citing *stare decisis* (respect for past rulings), O'Connor refused to overturn *Roe*, saying that *Roe* had been accepted by society. Moreover, she argued, if some states were allowed to ban abortion it would place too high a burden on a woman to travel to another state to get an abortion.

US v. Nixon **(1974):** During an investigation of the Watergate scandal, it was discovered that President Richard Nixon recorded his Oval Office conversations. The special prosecutor demanded that Nixon release the tapes but he refused, citing *executive privilege*: the right of the president to maintain private council. The Supreme Court, however, ruled that President Nixon had to release his tapes. The Court acknowledged the principle of executive privilege was valid, but in criminal investigations the president must provide all information requested. Chief Justice Warren Burger, a Nixon appointee, wrote that no man is above the law, not even the president. Likewise, in ***Clinton v. Jones*** **(1997),** the Court ruled that no president is above the law and ordered President Bill Clinton to testify in a sexual harassment case during his presidency—which eventually led to his impeachment.

Regents of UC v. Bakke **(1978):** Allan Bakke, a former honor student and medic in the US Marines, was rejected admission to the medical school at UC Davis even though his grades and test scores were higher than the minority students who were accepted under the university's affirmative action program. UC Davis used a quota system that set aside sixteen of one hundred seats for minority students. In a 5-4 decision, the Court sided with Bakke by declaring that quotas were an unconstitutional violation of the equal protection clause. But in Lewis Powell's concurring opinion, he said that colleges have a compelling justification for promoting diversity—it is good for students to be exposed to other students of different backgrounds and it is beneficial for the country to get minorities into the professions. As a result of his comments, colleges across the country catered their affirmative action programs to fit the Powell doctrine.

In another landmark affirmative action case, *Grutter v. Bollinger* **(2003),** the Court essentially upheld the Powell doctrine. They affirmed that all quotas and numerical systems giving an advantage to one racial group violated the equal protection clause. But colleges do have a compelling justification to promote diversity. This can be achieved by assessing students on a case-by-case basis and by adopting a "holistic" admission policy.

US v. Lopez **(1995):** This case exemplifies the conservative Rehnquist Court's attempt to restore some power back to the state, sometimes called the "New Federalism." Responding to a wave of school shootings, in 1990 Congress passed a law making it a crime to carry a firearm within 1,000 feet of a school. In the 5-4 decision, Chief Justice William Rehnquist said that this type of law may be a good thing, but it is up to the states, not the national government, to do it. In no way do local gun laws fall under the national government's interstate commerce authority, but instead they do fall under the state's traditional "police powers." This was the first time since the early years of the New Deal that the Supreme Court ruled a congressional act unconstitutional by denying a broad interpretation of the commerce clause.

Lawrence v. Texas **(2003):** In 1986, the Court upheld state sodomy laws in *Hardwick v. Bowers* **(1986),** ruling that it had always been a state prerogative to uphold morals under their police powers. Now, in *Lawrence v. Texas*, the Court ruled that sodomy laws have no rational purpose except to hold up a morality that disapproved of homosexuality. They concluded that the majority may not use the power of the state to impose its morality on a minority through the criminal code. In dissent, Scalia said that by this standard of enforcing morality, all sorts of current laws fall under danger of attack: same sex marriage, bigamy, incest, prostitution, masturbation, adultery, bestiality, and obscenity.

In one regard, Scalia's prediction came true. In *Obergefell v. Hodges* **(2015),** the Supreme Court ruled that state laws and state constitutional amendments (even if approved by the people) that defined marriage as between one man and one woman violates the US Constitution. The court acknowledged that marriage certificates have always been granted by state governments, but denying gays the ability to get married violates their right to privacy and their right to the equal protection of the laws.

DC v. Heller **(2008):** In *DC v. Heller*, the Supreme Court overturned a District of Columbia law that banned handguns as a violation of the 2nd Amendment. In the 5-4 decision, Justice Antonin Scalia wrote that the 2nd Amendment protects an individual's right to possess firearms unconnected with service in a militia. Scalia said that when the 2nd Amendment states "the right of the people," it is referring to the same people cited in the 1st Amendment, and therefore it was an individual right, not a collective right as Justice John Paul Stevens asserted in his dissent. Two years later, in *McDonald v. Chicago,* the Court selectively incorporated the individual "right to bear arms" as applying to the states. For most of American history, the Supreme Court did not think the Bill of Rights applied to the states. But since *Gitlow v. New York* (1925), when the Court ruled that the 1st Amendment right of freedom of speech must also be protected by state governments, the Supreme Court had been *selectively incorporating* through the 14th Amendment provisions of the Bill of Rights as applying not only to the federal government but also to state and local governments. With *McDonald v. Chicago,* the Court finally incorporated the 2nd Amendment as applying to the state and local governments. This is the last major provision of the Bill of Rights that has been incorporated.

Boumediene v. Bush (2008): The Supreme Court held that enemy combatants held overseas—at Guantánamo Bay—enjoy exactly the same habeas corpus rights as US citizens under article 1, section 9. But the majority said the enemy combatants would not be afforded any other constitutional rights. This Court ruling, along with *Hamdan* and *Rasul*, established the federal government's policy related to holding and trying terrorists. In *Hamdan v. Rumsfeld* (2006), the Court ruled that the president does not have the authority to establish a separate set of military courts in order to try non-citizen combatants, as the Bush Administration had started to do. And in *Rasul v. Bush* (2004), the Supreme Court determined the federal courts could hear cases in which foreign enemy combatants challenge their detention.

Citizens United v. FEC (2010): In 2002, Congress passed the Bipartisan Campaign Reform Act, often called the McCain-Feingold Act. One provision of the law prohibited corporations or unions from paying for "electioneering" campaign commercials thirty days before a primary or sixty days prior to a general election. In 2008, a conservative non-profit group, called Citizens United, planned on running a commercial publicizing its upcoming film to be shown on DirecTV. The film was called *Hillary: the Movie*, a documentary critical of Hillary Clinton, who was running for president. The Federal Elections Commission (FEC), however, stopped the commercial on the grounds that it violated the McCain-Feingold Act.

In a 5-4 decision, the Supreme Court voided the provision of McCain-Feingold, ruling that the law violated the 1st Amendment rights of Citizens United. The 1st Amendment states that "Congress shall make no law . . . abridging the freedom of speech . . . or the right of the people to peaceably assemble, and to petition the government." The Court ruled that individuals clearly have the right to form groups in order to make political speeches. In response to this, Democrats have suggested that a constitutional amendment be ratified that prohibits corporations and unions from making political commercials.

National Federation of Independent Business v. Sebelius (2012): In 2005, when George W. Bush nominated John Roberts to be the next Chief Justice, he said that he was seeking a justice that wouldn't slide to the left, as many other justices like Harry Blackman or David Souter had done. Thinking Roberts was a solid conservative, and knowing that he approved of a narrow interpretation of the commerce clause, most Supreme Court observers were shocked when Roberts refused to overturn the Affordable Care Act's federal mandate to buy health insurance.

Chief Justice Roberts, however, remained true to his conservative convictions, just not in a way that many conservatives had expected. Roberts always opposed activist Courts and believed that in most cases the Court should defer to the political branches. The people elected a Democratic president and a Democratic Congress, which passed the Affordable Care Act. Roberts believed unless the Constitution was clearly violated, the Court should respect the democratic process. Also, he remained true to his conservative principles by keeping a narrow interpretation of the commerce clause. In *Sebelius*, Roberts upheld the ACA not under the commerce clause but under the federal government's tax authority, which is clearly granted in Article I, Section 8.

NOTES

To find the full text of Supreme Court opinions go to the Supreme Court website (www.supreme court.gov) or go to Findlaw.com, United States Supreme Court Cases (caselaw.findlaw.com/court/us-supreme-court)

Erwin Chemerinsky. *Constitutional Law: Principles and Policies*. 3rd edition. New York: Aspen Publishers, 2006.

Adam Freedman. *The Naked Constitution: What the Founders Said and Why it Still Matters*. New York: Broadside Books, 2012.

Alfred H. Kelly et al. The American Constitution: Its Origins and Developments. Vol I & II. New York: Norton & Co., 1991.

Michael Les Benedict. *The Blessings of Liberty: A Concise History of the Supreme Court*. Boston: Wadsworth, 2006.

Donald E. Lively. *Landmark Supreme Court Cases: A Reference Guide*. Connecticut: Greenwood Press, 1999.

APPENDIX C

Declaration of Independence (1776)

When in the Course of human events, it becomes necessary for one people to dissolve the political bands which have connected them with another, and to assume among the powers of the earth, the separate and equal station to which the Laws of Nature and of Nature's God entitle them, a decent respect to the opinions of mankind requires that they should declare the causes which impel them to the separation.

We hold these truths to be self-evident, that all men are created equal, that they are endowed by their Creator with certain unalienable Rights, that among these are Life, Liberty and the pursuit of Happiness.—That to secure these rights, Governments are instituted among Men, deriving their just powers from the consent of the governed,—That whenever any Form of Government becomes destructive of these ends, it is the Right of the People to alter or to abolish it, and to institute new Government, laying its foundation on such principles and organizing its powers in such form, as to them shall seem most likely to effect their Safety and Happiness. Prudence, indeed, will dictate that Governments long established should not be changed for light and transient causes; and accordingly all experience hath shewn, that mankind are more disposed to suffer, while evils are sufferable, than to right themselves by abolishing the forms to which they are accustomed. But when a long train of abuses and usurpations, pursuing invariably the same Object evinces a design to reduce them under absolute Despotism, it is their right, it is their duty, to throw off such Government, and to provide new Guards for their future security.—Such has been the patient sufferance of these Colonies; and such is now the necessity which constrains them to alter their former Systems of Government. The history of the present King of Great Britain is a history of repeated injuries and usurpations, all having in direct object the establishment of an absolute Tyranny over these States. To prove this, let Facts be submitted to a candid world.

He has refused his Assent to Laws, the most wholesome and necessary for the public good.

He has forbidden his Governors to pass Laws of immediate and pressing importance, unless suspended in their operation till his Assent should be obtained; and when so suspended, he has utterly neglected to attend to them.

He has refused to pass other Laws for the accommodation of large districts of people, unless those people would relinquish the right of Representation in the Legislature, a right inestimable to them and formidable to tyrants only.

He has called together legislative bodies at places unusual, uncomfortable, and distant from the depository of their public Records, for the sole purpose of fatiguing them into compliance with his measures.

He has dissolved Representative Houses repeatedly, for opposing with manly firmness his invasions on the rights of the people.

He has refused for a long time, after such dissolutions, to cause others to be elected; whereby the Legislative powers, incapable of Annihilation, have returned to the People at large for their exercise; the State remaining in the mean time exposed to all the dangers of invasion from without, and convulsions within.

He has endeavoured to prevent the population of these States; for that purpose obstructing the Laws for Naturalization of Foreigners; refusing to pass others to encourage their migrations hither, and raising the conditions of new Appropriations of Lands.

He has obstructed the Administration of Justice, by refusing his Assent to Laws for establishing Judiciary powers.

He has made Judges dependent on his Will alone, for the tenure of their offices, and the amount and payment of their salaries.

He has erected a multitude of New Offices, and sent hither swarms of Officers to harrass our people, and eat out their substance.

He has kept among us, in times of peace, Standing Armies without the Consent of our legislatures.

He has affected to render the Military independent of and superior to the Civil power.

He has combined with others to subject us to a jurisdiction foreign to our constitution, and unacknowledged by our laws; giving his Assent to their Acts of pretended Legislation:

For Quartering large bodies of armed troops among us:

For protecting them, by a mock Trial, from punishment for any Murders which they should commit on the Inhabitants of these States:

For cutting off our Trade with all parts of the world:

For imposing Taxes on us without our Consent:

For depriving us in many cases, of the benefits of Trial by Jury:

For transporting us beyond Seas to be tried for pretended offences

For abolishing the free System of English Laws in a neighbouring Province, establishing therein an Arbitrary government, and enlarging its Boundaries so as to render it at once an example and fit instrument for introducing the same absolute rule into these Colonies:

For taking away our Charters, abolishing our most valuable Laws, and altering fundamentally the Forms of our Governments:

For suspending our own Legislatures, and declaring themselves invested with power to legislate for us in all cases whatsoever.

He has abdicated Government here, by declaring us out of his Protection and waging War against us.

He has plundered our seas, ravaged our Coasts, burnt our towns, and destroyed the lives of our people.

He is at this time transporting large Armies of foreign Mercenaries to compleat the works of death, desolation and tyranny, already begun with circumstances of Cruelty & perfidy scarcely paralleled in the most barbarous ages, and totally unworthy the Head of a civilized nation.

He has constrained our fellow Citizens taken Captive on the high Seas to bear Arms against their Country, to become the executioners of their friends and Brethren, or to fall themselves by their Hands.

He has excited domestic insurrections amongst us, and has endeavoured to bring on the inhabitants of our frontiers, the merciless Indian Savages, whose known rule of warfare, is an undistinguished destruction of all ages, sexes and conditions.

In every stage of these Oppressions We have Petitioned for Redress in the most humble terms: Our repeated Petitions have been answered only by repeated injury. A Prince whose character is thus marked by every act which may define a Tyrant, is unfit to be the ruler of a free people.

Nor have We been wanting in attentions to our Brittish brethren. We have warned them from time to time of attempts by their legislature to extend an unwarrantable jurisdiction over us. We have reminded them of the circumstances of our emigration and settlement here. We have appealed to their native justice and magnanimity, and we have conjured them by the ties of our common kindred to disavow these usurpations, which, would inevitably interrupt our connections and correspondence. They too have been deaf to the voice of justice and of consanguinity. We must, therefore, acquiesce in the necessity, which denounces our Separation, and hold them, as we hold the rest of mankind, Enemies in War, in Peace Friends.

We, therefore, the Representatives of the united States of America, in General Congress, Assembled, appealing to the Supreme Judge of the world for the rectitude of our intentions, do, in the Name, and by Authority of the good People of these Colonies, solemnly publish and declare, That these United Colonies are, and of Right ought to be Free and Independent States; that they are Absolved from all Allegiance to the British Crown, and that all political connection between them and the State of Great Britain, is and ought to be totally dissolved; and that as Free and Independent States, they have full Power to levy War, conclude Peace, contract Alliances, establish Commerce, and to do all other Acts and Things which Independent States may of right do. And for the support of this Declaration, with a firm reliance on the protection of divine Providence, we mutually pledge to each other our Lives, our Fortunes and our sacred Honor.

APPENDIX D

The Constitution of the United States of America

Preamble

We the People of the United States, in Order to form a more perfect Union, establish Justice, insure domestic Tranquility, provide for the common defence, promote the general Welfare, and secure the Blessings of Liberty to ourselves and our Posterity, do ordain and establish this Constitution for the United States of America.

Article I

SECTION. 1. All legislative Powers herein granted shall be vested in a Congress of the United States, which shall consist of a Senate and House of Representatives.

SECTION. 2. The House of Representatives shall be composed of Members chosen every second Year by the People of the several States, and the Electors in each State shall have the Qualifications requisite for Electors of the most numerous Branch of the State Legislature.

No Person shall be a Representative who shall not have attained to the Age of twenty five Years, and been seven Years a Citizen of the United States, and who shall not, when elected, be an Inhabitant of that State in which he shall be chosen.

Representatives and direct Taxes shall be apportioned among the several States which may be included within this Union, according to their respective Numbers, which shall be determined by adding to the whole Number of free Persons, including those bound to Service for a Term of Years, and excluding Indians not taxed, three fifths of all other Persons. The actual Enumeration shall be made within three Years after the first Meeting of the Congress of the United States, and within every subsequent Term of ten Years, in such Manner as they shall by Law direct. The number of Representatives shall not exceed one for every thirty Thousand, but each State shall have at Least one Representative; and until such enumeration shall be made, the State of New Hampshire shall be entitled to chuse three, Massachusetts eight, Rhode-Island and Providence Plantations one, Connecticut five, New-York six, New Jersey four, Pennsylvania eight, Delaware one, Maryland six, Virginia ten, North Carolina five, South Carolina five, and Georgia three.

When vacancies happen in the Representation from any State, the Executive Authority thereof shall issue Writs of Election to fill such Vacancies.

The House of Representatives shall chuse their Speaker and other Officers; and shall have the sole Power of Impeachment.

SECTION. 3. The Senate of the United States shall be composed of two Senators from each State, *chosen by the Legislature thereof*, for six Years; and each Senator shall have one Vote.

Immediately after they shall be assembled in Consequence of the first Election, they shall be divided as equally as may be into three Classes. The Seats of the Senators of the first Class shall be vacated at the Expiration of the second Year, of the second Class at the Expiration of the fourth Year, and of the third Class at the Expiration of the sixth Year, so that one third may be chosen every second Year; *and if Vacancies happen by Resignation, or otherwise, during the Recess of the Legislature of any State, the Executive thereof may make temporary Appointments until the next Meeting of the Legislature, which shall then fill such Vacancies.*

No Person shall be a Senator who shall not have attained to the Age of thirty Years, and been nine Years a Citizen of the United States, and who shall not, when elected, be an Inhabitant of that State for which he shall be chosen.

The Vice President of the United States shall be President of the Senate, but shall have no Vote, unless they be equally divided.

The Senate shall chuse their other Officers, and also a President pro tempore, in the Absence of the Vice President, or when he shall exercise the Office of President of the United States.

The Senate shall have the sole Power to try all Impeachments. When sitting for that Purpose, they shall be on Oath or Affirmation. When the President of the United States is tried, the Chief Justice shall preside: And no Person shall be convicted without the Concurrence of two thirds of the Members present.

Judgment in Cases of Impeachment shall not extend further than to removal from Office, and disqualification to hold and enjoy any Office of honor, Trust or Profit under the United States: but the Party convicted shall nevertheless be liable and subject to Indictment, Trial, Judgment and Punishment, according to Law.

SECTION. 4. The Times, Places and Manner of holding Elections for Senators and Representatives, shall be prescribed in each State by the Legislature thereof; but the Congress may at any time by Law make or alter such Regulations, except as to the Places of chusing Senators.

The Congress shall assemble at least once in every Year, and such Meeting shall be on the first Monday in December, unless they shall by Law appoint a different Day.

SECTION. 5. Each House shall be the Judge of the Elections, Returns and Qualifications of its own Members, and a Majority of each shall constitute a Quorum to do Business; but a smaller Number may adjourn from day to day, and may be authorized to compel the Attendance of absent Members, in such Manner, and under such Penalties as each House may provide.

Each House may determine the Rules of its Proceedings, punish its Members for disorderly Behaviour, and, with the Concurrence of two thirds, expel a Member.

Each House shall keep a Journal of its Proceedings, and from time to time publish the same, excepting such Parts as may in their Judgment require Secrecy; and the Yeas and Nays of the Members of either House on any question shall, at the Desire of one fifth of those Present, be entered on the Journal.

Neither House, during the Session of Congress, shall, without the Consent of the other, adjourn for more than three days, nor to any other Place than that in which the two Houses shall be sitting.

SECTION. 6. The Senators and Representatives shall receive a Compensation for their Services, to be ascertained by Law, and paid out of the Treasury of the United States. They shall in all Cases, except Treason, Felony and Breach of the Peace, be privileged from Arrest during their Attendance at the Session of their respective Houses, and in going to and returning from the same; and for any Speech or Debate in either House, they shall not be questioned in any other Place.

No Senator or Representative shall, during the Time for which he was elected, be appointed to any civil Office under the Authority of the United States, which shall have been created, or the Emoluments whereof shall have been encreased during such time; and no Person holding any Office under the United States, shall be a Member of either House during his Continuance in Office.

SECTION. 7. All Bills for raising Revenue shall originate in the House of Representatives; but the Senate may propose or concur with Amendments as on other Bills.

Every Bill which shall have passed the House of Representatives and the Senate, shall, before it become a Law, be presented to the President of the United States; If he approve he shall sign it, but if not he shall return it, with his Objections to that House in which it shall have originated, who shall enter the Objections at large on their Journal, and proceed to reconsider it. If after such Reconsideration two thirds of that House shall agree to pass the Bill, it shall be sent, together with the Objections, to the other House, by which it shall likewise be reconsidered, and if approved by two thirds of that House, it shall become a Law. But in all such Cases the Votes of both Houses shall be determined by Yeas and Nays, and the Names of the Persons voting for and against the Bill shall be entered on the Journal of each House respectively. If any Bill shall not be returned by the President within ten Days (Sundays excepted) after it shall have been presented to him, the Same shall be a Law, in like Manner as if he had signed it, unless the Congress by their Adjournment prevent its Return, in which Case it shall not be a Law.

Every Order, Resolution, or Vote to which the Concurrence of the Senate and House of Representatives may be necessary (except on a question of Adjournment) shall be presented to the President of the United States; and before the Same shall take Effect, shall be approved by him, or being disapproved by him, shall be repassed by two thirds of the Senate and House of Representatives, according to the Rules and Limitations prescribed in the Case of a Bill.

SECTION. 8. The Congress shall have Power To lay and collect Taxes, Duties, Imposts and Excises, to pay the Debts and provide for the common Defence and general Welfare of the United States; but all Duties, Imposts and Excises shall be uniform throughout the United States;

To borrow Money on the credit of the United States;

To regulate Commerce with foreign Nations, and among the several States, and with the Indian Tribes;

To establish an uniform Rule of Naturalization, and uniform Laws on the subject of Bankruptcies throughout the United States;

To coin Money, regulate the Value thereof, and of foreign Coin, and fix the Standard of Weights and Measures;

To provide for the Punishment of counterfeiting the Securities and current Coin of the United States;

To establish Post Offices and post Roads;

To promote the Progress of Science and useful Arts, by securing for limited Times to Authors and Inventors the exclusive Right to their respective Writings and Discoveries;

To constitute Tribunals inferior to the supreme Court;

To define and punish Piracies and Felonies committed on the high Seas, and Offenses against the Law of Nations;

To declare War, grant Letters of Marque and Reprisal, and make Rules concerning Captures on Land and Water;

To raise and support Armies, but no Appropriation of Money to that Use shall be for a longer Term than two Years;

To provide and maintain a Navy; To make Rules for the Government and Regulation of the land and naval Forces;

To provide for calling forth the Militia to execute the Laws of the Union, suppress Insurrections and repel Invasions;

To provide for organizing, arming, and disciplining, the Militia, and for governing such Part of them as may be employed in the Service of the United States, reserving to the States respectively, the Appointment of the Officers, and the Authority of training the Militia according to the discipline prescribed by Congress;

To exercise exclusive Legislation in all Cases whatsoever, over such District (not exceeding ten Miles square) as may, by Cession of particular States, and the Acceptance of Congress, become the Seat of the Government of the United States, and to exercise like Authority over all Places purchased by the Consent of the Legislature of the State in which the Same shall be, for the Erection of Forts, Magazines, Arsenals, dock-Yards and other needful Buildings;-And

To make all Laws which shall be necessary and proper for carrying into Execution the foregoing Powers, and all other Powers vested by this Constitution in the Government of the United States, or in any Department or Officer thereof.

SECTION. 9. The Migration or Importation of such Persons as any of the States now existing shall think proper to admit, shall not be prohibited by the Congress prior to the Year one thousand eight hundred and eight, but a Tax or duty may be imposed on such Importation, not exceeding ten dollars for each Person.

The Privilege of the Writ of Habeas Corpus shall not be suspended, unless when in Cases of Rebellion or Invasion the public Safety may require it.

No Bill of Attainder or ex post facto Law shall be passed.

No Capitation, or other direct, Tax shall be laid, *unless in Proportion to the Census or Enumeration herein before directed to be taken.*

No Tax or Duty shall be laid on Articles exported from any State.

No Preference shall be given by any Regulation of Commerce or Revenue to the Ports of one State over those of another: nor shall Vessels bound to, or from, one State, be obliged to enter, clear, or pay Duties in another.

No Money shall be drawn from the Treasury, but in Consequence of Appropriations made by Law; and a regular Statement and Account of the Receipts and Expenditures of all public Money shall be published from time to time.

No Title of Nobility shall be granted by the United States: And no Person holding any Office of Profit or Trust under them, shall, without the Consent of the Congress, accept of any present, Emolument, Office, or Title, of any kind whatever, from any King, Prince, or foreign State.

SECTION. 10. No State shall enter into any Treaty, Alliance, or Confederation; grant Letters of Marque and Reprisal; coin Money; emit Bills of Credit; make any Thing but gold and silver Coin a Tender in Payment of Debts; pass any Bill of Attainder, ex post facto Law, or Law impairing the Obligation of Contracts, or grant any Title of Nobility.

No State shall, without the Consent of the Congress, lay any Imposts or Duties on Imports or Exports, except what may be absolutely necessary for executing it's inspection Laws: and the net Produce of all Duties and Imposts, laid by any State on Imports or Exports, shall be for the Use of the Treasury of the United States; and all such Laws shall be subject to the Revision and Controul of the Congress.

No State shall, without the Consent of Congress, lay any Duty of Tonnage, keep Troops, or Ships of War in time of Peace, enter into any Agreement or Compact with another State, or with a foreign Power, or engage in War, unless actually invaded, or in such imminent Danger as will not admit of delay.

Article II

SECTION. 1. The executive Power shall be vested in a President of the United States of America. He shall hold his Office during the Term of four Years, and, together with the Vice President, chosen for the same Term, be elected, as follows:

Each State shall appoint, in such Manner as the Legislature thereof may direct, a Number of Electors, equal to the whole Number of Senators and Representatives to which the State may be entitled in the Congress: but no Senator or Representative, or Person holding an Office of Trust or Profit under the United States, shall be appointed an Elector.

The Electors shall meet in their respective States, and vote by Ballot for two Persons, of whom one at least shall not be an Inhabitant of the same State with themselves. And they shall make a List of all the Persons voted for, and of the Number of Votes for each; which List they shall sign and certify, and transmit sealed to the Seat of the Government of the United States, directed to the President of the Senate. The President of the Senate shall, in the Presence of the Senate and House of Representatives, open all the Certificates, and the Votes shall then be counted. The Person having the greatest Number of Votes shall be the President, if such Number be a Majority of the whole Number of Electors appointed; and if there be more than one who have such Majority, and have an equal Number of Votes, then the House of Representatives shall immediately chuse by Ballot one of them for President; and if no Person have a Majority, then from the five highest on the List the said House shall in like Manner chuse the President. But in chusing the President, the Votes shall be taken by States, the Representation from each State having one Vote; A quorum for this Purpose shall consist of a Member or Members from two thirds of the States, and a Majority of all the States shall be necessary to a Choice. In every Case, after the Choice of the President, the Person having the greatest Number of Votes of the Electors shall be the Vice President. But if there should remain two or more who have equal Votes, the Senate shall chuse from them by Ballot the Vice President.

The Congress may determine the Time of chusing the Electors, and the Day on which they shall give their Votes; which Day shall be the same throughout the United States.

No Person except a natural born Citizen, or a Citizen of the United States, at the time of the Adoption of this Constitution, shall be eligible to the Office of President; neither shall any person be eligible to that Office who shall not have attained to the Age of thirty five Years, and been fourteen Years a Resident within the United States.

In Case of the Removal of the President from Office, or of his Death, Resignation, or Inability to discharge the Powers and Duties of the said Office, the Same shall devolve on the Vice President, and the Congress may by Law provide for the Case of Removal, Death, Resignation or Inability, both of the President and Vice President, declaring what Officer shall then act as President, and such Officer shall act accordingly, until the Disability be removed, or a President shall be elected.

The President shall, at stated Times, receive for his Services, a Compensation, which shall neither be increased nor diminished during the Period for which he shall have been elected, and he shall not receive within that Period any other Emolument from the United States, or any of them.

Before he enter on the Execution of his Office, he shall take the following Oath or Affirmation:—"I do solemnly swear (or affirm) that I will faithfully execute the Office of President of the United States, and will to the best of my Ability, preserve, protect and defend the Constitution of the United States."

SECTION. 2. The President shall be Commander in Chief of the Army and Navy of the United States, and of the Militia of the several States, when called into the actual Service of the United States; he may require the Opinion, in writing, of the principal Officer in each of the executive Departments, upon any Subject relating to the Duties of their respective Offices, and he shall have Power to grant Reprieves and Pardons for Offenses against the United States, except in Cases of Impeachment.

He shall have Power, by and with the Advice and Consent of the Senate, to make Treaties, provided two thirds of the Senators present concur; and he shall nominate, and by and with the Advice and Consent of the Senate, shall appoint Ambassadors, other public Ministers and Consuls, Judges of the supreme Court, and all other Officers of the United States, whose Appointments are not herein otherwise provided for, and which shall be established by Law: but the Congress may by Law vest the Appointment of such inferior Officers, as they think proper, in the President alone, in the Courts of Law, or in the Heads of Departments.

The President shall have Power to fill up all Vacancies that may happen during the Recess of the Senate, by granting Commissions which shall expire at the End of their next Session.

SECTION. 3. He shall from time to time give to the Congress Information of the State of the Union, and recommend to their Consideration such Measures as he shall judge necessary and expedient; he may, on extraordinary Occasions, convene both Houses, or either of them, and in Case of Disagreement between them, with Respect to the Time of Adjournment, he may adjourn them to such Time as he shall think proper; he shall receive Ambassadors and other public Ministers; he shall take Care that the Laws be faithfully executed, and shall Commission all the Officers of the United States.

SECTION. 4. The President, Vice President and all civil Officers of the United States, shall be removed from Office on Impeachment for, and Conviction of, Treason, Bribery, or other high Crimes and Misdemeanors.

Article III

SECTION. 1. The judicial Power of the United States, shall be vested in one supreme Court, and in such inferior Courts as the Congress may from time to time ordain and establish. The Judges, both of the supreme and inferior Courts, shall hold their Offices during good Behaviour, and shall, at stated Times, receive for their Services, a Compensation, which shall not be diminished during their Continuance in Office.

SECTION. 2. The judicial Power shall extend to all Cases, in Law and Equity, arising under this Constitution, the Laws of the United States, and Treaties made, or which shall be made, under their Authority;—to all Cases affecting Ambassadors, other public Ministers and Consuls;—to all Cases of admiralty and maritime Jurisdiction;—to Controversies to which the United States shall be a Party;—to Controversies between two or more States;—*between a State and Citizens of another State*;—between Citizens of different States;—between Citizens of the same State claiming Lands under Grants of different States, *and between a State, or the Citizens thereof, and foreign States, Citizens or Subjects.*

In all Cases affecting Ambassadors, other public Ministers and Consuls, and those in which a State shall be Party, the supreme Court shall have original Jurisdiction. In all the other Cases before mentioned, the supreme Court shall have appellate Jurisdiction, both as to Law and Fact, with such Exceptions, and under such Regulations as the Congress shall make.

The Trial of all Crimes, except in Cases of Impeachment; shall be by Jury; and such Trial shall be held in the State where the said Crimes shall have been committed; but when not committed within any State, the Trial shall be at such Place or Places as the Congress may by Law have directed.

SECTION. 3. Treason against the United States, shall consist only in levying War against them, or in adhering to their Enemies, giving them Aid and Comfort. No Person shall be convicted of Treason unless on the Testimony of two Witnesses to the same overt Act, or on Confession in open Court.

The Congress shall have Power to declare the Punishment of Treason, but no Attainder of Treason shall work Corruption of Blood, or Forfeiture except during the Life of the Person attainted.

Article IV

SECTION. 1. Full Faith and Credit shall be given in each State to the public Acts, Records, and judicial Proceedings of every other State. And the Congress may by general Laws prescribe the Manner in which such Acts, Records and Proceedings shall be proved, and the Effect thereof.

SECTION. 2. The Citizens of each State shall be entitled to all Privileges and Immunities of Citizens in the several States.

A Person charged in any State with Treason, Felony, or other Crime, who shall flee from Justice, and be found in another State, shall on Demand of the executive Authority of the State from which he fled, be delivered up, to be removed to the State having Jurisdiction of the Crime.

No Person held to Service or Labour in one State, under the Laws thereof, escaping into another, shall, in Consequence of any Law or Regulation therein, be discharged from such Service or Labour, but shall be delivered up on Claim of the Party to whom such Service or Labour may be due.

SECTION. 3. New States may be admitted by the Congress into this Union; but no new State shall be formed or erected within the Jurisdiction of any other State; nor any State be formed by the Junction of two or more States, or Parts of States, without the Consent of the Legislatures of the States concerned as well as of the Congress.

The Congress shall have Power to dispose of and make all needful Rules and Regulations respecting the Territory or other Property belonging to the United States; and nothing in this Constitution shall be so construed as to Prejudice any Claims of the United States, or of any particular State.

SECTION. 4. The United States shall guarantee to every State in this Union a Republican Form of Government, and shall protect each of them against Invasion; and on Application of the Legislature, or of the Executive (when the Legislature cannot be convened) against domestic Violence.

Article V

The Congress, whenever two thirds of both Houses shall deem it necessary, shall propose Amendments to this Constitution, or, on the Application of the Legislatures of two thirds of the several States, shall call a Convention for proposing Amendments, which, in either Case, shall be valid to all Intents and Purposes, as Part of this Constitution, when ratified by the Legislatures of three fourths of the several States, or by Conventions in three fourths thereof, as the one or the other Mode of Ratification may be proposed by the Congress; Provided that no Amendment which may be made prior to the Year One thousand eight hundred and eight shall in any Manner affect the first and fourth Clauses in the

Ninth Section of the first Article; and that no State, without its Consent, shall be deprived of its equal Suffrage in the Senate.

Article VI

All Debts contracted and Engagements entered into, before the Adoption of this Constitution, shall be as valid against the United States under this Constitution, as under the Confederation.

This Constitution, and the Laws of the United States which shall be made in Pursuance thereof; and all Treaties made, or which shall be made, under the Authority of the United States, shall be the supreme Law of the Land; and the Judges in every State shall be bound thereby, any Thing in the Constitution or Laws of any State to the Contrary notwithstanding.

The Senators and Representatives before mentioned, and the Members of the several State Legislatures, and all executive and judicial Officers, both of the United States and of the several States, shall be bound by Oath or Affirmation, to support this Constitution; but no religious Test shall ever be required as a Qualification to any Office or public Trust under the United States.

Article VII

The Ratification of the Conventions of nine States, shall be sufficient for the Establishment of this Constitution between the States so ratifying the Same.

Amendment I

Congress shall make no law respecting an establishment of religion, or prohibiting the free exercise thereof; or abridging the freedom of speech, or of the press; or the right of the people peaceably to assemble, and to petition the Government for a redress of grievances.

Amendment II

A well-regulated Militia, being necessary to the security of a free State, the right of the people to keep and bear Arms, shall not be infringed.

Amendment III

No Soldier shall, in time of peace be quartered in any house, without the consent of the Owner, nor in time of war, but in a manner to be prescribed by law.

Amendment IV

The right of the people to be secure in their persons, houses, papers, and effects, against unreasonable searches and seizures, shall not be violated, and no Warrants shall issue, but upon probable cause, supported by Oath or affirmation, and particularly describing the place to be searched, and the persons or things to be seized.

Amendment V

No person shall be held to answer for a capital, or otherwise infamous crime, unless on a presentment or indictment of a Grand Jury, except in cases arising in the land or naval forces, or in the Militia, when in actual service in time of War or public danger; nor shall any person be subject for the same offence to be twice put in jeopardy of life or limb; nor shall be compelled in any criminal case to be a witness against himself, nor be deprived of life, liberty, or property, without due process of law; nor shall private property be taken for public use, without just compensation.

Amendment VI

In all criminal prosecutions, the accused shall enjoy the right to a speedy and public trial, by an impartial jury of the State and district wherein the crime shall have been committed, which district shall have been previously ascertained by law, and to be informed of the nature and cause of the accusation; to be confronted with the witnesses against him; to have compulsory process for obtaining witnesses in his favor, and to have the Assistance of Counsel for his defence.

Amendment VII

In suits at common law, where the value in controversy shall exceed twenty dollars, the right of trial by jury shall be preserved, and no fact tried by a jury, shall be otherwise reexamined in any Court of the United States, than according to the rules of the common law.

Amendment VIII

Excessive bail shall not be required, nor excessive fines imposed, nor cruel and unusual punishments inflicted.

Amendment IX

The enumeration in the Constitution, of certain rights, shall not be construed to deny or disparage others retained by the people.

Amendment X

The powers not delegated to the United States by the Constitution, nor prohibited by it to the States, are reserved to the States respectively, or to the people.

Amendment XI

The Judicial power of the United States shall not be construed to extend to any suit in law or equity, commenced or prosecuted against one of the United States by Citizens of another State, or by Citizens or Subjects of any Foreign State.

Amendment XII

The Electors shall meet in their respective states and vote by ballot for President and Vice-President, one of whom, at least, shall not be an inhabitant of the same state with themselves; they shall name in their ballots the person voted for as President, and in distinct ballots the person voted for as Vice-President, and they shall make distinct lists of all persons voted for as President, and of all persons voted for as Vice-President, and of the number of votes for each, which lists they shall sign and certify, and transmit sealed to the seat of the government of the United States, directed to the President of the Senate;—The President of the Senate shall, in the presence of the Senate and House of Representatives, open all the certificates and the votes shall then be counted;—The person having the greatest number of votes for President, shall be the President, if such number be a majority of the whole number of Electors appointed; and if no person have such majority, then from the persons having the highest numbers not exceeding three on the list of those voted for as President, the House of Representatives shall choose immediately, by ballot, the President. But in choosing the President, the votes shall be taken by states, the representation from each state having one vote; a quorum for this purpose shall consist of a member or members from two-thirds of the states, and a majority of all the states shall be necessary to a choice. *And if the House of Representatives shall not choose a President whenever the right of choice shall devolve upon them, before the fourth day of March next following, then the Vice-President shall act as President, as in case of the death or other constitutional disability of the President.*—The person having the greatest number of votes as Vice-President, shall be the Vice-President, if such number be a majority of the whole number of Electors appointed, and if no person have a majority, then from the two highest numbers on the list, the Senate shall choose the Vice-President; a quorum for the purpose shall consist of two-thirds of the whole number of Senators, and a majority of the whole number shall be necessary to a choice. But no person constitutionally ineligible to the office of President shall be eligible to that of Vice-President of the United States.

Amendment XIII

SECTION. 1. Neither slavery nor involuntary servitude, except as a punishment for crime whereof the party shall have been duly convicted, shall exist within the United States, or any place subject to their jurisdiction.

SECTION. 2. Congress shall have power to enforce this article by appropriate legislation.

Amendment XIV

SECTION. 1. All persons born or naturalized in the United States, and subject to the jurisdiction thereof, are citizens of the United States and of the State wherein they reside. No State shall make or enforce any law which shall abridge the privileges or immunities of citizens of the United States; nor shall any State deprive any person of life, liberty, or property, without due process of law; nor deny to any person within its jurisdiction the equal protection of the laws.

SECTION. 2. Representatives shall be apportioned among the several States according to their respective numbers, counting the whole number of persons in each State, excluding Indians not taxed. But when the right to vote at any election for the choice of electors for President and Vice-President of the United States, Representatives in Congress, the Executive and Judicial officers of a State, or the members of the Legislature thereof, is denied to any of the male inhabitants of such State, being twenty-one years of age, and citizens of the United States, or in any way abridged, except for participation in rebellion, or other crime, the basis of representation therein shall be reduced in the proportion which the number of such male citizens shall bear to the whole number of male citizens twenty-one years of age in such State.

SECTION. 3. No person shall be a Senator or Representative in Congress, or elector of President and Vice-President, or hold any office, civil or military, under the United States, or under any State, who, having previously taken an oath, as a member of Congress, or as an officer of the United States, or as a member of any State legislature, or as an executive or judicial officer of any State, to support the Constitution of the United States, shall have engaged in insurrection or rebellion against the same, or given aid or comfort to the enemies thereof. But Congress may by a vote of two-thirds of each House, remove such disability.

SECTION. 4. The validity of the public debt of the United States, authorized by law, including debts incurred for payment of pensions and bounties for services in suppressing insurrection or rebellion, shall not be questioned. But neither the United States nor any State shall assume or pay any debt or obligation incurred in aid of insurrection or rebellion against the United States, or any claim for the loss or emancipation of any slave; but all such debts, obligations and claims shall be held illegal and void.

SECTION. 5. The Congress shall have the power to enforce, by appropriate legislation, the provisions of this article.

Amendment XV

SECTION. 1. The right of citizens of the United States to vote shall not be denied or abridged by the United States or by any State on account of race, color, or previous condition of servitude.

SECTION. 2. The Congress shall have the power to enforce this article by appropriate legislation.

Amendment XVI

The Congress shall have power to lay and collect taxes on incomes, from whatever source derived, without apportionment among the several States, and without regard to any census or enumeration.

Amendment XVII

The Senate of the United States shall be composed of two Senators from each State, elected by the people thereof, for six years; and each Senator shall have one vote. The electors in each State shall have the qualifications requisite for electors of the most numerous branch of the State legislatures.

When vacancies happen in the representation of any State in the Senate, the executive authority of such State shall issue writs of election to fill such vacancies: Provided, That the legislature of any State may empower the executive thereof to make temporary appointments until the people fill the vacancies by election as the legislature may direct.

This amendment shall not be so construed as to affect the election or term of any Senator chosen before it becomes valid as part of the Constitution.

Amendment XVIII

SECTION. 1. *After one year from the ratification of this article the manufacture, sale, or transportation of intoxicating liquors within, the importation thereof into, or the exportation thereof from the United States and all territory subject to the jurisdiction thereof for beverage purposes is hereby prohibited.*

SECTION. 2. *The Congress and the several States shall have concurrent power to enforce this article by appropriate legislation.*

SECTION. 3. *This article shall be inoperative unless it shall have been ratified as an amendment to the Constitution by the legislatures of the several States, as provided in the Constitution, within seven years from the date of the submission hereof to the States by the Congress.*

Amendment XIX

The right of citizens of the United States to vote shall not be denied or abridged by the United States or by any State on account of sex.

Congress shall have power to enforce this article by appropriate legislation.

Amendment XX

SECTION. 1. The terms of the President and the Vice President shall end at noon on the 20th day of January, and the terms of Senators and Representatives at noon on the 3d day of January, of the years in which such terms would have ended if this article had not been ratified; and the terms of their successors shall then begin.

SECTION. 2. The Congress shall assemble at least once in every year, and such meeting shall begin at noon on the 3d day of January, unless they shall by law appoint a different day.

SECTION. 3. If, at the time fixed for the beginning of the term of the President, the President elect shall have died, the Vice President elect shall become President. If a President shall not have been chosen before the time fixed for the beginning of his term, or if the President elect shall have failed to qualify, then the Vice President elect shall act as President until a President shall have qualified; and the Congress may by law provide for the case wherein neither a President elect nor a Vice President shall have qualified, declaring who shall then act as President, or the manner in which one who is to act shall be selected, and such person shall act accordingly until a President or Vice President shall have qualified.

SECTION. 4. The Congress may by law provide for the case of the death of any of the persons from whom the House of Representatives may choose a President whenever the right of choice shall have devolved upon them, and for the case of the death of any of the persons from whom the Senate may choose a Vice President whenever the right of choice shall have devolved upon them.

SECTION. 5. Sections 1 and 2 shall take effect on the 15th day of October following the ratification of this article.

SECTION. 6. This article shall be inoperative unless it shall have been ratified as an amendment to the Constitution by the legislatures of three-fourths of the several States within seven years from the date of its submission.

Amendment XXI

SECTION. 1. The eighteenth article of amendment to the Constitution of the United States is hereby repealed.

SECTION. 2. The transportation or importation into any State, Territory, or Possession of the United States for delivery or use therein of intoxicating liquors, in violation of the laws thereof, is hereby prohibited.

SECTION. 3. This article shall be inoperative unless it shall have been ratified as an amendment to the Constitution by conventions in the several States, as provided in the Constitution, within seven years from the date of the submission hereof to the States by the Congress.

Amendment XXII

SECTION. 1. No person shall be elected to the office of the President more than twice, and no person who has held the office of President, or acted as President, for more than two years of a term to which some other person was elected President shall be elected to the office of President more than once. But this Article shall not apply to any person holding the office of President when this Article was proposed by Congress, and shall not prevent any person who may be holding the office of President, or acting as President, during the term within which this Article becomes operative from holding the office of President or acting as President during the remainder of such term.

SECTION. 2. This article shall be inoperative unless it shall have been ratified as an amendment to the Constitution by the legislatures of three-fourths of the several States within seven years from the date of its submission to the States by the Congress.

Amendment XXIII

SECTION. 1. The District constituting the seat of Government of the United States shall appoint in such manner as Congress may direct:

A number of electors of President and Vice President equal to the whole number of Senators and Representatives in Congress to which the District would be entitled if it were a State, but in no event more than the least populous State; they shall be in addition to those appointed by the States, but they shall be considered, for the purposes of the election of President and Vice President, to be electors appointed by a State; and they shall meet in the District and perform such duties as provided by the twelfth article of amendment.

SECTION. 2. The Congress shall have power to enforce this article by appropriate legislation.

Amendment XXIV

SECTION. 1. The right of citizens of the United States to vote in any primary or other election for President or Vice President, for electors for President or Vice President, or for Senator or Representative in Congress, shall not be denied or abridged by the United States or any State by reason of failure to pay poll tax or other tax.

SECTION. 2. The Congress shall have power to enforce this article by appropriate legislation.

Amendment XXV

SECTION. 1. In case of the removal of the President from office or of his death or resignation, the Vice President shall become President.

SECTION. 2. Whenever there is a vacancy in the office of the Vice President, the President shall nominate a Vice President who shall take office upon confirmation by a majority vote of both Houses of Congress.

SECTION. 3. Whenever the President transmits to the President pro tempore of the Senate and the Speaker of the House of Representatives his written declaration that he is unable to discharge the powers and duties of his office, and until he transmits to them a written declaration to the contrary, such powers and duties shall be discharged by the Vice President as Acting President.

SECTION. 4. Whenever the Vice President and a majority of either the principal officers of the executive departments or of such other body as Congress may by law provide, transmit to the President pro tempore of the Senate and the Speaker of the House of Representatives their written declaration that the President is unable to discharge the powers and duties of his office, the Vice President shall immediately assume the powers and duties of the office as Acting President.

Thereafter, when the President transmits to the President pro tempore of the Senate and the Speaker of the House of Representatives his written declaration that no inability exists, he shall resume the powers and duties of his office unless the Vice President and a majority of either the principal officers of the executive department or of such other body as Congress may by law provide, transmit within four days to the President pro tempore of the Senate and the Speaker of the House of Representatives their written declaration that the President is unable to discharge the powers and duties of his office. Thereupon Congress shall decide the issue, assembling within forty-eight hours for that purpose if not in session. If the Congress, within twenty-one days after receipt of the latter written declaration, or, if Congress is not in session, within twenty-one days after Congress is required to assemble, determines by two-thirds vote of both Houses that the President is unable to discharge the powers and duties of his office, the Vice President shall continue to discharge the same as Acting President; otherwise, the President shall resume the powers and duties of his office.

Amendment XXVI

SECTION. 1. The right of citizens of the United States, who are eighteen years of age or older, to vote shall not be denied or abridged by the United States or by any State on account of age.

SECTION. 2. The Congress shall have power to enforce this article by appropriate legislation.

Amendment XXVII

No law, varying the compensation for the services of the Senators and Representatives, shall take effect, until an election of representatives shall have intervened.

CLASS ACTIVITIES

Since each chapter concisely provides the students with the fundamental concepts of US government, instructors do not need to spend the whole class period lecturing on the chapter topic. Instead, a portion of the period can be devoted to engaging the students in class activities. The following include recommended class activities for each chapter.

CHAPTER 1—CLASS ACTIVITIES

1. Primary Sources: Read the Preamble of the Constitution and discuss its ideas.
2. Class Discussion: Do you think democracy is the best form of government for all people in the world? What values do people need to maintain a democracy?
3. Class Discussion: Look at Aristotle's three criteria for good government. Would Aristotle think America has a good government?
4. Class Assignment: If your family were a government, how does it function? How are decisions made? Is your family a democracy or a benign dictatorship? After the students write a paragraph on their family government, the class will have a discussion.

CHAPTER 2—CLASS ACTIVITIES

1. Primary Sources: Read and discuss the Declaration of Independence in class.
2. Group Project: Divide the class into groups and have them go to the computer lab. Each group must find three symbols of America on a monument, statue, building, coin, or holiday decoration. Print the three pictures and interpret the meaning. Then the class will have a discussion about what these symbols tell us about the ideas America is founded on.
3. Class Discussion: Have the class discuss what liberty and equality mean to each student.
4. Class Discussion: Have the class discuss the concept of E Pluribus Unum. Do the students identify more with their ethnicity, class, or gender than with being an American citizen?

CHAPTER 3—CLASS ACTIVITIES

1. Primary Sources: Read some of the excerpts from the speeches on slavery at the Constitutional Convention from Madison's Notes.
2. Class Discussion: Discuss some examples when the Constitution failed to work properly and did not protect minority rights.
3. Class Discussion: What are some of the undemocratic elements of the Constitution?
4. Class Discussion: Do you think the Founder's worst fears came true when they worried about whether American culture would retain "republican virtue" and be able to maintain a republic? In general, what values do people need to maintain a democracy?

CHAPTER 4—CLASS ACTIVITIES

1. Video: Watch video on *Marbury v. Madison.*
2. Class Discussion: What do we do if Congress passes an unconstitutional law? What do we do if Congress passes, the president signs, and the Supreme Court upholds an unconstitutional law?
3. Class Discussion: Has the press become too powerful?
4. Class Discussion: Provide examples of executive department czars and have the class discuss whether they pose constitutional problems or not.
5. Class Activity: Have the class break up into groups and have each group propose an amendment to the Constitution. Then have the class as a whole vote for the best proposal.

CHAPTER 5—CLASS ACTIVITIES

1. Class Quiz: Have the students individually or as a class take an online test on whether they are liberal or conservative. Discuss the questions.
2. Class Discussion: Select several issues and discuss the liberal and conservative position on each issue.
3. Class Discussion: Communism has been tried many times in world history. Why does it always fail? And what is the attraction of communism?
4. Analyze Polls: Look at recent polls to understand American's political ideology. Why do so many young people say they like socialism?
5. Class Discussion: Polls show that twice as many Americans identify as conservative than liberal, then why have Republicans failed to win more elections?

CHAPTER 6—CLASS ACTIVITIES

1. Class Discussion: Do you think there are any areas over which the states should have complete power?
2. Class Discussion: Should laws related to abortion, marijuana, prostitution, drinking age, and gay marriage be decided by each state or should we have one national policy for these issues?
3. Class Discussion: What laws work in your state that would not work in other states?
4. Research: Go to the computer lab and find five strange state laws.

CHAPTER 7—CLASS ACTIVITIES

1. Class Discussion: From the above chapter, can you cite some failures of the states that the national government had to come in to rectify?
2. Class Discussion: Are there problems today that the states are incapable of solving?
3. Class Discussion: Are there problems that the states are better able to solve than the national government?
4. Class Discussion: Would Southern states have changed their racist laws without federal pressure?

CHAPTER 8—CLASS ACTIVITIES

1. Class Discussion: Do you think the speech of high school students should be limited to a greater extent than adults?
2. Class Discussion: Should high school or colleges be allowed to say a prayer at graduation ceremonies or before sports events?
3. Class Discussion: Should your local government decorate your town during Christmas? What kind of decorations? Is Christmas a secular or religious holiday?
4. Class Discussion: What words or symbolic speech would you ban at school, work, or in public places?
5. Group Project: Have groups go online and collect actual college speech codes. Then have a class discussion on whether these codes are proper.
6. Group Project: Have groups go online and research news stories about college students protesting politically incorrect speech. Then have a class discussion on whether the students made valid arguments.

CHAPTER 9—CLASS ACTIVITIES

1. Class Project: Organize the class into small groups. Have each group create a mythic evil dictator that abuses one provision in the Bill of Rights. Have each group write the original part of the Bill of Rights and then write the evil version.
2. Class Discussion: In what ways should the government be able to limit your gun rights? What weapons should no citizen be able to possess?
3. Class Discussion: Do you agree with the concept of a right to privacy?
4. Class Discussion: Do you think each state should have their own abortion laws?
5. Class Discussion: What positive rights ought the government provide?

CHAPTER 10—CLASS ACTIVITIES

1. Class Discussion: Do you support or disapprove of affirmative action?
2. Class Discussion: How much racism still exists in America today?
3. Class Discussion: Have you ever experienced discrimination or do you know somebody who has?
4. Class Discussion: Is gay marriage a constitutional right or is marriage something the majority population of each state can define?

CHAPTER 11—CLASS ACTIVITIES

1. Class Discussion: Have the class examine a historical international conflict and discuss whether the president should have gone to war without congressional approval.
2. Video: Watch a video of Watergate and discuss what constitutional limits Richard Nixon crossed.

3. Class Project: Have groups look at a list of executive orders or executive pardons and determine if the president should have made them. Then have each group present their findings to the class.

4. Video: Watch video about the impeachment of Bill Clinton. Should he have been impeached?

CHAPTER 12—CLASS ACTIVITIES

1. Class Discussion: What do you think are the most important qualities of a good president? What presidents do you remember and who was good or bad?

2. Video: Compare clips of news conferences of JFK and George W. Bush and discuss the relationship between the media and the president.

3. Video: Show clips of Nixon's resignation speech.

4. Video: Show clips of Reagan's D-day speech or Statue of Liberty speech and talk about how a president can inspire and teach a nation.

CHAPTER 13—CLASS ACTIVITIES

1. Class Discussion: Why do you think Congress is so unpopular?

2. Class Discussion: Should Congress have caucuses based solely on race or ethnicity? Should college campuses have clubs or organizations based solely on race?

3. Video: Show clips of filibusters or congressional speeches.

4. Video: Watch the movie *Mr. Smith Goes to Washington*.

CHAPTER 14—CLASS ACTIVITIES

1. Class Discussion: Have the class answer this question: "There oughta be a law against that."

2. Group Project: Have the class split up into groups and make a list of bills to propose.

3. Video: Show the famous School House Rock episode, "I'm Just a Bill."

CHAPTER 15—CLASS ACTIVITIES

1. Video: Watch clips on the Clarence Thomas hearings, followed by class discussion.

2. Video: Watch a documentary of *Roe v. Wade*.

3. Class Discussion: Do you think judges should serve for life? Should federal courts adopt mandatory retirement ages?

4. Class Discussion: Debate the merits of the conservative and liberal judicial philosophies.

5. Class Discussion: Considering that the Supreme Court decides so many political issues, do you think justices should be elected, as they are in Texas?

CHAPTER 16—CLASS ACTIVITIES

1. Class Discussion: Do you vote the same way as your parents?
2. Class Discussion: Do you trust the polls?
3. Class Activity: The instructor can cite a couple of demographic facts about an imaginary voter, and the class can guess how he or she will likely vote. For example, John Smith is a 45-year-old white man who goes to church twice a week. Statistically, who is he more likely to vote for: the Republicans or Democrats?

CHAPTER 17—CLASS ACTIVITIES

1. Primary Sources: Show the class examples of a literacy test.
2. Class Discussion: Do you vote, why or why not?
3. Class Discussion: Do you think voter ID laws are racist?
4. Video: Watch a video on the electoral college: go to Khan Academy (http://www.khanacademy.org) or Prager University (www.prageru.com).

CHAPTER 18—CLASS ACTIVITIES

1. Video: Watch clips from past presidential debates and analyze their performances.
2. Video: Watch acceptance speeches from past national party conventions and analyze what speeches were most effective.
3. Video: Watch famous presidential campaign commercials. Are negative or positive ads more influential?
4. Class Discussion: Discuss the most recent or current presidential election and determine what made the candidates likable or not. Was likability the reason some contenders lost the primary or general election?

CHAPTER 19—CLASS ACTIVITIES

1. Primary Source: Have the class read examples of party platforms.
2. Video: Watch documentary on what goes into preparing a national party convention.
3. Video: Watch documentary on why Teddy Roosevelt created the Progressive Party of 1912.
4. Video: Watch examples of past and current unconventional political participation: PETA demonstrations, Code Pink, anti-Vietnam War, the Weather Underground, and the Black Panthers.
5. Class Discussion: What are the political and social goals of radical Islamist terrorists?

CHAPTER 20—CLASS ACTIVITIES

1. Video: Watch videos of Charles Coughlin's speeches.
2. Video: Watch a documentary on Watergate.
3. Class Discussion: How should the media cover wars? Should journalists be able to report from the front lines?
4. Class Activities: Get a copy of *The New York Times* (liberal leaning) and *The Washington Times* (conservative leaning) and compare stories about the identical subject. How do they differ?
5. Class Activity: Watch a video of Jimmy Fallon's monologue or a *Saturday Night Live* skit and analyze whether it conveys a liberal or conservative perspective.

CHAPTER 21—CLASS ACTIVITIES

1. Video: Watch a video on interest groups, such as the AARP or AIPAC.
2. Class Discussion: What interest group would you join?
3. Class Activity: Look at the Center for Responsive Politics website and look over the lists of the interest groups that give the most money. What are these groups seeking to achieve?
4. Class Discussion: Do you agree with the concept of social capital? Do you think it is beneficial for individuals and society to have many groups? What non-political groups do you belong to?

CHAPTER 22 —CLASS ACTIVITIES

1. Class Discussion: Can you describe a time when you had a difficult time dealing with a bureaucrat?
2. Video: Show an interview of Edward Snowden. Would Whistleblower laws have protected him? Did he do the right thing?
3. Class Discussion: What things can private companies do better than government: Run welfare programs? Conduct military operations? Deliver the mail? Build roads?

CHAPTER 23—CLASS ACTIVITIES

1. Video: Watch the PBS documentary featuring Keynes and Hayek, "Commanding Heights."
2. Video: Watch a segment of Milton Friedman's PBS TV series: "Free to Choose."
3. Video: Watch PBS Frontline documentary on the 2008 financial crisis: "Money, Power & Wall Street."
4. Class Discussion: After reading the Final thought, ask the students if they would rather have economy (a) more equality and safety but slower growth and higher unemployment or (b) higher growth and lower unemployment but more individual responsibility.

CHAPTER 24—CLASS ACTIVITIES

1. Class Activity: Have the class watch the "debt clock" and discuss what the different numbers mean.
2. Video: Watch a video on the dangers of the debt.
3. Class Discussion: Talk about the dangers of taking on too much student debt. Ask students how they are paying for college.
4. Class Discussion: What is a fair tax? What is the maximum amount somebody should pay in personal income tax? Conversely, is it right that some people pay no income tax?

CHAPTER 25—CLASS ACTIVITIES

1. Video: Watch video on the Vietnam War. What was America's motive for fighting the war? What mistakes were made?
2. Video: Watch video on dropping the atom bomb on Japan. Follow this with a class discussion of whether the students think it was justified.
3. Video: Watch video on 9/11 or War on Terror.
4. Class Discussion: When is war justified? Is there such a thing as a "good war"?

GLOSSARY

A

accommodationism: This view of the establishment clause allows government to aid any or all religious groups as long as it does not favor one church over another or establish an official religion.

administrative discretion: The authority of bureaucrats to make reasonable judgments or choices when implementing congressional law or executive orders.

affirmative action: Laws and policies designed to give preference to minority groups in employment and college enrollment.

agenda setting: The process by which government decides that a problem exists and that it needs an imminent solution.

amicus brief: If a person or group has a particular interest in a case or can provide important information to the Supreme Court, they can file a "friend of the court" brief.

anarchists: They oppose government in any form.

annual deficit: When annual government spending exceeds annual tax revenue, the result is a budget annual deficit.

anti-federalists: During the debate to ratify the Constitution, they were either outright opposed to the Constitution or would approve it only with certain amendments.

appellate jurisdiction: The Supreme Court has the power to review decisions from lower courts.

Aristotle (384–322 BC): A Greek philosopher who taught in ancient Athens in the school he established, the Lyceum.

Australian ballot: A ballot printed by the state, showing the candidates from both parties, and submitted in a private voting booth.

B

bad tendency test: The legal principle that permits restriction of freedom of speech by government if it is believed that speech has a sole tendency to incite illegal activity or bad morals.

bicameral: A legislature with two chambers.

Bill of Rights: Consisting of the first ten amendments to the Constitution, it protects the individual against the encroachment of the federal government.

bills of attainder: Punishment by a legislative body on an individual, including the confiscation of property.

block grants: Federal monetary transfers to states with no strings attached to be used for general purposes.

blue states: Due to the demographic makeup of the state or region, residents in this area consistently vote for Democrats.

Brandenburg v. Ohio **(1969):** In this case, the Supreme Court more narrowly interpreted the clear and present danger test to only include speech that can reasonably lead to imminent lawless actions.

Brown v. the Board of Education **(1954):** In this case, the Supreme Court overturned Plessy's "separate but equal doctrine" and banned segregated schools in America.

bundling: The process by which individuals give a limited amount of money to a fundraiser, and that fundraiser gives all the money (in a bundle) to a candidate.

bureaucratic state: A government dominated by non-elected officials that creates a complex maze of rules and regulations that burdens the economy and individual liberty.

C

campaign manager: This person heads a political campaign.

candidate appeal: The positive feeling a voter gets about an individual candidate.

capitalism: An economic system characterized by private property by which the allocation of labor and recourses is determined by competition in free markets.

capitalistic system: Free enterprise sets prices, allocates natural resources, establishes wages, distributes goods and services, and regulates production, while providing the individual with the incentive to succeed.

categorical grant: Federal monetary grants to the states for specific purposes, which comes with federal rules and regulations.

caucuses: Informal groups of congressmen that meet on like-minded issues.

checks and balances: Each branch of government has some power over the other branches.

civil rights: This term refers to the constitutionally protected rights of all persons to due process, the equal protection of the law, and the right not to be discriminated against.

Civil Rights Act of 1964: This law made it a federal crime to discriminate in America.

classical liberalism: Holds that limited government should leave citizens free to further their individual pursuits, which will enhance the public good in the aggregate.

closed primaries: State primaries in which only registered party members can vote for a candidate of that party.

collegial style: A loose management method that does not follow a strict organizational chart but provides the president with advice from a wider circle of people.

commander in chief: The role of the president as the functioning head of the military, approving the strategy and picking the generals.

commerce clause: Found in Article I, Section 8, it states that Congress shall have the power to "regulate commerce . . . among the several states."

communications director: The head of the president's communication team responsible for crafting the administration's political themes, orchestrating public relations, and articulating policy issues in the most favorable way.

communism: A political system in which the central government owns the means of production (factories and farms) and uses a central government to allocate resources and manage the economy.

compounded interest: Interest paid on the original amount of money, plus the interest paid on the interest already earned.

concurrent powers: As long as there is no conflict, powers not exclusively given to the national government may be exercised concurrently by the states.

conference committee: A special type of joint committee with members of both congressional chambers which settle the difference between two bills from each chamber.

Congressional Budget Office (CBO): An independent government agency staffed by professional economists, examines the budget and conducts a cost analysis for Congress.

conservatives: They believe in limited government, traditional values, and personal responsibility and liberty, especially economic liberty.

constitutional democratic republic: This is the best way to describe the US government because it contains elements of republicanism, democracy, and limited government.

containment policy: During the Cold War, it was America's commitment to stop the spread of communism around the globe.

conventional political participation: The routine and culturally acceptable political activities that citizens use to engage in the political process.

cooperative federalism: The model of federalism that asserts that the national government and the state governments should cooperate and work together to serve the public.

crony capitalism: A system in which business success is enhanced by connections to government officials, knowledge of legal loopholes (and tax breaks), and by government favoritism.

czars: Executive department officials appointed by the president with ad hoc responsibilities, such as "drug czar" or "environmental czar."

D

deficit spending: When government spending exceeds tax revenues.

Delegate Model: the lawmaker votes in accordance with the wishes of the majority of his or her constituents, even if those views are contrary to the lawmaker's.

demagogues: Politicians with great rhetorical skills that appealed to the public's baser emotions of greed and fear.

democracy: Rule by the people.

deregulation: Ending or reducing government regulation of an industry to create more competition.

détente: Started by President Richard Nixon, it was a foreign policy initiative designed to reduce tensions and improve relations with the Soviet Union during the Cold War.

diplomacy: when countries use diplomats or other public officials to negotiate with the leaders of other countries to try to influence them.

direct democracy: The people made the laws and determined policy by immediate majority vote, sometimes without regard to established law.

discretionary spending: Non-entitlement spending that is up to the "discretion" of Congress and the president to spend each year.

dissenting opinion: The non-legally binding opinion issued by the minority of justices of the Supreme Court that disagrees with the majority opinion.

divided government: This is when the executive branch and one or both chambers of Congress are controlled by different political parties.

***Dred Scott v Sanford* (1857):** In this case, the Supreme Court declared a congressional act unconstitutional—the Missouri Compromise, which prohibited slavery in the Northern territories.

dual federalism: The model of federalism that asserts that the national government should operate only within its limited enumerated powers while the states retain their sovereign powers, and the two layers of government have separate functions and responsibilities.

due process: The procedures that governments must follow to protect individual rights and provide equal justice.

during good behavior: The language in the Constitution that means federal judges serve lifetime terms.

E

e pluribus unum: Latin for "from the many one." The American motto that represents the idea that individuals with a diversity of backgrounds come together to form one nation.

economic interest groups: Interest groups that promote the financial concerns of its members, such as corporations or unions.

Electoral College: The body today, consisting of 538 electors, that selects the president in state-by-state elections.

electoral realignment: This is when the majority of voters switch from one party to another and remain loyal to the new party for a generation.

elite theory: The idea that a small group of the wealthy and highly educated elites use interest groups for their own advantage at the expense of the general public.

eminent domain: The power of the government to take private property for public use as long as the government pays a fair market price.

empire: Refers to when one nations takes over other nations and maintains military and political control over the conquered nation for economic and geo-political advantage.

Engel v. Vital **(1962):** In this case, the Supreme Court ended prayer in all US public schools.

entrepreneur: A person who risks his or her money and time to start a business.

environmentalists: They support a liberal agenda with the primary focus on protecting the environment.

equal opportunity: Regardless of wealth or background, all people should have an equal chance in life.

equal outcome: The attempt to achieve equal economic conditions.

equal protection clause: Found in the 14th Amendment, it states that "No state shall . . . deny any person within its jurisdiction the equal protection of the laws."

establishment clause: Found in the 1st Amendment, it states that "Congress shall make no law respecting the establishment of religion."

excise taxes: Taxes on luxury consumer items, such as cigarettes, liquor, and gasoline.

ex post facto laws: Laws that retroactively punish an act that was legal at the time it was committed.

executive orders: Executive branch directives that have the force of law.

executive privilege: The right of the executive to keep communications confidential.

exit polls: Surveys of voters taken right after they exited the voting booths, collecting data about the voter's opinions and demographics.

expressed powers: The national powers explicitly enumerated or listed in the Constitution.

F

Fairness Doctrine: in order to further the "public good," broadcasters were required to provide a "reasonable" amount of time to public policy issues and provide diverse opinions.

Federal Communications Commission (FCC): a federal agency that was created to regulate the broadcast media

Federal Elections Commission (FEC): A federal regulatory agency that oversees all federal elections and enforces federal election laws.

Federal Reserve: The central bank of the US.

federal system: National and states' governments share power.

Federalist Papers: The most famous Federalists essays written in support of the new Constitution.

federalists: During the debate to ratify the Constitution, they approved of the Constitution as it stood.

15th Amendment: It prohibits the states from denying people the right to vote on account of race, color, or previous condition of servitude.

filibuster: A long speech delivered by a senator in order to delay a vote on a bill.

FISA Court: The US Foreign Intelligence Surveillance Court was established to grant surveillance warrants on suspected foreign intelligence agents or terrorists.

fiscal policy: A government's spending and taxing policies.

foreign policy: A nation's set of policies and objectives in dealing with other nations.

formula for adding amendments: A proposal must pass two-thirds of both chambers of Congress, and it must be ratified by three-fourths of the state legislatures.

14th Amendment: guarantees that all people born in America, even if they were once a slave, are citizens. Furthermore, it prohibits the states from depriving any person within its jurisdiction "the equal protection of the laws."

framing: is when the professional press determines the premise or the questions of an issue.

free exercise clause: Found in the 1st Amendment, it states that "Congress shall make no law . . . prohibiting the free exercise thereof" (of religion).

front-loading: In recent decades, more and more states have moved their primaries to an earlier date in order to have more influence on presidential elections.

G

gatekeepers: the people that decide what news stories to print or broadcast on a daily and weekly news cycle.

general election: Voters select the person who will actually fill the seat of office in the government.

gerrymandering: when a district is drawn in an irregular shape in order to maximize the benefits for one party The party that controls a state tries to draw congressional districts in a way that will give members of that party the most "safe seats."

getting-out-the-vote: The effort campaigns and political parties make to get people to the polls on Election Day.

Gibbons v. Ogden **(1824):** In this case, the Marshall Court established for the national government far-reaching powers to regulate business and the economy under the commerce clause.

GNP: The total market value of all the goods and services produced within a country in one year.

going public: In order to put pressure on Congress to support the President's proposal, the president will go on a media campaign, sidestepping the press, and directly appeal for public support.

government: An entity that uses legitimate force to make policy, conducts affairs of the state, and enacts laws guiding its citizens.

government corporations: Independent agencies that are owned by the federal government and operate by charging a fee for a service.

great compromise: Each state will have an equal vote in the Senate, and representation in the House will be based on population.

Grutter v. Bollinger **(2003):** In this case, the Supreme Court upheld the law school's affirmative action program because it was not a mechanical point system, rather it evaluated each applicant in a holistic manner.

H

habeas corpus: An official holding a person as prisoner must demonstrate the legal basis for continuing to hold that person.

hierarchical management system: This management method assigns a clear chain of command up the organizational chart, giving each staff member a decision role according to their area of expertise.

honeymoon period: A time of high approval ratings and goodwill that a newly elected president experiences.

I

identity politics: Political activity that appeals to a citizen's identity as a member of an ethnic or social group and its perceived mistreatment.

impeachment process: The House must approve the articles of impeachment with a majority vote. And the Senate, with the Chief Justice presiding, must conduct a trial based on those articles, with the president being removed from office with a two-thirds vote.

imperial presidency: A presidency that is characterized by greater power than the Constitution allows.

implied powers: As articulated in the necessary and proper clause, these are powers not enumerated in the text of the Constitution but implied as a means of carrying out the expressed powers.

income disparity: The unequal distribution of individual or household income in society.

individual income tax: A direct tax on the income an individual earns in one year.

inflation: The rate at which prices rise for goods and services.

Infotainment: mixing news with entertainment to increase ratings.

inherent powers: Powers not expressed or implied in the text of the Constitution, but inherent in the function and responsibility of the office.

initiative: A ballot measure which allows citizens the ability to craft their own laws.

interest group: An organized group of people that get together in order to change public policy.

isolationism: The belief that America should not be involved with other countries and should not go to war unless attacked.

J

Jim Crow laws: These laws accomplished two major objectives: they made it more difficult for blacks to vote, and they segregated or separated the black population from the white population.

joint committees: This type of committee consists of members from both the House and the Senate to oversee something that is of interest to the entire Congress.

judicial activism: When judges broadly interpret the Constitution in order to achieve the values of the judge, and in essence making law.

judicial restraint: Judges should only hear cases that deal with explicit constitutional issues, and allow other issues to be resolved by the political process.

judicial review: The power of the Supreme Court to declare a congressional act null and void if it is found to be unconstitutional.

L

Laffer-Curve: A graph that illustrates how higher taxes reduces government revenues.

laissez-faire: Economies run by free market capitalism with little or no government regulation.

law of unintended consequences: When lawmakers pass a law intending to solve one problem but end up making other problems worse.

leak: Information provided by a government official to a reporter for political advantage.

Lemon v. Kurtzman **(1971):** In this case, the Supreme Court tried to formulate clear establishment clause guidelines for legislatures to follow, called the "Lemon Test."

libel: False written statements about others that harm their reputations.

liberals: They believe in the positive use of government to promote economic and social equality.

libertarians: They believe that the federal government should be limited to the most essential functions in order to protect individual liberty.

liberty: Individual freedom from undo government interference and the freedom to pursue happiness.

Linkage Institution: the press links government officials to the people, and it links the people to government officials.

lobbyists: People hired by interest groups to meet with lawmakers or administrators to persuade them to change a law or policy.

logrolling: vote trading.

loose construction: When judges broadly interpret the Constitution.

M

majority opinion: The official, legally binding ruling of the Supreme Court, backed by a majority of the justices.

mandate: When a president wins an election by a large margin, Congress recognizes that they should implement the president's agenda and comply with the will of the people.

mandatory spending: Spending on entitlement programs such as Social Security and Medicare that require no congressional authorization but are automatically paid for according to a formula.

Marbury v. Madison (1803): In this landmark case, the Supreme Court established the power of judicial review.

margin of error: The sampling error of an opinion poll.

market driven: the media must attract readers and viewers in order to make a profit.

marketplace of ideas: another way to think of the press is that it serves as a public forum to debate and test ideas.

John Marshall: Serving as Chief Justice from 1801 to 1835, Marshall was the most influential jurist in Supreme Court history.

McCulloch v. Maryland (1819): In this case, the Marshall Court established the constitutional approach to federalism that would guide the national government for centuries by upholding the establishment of a national bank.

McDonald v. Chicago (2010): In this case, the Supreme Court upheld the right to keep and bear arms as an individual right applicable to the states.

Miranda warning: The police must inform any person held in custody of their constitutional rights.

monarchy: Power given to a hereditary king or queen.

monetary policy: Government policies concerning the money supply and interest rates through a central bank.

N

national debt: The accumulated annual deficits.

necessary and proper clause: Found in Article I, Section 8, it states that the national government possesses the power "to make all laws which shall be necessary and proper for carrying into Execution the foregoing powers, and all other Powers vested by this Constitution."

negative ads: Campaign commercials that attack the opponent.

negative rights: These are proscriptions that limit the government in order to protect individual rights.

neutral questions: Non-biased and non-leading questions that seek true and honest responses in opinion polls.

new federalism: A conservative effort to restore some power and responsibility to the states.

New Jersey Plan: This plan that was presented at the Constitutional Convention would have retained equal state representation in the legislature just as they did under the Articles of Confederation.

19th Amendment: It gave women the right to vote in all state and national elections.

O

Office of Management and Budget (OMB): It reviews the spending requests of each department and agency of the executive branch and helps the president prepare the budget.

oligarchy: Rule by the few, usually the rich.

open primaries: In this type of primary, people are allowed to vote for any candidate, regardless of what party they are registered with.

order: The primary function and responsibility of government. Governments provide armies, laws, and police to protect people and property in order to establish *order*.

original intent: When interpreting the meaning of the Constitution, judges should understand the original goals and the historical context of the provision written by the Framers.

P

party identification: The personal affiliation that a person has for a political party.

party platform: A document released by a political party at the national convention that lists the party's positions on the issue and its political values.

payroll taxes: A tax paid jointly by employers and employees out of a worker's paycheck.

permanent campaign: This is when a president maintains a constant media campaign to support his agenda and attack his opponents.

pluralistic theory: The idea that many interest groups representing a wide variety of economic and ideological interests compete with each other.

pocket veto: When Congress is adjourned the president need not sign a veto for it to die within ten days.

police powers: The traditional state powers related to the health and safety of its citizens.

policy implementation: The process of setting up and carrying out the actual reform.

political action committees (PACS): Entities formed by interest groups to give money directly to candidates.

political culture: The widely shared beliefs, values, and norms concerning the relationship of citizens to their government and to one another.

political equality: The idea that all Americans should enjoy equal protection under the law, equal voting rights, and equal access to office.

political ideology: A consistent set of values and beliefs about the proper purpose and scope of government.

political party: Organized groups of people united by a common political goal that try to get their candidates elected to office in order to implement a political agenda.

political socialization: The process by which people develop their political orientation and values as they grow up.

poll tax: A tax to register to vote designed to discourage the black franchise.

popular sovereignty: The idea that ultimate power resides in the people.

population: The target group of people a particular poll attempts to gauge.

populism: A political approach that appeals to the concerns and prejudices of the ordinary people against the financial or cultural elites.

positive ads: Campaign commercials that depict the candidate in the most positive light, highlighting the candidate's ideas, accomplishments, and values.

positive right: The government must provide something to the people, as part of their human rights, such as education, medical support, housing, or welfare.

President Pro Tempore: The official presiding officer of the Senate when the vice president is not present.

press conference: This is when the president stands before the press corps and answers questions.

primary: The voters select the candidate to represent the party in the general election.

privatization: Transferring management of a government agency to a private company.

progressive taxes: Taxes in which wealthy people pay a higher percentage of their income.

progressives: They believed good laws and institutions could eradicate corrupt business and government and aid the enlightened progress of mankind.

promote the general good: Providing for the best long-term interest for the greatest number of people in the country.

proportional system: Seats in the legislature are allocated according to what percentage of the vote each party receives.

prospective issue voting: The issues a candidate says he is for during the campaign; campaign promises.

Protestant ethic: A set of virtues especially strong in Puritan America that valued hard work, self-reliance, thrift, honesty, religiosity, and moderation.

public advocacy: holding that it is the mission of the news media to enlighten the public in order to achieve greater social justice.

public opinion: The views held by the population about issues, individuals, and institutions.

public opinion poll: A scientific survey of public opinion at a point in time.

public policy: All the laws, rules, regulations, codes, programs, and recommendations of government.

Q

qualified veto: The president can veto any bill, but a veto can be overridden by a two-thirds vote of both chambers of Congress.

R

radical Islamists: They believe that all of mankind should be converted to Islam, by violent means if necessary, and that all Muslims should be governed by Sharia, a law code derived from the Koran which is administered by Islamic leaders (a caliphate).

random sample: A sample is truly random only if every person in that population has an equal chance of being selected for an opinion poll.

realpolitik: The diplomatic approach based on the practical calculations of power, material gain, and other realistic factors of international relationships.

reapportioning: if a state's population increases or decreases by more than the average number of people in a district (today 710,000), then the state will either gain or lose a representative.

red state: Due to the demographic makeup of the state or region, residents in this area consistently vote for Republicans.

regressive taxes: Taxes in which poor people pay a higher percentage of their income in taxes.

republic: A representative form of government in which elected officials make laws on behalf of the people.

retrospective issue voting: The actual issues that a candidate supported or voted for over their career.

rights: Legal freedoms or entitlements that structure the form of government and the content of the law.

Roe v. Wade **(1973)**: In this case, the Supreme Court extended the concept of privacy to include the right to have an abortion.

S

safety net: A set of government programs designed to catch Americans if they fall on hard times and to provide basic support for the poor.

Schenck v. United States **(1919):** In this case, the Supreme Court established the clear and present danger doctrine to limit dangerous speech.

second term curse: The recognition that presidents' second terms are always less successful than their first terms.

select committees: Congressional committees created for a special purpose, often to conduct an investigation.

selective incorporation: The Supreme Court, on a case-by-case basis, has applied the Bill of Rights through the due process clause of the 14th Amendment to apply to the states.

selective perception: if a conservative or a liberal watches a biased news broadcast, he or she will interpret the story to fit their ideology.

selective viewership: since most people are aware of their own ideology, they select news outlets that support their beliefs.

Senate Majority Leader: The top leadership position in the US Senate.

separate but equal doctrine: In *Plessy v. Ferguson*, the Supreme Court ruled that as long as cities and states provide separate but equal facilities, segregation doesn't violate the 14th amendment.

separation of powers: A government with three branches of government: executive, legislative, and judicial.

17th Amendment: It gave the people of the state the power to vote for their two US Senators, not the state legislatures.

16th Amendment: It created the national income tax.

social capital: The interconnection fostered by people joining groups that benefited the society and the individual.

social contract theory: States that people must give up certain liberties when they enter into society, but the resulting order and safety is worth the loss of freedom.

social interest groups: Interest groups that seek to change society for the better, they include ideological or single issue groups.

socialism: Asserts that strong central government authority is needed to regulate private property, to nationalize industry, and to distribute the wealth in order to achieve equality.

socialization: Teaching or socializing proceeding generations certain values that society holds dear.

solicitor general: This official represents the federal government before the Supreme Court.

Speaker of the House: The presiding officer and leader of the House of Representatives.

speech codes: Policies that ban speech that may disparage somebody's race, ethnicity, gender, sexual orientation, or disability; or any speech that might be intimidating or offensive.

spoil system: When elected public officials would distribute government jobs to loyal members of their political party.

standing committees: Permanent congressional committees in session year in and year out, producing most of the bills.

stare decisis: In order to provide stability, uniformity, and clarity, the Supreme Court tries to abide by the precedents established by previous Courts.

strict construction: When interpreting the meaning of the Constitution, judges should primarily focus on the clear, explicit, and literal meaning of the text.

strict separation of church and state: This view of the establishment clause asserts that the government should do nothing to aid any religious activity and that government and public spaces ought to be secular.

Super PACs: Groups that must report their contributions to the FEC, but can raise unlimited money for campaigns as long as they don't coordinate with a candidate.

Superdelegates: Delegates at the Democratic National Convention consisting of party leaders who are not pledged on the basis of primary votes.

supply-side economics: The government's attempt to stimulate long-term economic growth by bolstering the supply of goods and services through policies of lower taxes, less government regulations, and less government spending.

supremacy clause: Contained in Article VI, it states that "This Constitution and the laws of the United States . . . shall be the supreme laws of the land."

swing states: The states, sometimes called "battleground states," that have populations evenly divided between Democrats and Republicans and that swing back and forth between both parties in presidential elections.

T

10th Amendment: It states that "the powers not delegated to the United States by the Constitution, nor prohibited to the states, are reserved to the states respectively, or to the people."

terrorism: Premeditated, politically motivated violence perpetrated against civilian targets by people who want to bring about political or social change.

think tanks: Organizations that hire scholars to perform research and public education on issues in order to influence public policy.

13th Amendment: It states that "Neither slavery nor involuntary servitude shall exist with the United States."

three-fifths compromise: A phrase in the original Constitution that stated that for purposes of representation in Congress five slaves will be counted as three citizens in the census.

Title IX: It prohibits sex-based discrimination on college campuses that received federal funds.

total war: A war that uses all of a nation's recourses to target any or all of another nation's recourses, including military installations, crops, factories, and civilian population centers.

totalitarian government: A political system that has total authority over all aspects of society, including the economy, the military, the press, education, the arts, and the legal system.

tracking poll: A survey that measures public opinion over a long period of time, perhaps even decades.

trustee model: sees Congress more as a national lawmaking institution, in which educated and experienced lawmakers craft legislation for the long-term benefit of the whole nation.

turnout: The percentage of eligible voters who actually cast a ballot in an election.

22nd Amendment: It limits the president to two elected terms.

tyranny: Government by a selfish, autocratic ruler.

U

unconventional participation: Political activities that are not socially acceptable, defy social norms, or are illegal.

unfunded mandates: Laws passed by Congress requiring the states to do something without providing the funds to do it.

unicameral: A legislative branch with only one chamber.

unitary system: One central government has the ultimate authority and control to run all regions of the country.

United Nations (UN): An intergovernmental organization headquartered in New York consisting of 193 member nations whose objective is to foster international peace.

V

Virginia plan: A plan written by James Madison and presented at the Constitutional Convention that specified that representation in Congress should be based on the population of the states.

Voting Rights Act of 1965: It made it a federal crime for state officials to discriminate at the voting booth and gave the federal government many tools to enforce the act.

W

wars for liberation: Wars primarily intended to bring freedom or liberation to a people subjugated by a colonial power or a dictator.

watchdog: this function of exposing wrongdoing or incompetence of government officials is often referred to as the watchdog role of the press.

welfare state: A government that uses the progressive income tax to distribute wealth and provide cradle to grave service to its citizens.

whip: An important congressional position that prepares summaries of bills, counts the votes, and pressures members to vote with the leadership.

whistle-blowers: Government employees that report acts of waste, corruption, and mismanagement.

winner-take-all: A rule of the Electoral College that says the candidate who wins the plurality of the state's popular vote wins ALL the electors.